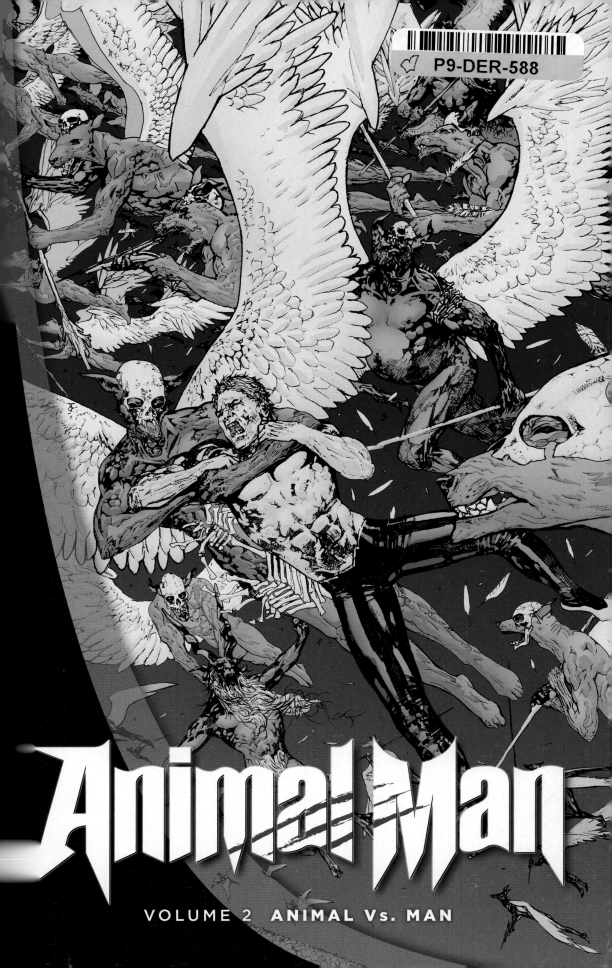

Animal Man

VOLUME 2   ANIMAL Vs. MAN

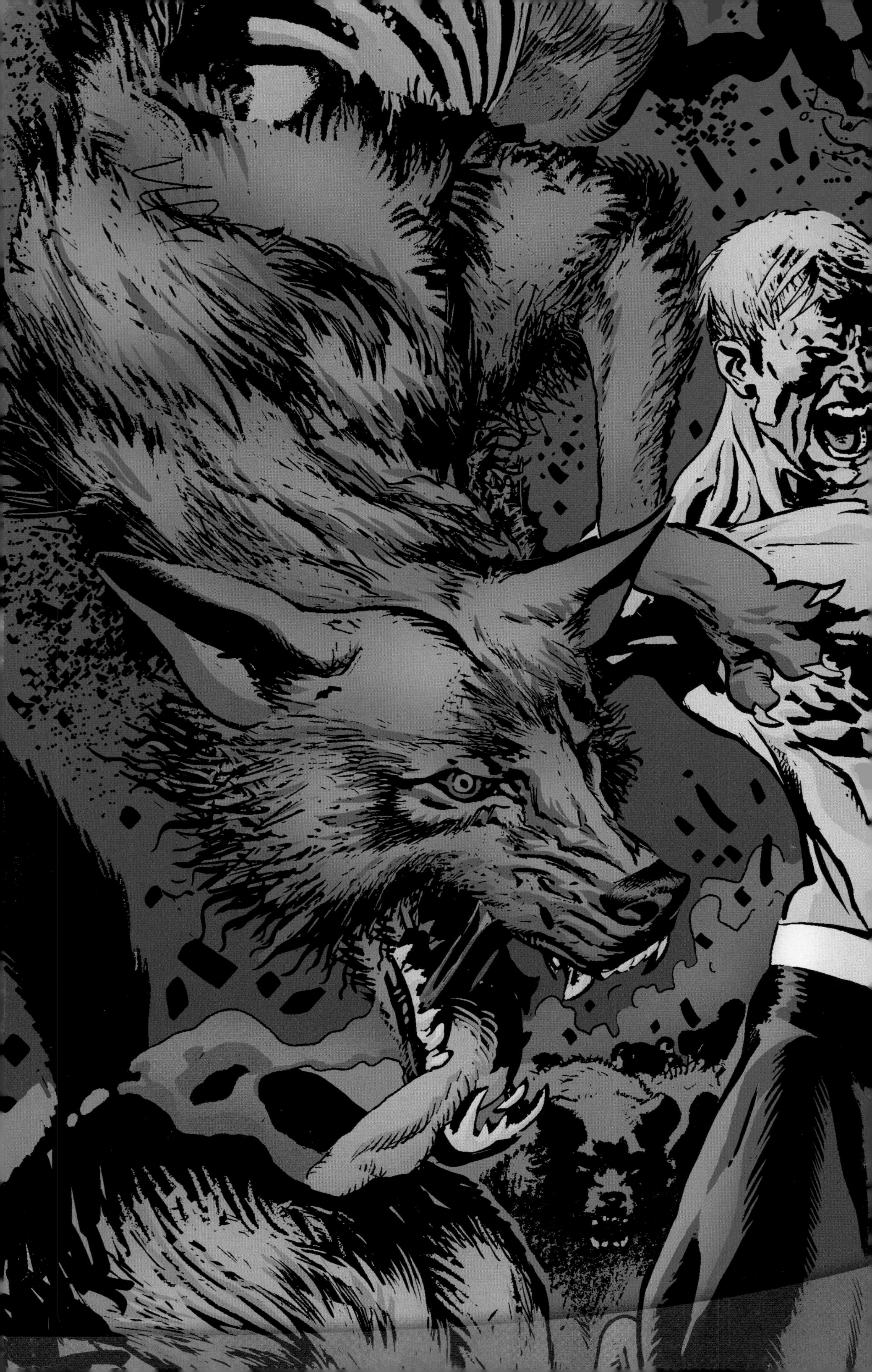

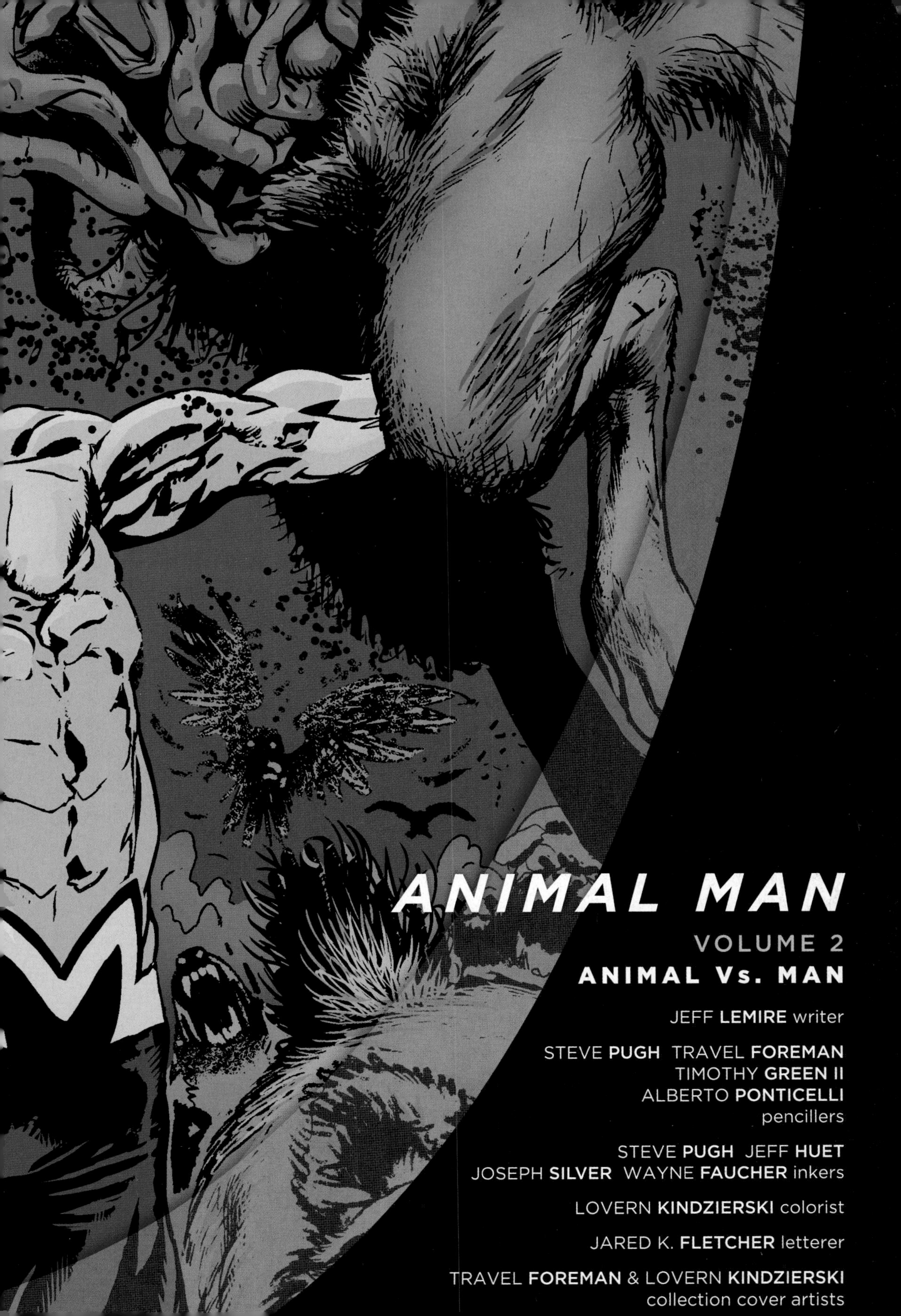

ANIMAL MAN

VOLUME 2

ANIMAL Vs. MAN

JEFF **LEMIRE** writer

STEVE **PUGH** TRAVEL **FOREMAN**
TIMOTHY **GREEN II**
ALBERTO **PONTICELLI**
pencillers

STEVE **PUGH** JEFF **HUET**
JOSEPH **SILVER** WAYNE **FAUCHER** inkers

LOVERN **KINDZIERSKI** colorist

JARED K. **FLETCHER** letterer

TRAVEL **FOREMAN** & LOVERN **KINDZIERSKI**
collection cover artists

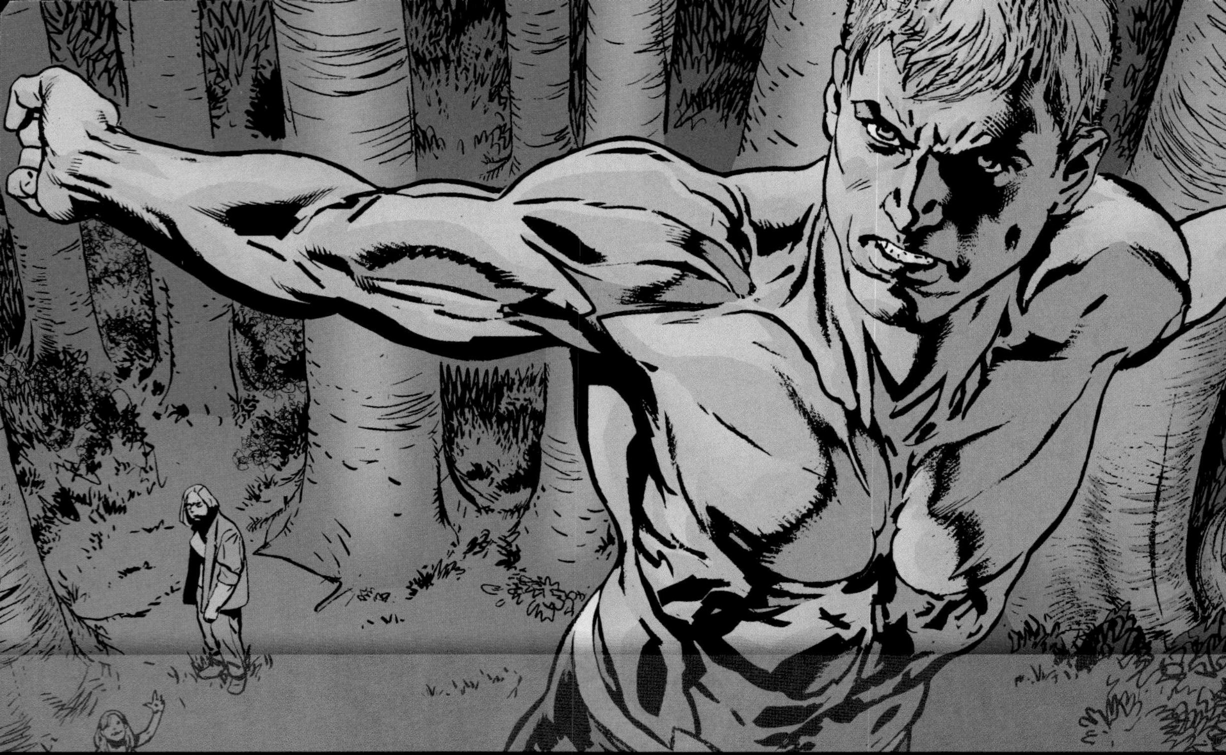

JOEY CAVALIERI Editor - Original Series KATE STEWART Assistant Editor - Original Series
ROBIN WILDMAN Editor ROBBIN BROSTERMAN Design Director - Books ROBBIE BIEDERMAN Publication Design

BOB HARRAS VP - Editor-in-Chief

DIANE NELSON President DAN DIDIO and JIM LEE Co-Publishers
GEOFF JOHNS Chief Creative Officer JOHN ROOD Executive VP - Sales, Marketing and Business Development
AMY GENKINS Senior VP - Business and Legal Affairs NAIRI GARDINER Senior VP - Finance
JEFF BOISON VP - Publishing Operations MARK CHIARELLO VP - Art Direction and Design
JOHN CUNNINGHAM VP - Marketing TERRI CUNNINGHAM VP - Talent Relations and Services
ALISON GILL Senior VP - Manufacturing and Operations HANK KANALZ Senior VP - Digital
JAY KOGAN VP - Business and Legal Affairs, Publishing JACK MAHAN VP - Business Affairs, Talent
NICK NAPOLITANO VP - Manufacturing Administration SUE POHJA VP - Book Sales
COURTNEY SIMMONS Senior VP - Publicity BOB WAYNE Senior VP - Sales

ANIMAL MAN VOLUME 2: ANIMAL Vs. MAN

DC Comics, 1700 Broadway, New York, NY 10019
A Warner Bros. Entertainment Company.
Printed by RR Donnelley, Salem, VA, USA. 12/7/12. First Printing.

ISBN: 978-1-4012-3800-1

Library of Congress Cataloging-in-Publication Data

Lemire, Jeff.
Animal Man. Volume 2, Animal vs. man / Jeff Lemire, Steve Pugh, Timothy Green II, Travel Foreman.
p. cm.
"Originally published in single magazine form in Animal Man 0, 7-11, Animal Man Annual 1."
ISBN 978-1-4012-3800-1
1. Graphic novels. I. Pugh, Steve. II. Green, Timothy, 1975- III. Foreman, Travel. IV. Title. V. Title: Animal vs. man.
PN6728.A58L47 2012
741.5'973—dc23
2012032137

SUSTAINABLE FORESTRY INITIATIVE
Certified Chain of Custody
At Least 20% Certified Forest Content
www.sfiprogram.org
SFI-01042

PREVIOUSLY...

Since the dawn of time, the fate of the Earth has depended on the balance between three forces: THE RED, THE GREEN, and THE ROT.

The Red connects all living animals; The Green, all plant life. Both fight to maintain power over the forces of death and decay.

Every generation The Red selects an avatar as a protector, and its newest is four-year-old Maxine Baker, daughter of Buddy Baker, the super hero called ANIMAL MAN.

But the moment Maxine revealed her powers, agents of The Rot were dispatched to destroy her. Forced from their home, the Baker family must go on the run, aided only by their guide "Socks," a housecat and former avatar of The Red.

Now, the family's best shot at stopping the forces of death is to join with The Rot's other great enemy — avatar of The Green, the SWAMP THING.

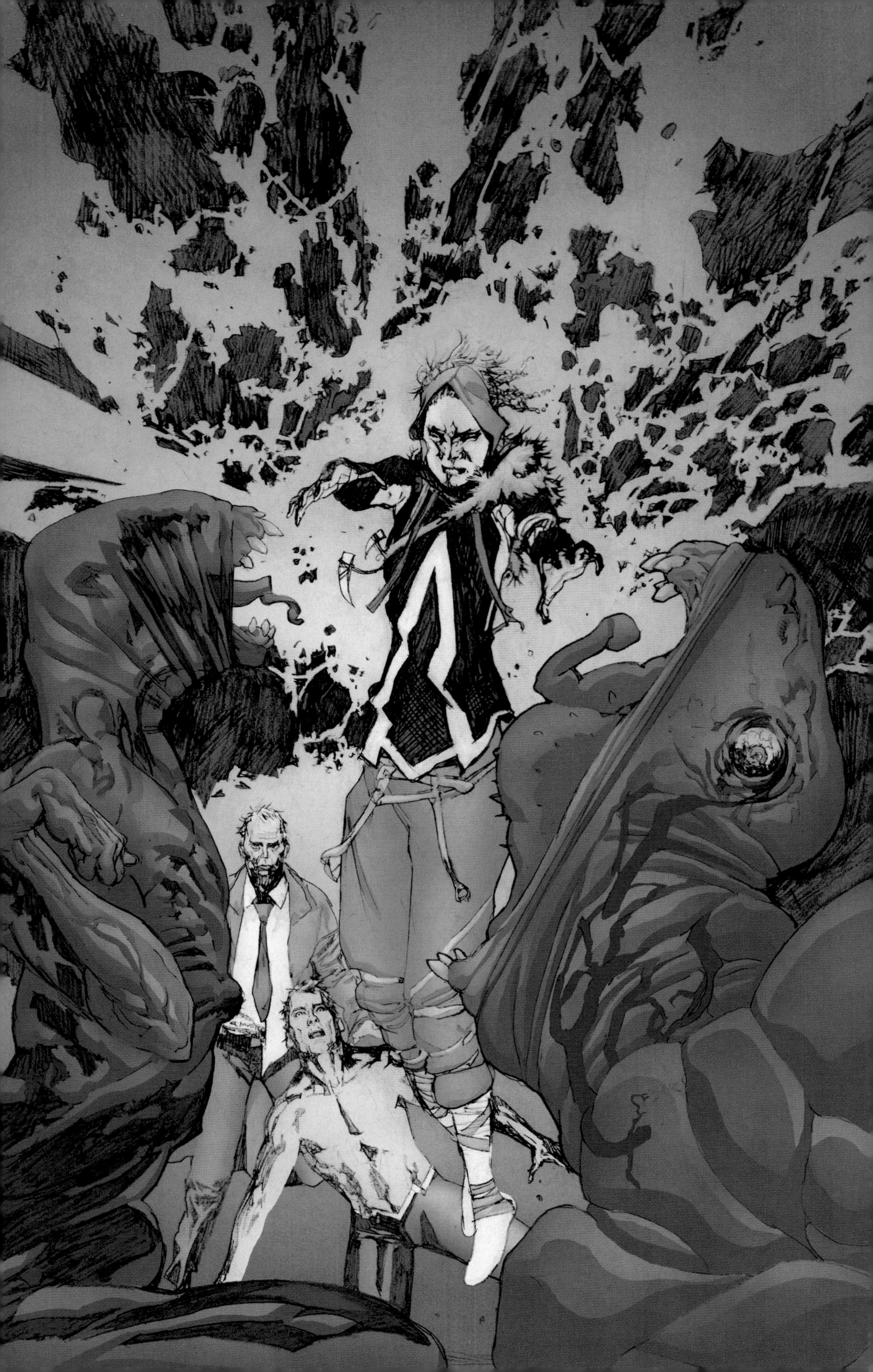

JEFF LEMIRE writer STEVE PUGH artist TRAVEL FOREMAN with JEFF HUET additional art
cover by TRAVEL FOREMAN with LOVERN KINDZIERSKI

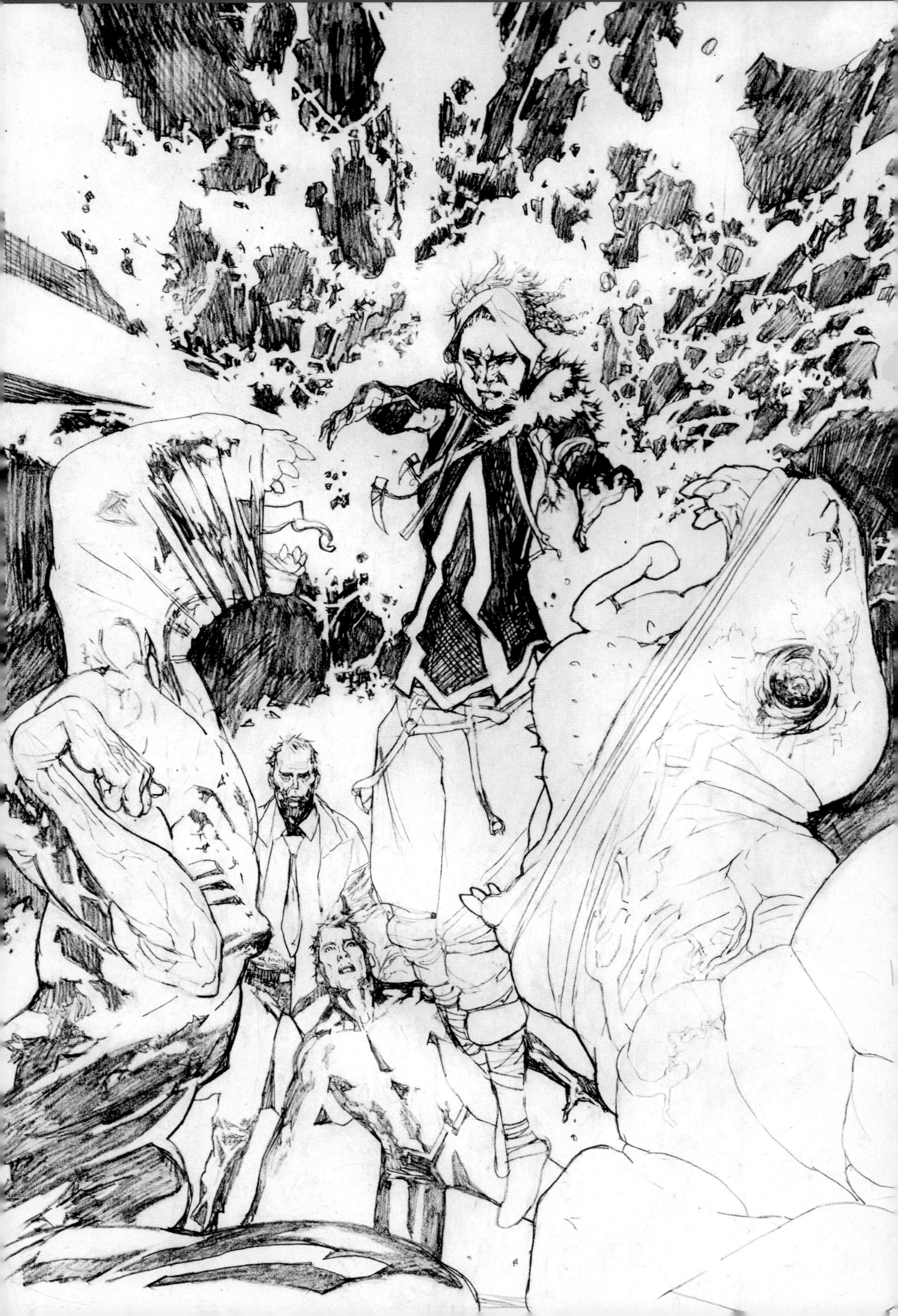

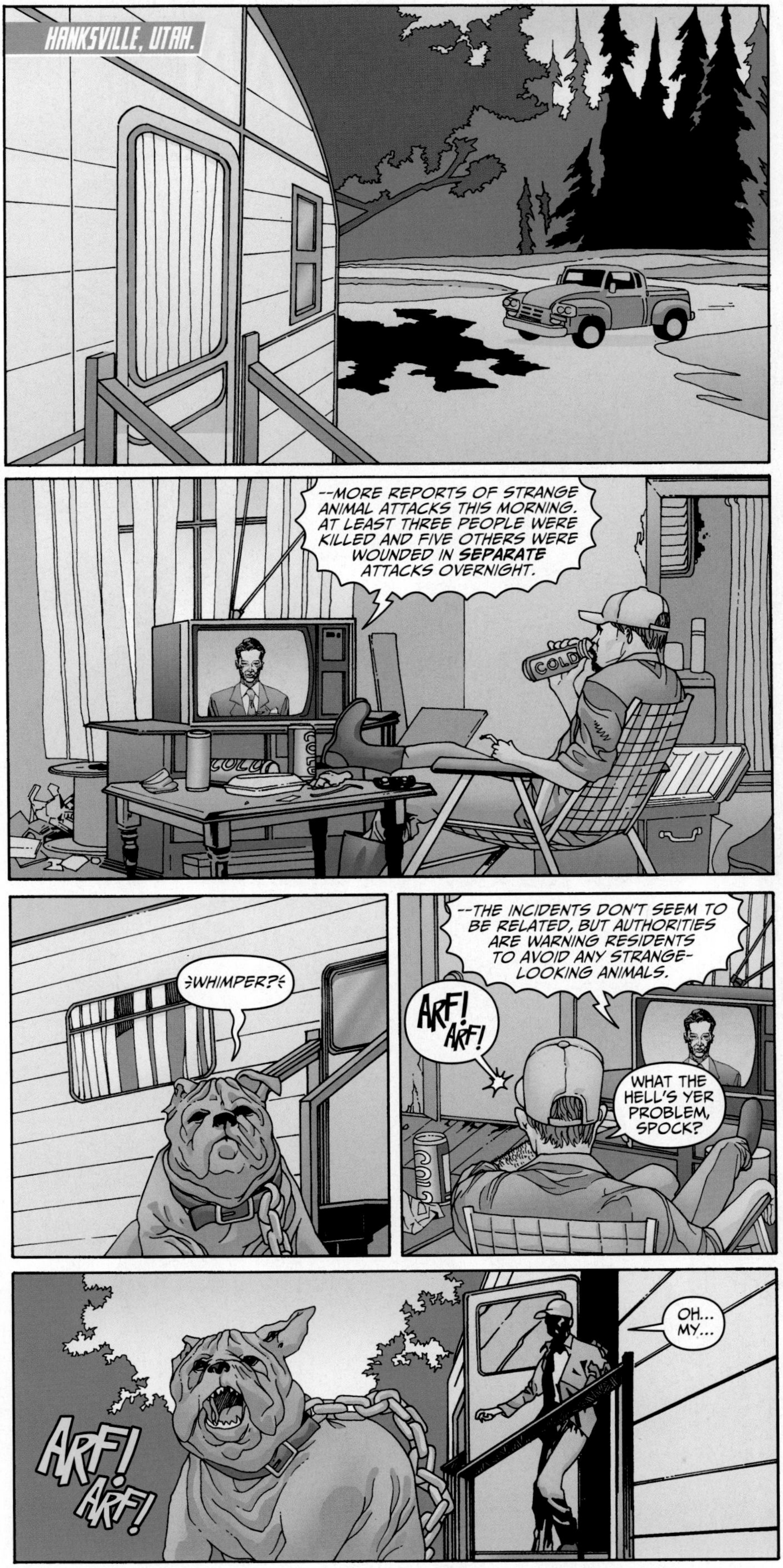
HANKSVILLE, UTAH.
--MORE REPORTS OF STRANGE ANIMAL ATTACKS THIS MORNING. AT LEAST THREE PEOPLE WERE KILLED AND FIVE OTHERS WERE WOUNDED IN SEPARATE ATTACKS OVERNIGHT.
COLD
WHIMPER?
--THE INCIDENTS DON'T SEEM TO BE RELATED, BUT AUTHORITIES ARE WARNING RESIDENTS TO AVOID ANY STRANGE-LOOKING ANIMALS.
ARF! ARF!
WHAT THE HELL'S YER PROBLEM, SPOCK?
OH... MY...
ARF! ARF!

ANIMAL vs. MAN part one

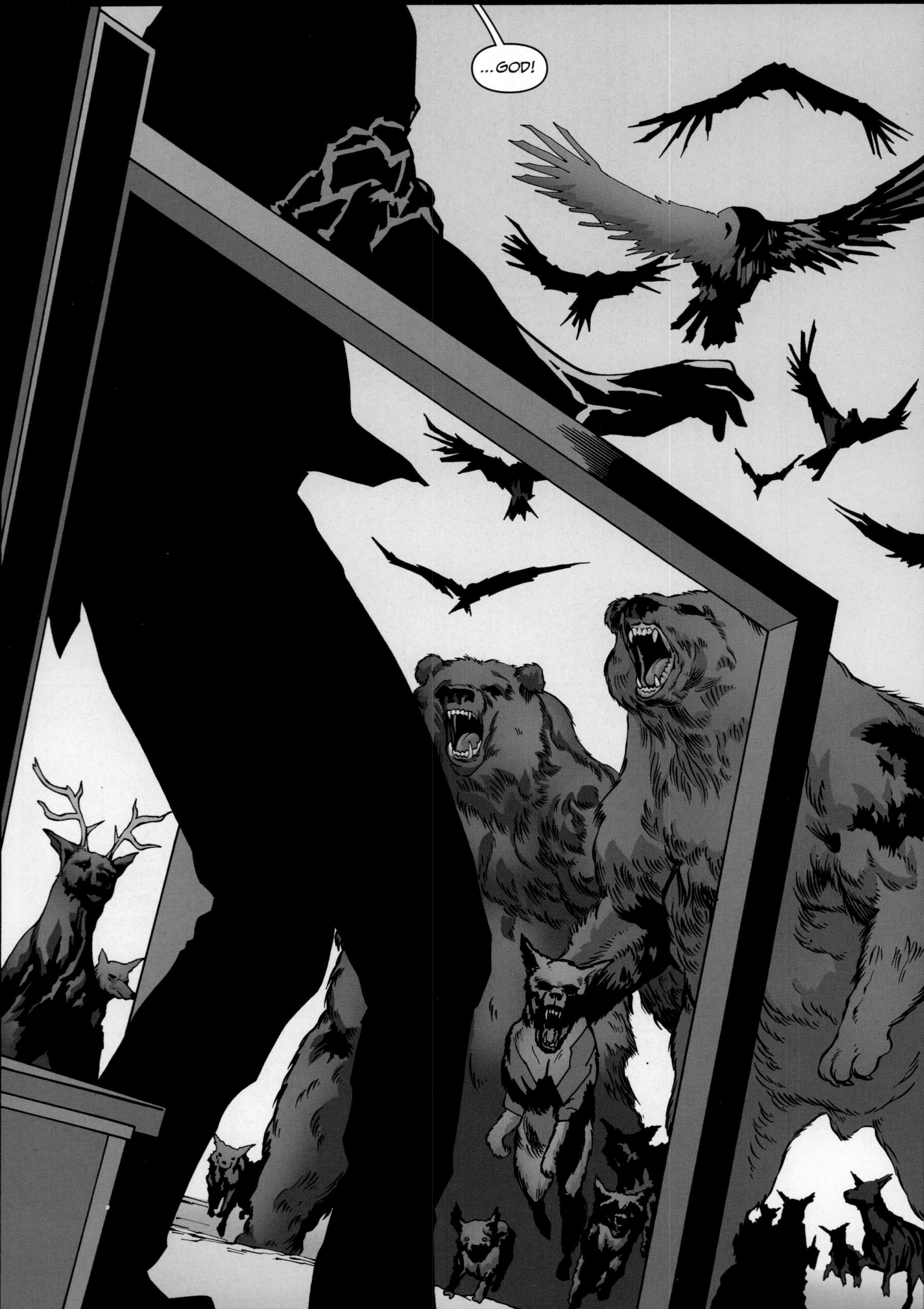
...GOD!

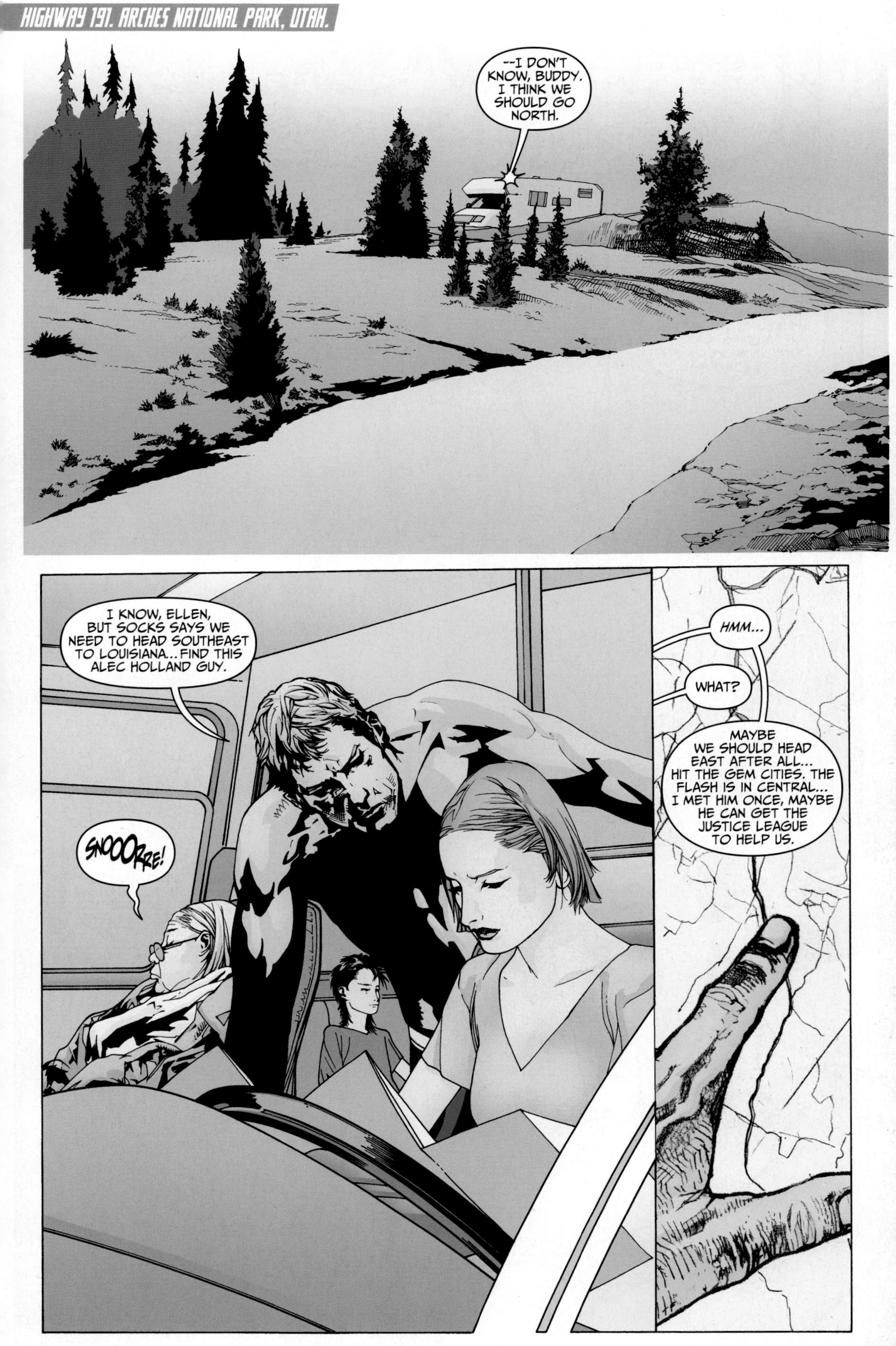
HIGHWAY 191. ARCHES NATIONAL PARK, UTAH.
--I DON'T KNOW, BUDDY. I THINK WE SHOULD GO NORTH.
I KNOW, ELLEN, BUT SOCKS SAYS WE NEED TO HEAD SOUTHEAST TO LOUISIANA...FIND THIS ALEC HOLLAND GUY.
SNOOORRE!
HMM...
WHAT?
MAYBE WE SHOULD HEAD EAST AFTER ALL... HIT THE GEM CITIES. THE FLASH IS IN CENTRAL... I MET HIM ONCE, MAYBE HE CAN GET THE JUSTICE LEAGUE TO HELP US.

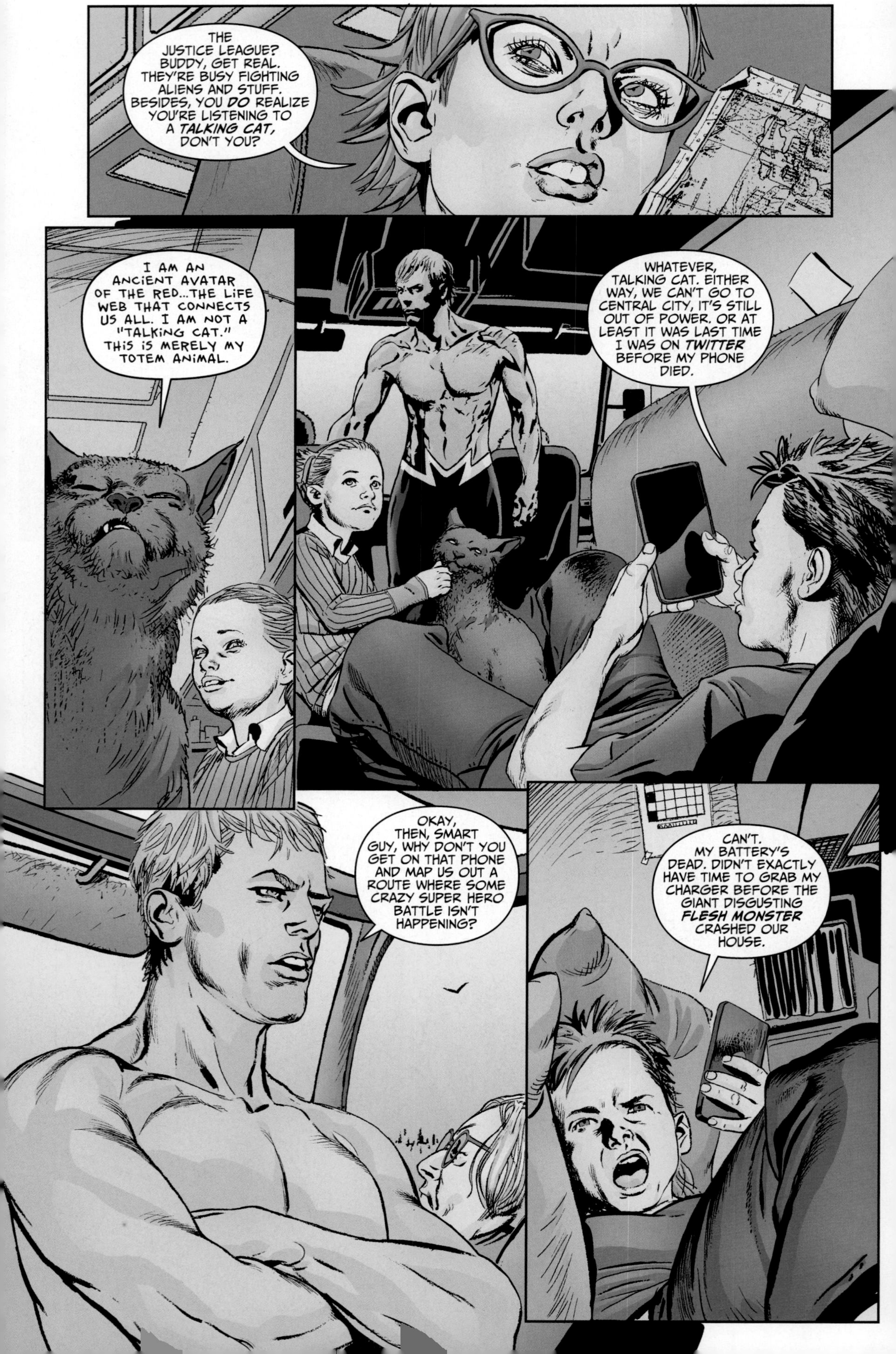
THE JUSTICE LEAGUE? BUDDY, GET REAL. THEY'RE BUSY FIGHTING ALIENS AND STUFF. BESIDES, YOU DO REALIZE YOU'RE LISTENING TO A TALKING CAT, DON'T YOU?
I AM AN ANCIENT AVATAR OF THE RED...THE LIFE WEB THAT CONNECTS US ALL. I AM NOT A "TALKING CAT." THIS IS MERELY MY TOTEM ANIMAL.
WHATEVER, TALKING CAT. EITHER WAY, WE CAN'T GO TO CENTRAL CITY, IT'S STILL OUT OF POWER. OR AT LEAST IT WAS LAST TIME I WAS ON TWITTER BEFORE MY PHONE DIED.
OKAY, THEN, SMART GUY, WHY DON'T YOU GET ON THAT PHONE AND MAP US OUT A ROUTE WHERE SOME CRAZY SUPER HERO BATTLE ISN'T HAPPENING?
CAN'T. MY BATTERY'S DEAD. DIDN'T EXACTLY HAVE TIME TO GRAB MY CHARGER BEFORE THE GIANT DISGUSTING FLESH MONSTER CRASHED OUR HOUSE.

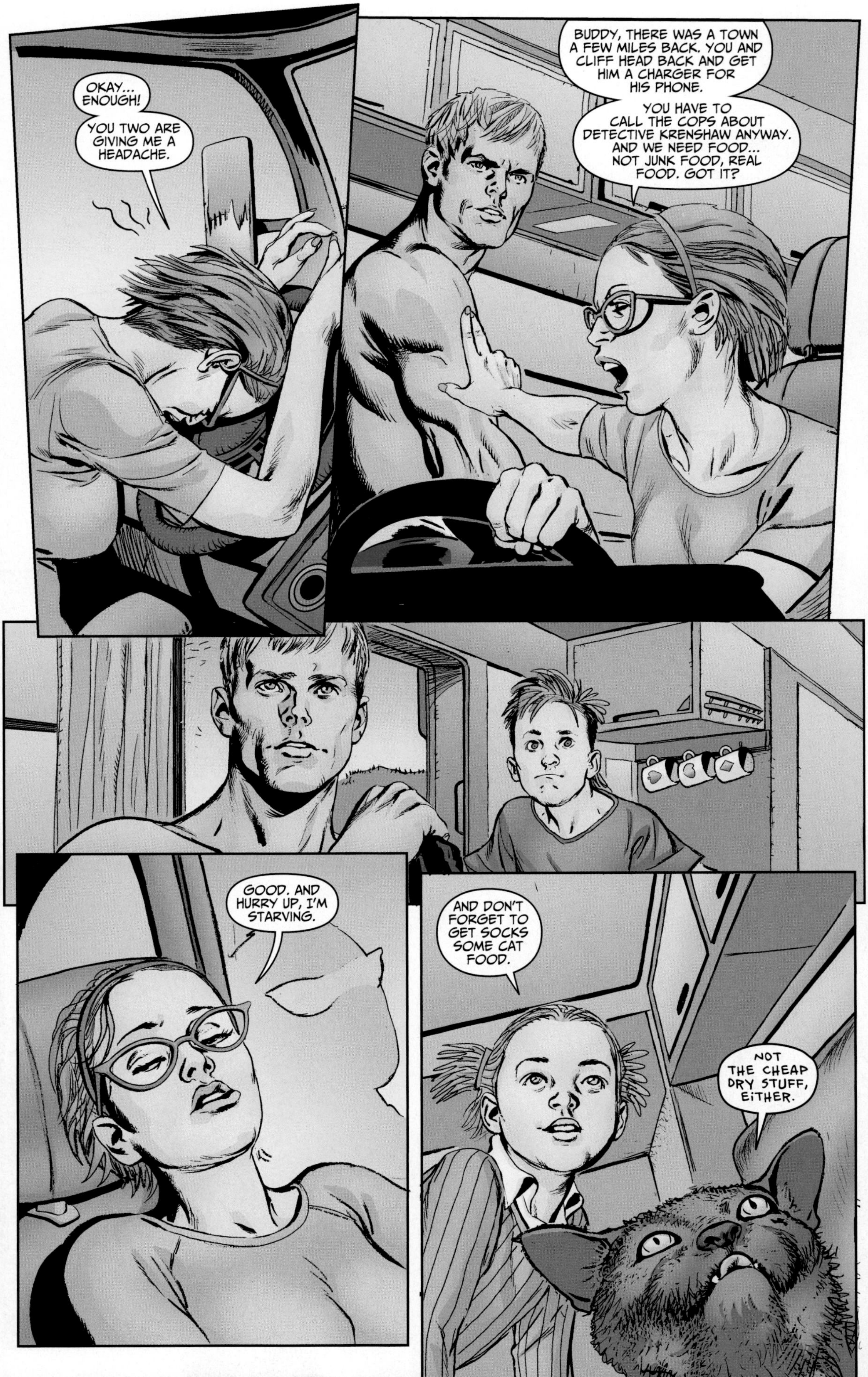
OKAY... ENOUGH!
YOU TWO ARE GIVING ME A HEADACHE.
BUDDY, THERE WAS A TOWN A FEW MILES BACK. YOU AND CLIFF HEAD BACK AND GET HIM A CHARGER FOR HIS PHONE.
YOU HAVE TO CALL THE COPS ABOUT DETECTIVE KRENSHAW ANYWAY. AND WE NEED FOOD... NOT JUNK FOOD, REAL FOOD. GOT IT?
GOOD. AND HURRY UP, I'M STARVING.
AND DON'T FORGET TO GET SOCKS SOME CAT FOOD.
NOT THE CHEAP DRY STUFF, EITHER.

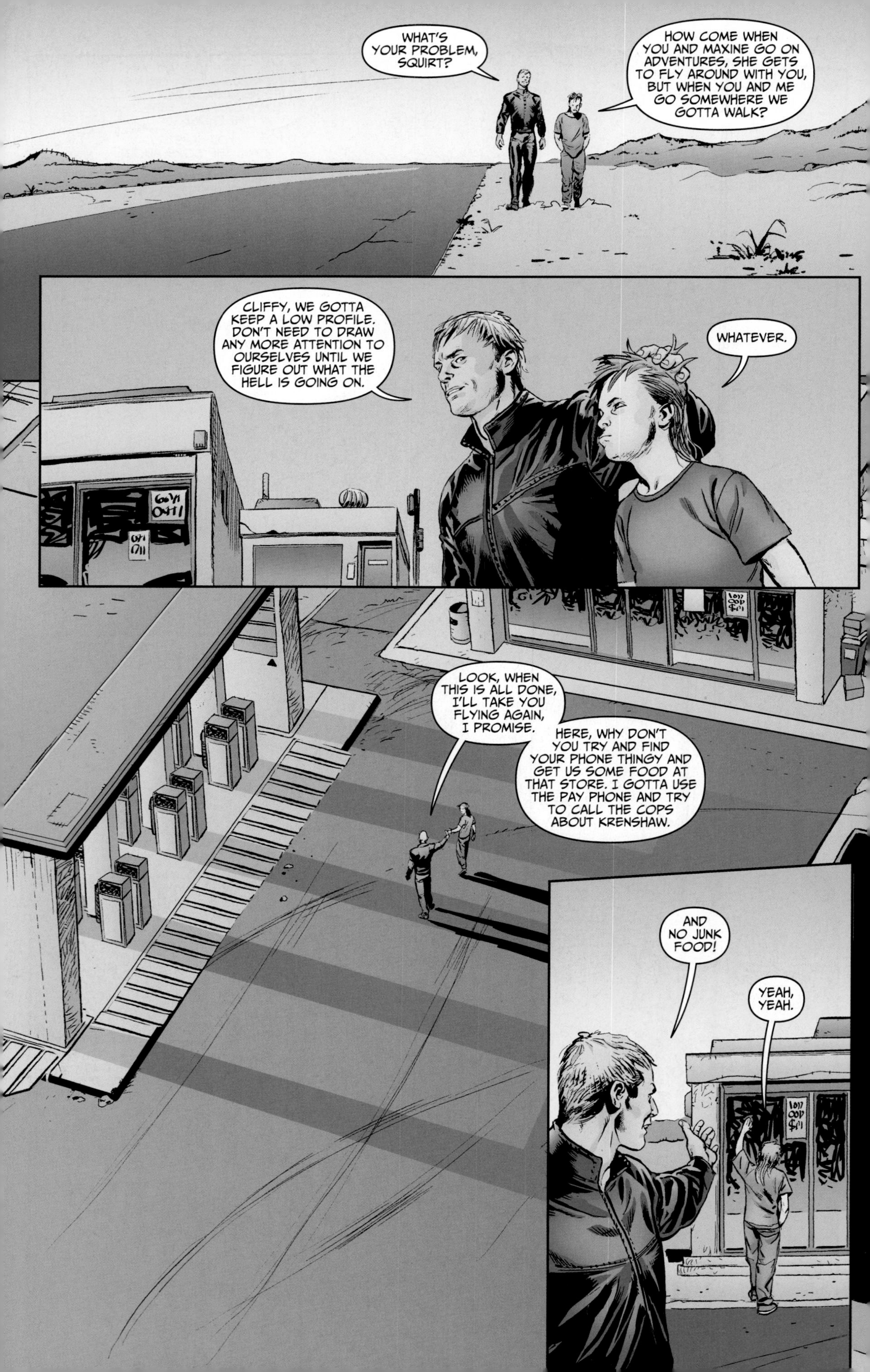
WHAT'S YOUR PROBLEM, SQUIRT?
HOW COME WHEN YOU AND MAXINE GO ON ADVENTURES, SHE GETS TO FLY AROUND WITH YOU, BUT WHEN YOU AND ME GO SOMEWHERE WE GOTTA WALK?
CLIFFY, WE GOTTA KEEP A LOW PROFILE. DON'T NEED TO DRAW ANY MORE ATTENTION TO OURSELVES UNTIL WE FIGURE OUT WHAT THE HELL IS GOING ON.
WHATEVER.
LOOK, WHEN THIS IS ALL DONE, I'LL TAKE YOU FLYING AGAIN, I PROMISE.
HERE, WHY DON'T YOU TRY AND FIND YOUR PHONE THINGY AND GET US SOME FOOD AT THAT STORE. I GOTTA USE THE PAY PHONE AND TRY TO CALL THE COPS ABOUT KRENSHAW.
AND NO JUNK FOOD!
YEAH, YEAH.

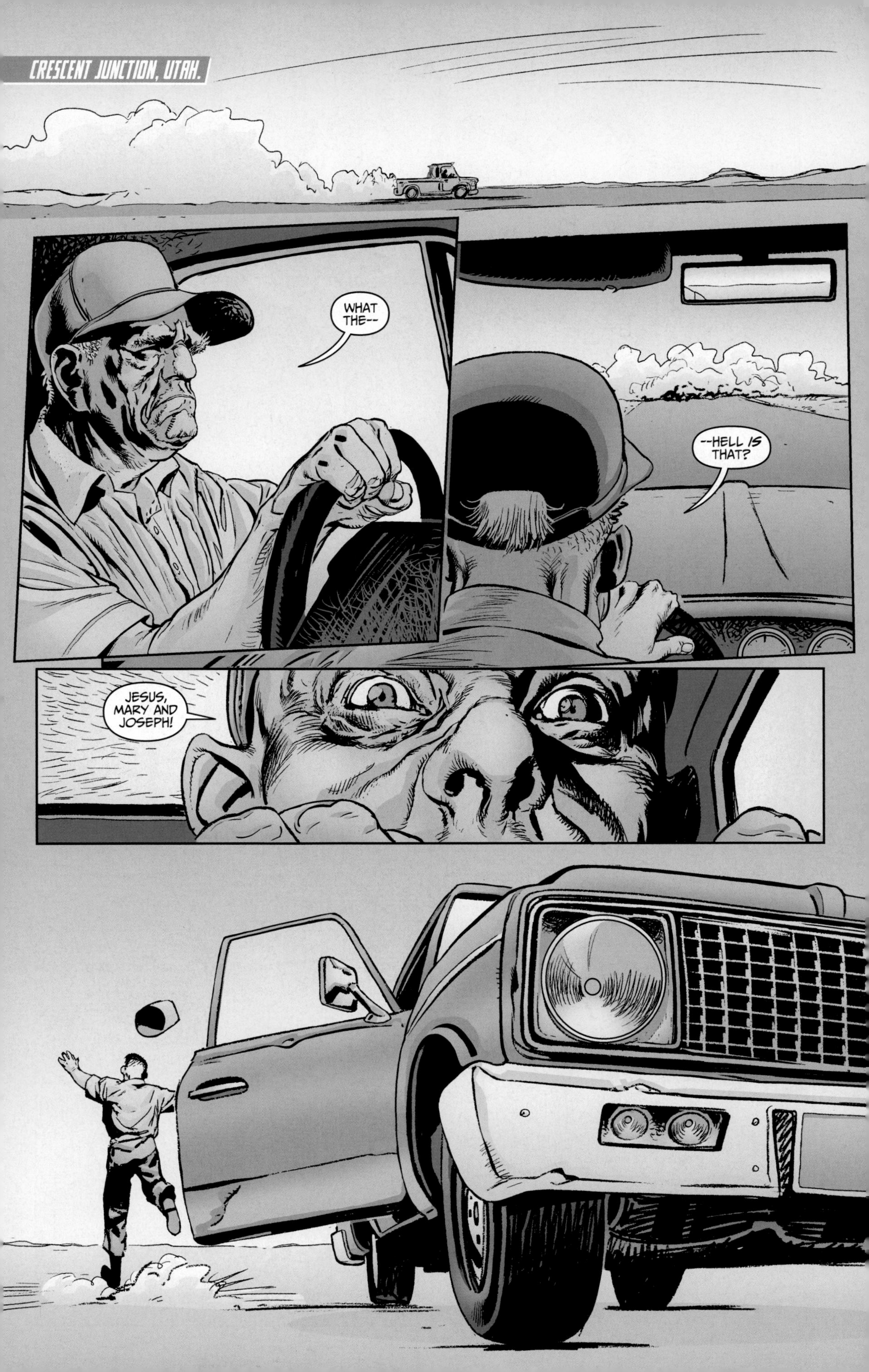
CRESCENT JUNCTION, UTAH.
WHAT THE--
--HELL IS THAT?
JESUS, MARY AND JOSEPH!

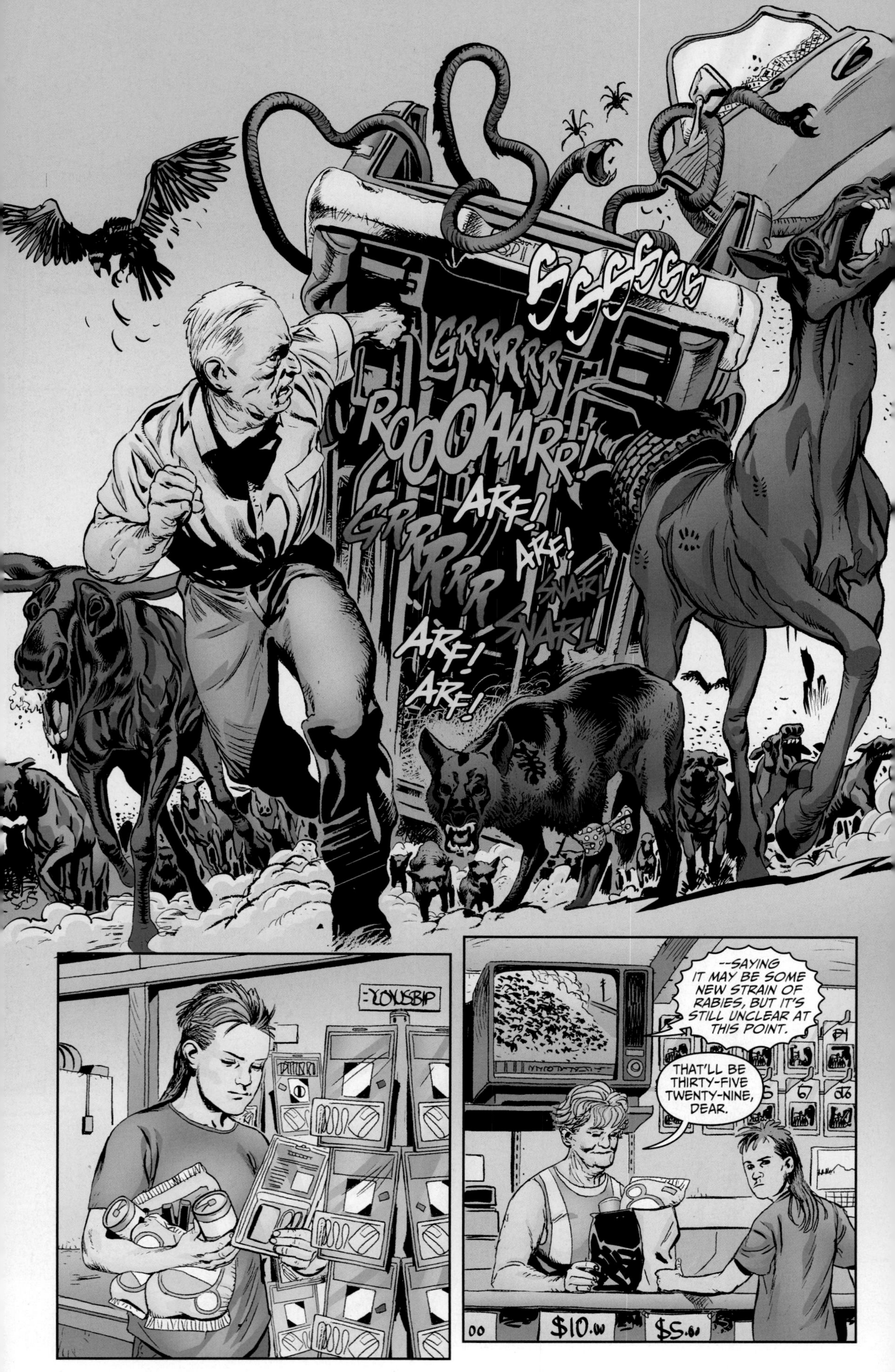
SSSSSS
GRRRRRR
ROOOAARRR!
ARF!
GRRRRRR
ARF!
SNARL
SNARL
ARF!
ARF!
--SAYING IT MAY BE SOME NEW STRAIN OF RABIES, BUT IT'S STILL UNCLEAR AT THIS POINT.
THAT'LL BE THIRTY-FIVE TWENTY-NINE, DEAR.

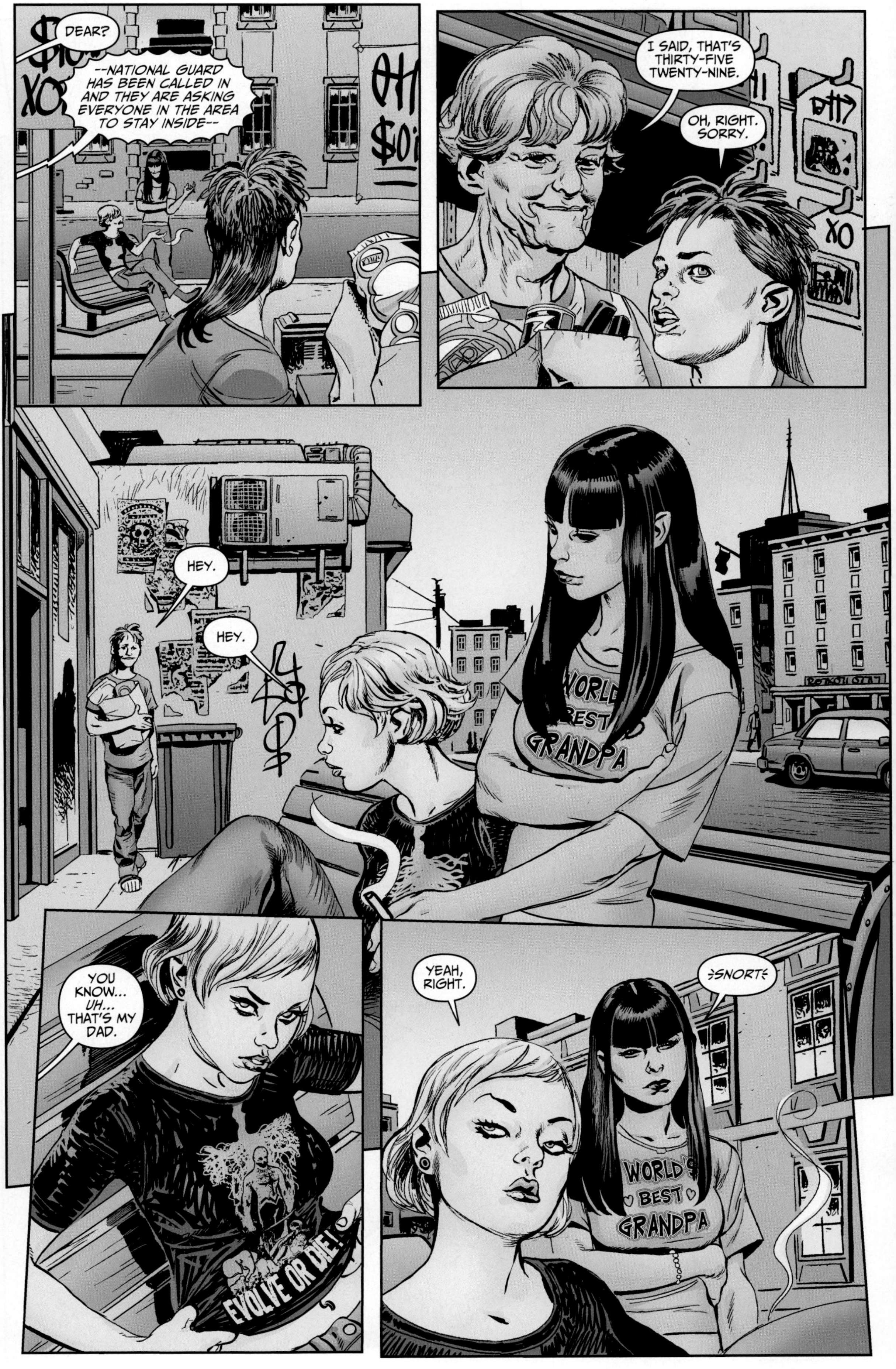
DEAR?
--NATIONAL GUARD HAS BEEN CALLED IN AND THEY ARE ASKING EVERYONE IN THE AREA TO STAY INSIDE--
I SAID, THAT'S THIRTY-FIVE TWENTY-NINE.
OH, RIGHT. SORRY.
HEY.
HEY.
WORLD'S BEST GRANDPA
YOU KNOW... UH... THAT'S MY DAD.
EVOLVE OR DIE!
YEAH, RIGHT.
SNORT
WORLD'S BEST GRANDPA

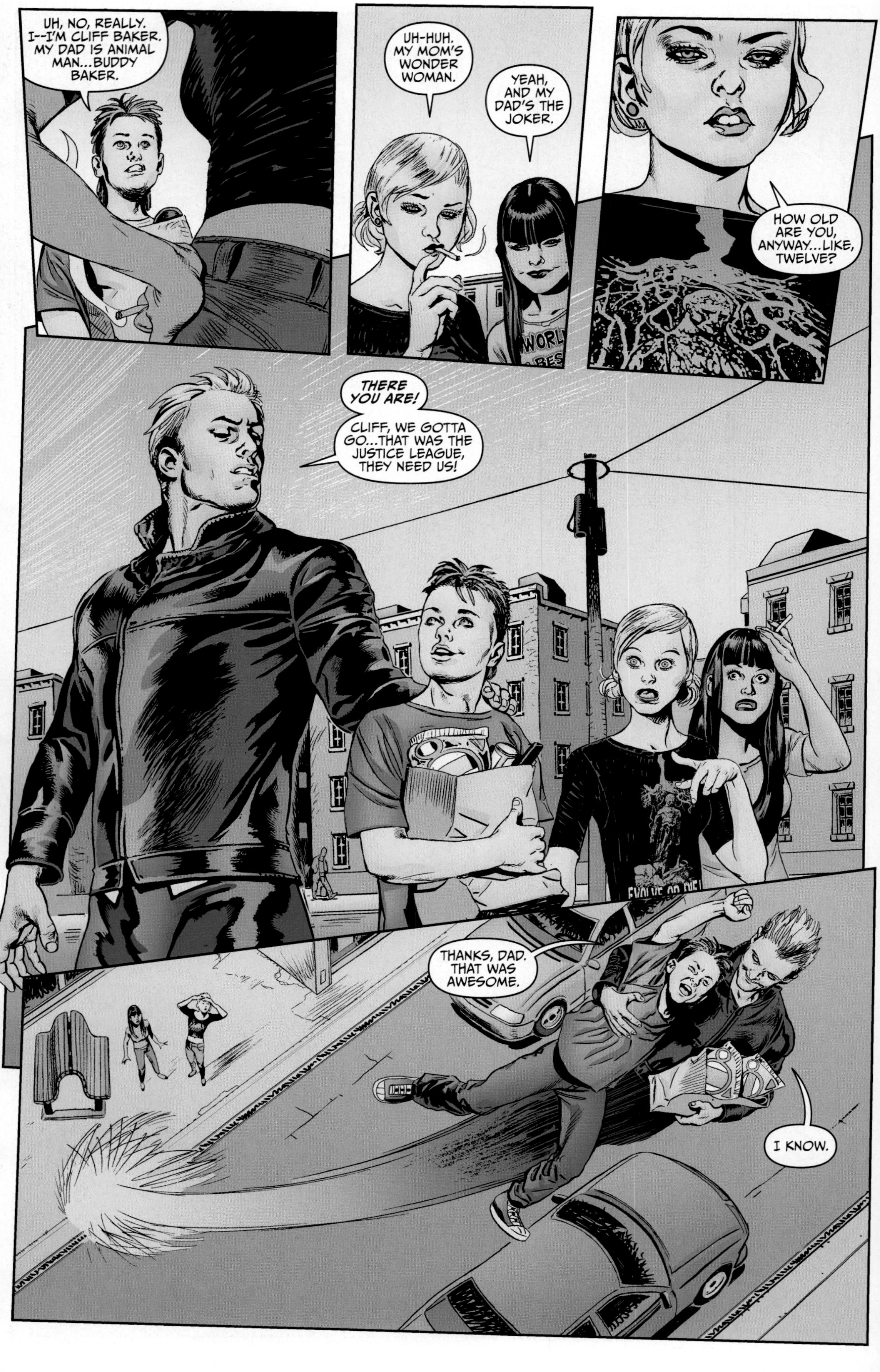
UH, NO, REALLY. I--I'M CLIFF BAKER. MY DAD IS ANIMAL MAN...BUDDY BAKER.
UH-HUH. MY MOM'S WONDER WOMAN.
YEAH, AND MY DAD'S THE JOKER.
HOW OLD ARE YOU, ANYWAY...LIKE, TWELVE?
THERE YOU ARE!
CLIFF, WE GOTTA GO...THAT WAS THE JUSTICE LEAGUE, THEY NEED US!
THANKS, DAD. THAT WAS AWESOME.
I KNOW.

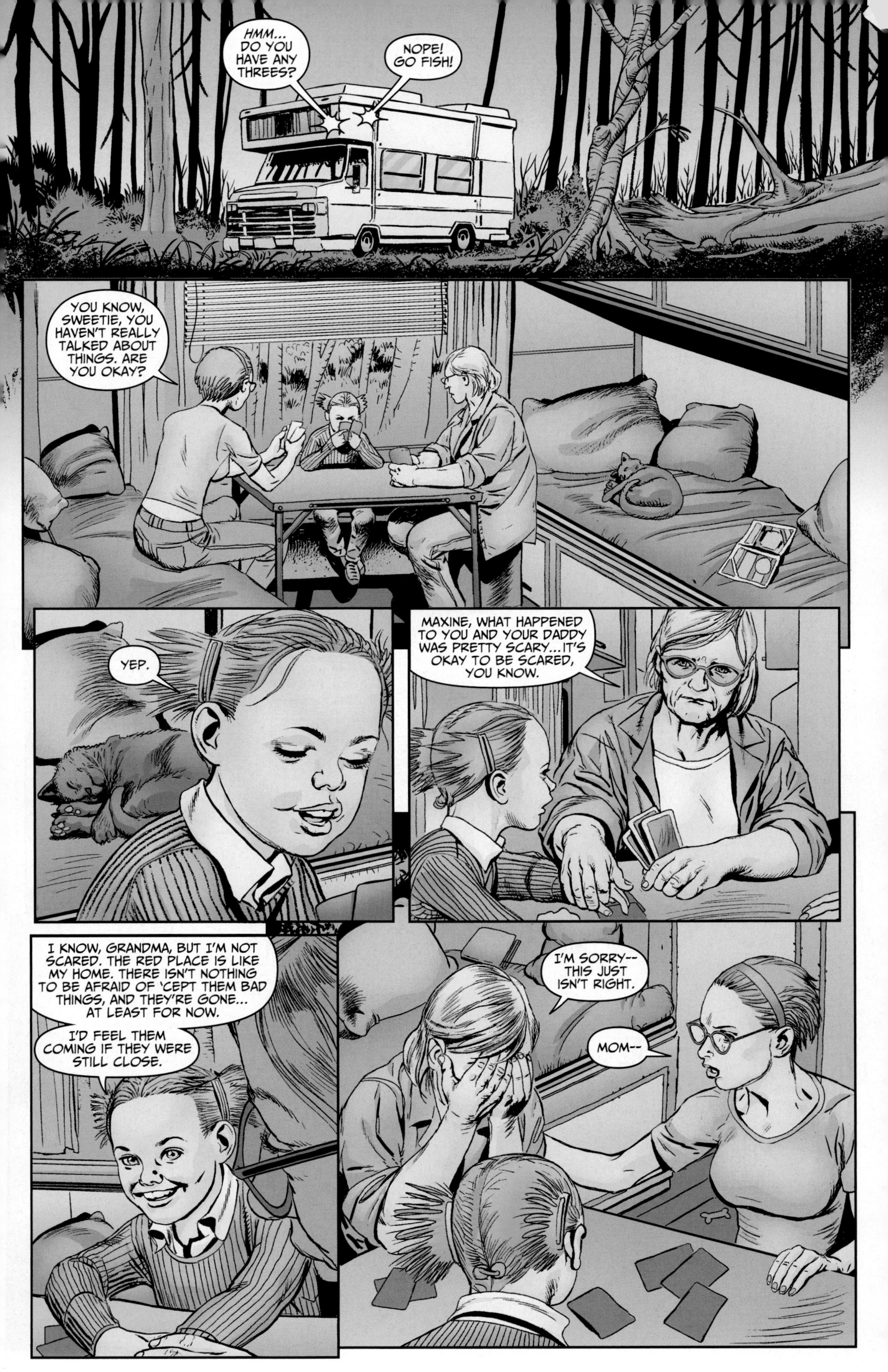
HMM... DO YOU HAVE ANY THREES?
NOPE! GO FISH!
YOU KNOW, SWEETIE, YOU HAVEN'T REALLY TALKED ABOUT THINGS. ARE YOU OKAY?
YEP.
MAXINE, WHAT HAPPENED TO YOU AND YOUR DADDY WAS PRETTY SCARY...IT'S OKAY TO BE SCARED, YOU KNOW.
I KNOW, GRANDMA, BUT I'M NOT SCARED. THE RED PLACE IS LIKE MY HOME. THERE ISN'T NOTHING TO BE AFRAID OF 'CEPT THEM BAD THINGS, AND THEY'RE GONE... AT LEAST FOR NOW.
I'D FEEL THEM COMING IF THEY WERE STILL CLOSE.
I'M SORRY-- THIS JUST ISN'T RIGHT.
MOM--

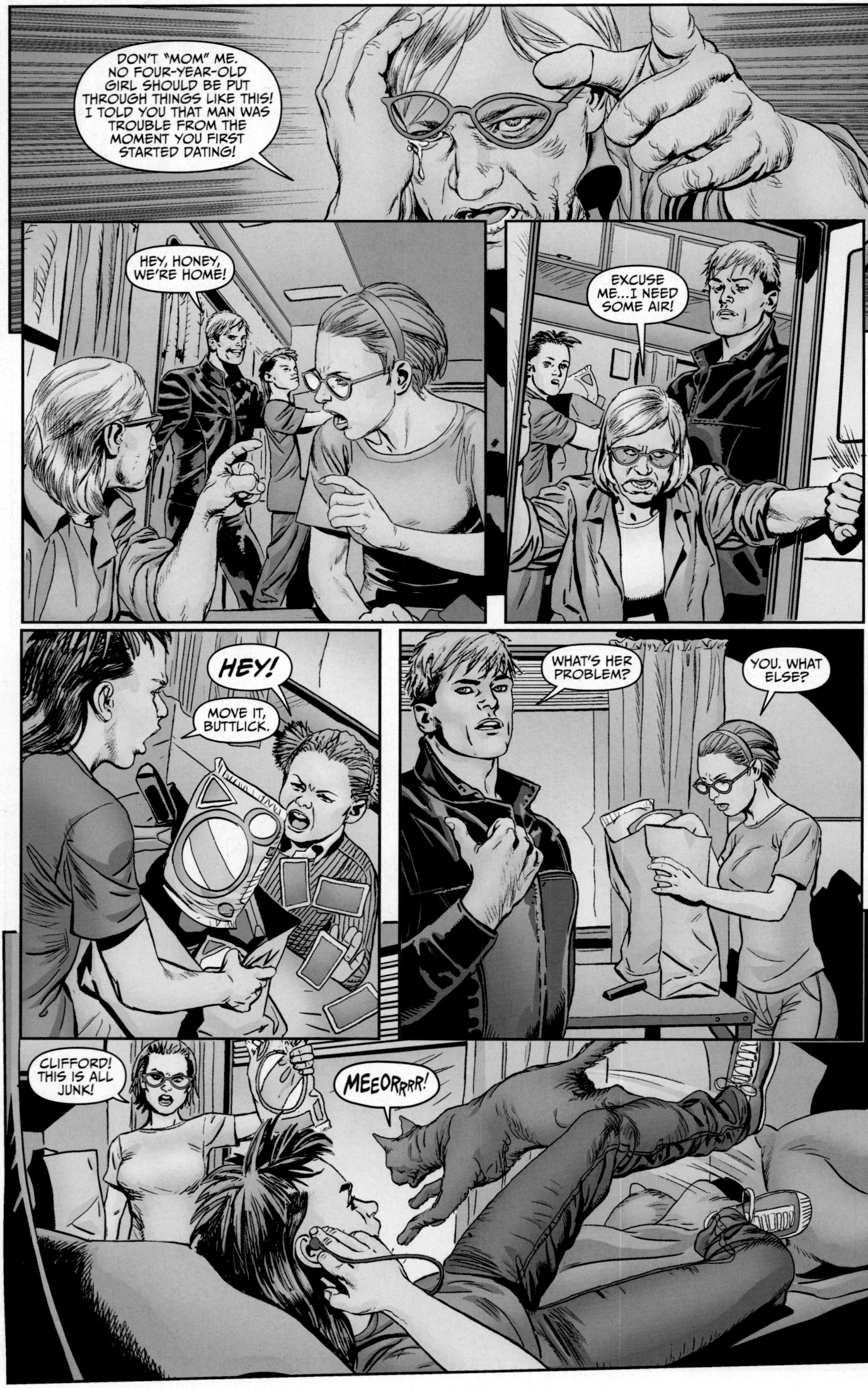
DON'T "MOM" ME. NO FOUR-YEAR-OLD GIRL SHOULD BE PUT THROUGH THINGS LIKE THIS! I TOLD YOU THAT MAN WAS TROUBLE FROM THE MOMENT YOU FIRST STARTED DATING!
HEY, HONEY, WE'RE HOME!
EXCUSE ME...I NEED SOME AIR!
HEY!
MOVE IT, BUTTLICK.
WHAT'S HER PROBLEM?
YOU. WHAT ELSE?
CLIFFORD! THIS IS ALL JUNK!
MEEORRRR!

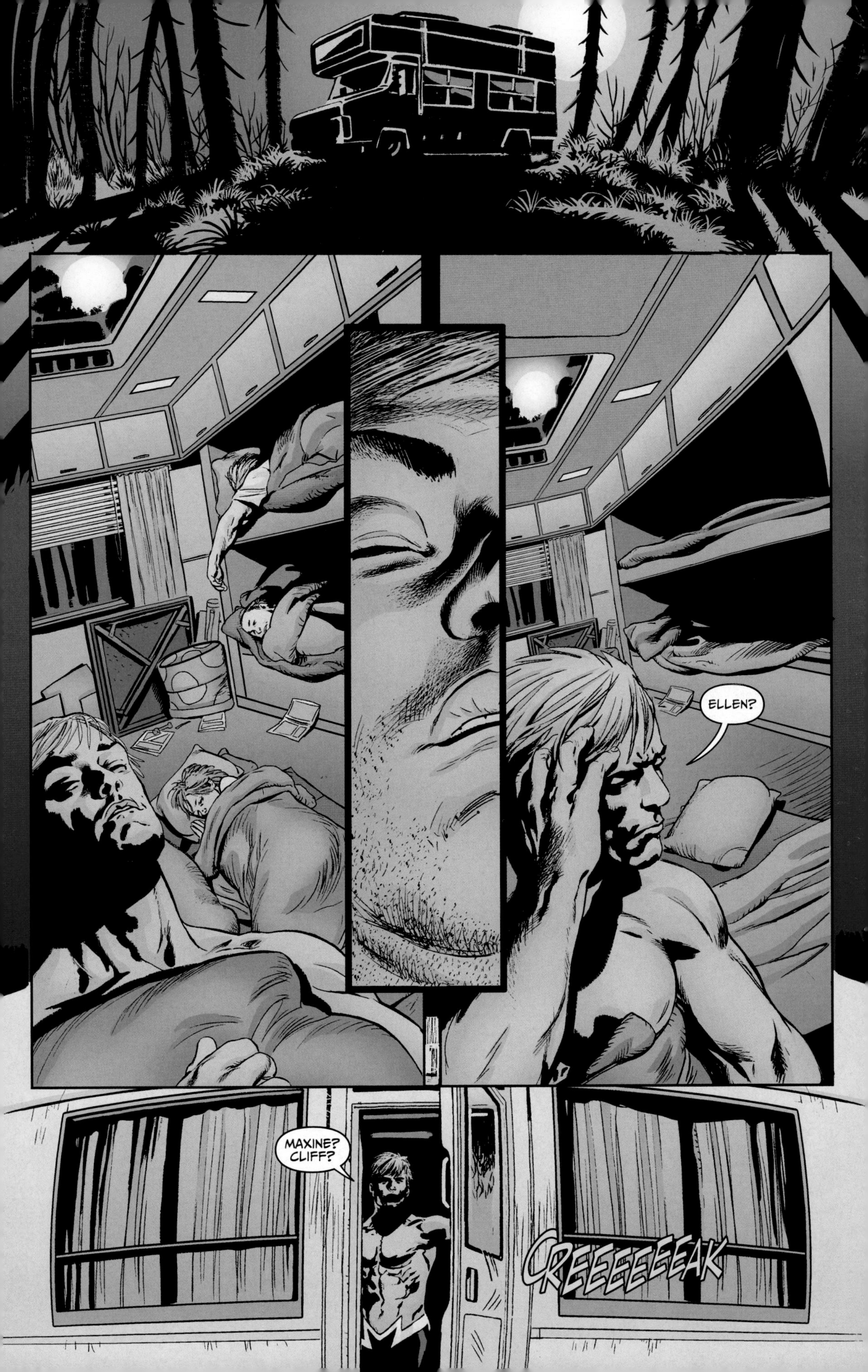
ELLEN?
MAXINE? CLIFF?
CREEEEEEAK

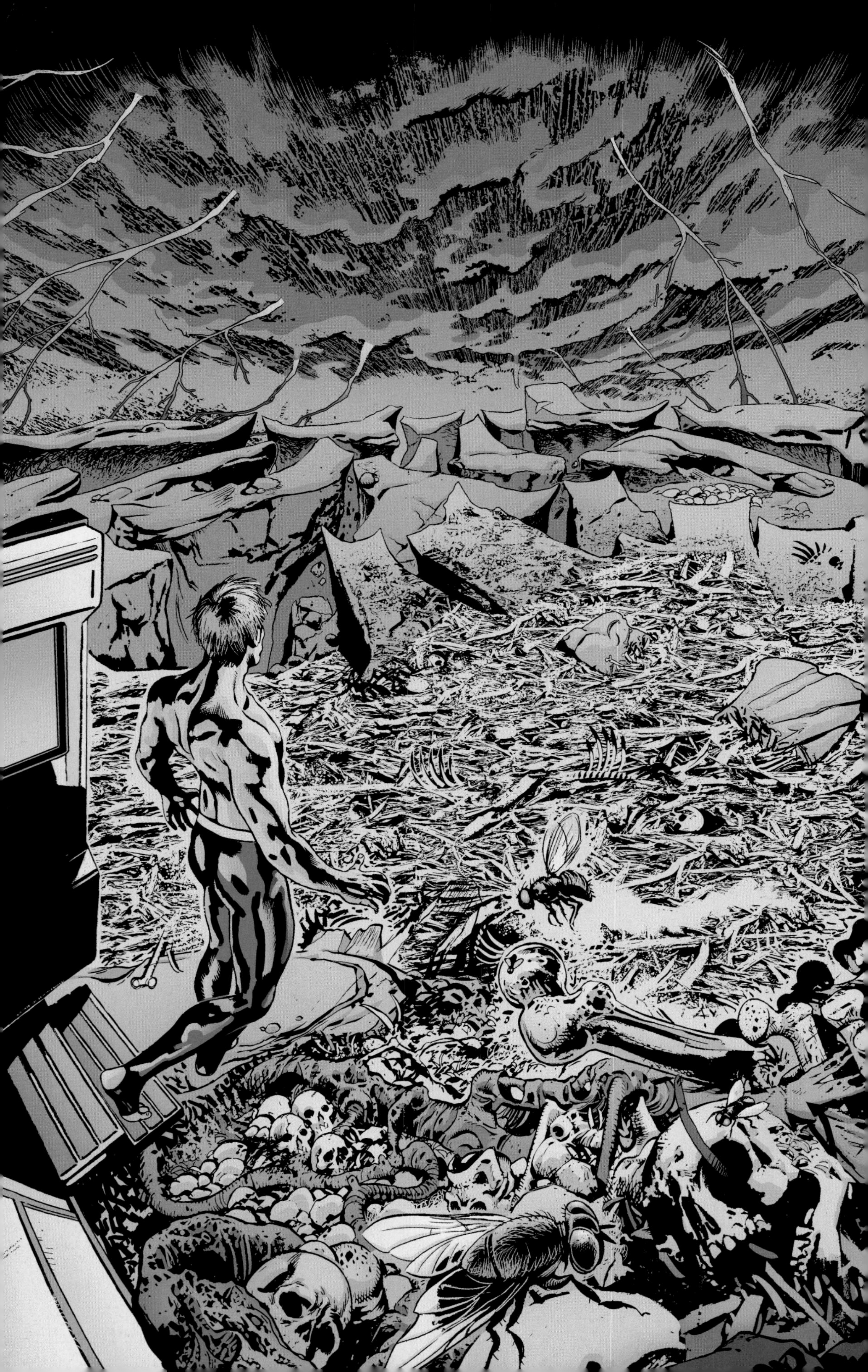

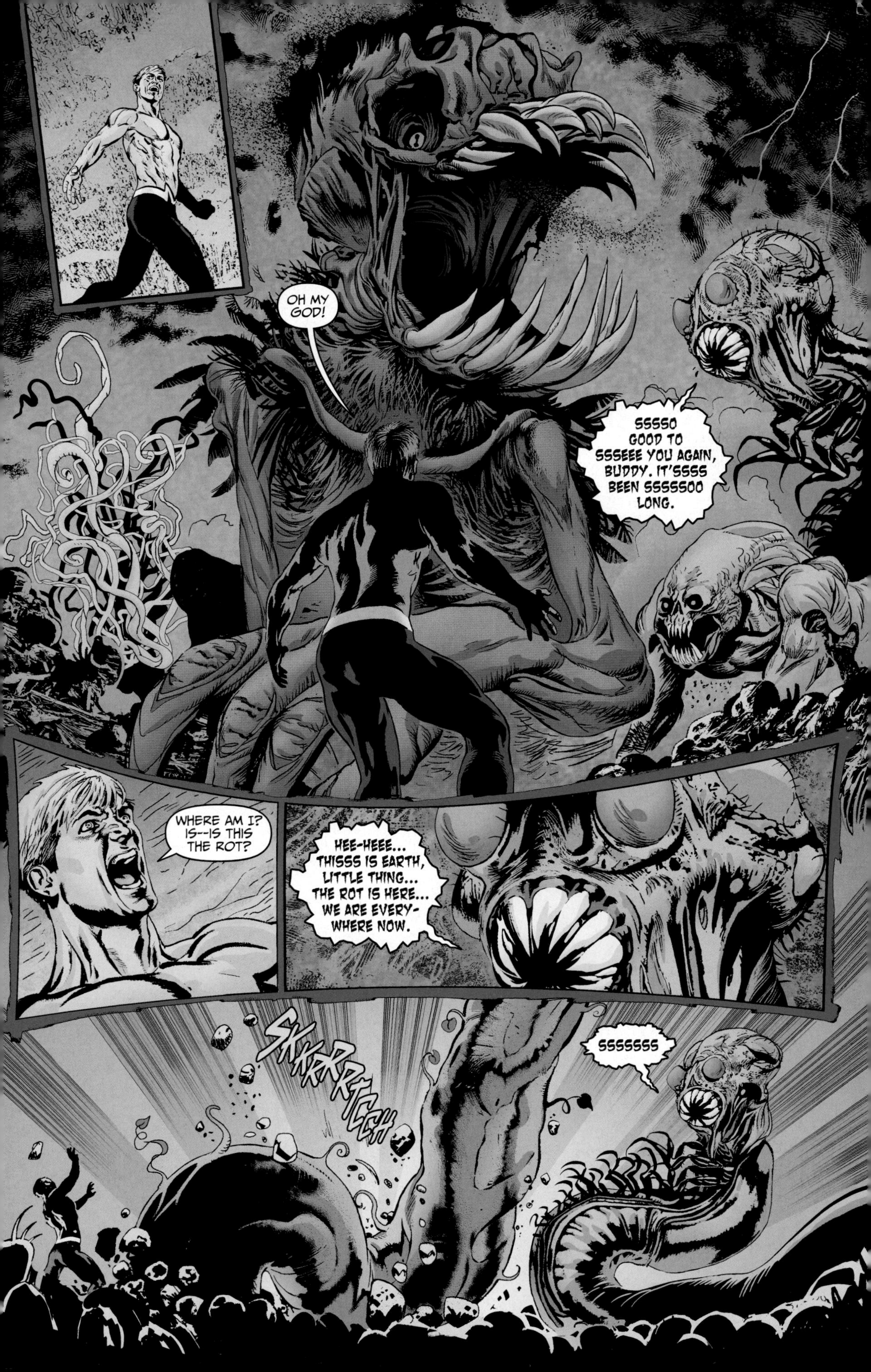
OH MY GOD!
SSSSO GOOD TO SSSEEE YOU AGAIN, BUDDY. IT'SSSS BEEN SSSSSOO LONG.
WHERE AM I? IS--IS THIS THE ROT?
HEE-HEEE... THISSS IS EARTH, LITTLE THING... THE ROT IS HERE... WE ARE EVERY-WHERE NOW.
SKKRRRTCH
SSSSSSS

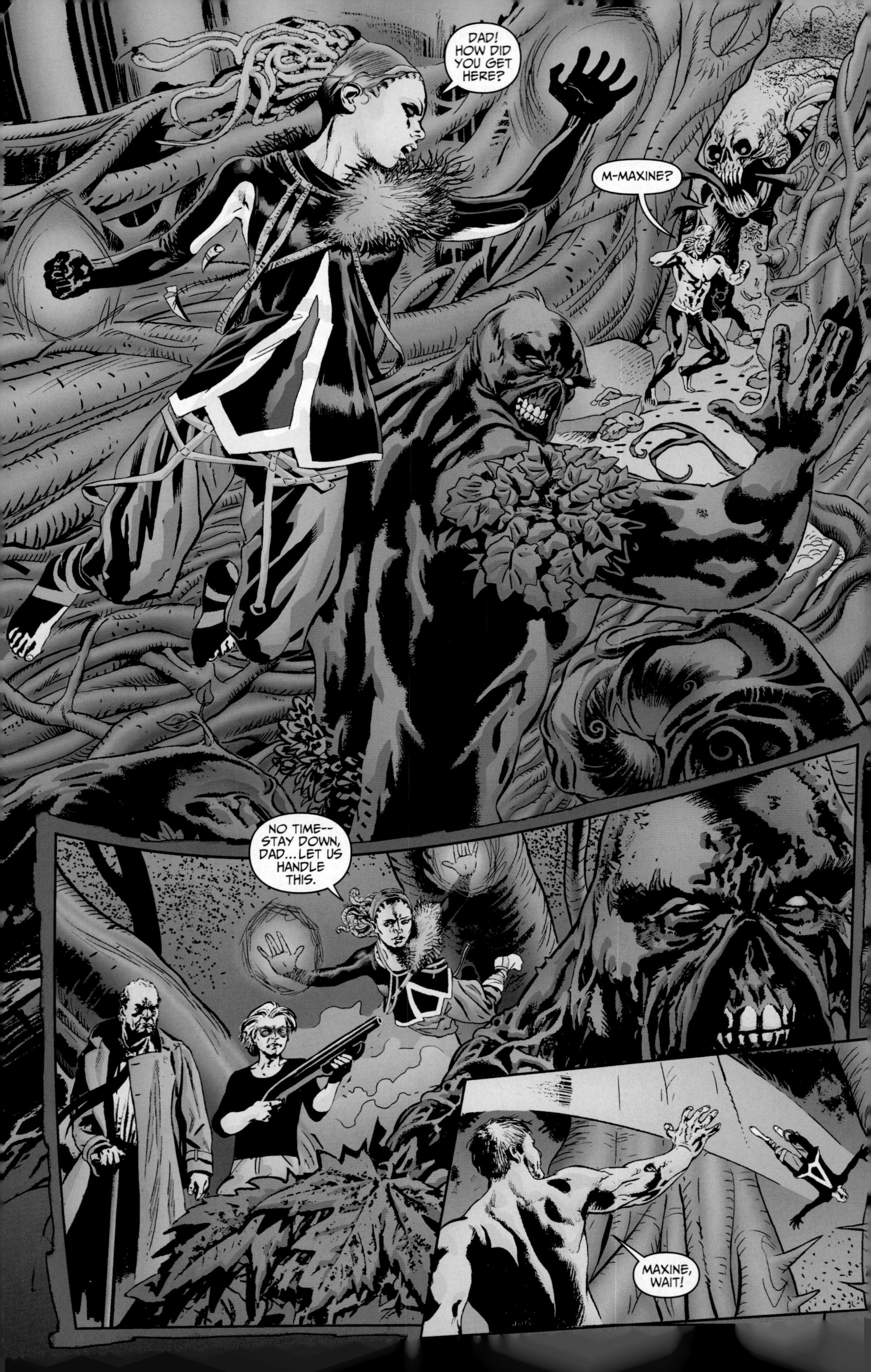
DAD! HOW DID YOU GET HERE?
M-MAXINE?
NO TIME-- STAY DOWN, DAD...LET US HANDLE THIS.
MAXINE, WAIT!

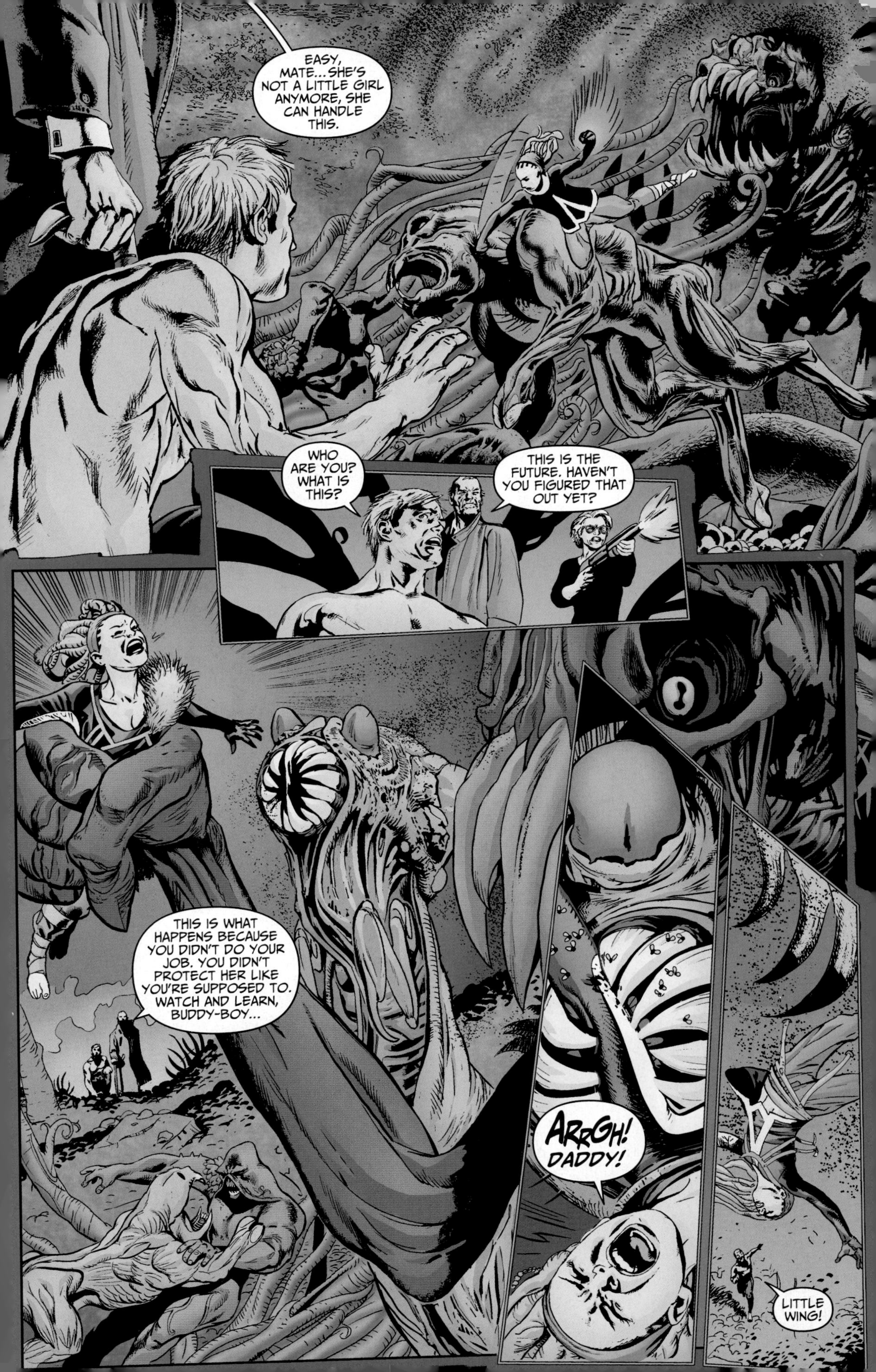
EASY, MATE...SHE'S NOT A LITTLE GIRL ANYMORE, SHE CAN HANDLE THIS.
WHO ARE YOU? WHAT IS THIS?
THIS IS THE FUTURE. HAVEN'T YOU FIGURED THAT OUT YET?
THIS IS WHAT HAPPENS BECAUSE YOU DIDN'T DO YOUR JOB. YOU DIDN'T PROTECT HER LIKE YOU'RE SUPPOSED TO. WATCH AND LEARN, BUDDY-BOY...
ARRGH! DADDY!
LITTLE WING!

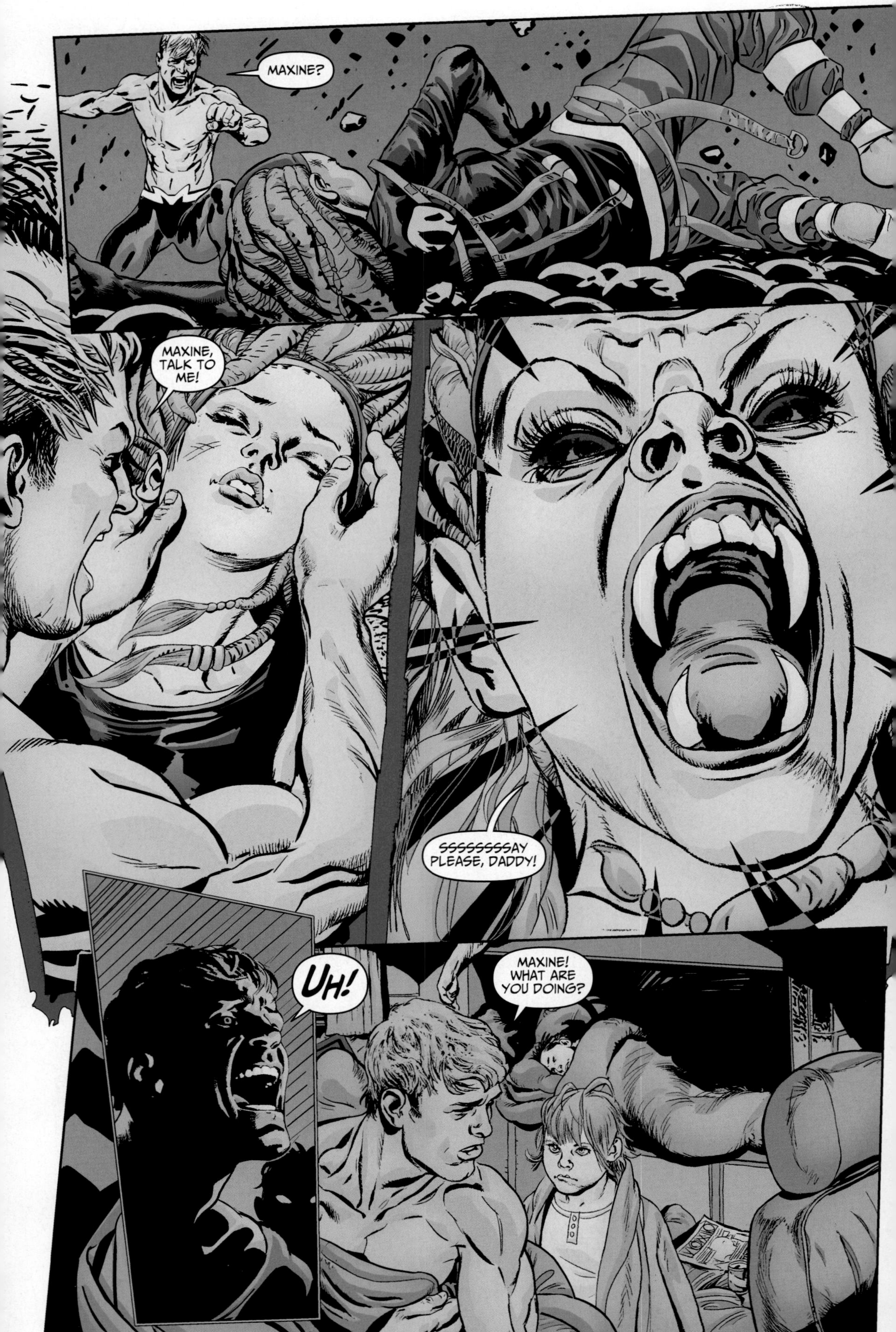
MAXINE?
MAXINE, TALK TO ME!
SSSSSSSSSAY PLEASE, DADDY!
UH!
MAXINE! WHAT ARE YOU DOING?

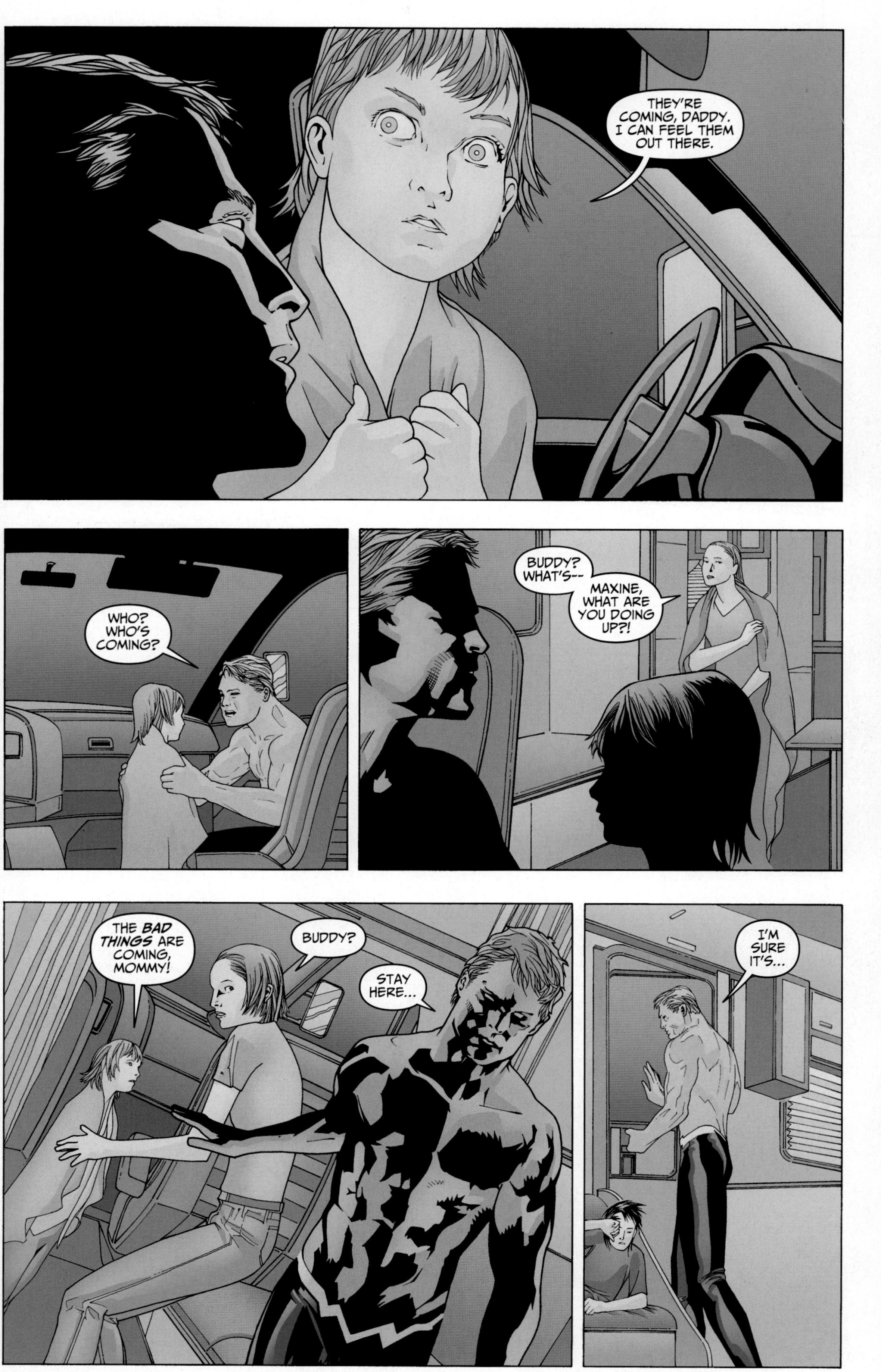
THEY'RE COMING, DADDY. I CAN FEEL THEM OUT THERE.
WHO? WHO'S COMING?
BUDDY? WHAT'S--
MAXINE, WHAT ARE YOU DOING UP?!
THE *BAD THINGS* ARE COMING, MOMMY!
BUDDY?
STAY HERE...
I'M SURE IT'S...

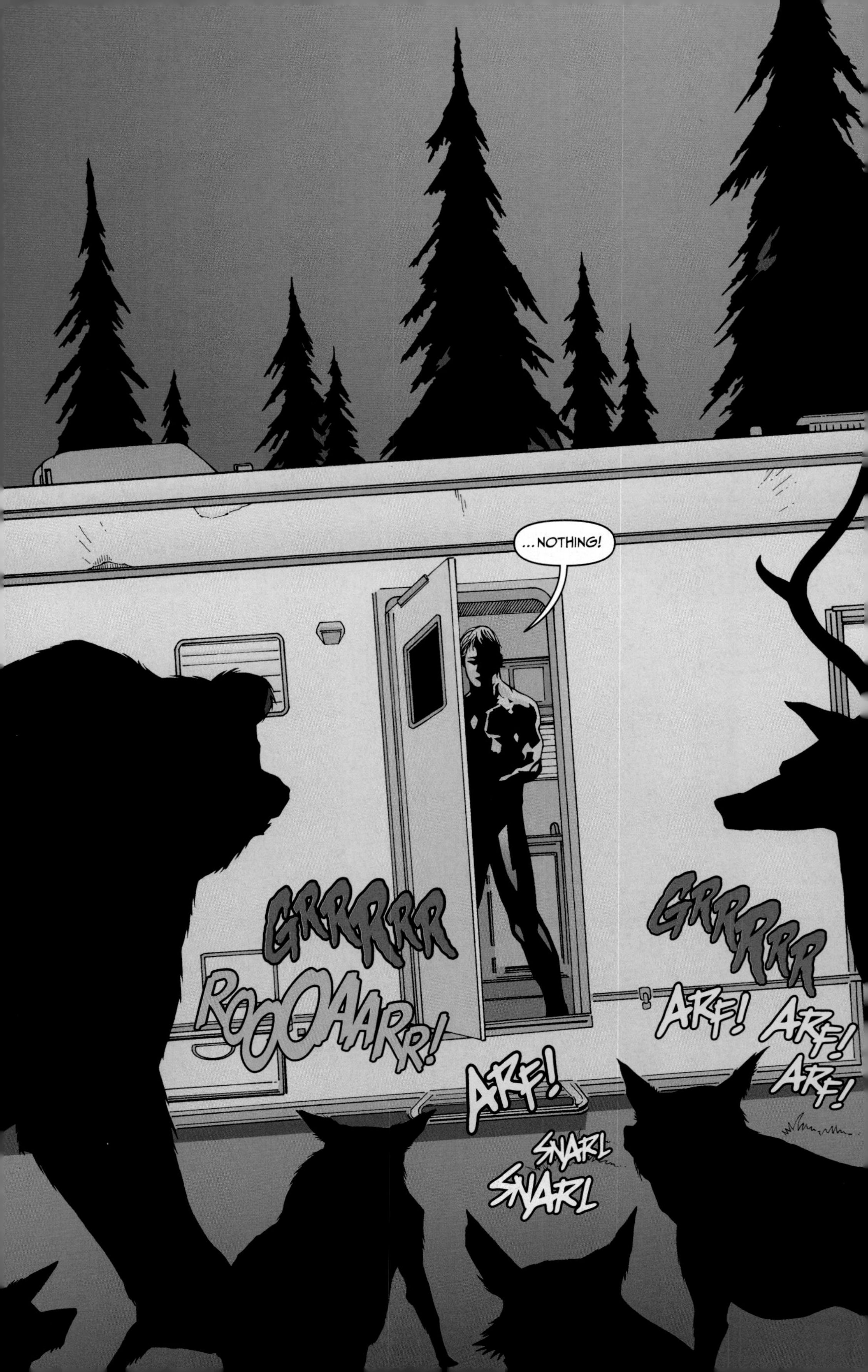
...NOTHING!
GRRRRR
ROOOAARR!
GRRRRR
ARF! ARF! ARF!
ARF!
SNARL
SNARL

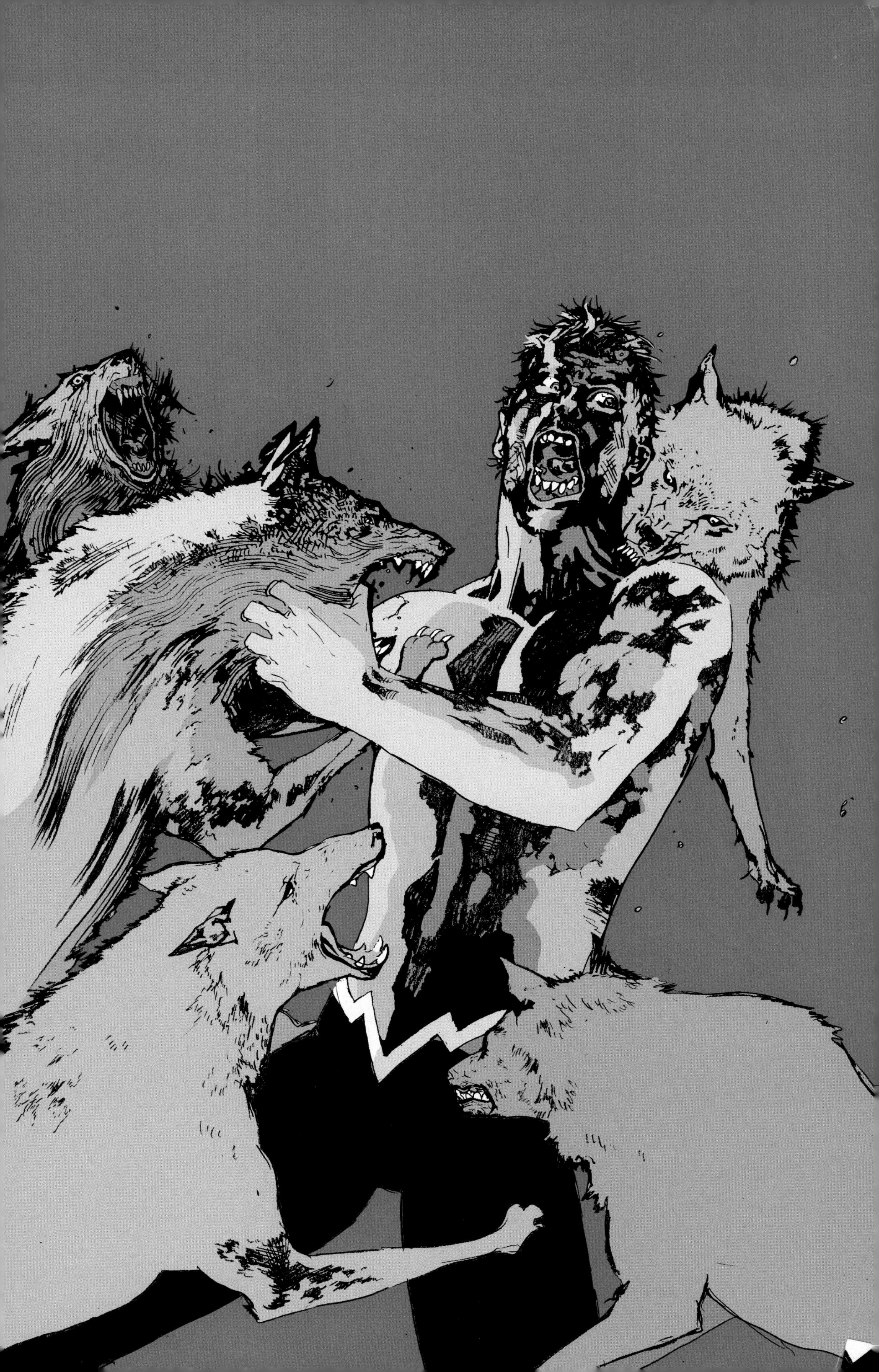

JEFF LEMIRE writer **STEVE PUGH** artist **TRAVEL FOREMAN with JEFF HUET** additional art
cover by **TRAVEL FOREMAN with LOVERN KINDZIERSKI**

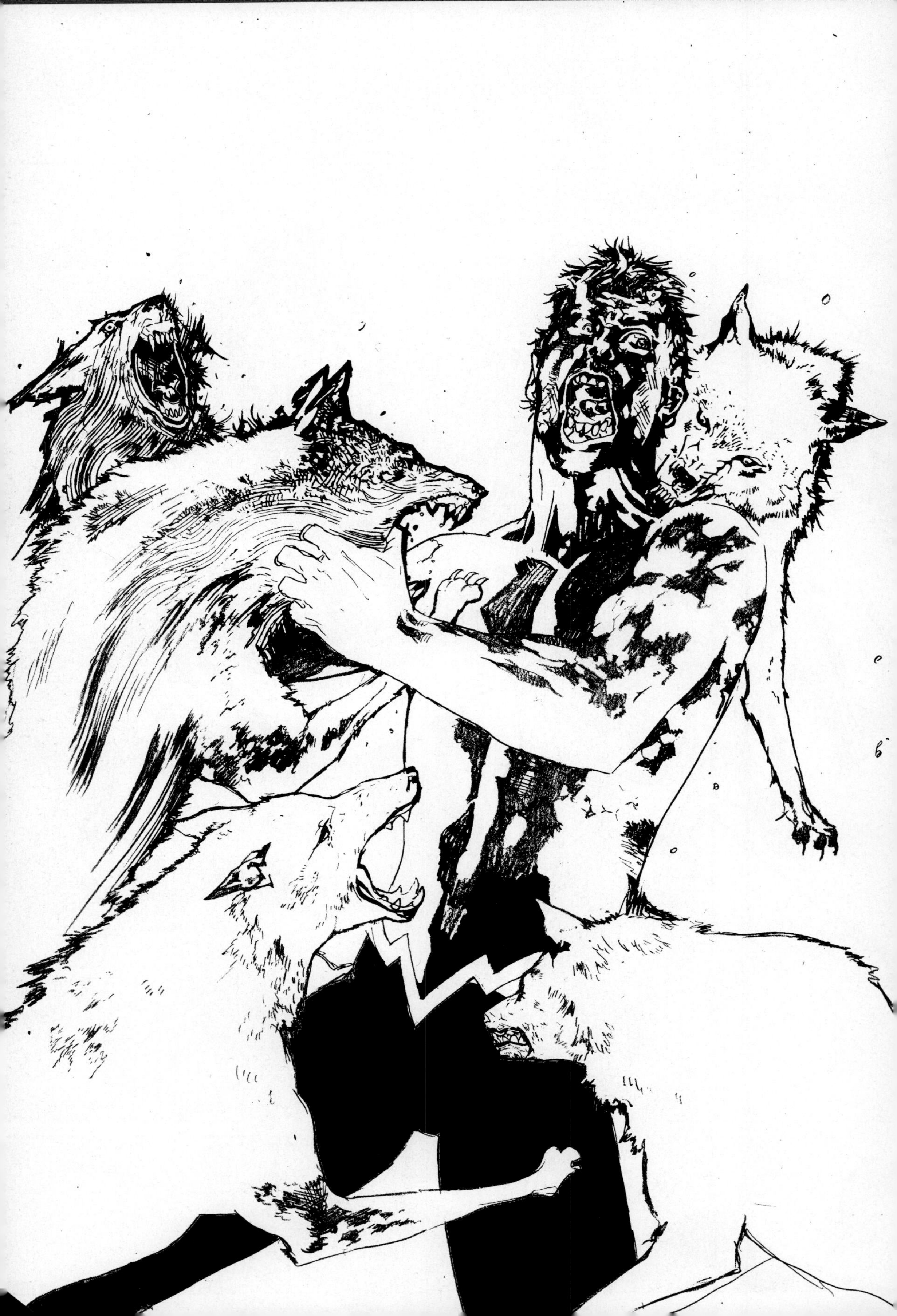

ANIMAL vs. MAN part two

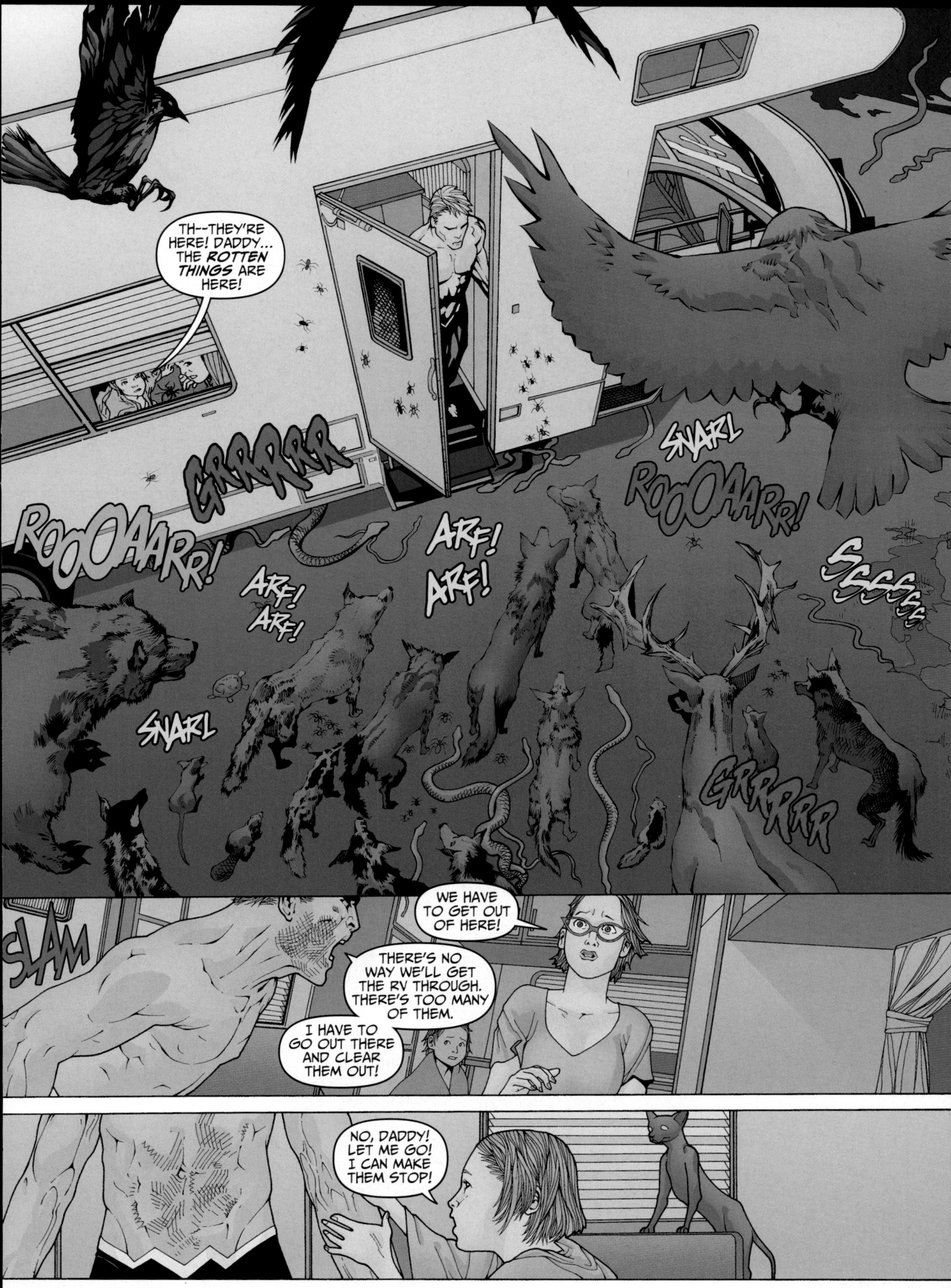
TH--THEY'RE HERE! DADDY... THE ROTTEN THINGS ARE HERE!
GRRRRR
ROOOAARR!
SNARL
ROOOAARR!
ARF! ARF!
ARF! ARF!
SSSSSS
SNARL
GRRRRR
SLAM
WE HAVE TO GET OUT OF HERE!
THERE'S NO WAY WE'LL GET THE RV THROUGH. THERE'S TOO MANY OF THEM.
I HAVE TO GO OUT THERE AND CLEAR THEM OUT!
NO, DADDY! LET ME GO! I CAN MAKE THEM STOP!

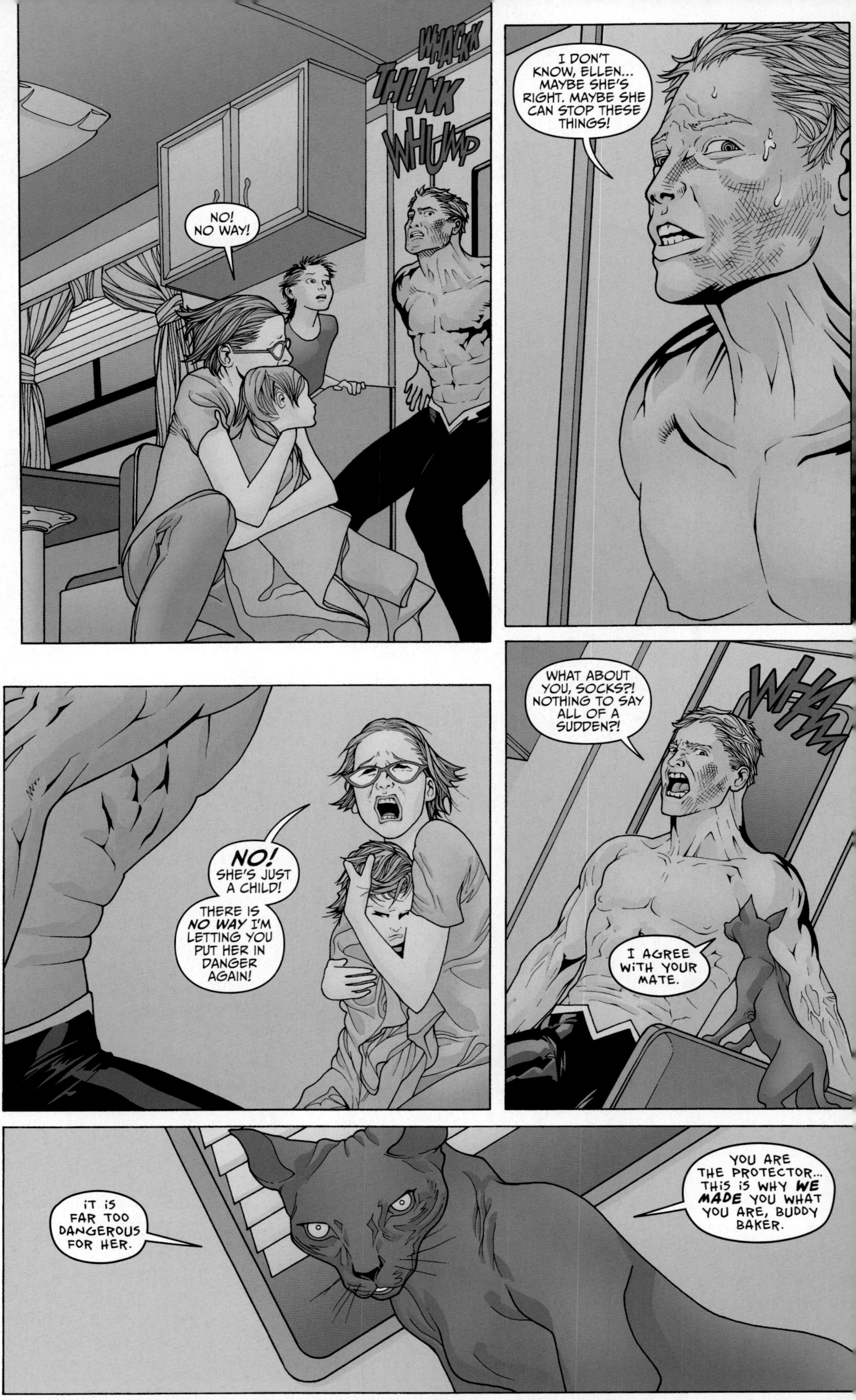
WHACKK
THUNK
WHUMP
NO! NO WAY!
I DON'T KNOW, ELLEN... MAYBE SHE'S RIGHT. MAYBE SHE CAN STOP THESE THINGS!
NO! SHE'S JUST A CHILD!
THERE IS NO WAY I'M LETTING YOU PUT HER IN DANGER AGAIN!
WHAM
WHAT ABOUT YOU, SOCKS?! NOTHING TO SAY ALL OF A SUDDEN?!
I AGREE WITH YOUR MATE.
IT IS FAR TOO DANGEROUS FOR HER.
YOU ARE THE PROTECTOR... THIS IS WHY WE MADE YOU WHAT YOU ARE, BUDDY BAKER.

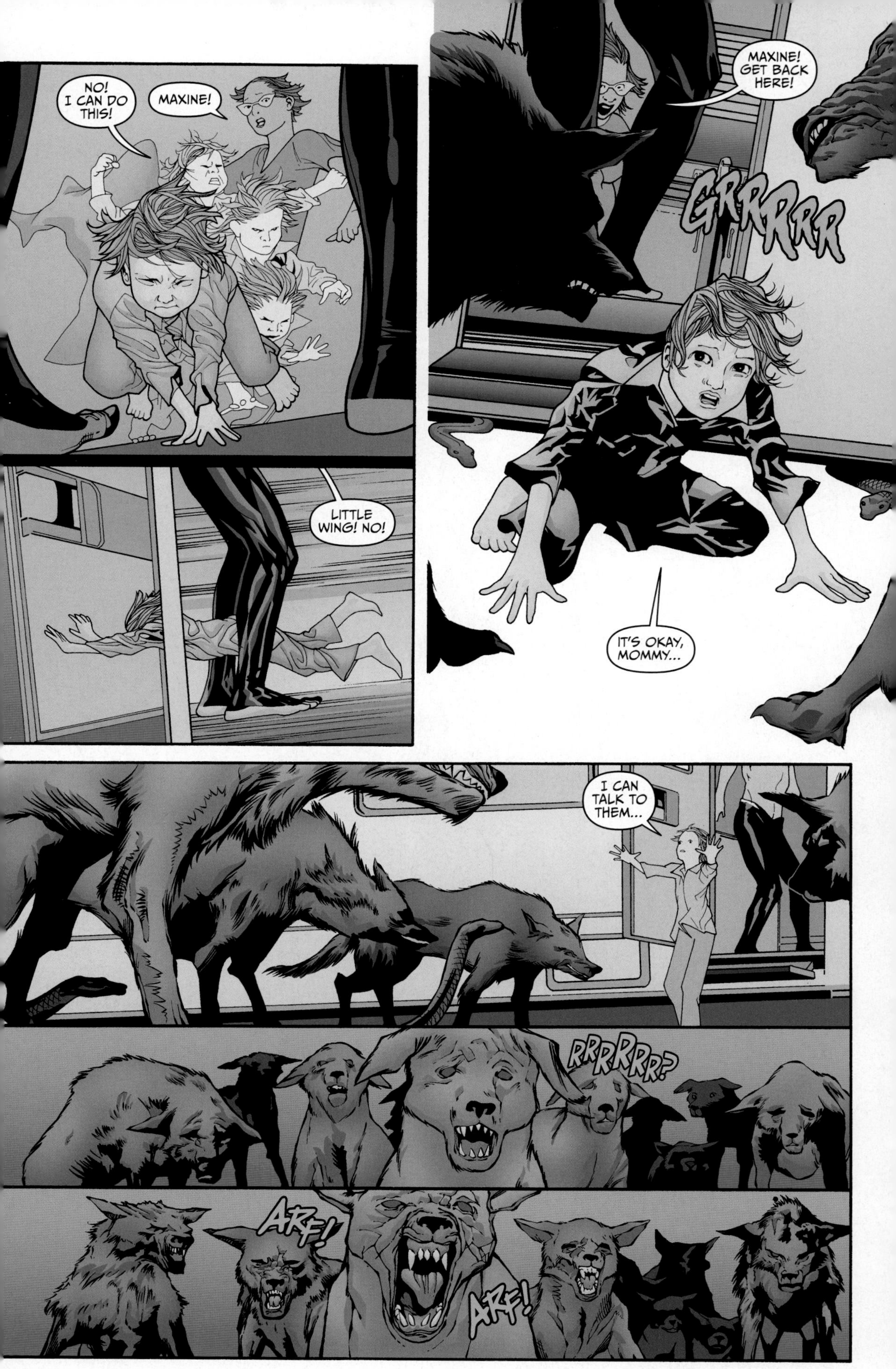
NO! I CAN DO THIS!
MAXINE!
MAXINE! GET BACK HERE!
GRRRRR
LITTLE WING! NO!
IT'S OKAY, MOMMY...
I CAN TALK TO THEM...
RRRRRR?
ARF!
ARF!

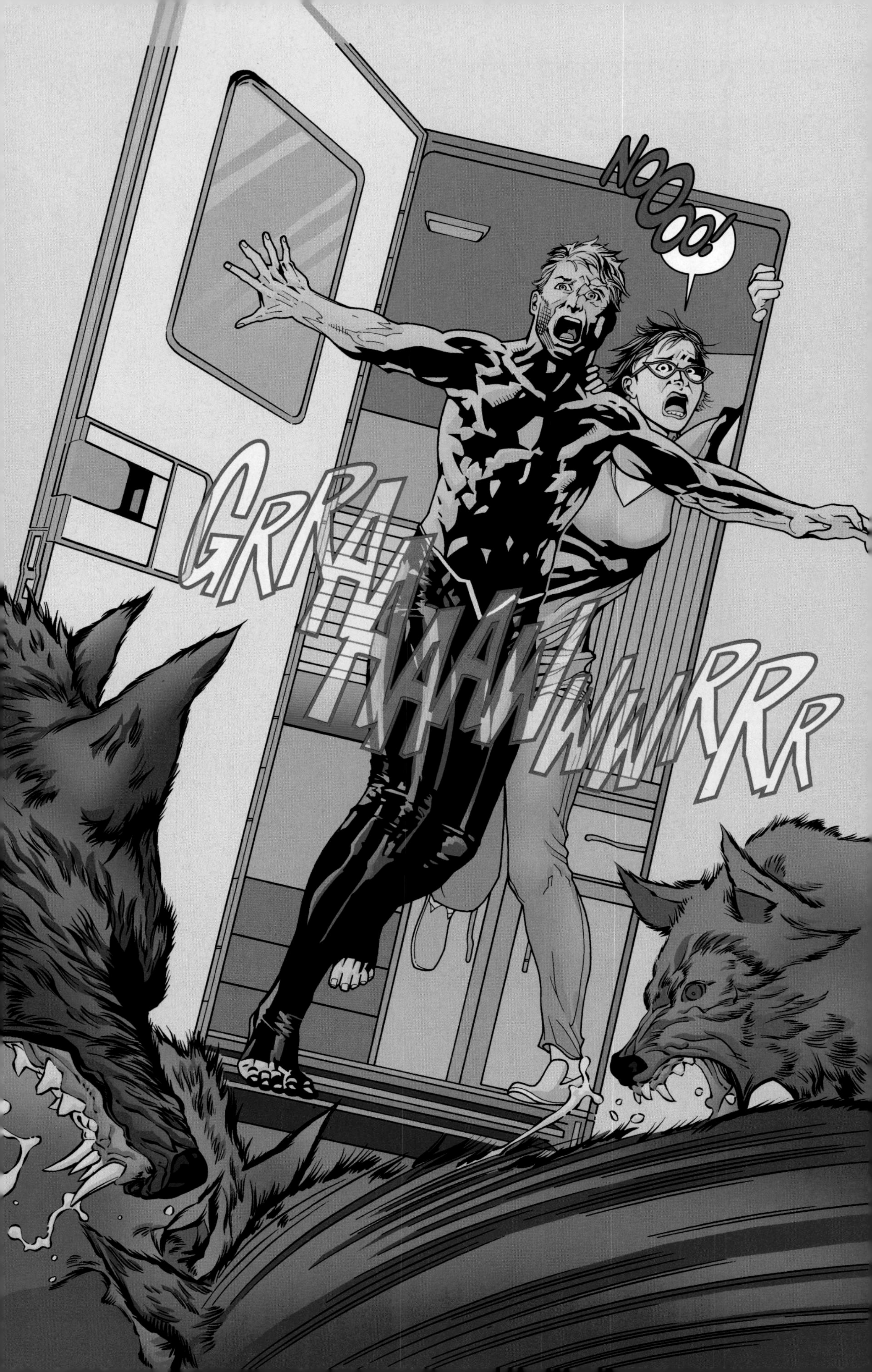
NOOOO!
GRRAAHHAAWWWRRRR

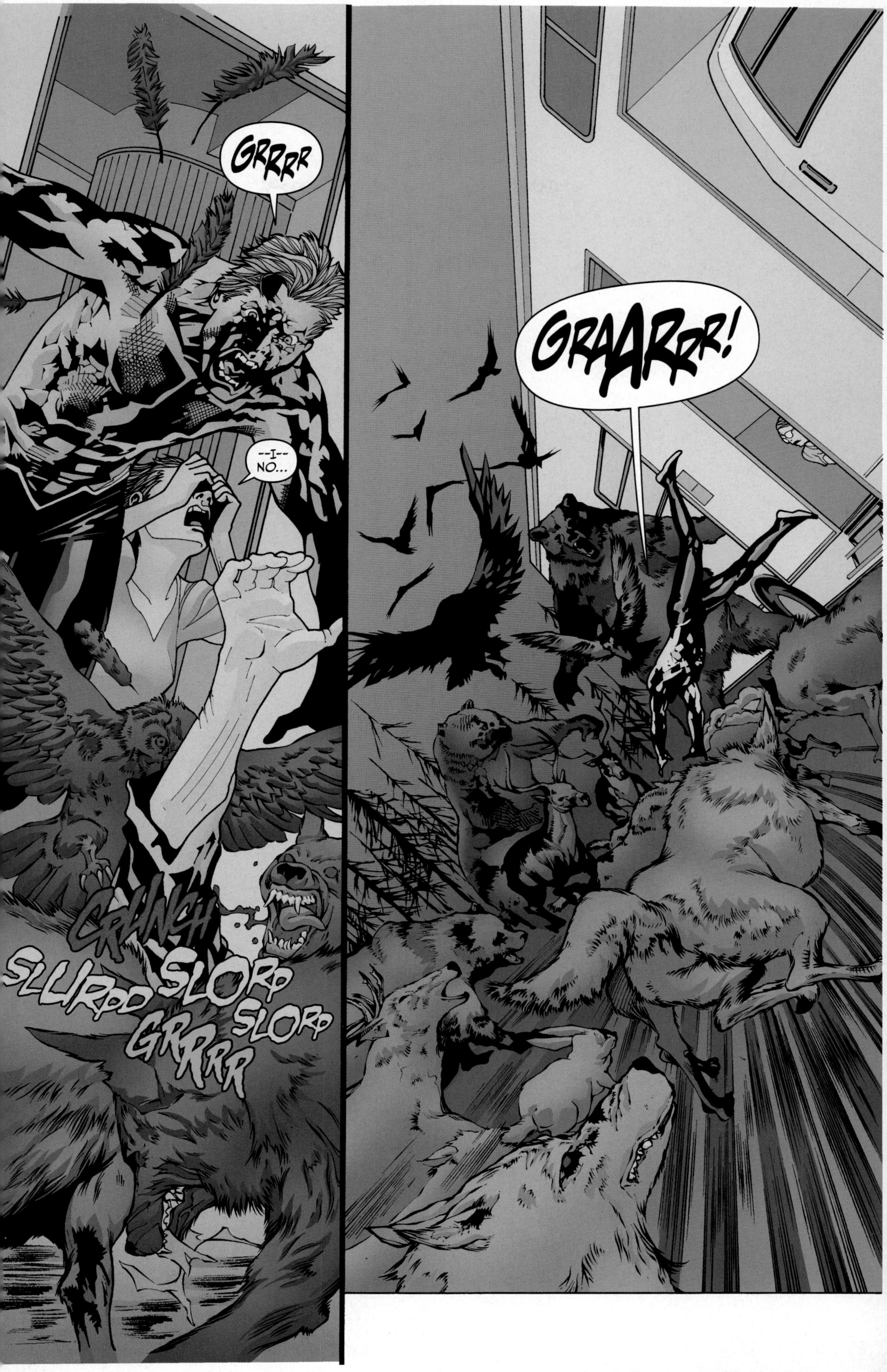
GRRRR
--I--
NO...
CRUNCH
SLURPP
SLORP
SLORP
GRRRR
GRAARRR!

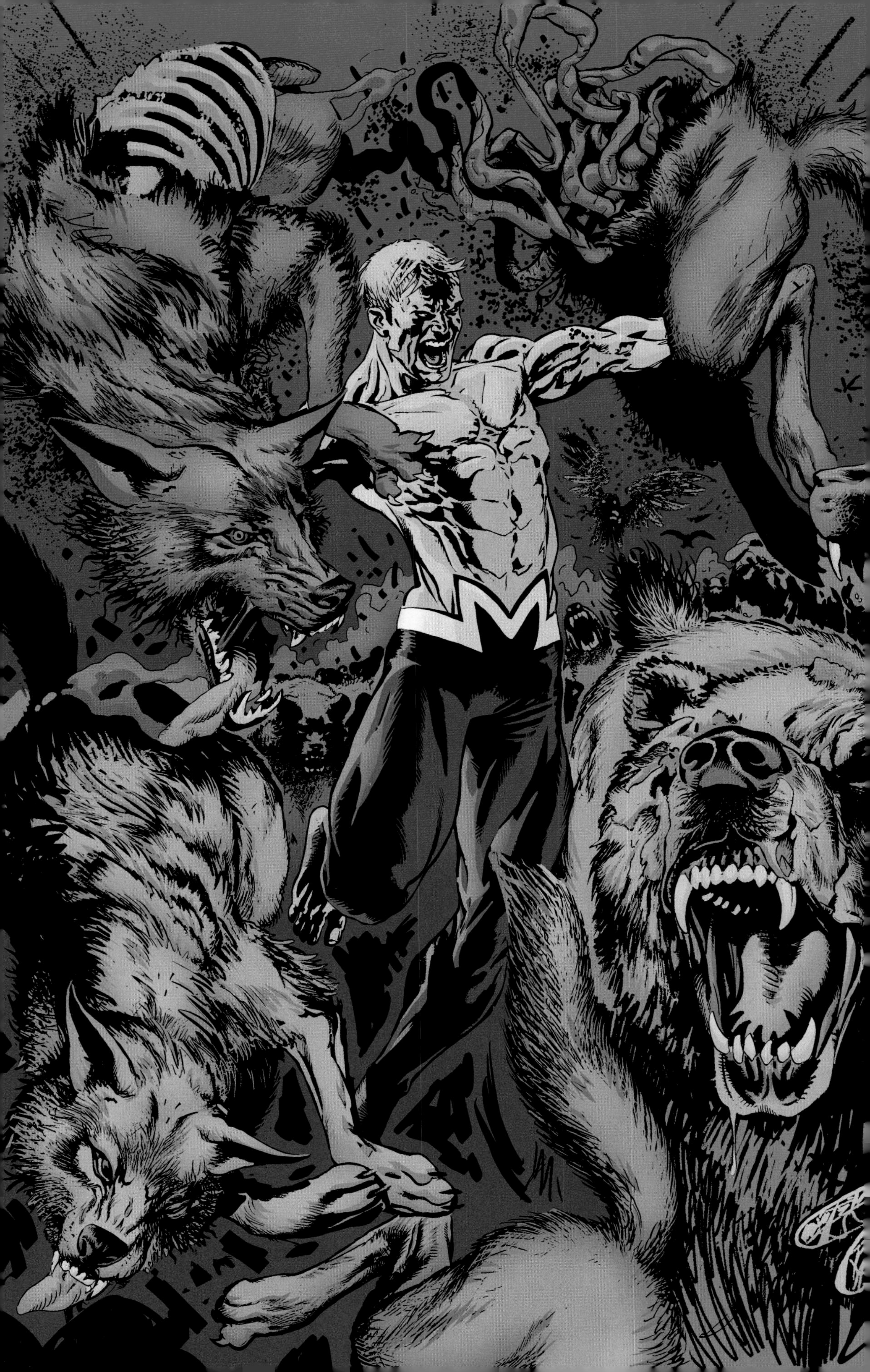

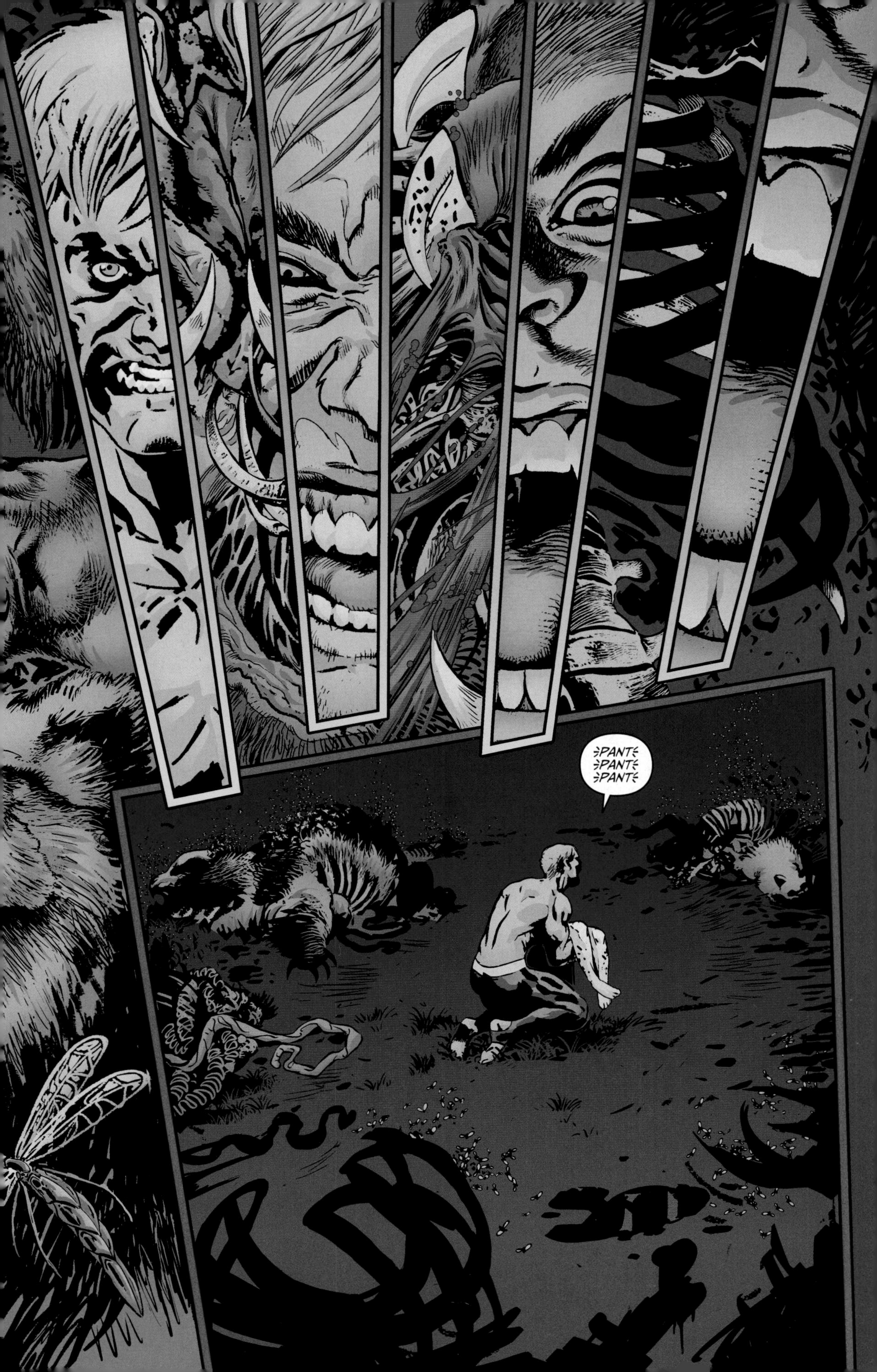
PANT PANT PANT

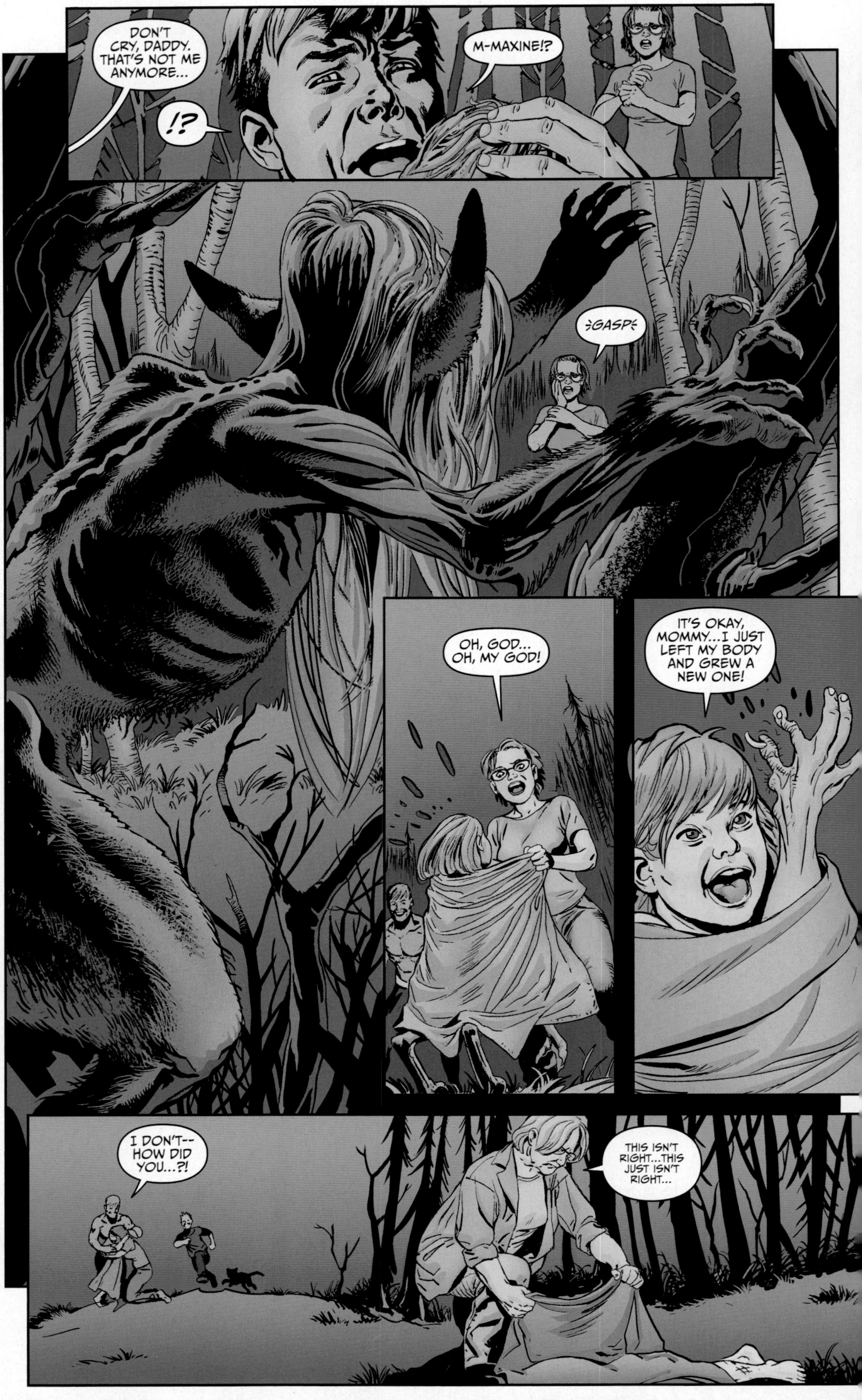
DON'T CRY, DADDY. THAT'S NOT ME ANYMORE...
!?
M-MAXINE!?
GASP
OH, GOD... OH, MY GOD!
IT'S OKAY, MOMMY...I JUST LEFT MY BODY AND GREW A NEW ONE!
I DON'T-- HOW DID YOU...?!
THIS ISN'T RIGHT...THIS JUST ISN'T RIGHT...

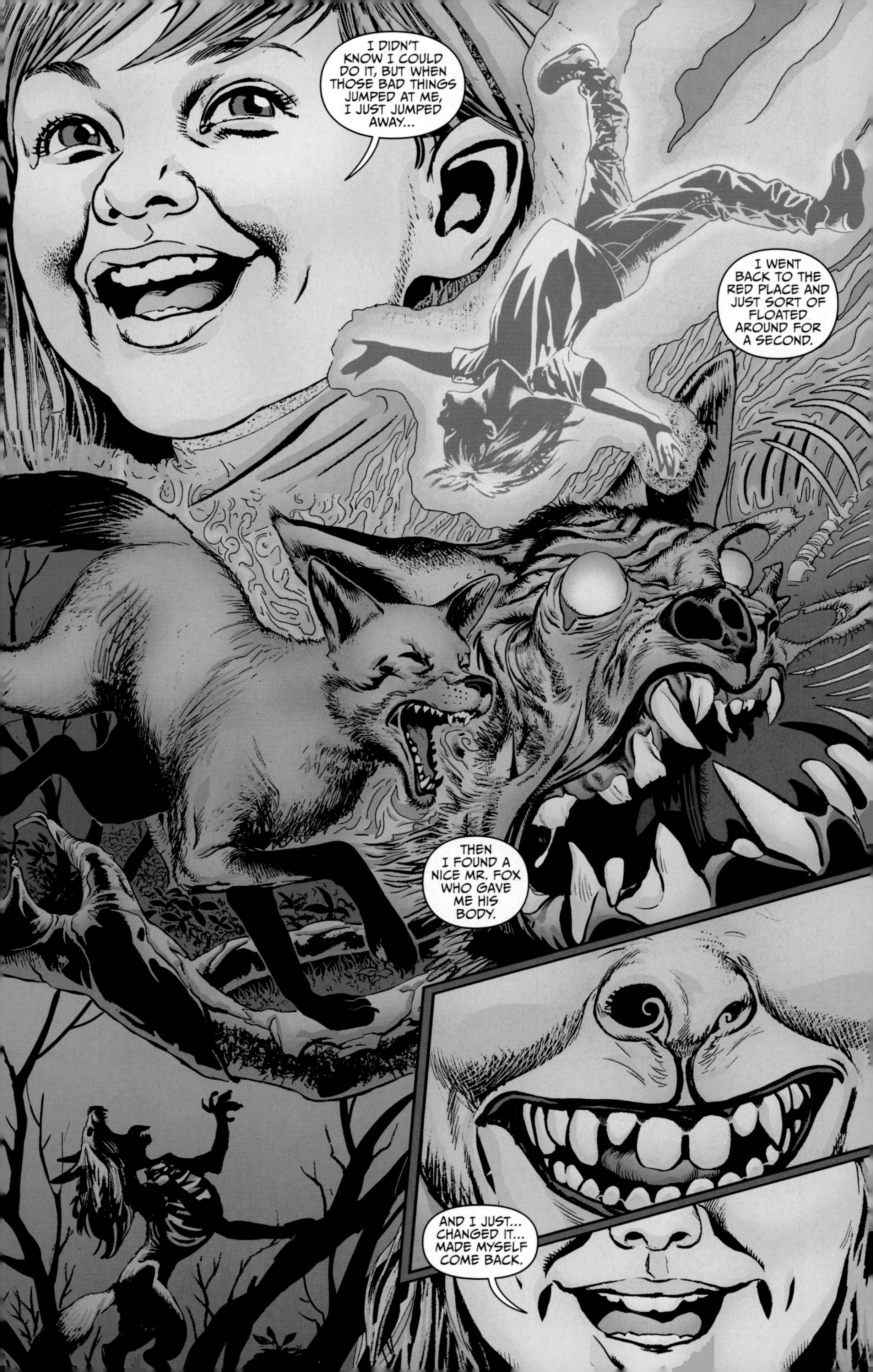
I DIDN'T KNOW I COULD DO IT, BUT WHEN THOSE BAD THINGS JUMPED AT ME, I JUST JUMPED AWAY...
I WENT BACK TO THE RED PLACE AND JUST SORT OF FLOATED AROUND FOR A SECOND.
THEN I FOUND A NICE MR. FOX WHO GAVE ME HIS BODY.
AND I JUST... CHANGED IT... MADE MYSELF COME BACK.

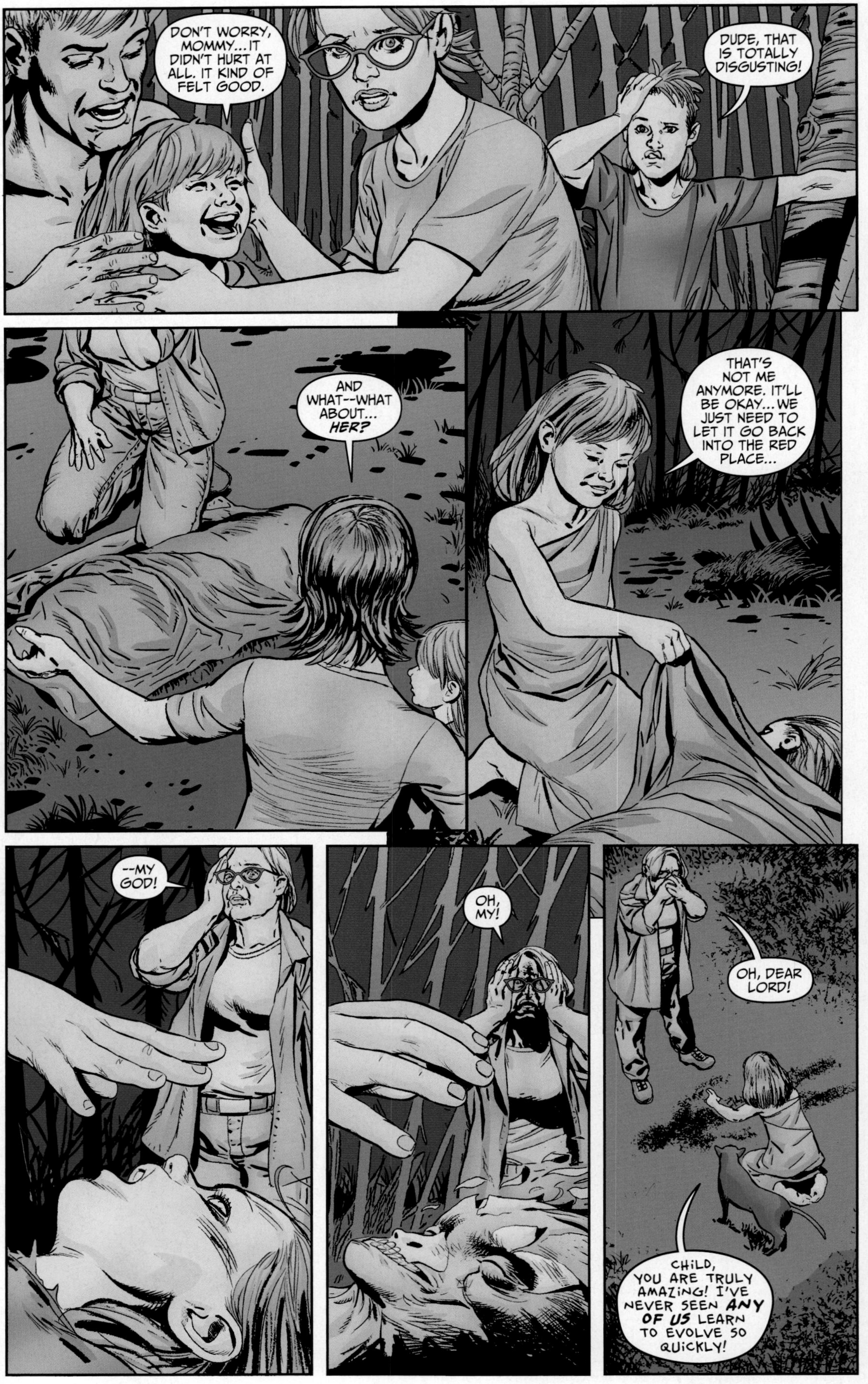
DON'T WORRY, MOMMY...IT DIDN'T HURT AT ALL. IT KIND OF FELT GOOD.
DUDE, THAT IS TOTALLY DISGUSTING!
AND WHAT--WHAT ABOUT... HER?
THAT'S NOT ME ANYMORE. IT'LL BE OKAY...WE JUST NEED TO LET IT GO BACK INTO THE RED PLACE...
--MY GOD!
OH, MY!
OH, DEAR LORD!
CHILD, YOU ARE TRULY AMAZING! I'VE NEVER SEEN ANY OF US LEARN TO EVOLVE SO QUICKLY!

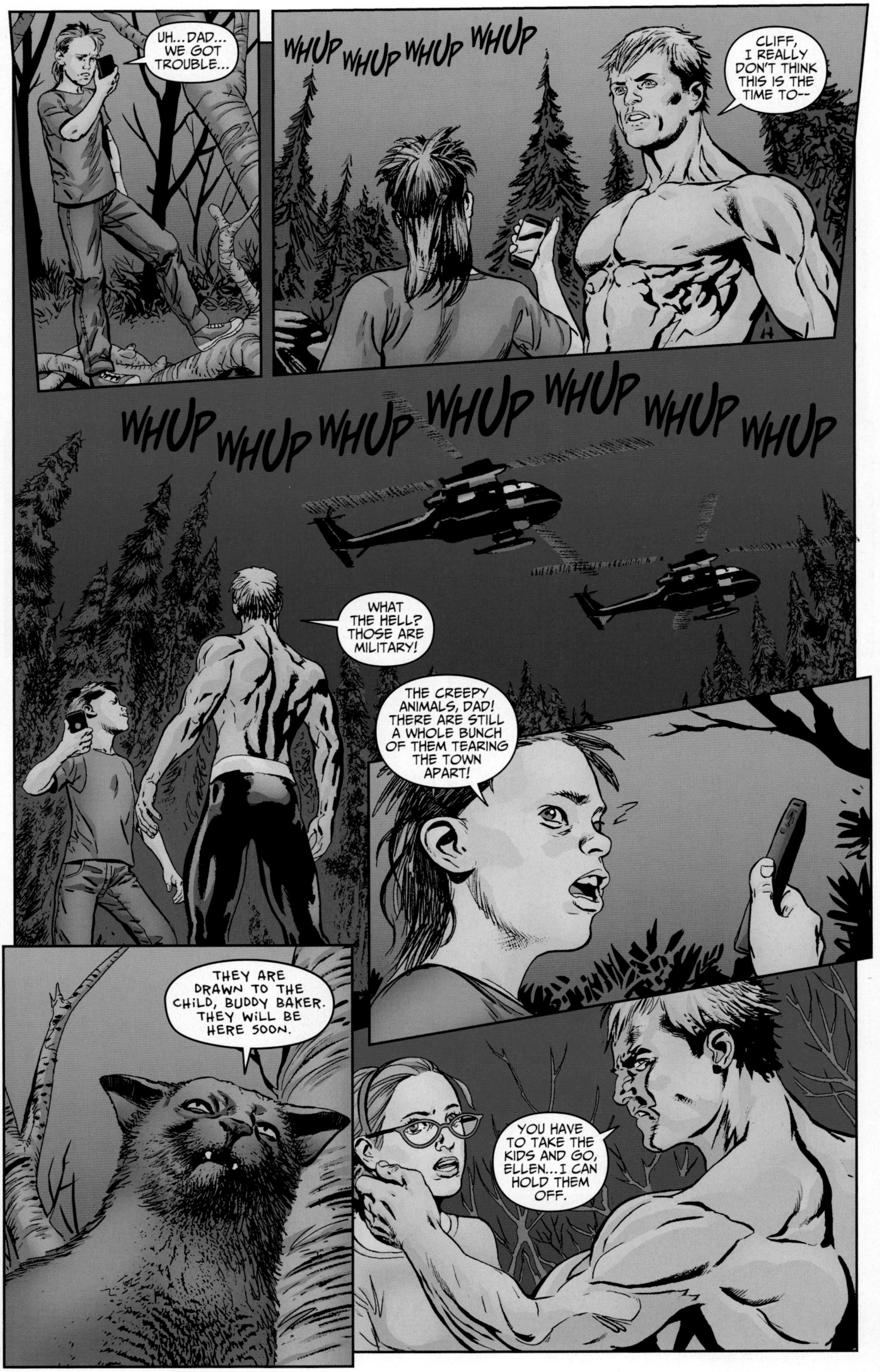
UH...DAD... WE GOT TROUBLE...
WHUP WHUP WHUP WHUP
CLIFF, I REALLY DON'T THINK THIS IS THE TIME TO--
WHUP WHUP WHUP WHUP WHUP WHUP WHUP
WHAT THE HELL? THOSE ARE MILITARY!
THE CREEPY ANIMALS, DAD! THERE ARE STILL A WHOLE BUNCH OF THEM TEARING THE TOWN APART!
THEY ARE DRAWN TO THE CHILD, BUDDY BAKER. THEY WILL BE HERE SOON.
YOU HAVE TO TAKE THE KIDS AND GO, ELLEN...I CAN HOLD THEM OFF.

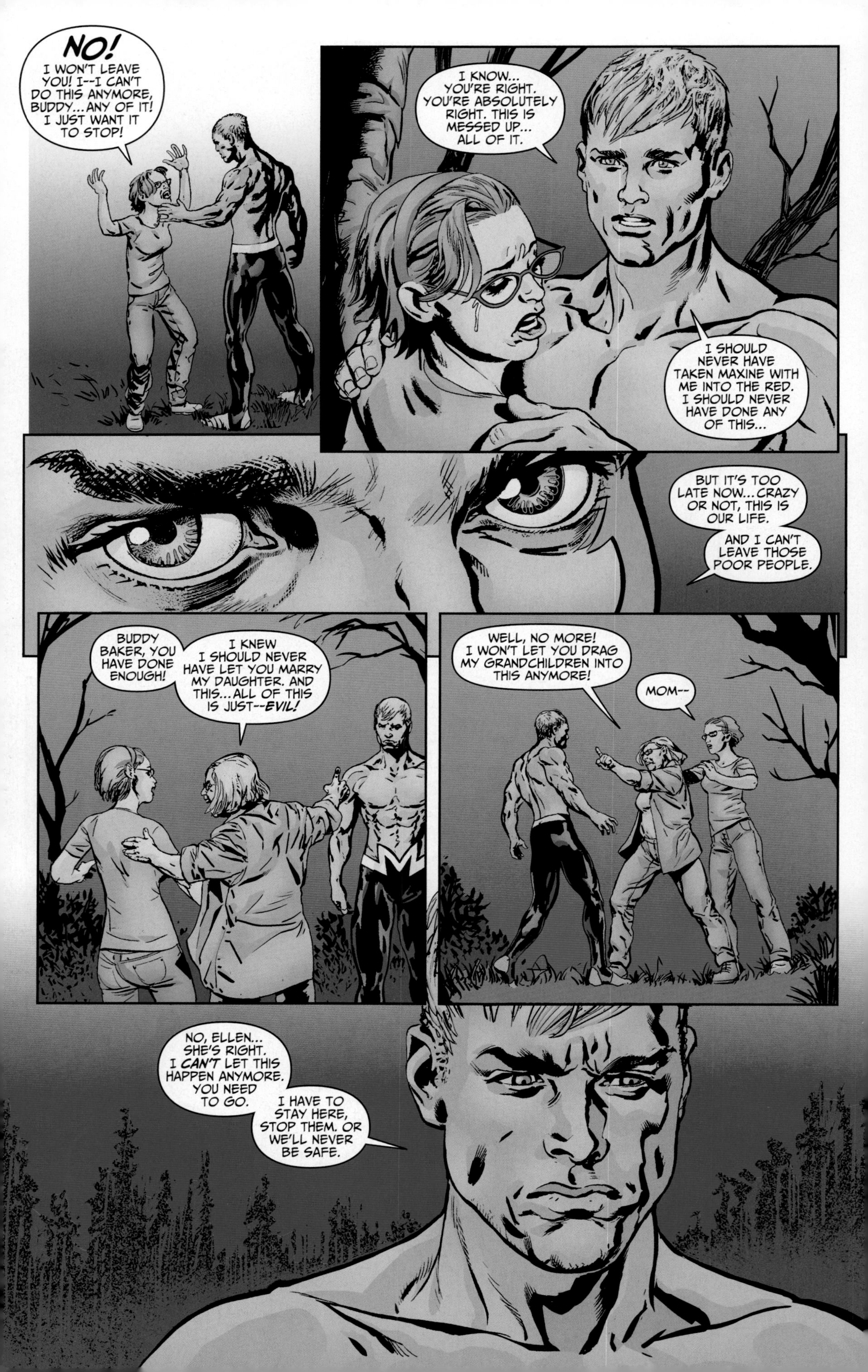
NO! I WON'T LEAVE YOU! I--I CAN'T DO THIS ANYMORE, BUDDY...ANY OF IT! I JUST WANT IT TO STOP!
I KNOW... YOU'RE RIGHT. YOU'RE ABSOLUTELY RIGHT. THIS IS MESSED UP... ALL OF IT.
I SHOULD NEVER HAVE TAKEN MAXINE WITH ME INTO THE RED. I SHOULD NEVER HAVE DONE ANY OF THIS...
BUT IT'S TOO LATE NOW...CRAZY OR NOT, THIS IS OUR LIFE.
AND I CAN'T LEAVE THOSE POOR PEOPLE.
BUDDY BAKER, YOU HAVE DONE ENOUGH!
I KNEW I SHOULD NEVER HAVE LET YOU MARRY MY DAUGHTER. AND THIS...ALL OF THIS IS JUST--EVIL!
WELL, NO MORE! I WON'T LET YOU DRAG MY GRANDCHILDREN INTO THIS ANYMORE!
MOM--
NO, ELLEN... SHE'S RIGHT. I CAN'T LET THIS HAPPEN ANYMORE. YOU NEED TO GO.
I HAVE TO STAY HERE, STOP THEM. OR WE'LL NEVER BE SAFE.

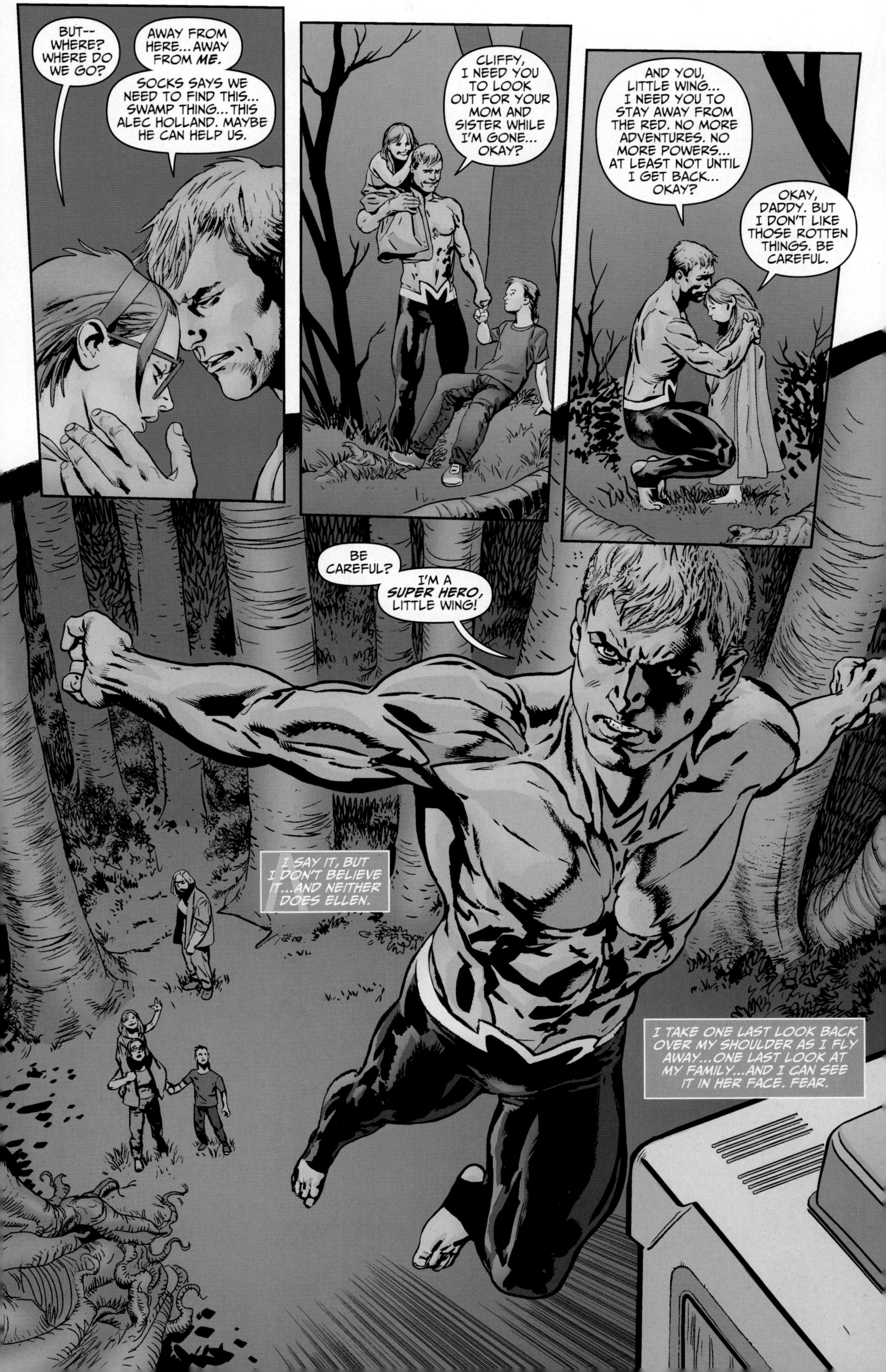
BUT-- WHERE? WHERE DO WE GO?
AWAY FROM HERE...AWAY FROM ME.
SOCKS SAYS WE NEED TO FIND THIS... SWAMP THING...THIS ALEC HOLLAND. MAYBE HE CAN HELP US.
CLIFFY, I NEED YOU TO LOOK OUT FOR YOUR MOM AND SISTER WHILE I'M GONE... OKAY?
AND YOU, LITTLE WING... I NEED YOU TO STAY AWAY FROM THE RED. NO MORE ADVENTURES. NO MORE POWERS... AT LEAST NOT UNTIL I GET BACK... OKAY?
OKAY, DADDY. BUT I DON'T LIKE THOSE ROTTEN THINGS. BE CAREFUL.
BE CAREFUL?
I'M A SUPER HERO, LITTLE WING!
I SAY IT, BUT I DON'T BELIEVE IT...AND NEITHER DOES ELLEN.
I TAKE ONE LAST LOOK BACK OVER MY SHOULDER AS I FLY AWAY...ONE LAST LOOK AT MY FAMILY...AND I CAN SEE IT IN HER FACE. FEAR.

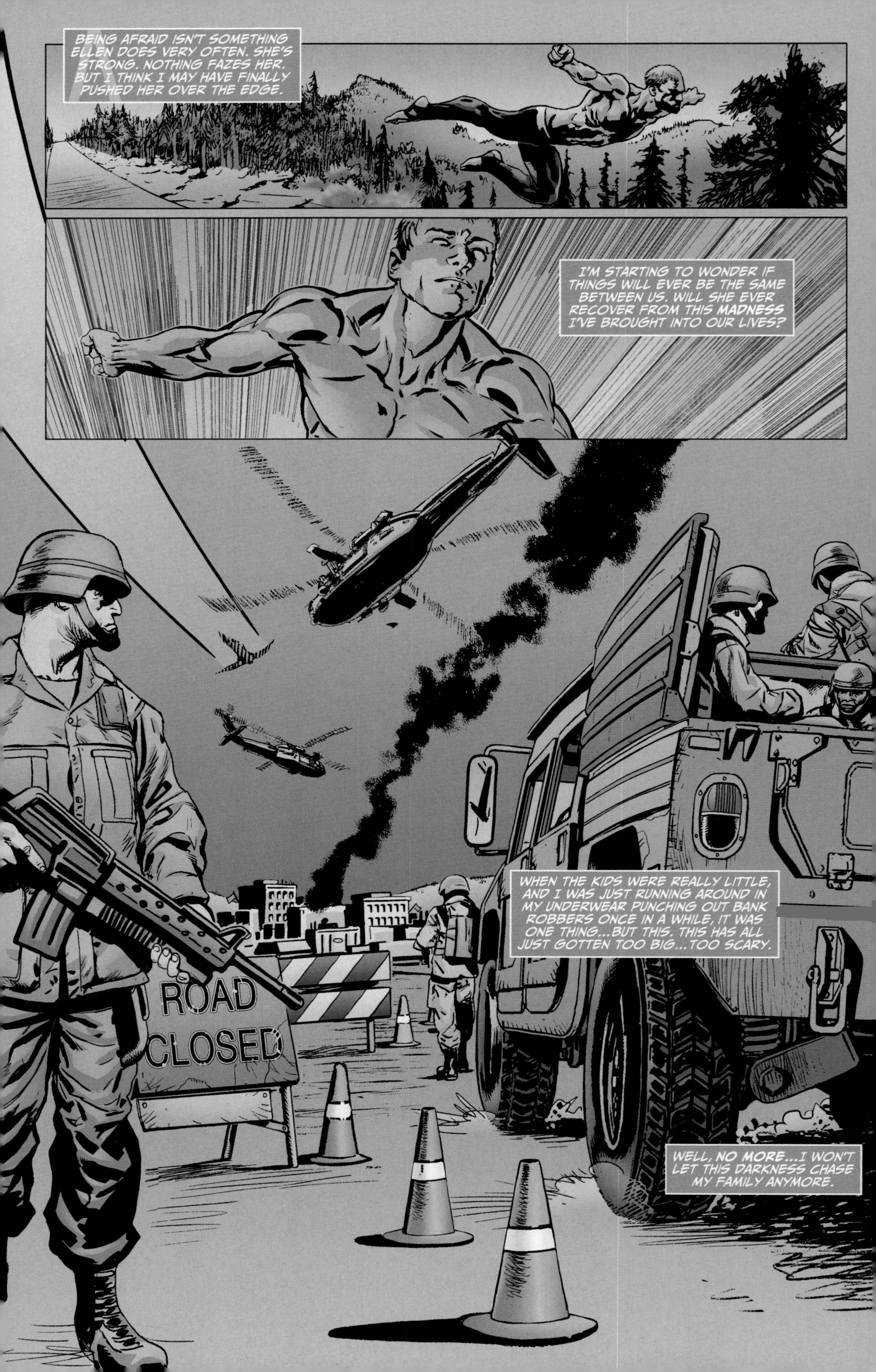
BEING AFRAID ISN'T SOMETHING ELLEN DOES VERY OFTEN. SHE'S STRONG. NOTHING FAZES HER. BUT I THINK I MAY HAVE FINALLY PUSHED HER OVER THE EDGE.
I'M STARTING TO WONDER IF THINGS WILL EVER BE THE SAME BETWEEN US. WILL SHE EVER RECOVER FROM THIS MADNESS I'VE BROUGHT INTO OUR LIVES?
WHEN THE KIDS WERE REALLY LITTLE, AND I WAS JUST RUNNING AROUND IN MY UNDERWEAR PUNCHING OUT BANK ROBBERS ONCE IN A WHILE, IT WAS ONE THING...BUT THIS. THIS HAS ALL JUST GOTTEN TOO BIG...TOO SCARY.
ROAD CLOSED
WELL, NO MORE...I WON'T LET THIS DARKNESS CHASE MY FAMILY ANYMORE.

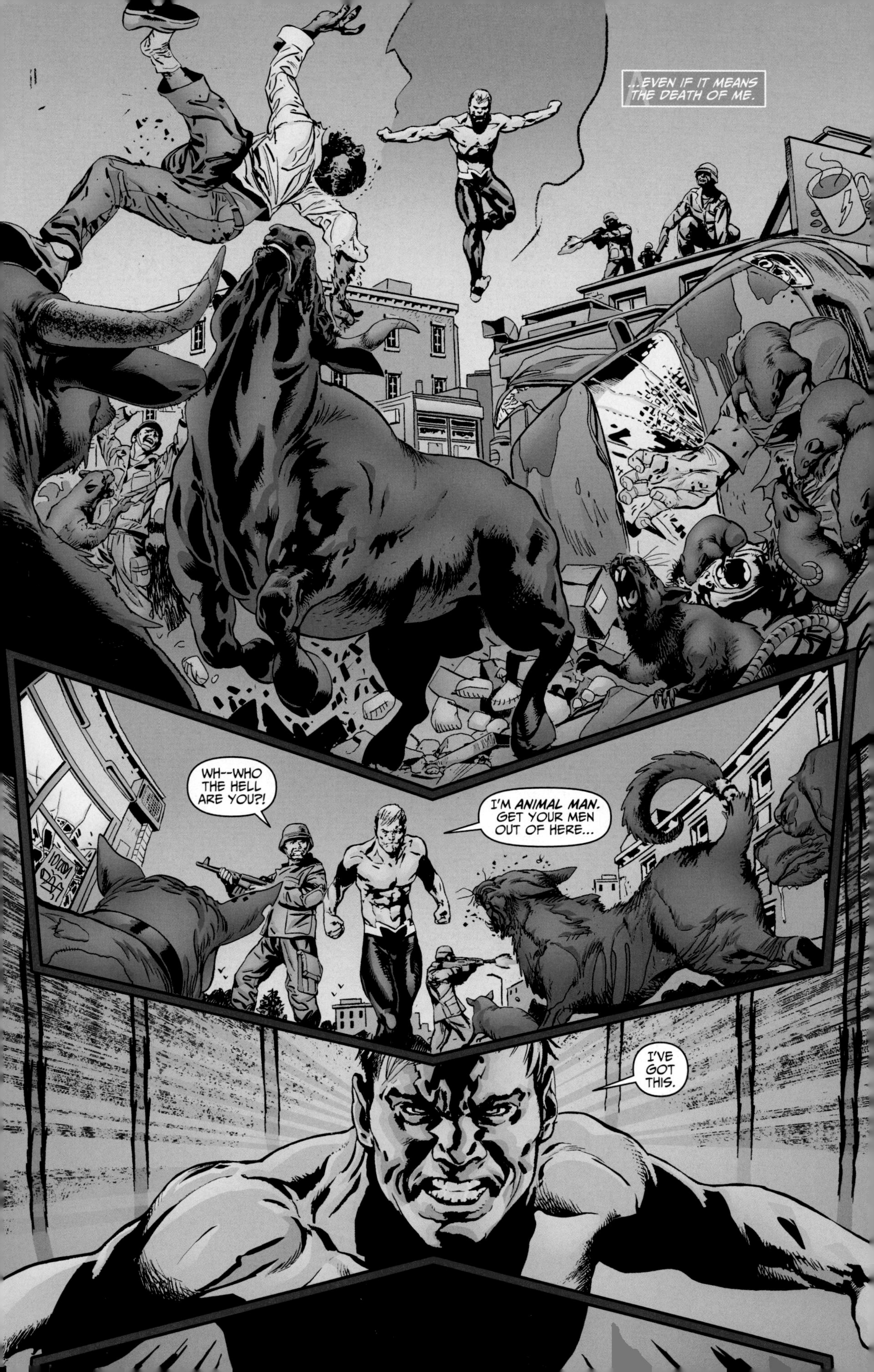
...EVEN IF IT MEANS THE DEATH OF ME.
WH--WHO THE HELL ARE YOU?!
I'M *ANIMAL MAN.* GET YOUR MEN OUT OF HERE...
I'VE GOT THIS.

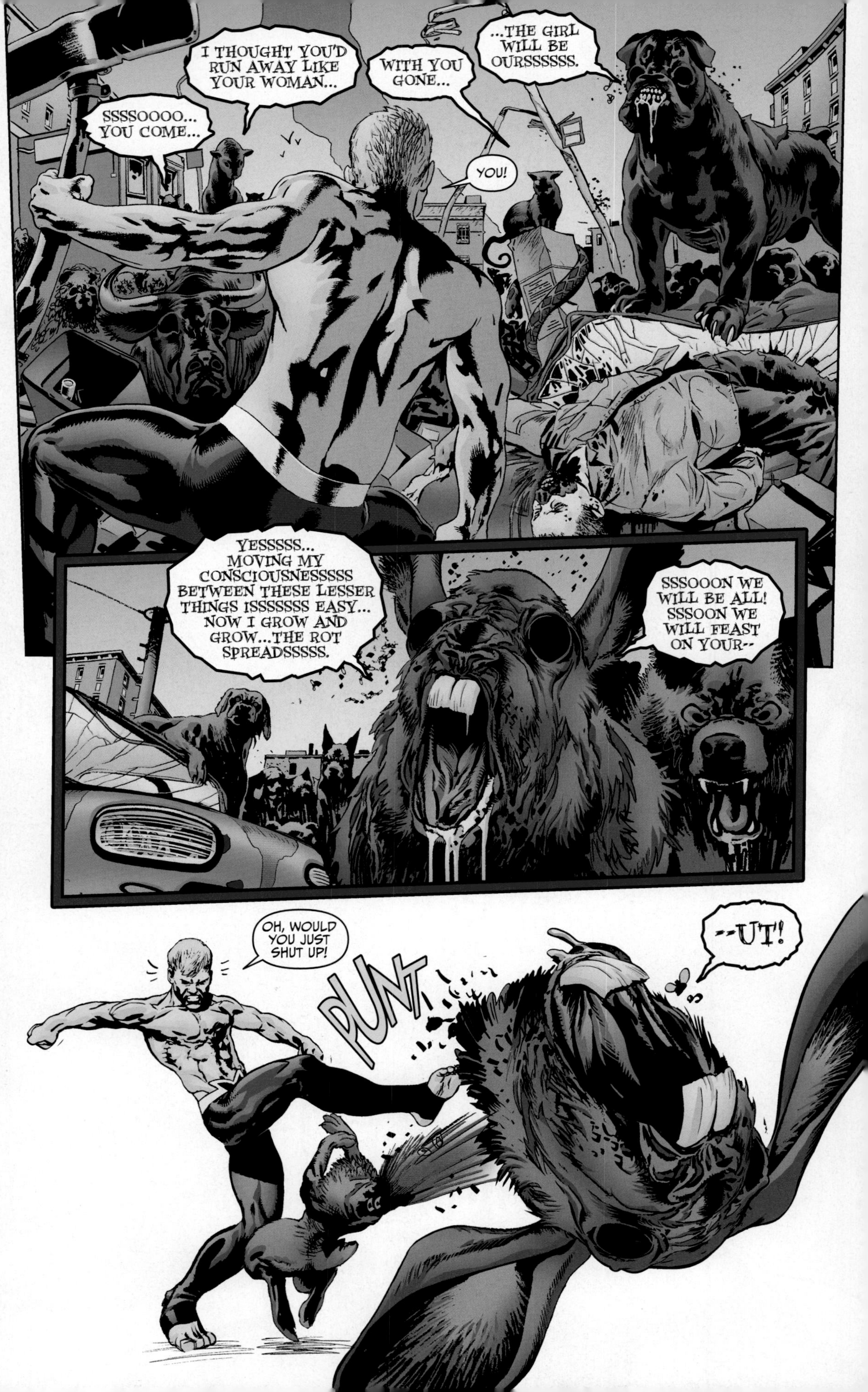
SSSSOOOO... YOU COME...
I THOUGHT YOU'D RUN AWAY LIKE YOUR WOMAN...
WITH YOU GONE...
...THE GIRL WILL BE OURSSSSSS.
YOU!
YESSSSS... MOVING MY CONSCIOUSNESSSSS BETWEEN THESE LESSER THINGS ISSSSSSS EASY... NOW I GROW AND GROW...THE ROT SPREADSSSSS.
SSSOOON WE WILL BE ALL! SSSOON WE WILL FEAST ON YOUR--
OH, WOULD YOU JUST SHUT UP!
PUNT
--UT!

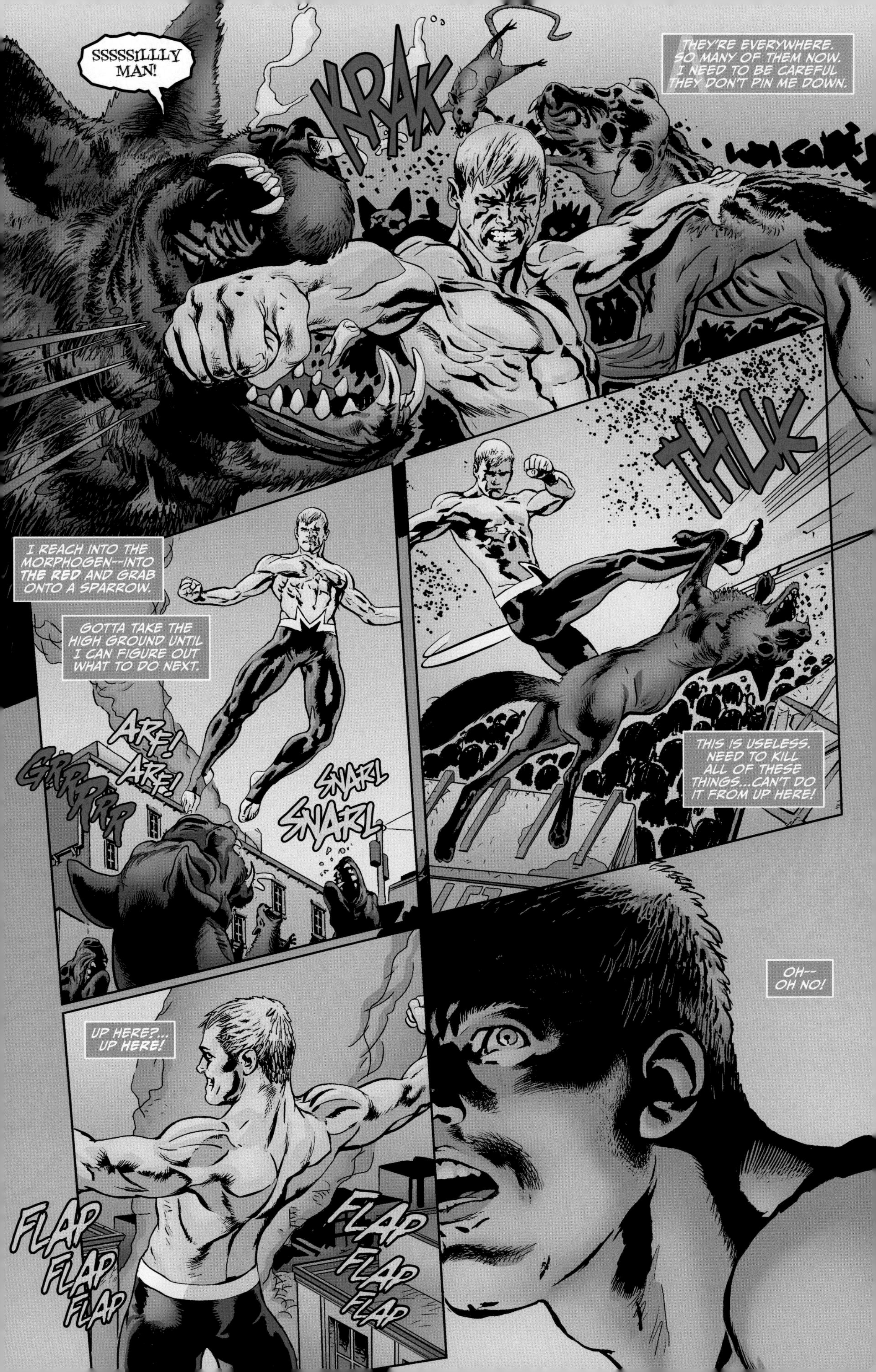

SSSSSILLLY MAN!
KRAK
THEY'RE EVERYWHERE. SO MANY OF THEM NOW. I NEED TO BE CAREFUL THEY DON'T PIN ME DOWN.
I REACH INTO THE MORPHOGEN--INTO THE RED AND GRAB ONTO A SPARROW.
GOTTA TAKE THE HIGH GROUND UNTIL I CAN FIGURE OUT WHAT TO DO NEXT.
ARF! ARF!
SNARL SNARL
THLK
THIS IS USELESS. NEED TO KILL ALL OF THESE THINGS...CAN'T DO IT FROM UP HERE!
UP HERE?... UP HERE!
FLAP FLAP FLAP
FLAP FLAP FLAP
OH-- OH NO!

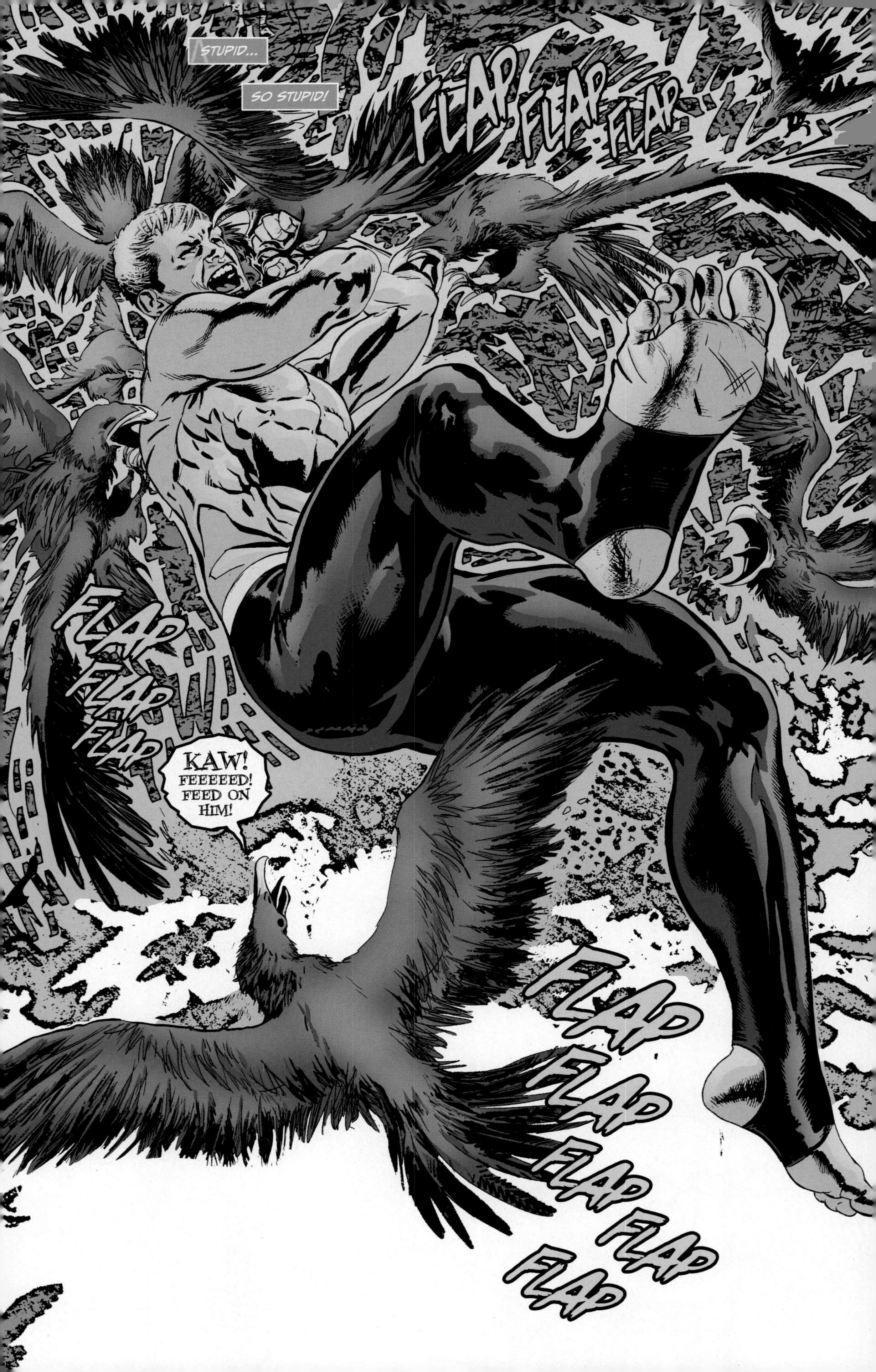
STUPID...
SO STUPID!
FLAP FLAP FLAP
FLAP FLAP FLAP
KAW! FEEEEED! FEED ON HIM!
FLAP FLAP FLAP FLAP FLAP

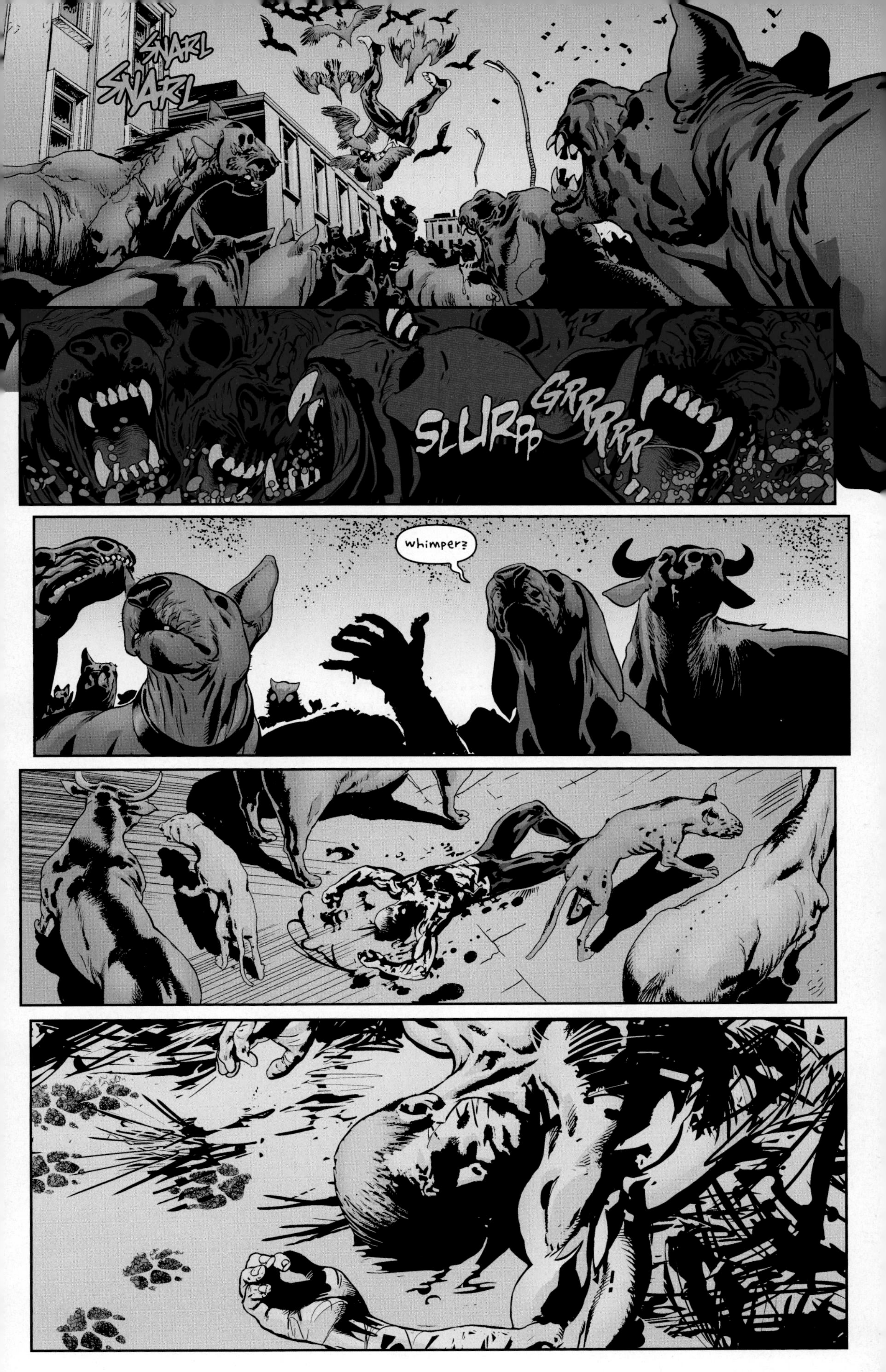

SNARL
SNARL
SLURPP
GRRRRRR
whimperz

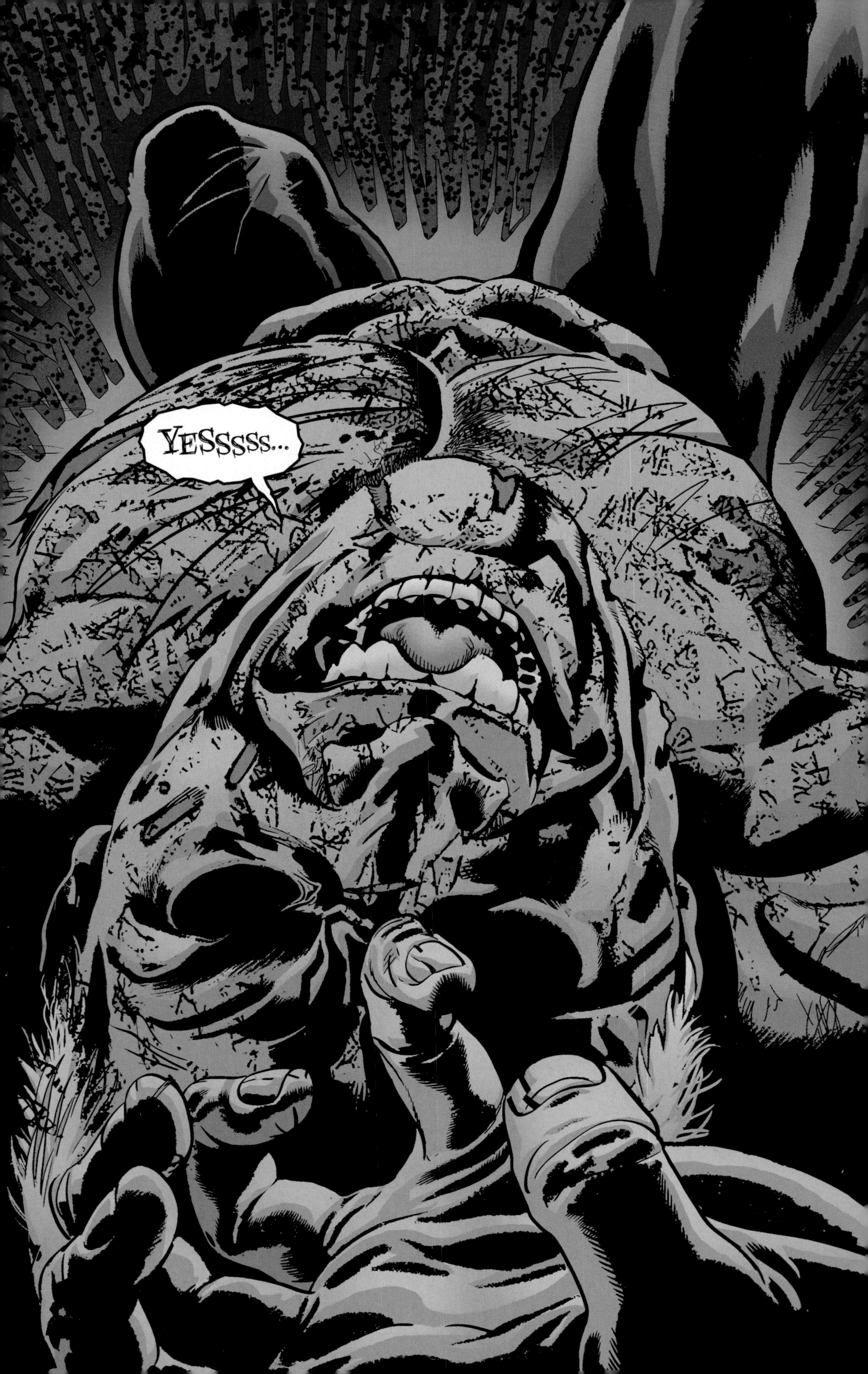
YESSSSS...

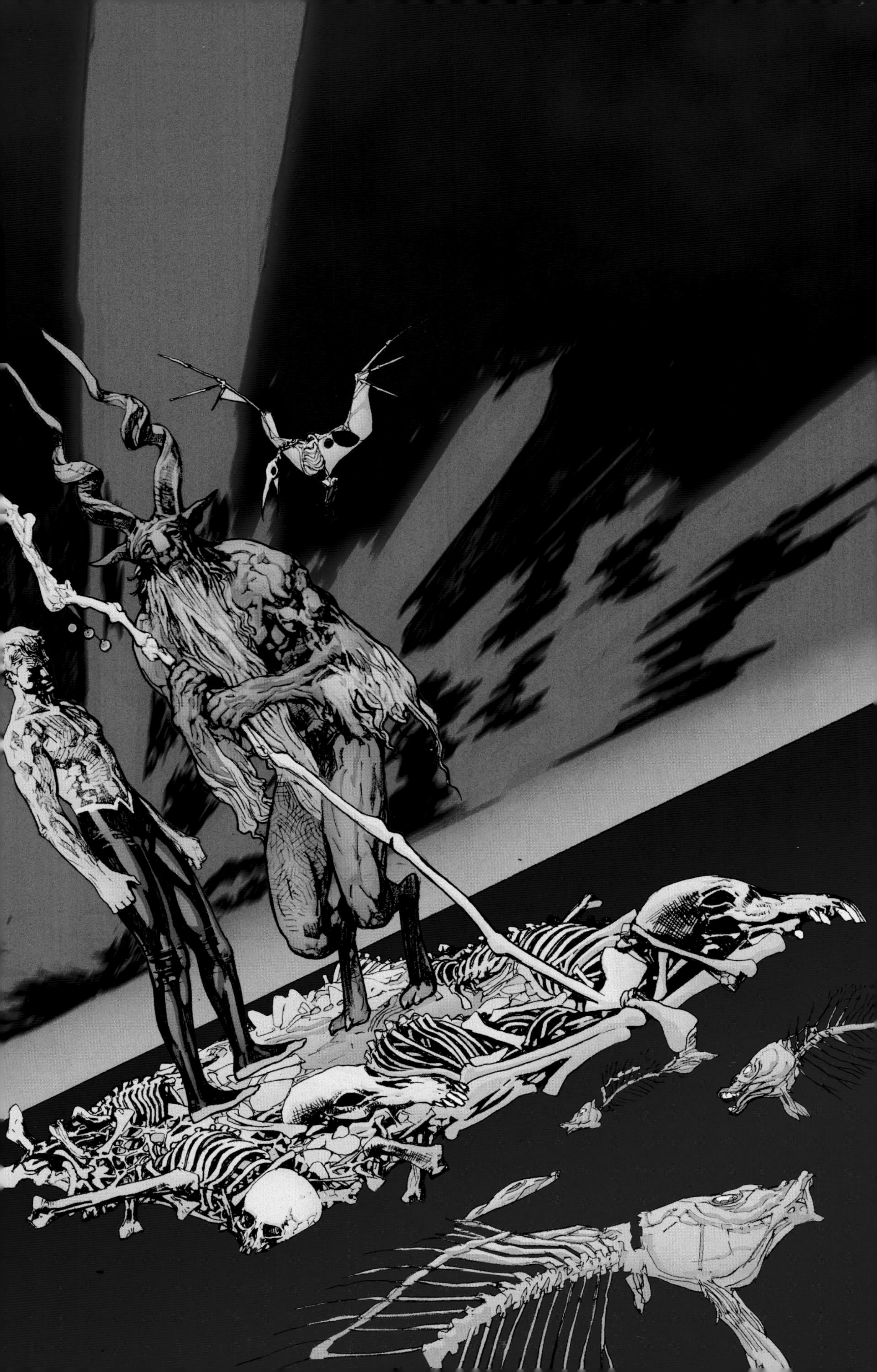

JEFF LEMIRE writer **STEVE PUGH** artist
cover by **TRAVEL FOREMAN** with **LOVERN KINDZIERSKI**

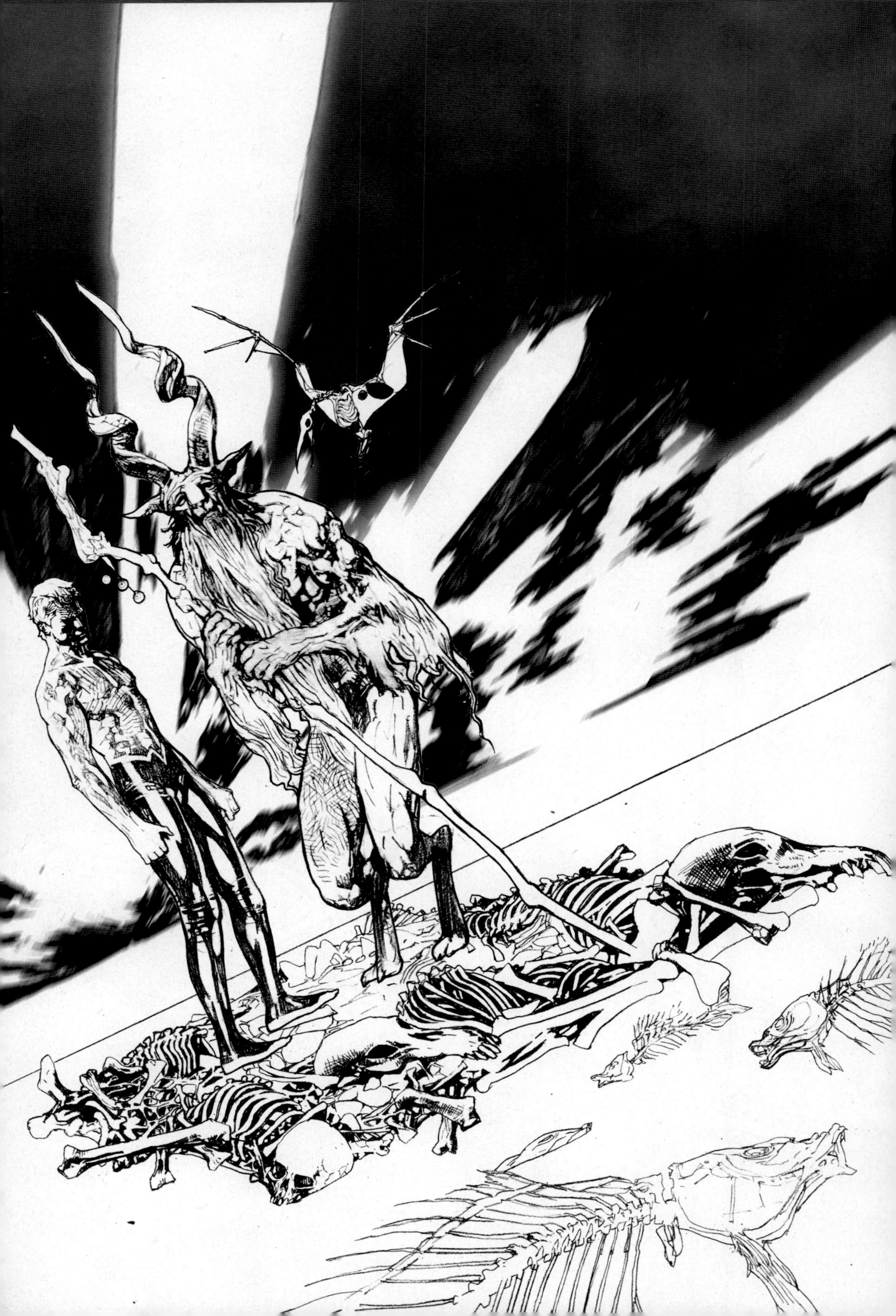

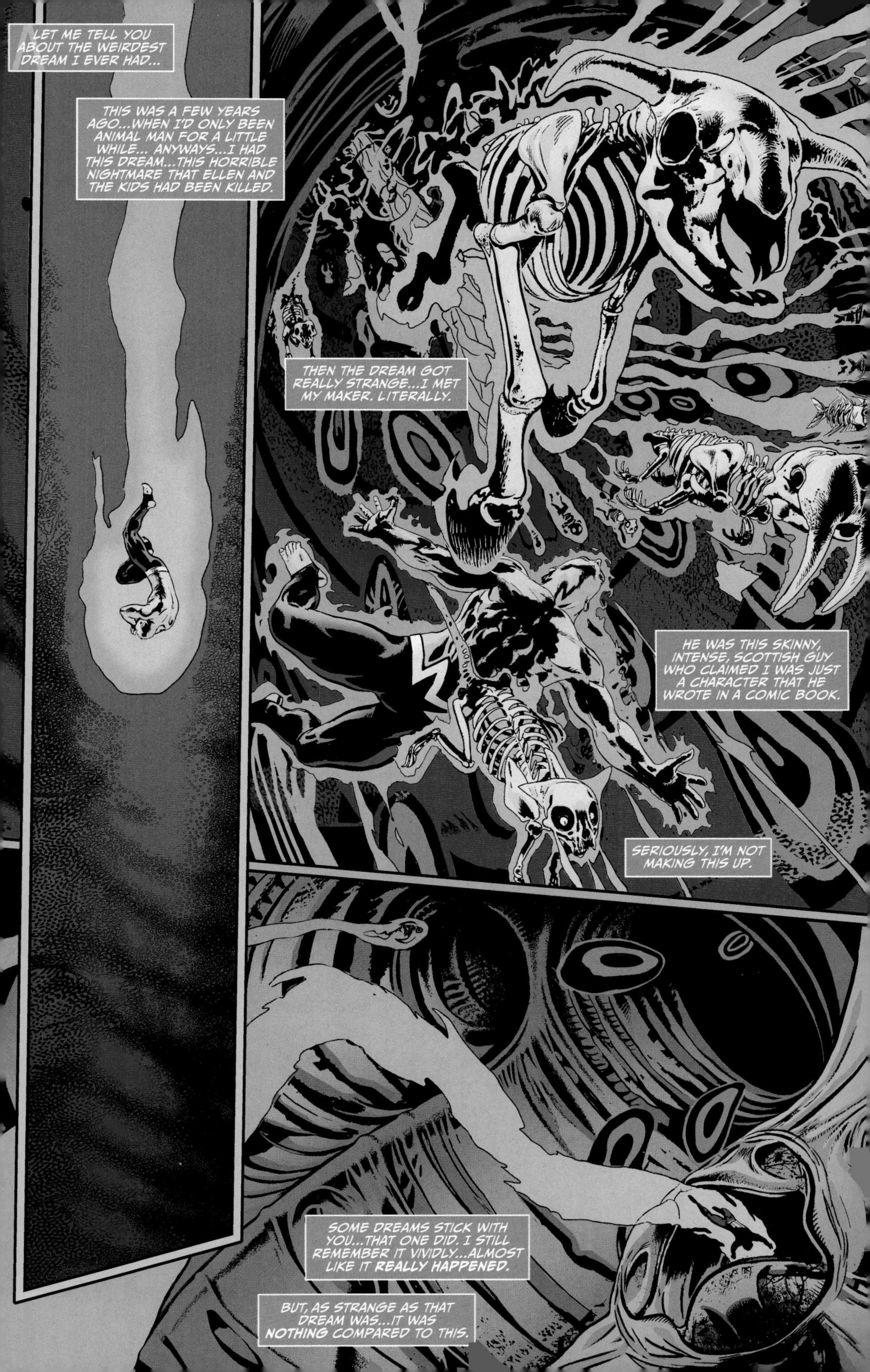
LET ME TELL YOU ABOUT THE WEIRDEST DREAM I EVER HAD...
THIS WAS A FEW YEARS AGO...WHEN I'D ONLY BEEN ANIMAL MAN FOR A LITTLE WHILE... ANYWAYS...I HAD THIS DREAM...THIS HORRIBLE NIGHTMARE THAT ELLEN AND THE KIDS HAD BEEN KILLED.
THEN THE DREAM GOT REALLY STRANGE...I MET MY MAKER. LITERALLY.
HE WAS THIS SKINNY, INTENSE, SCOTTISH GUY WHO CLAIMED I WAS JUST A CHARACTER THAT HE WROTE IN A COMIC BOOK.
SERIOUSLY, I'M NOT MAKING THIS UP.
SOME DREAMS STICK WITH YOU...THAT ONE DID. I STILL REMEMBER IT VIVIDLY...ALMOST LIKE IT REALLY HAPPENED.
BUT, AS STRANGE AS THAT DREAM WAS...IT WAS NOTHING COMPARED TO THIS.

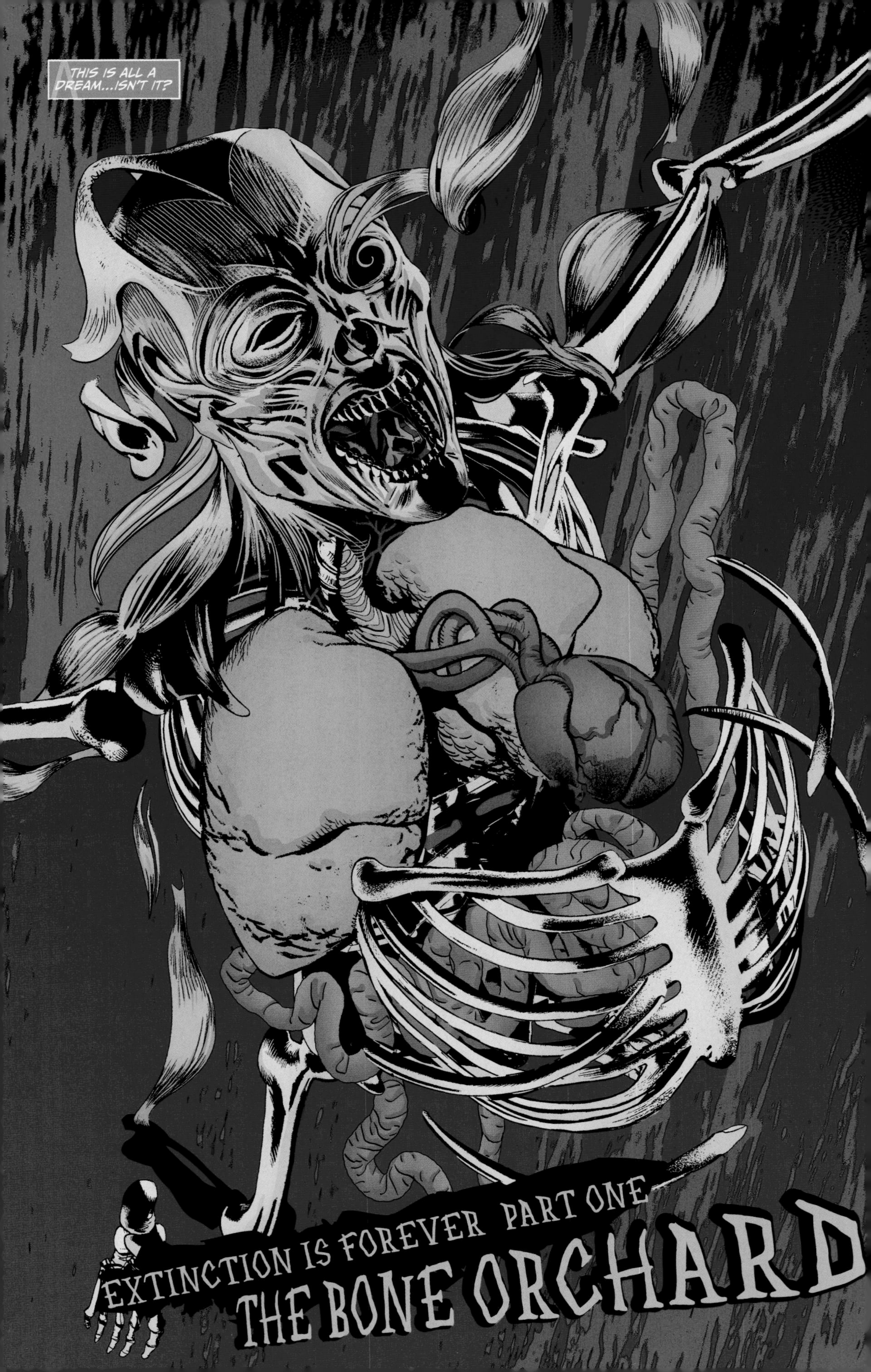
THIS IS ALL A DREAM...ISN'T IT?
EXTINCTION IS FOREVER PART ONE
THE BONE ORCHARD

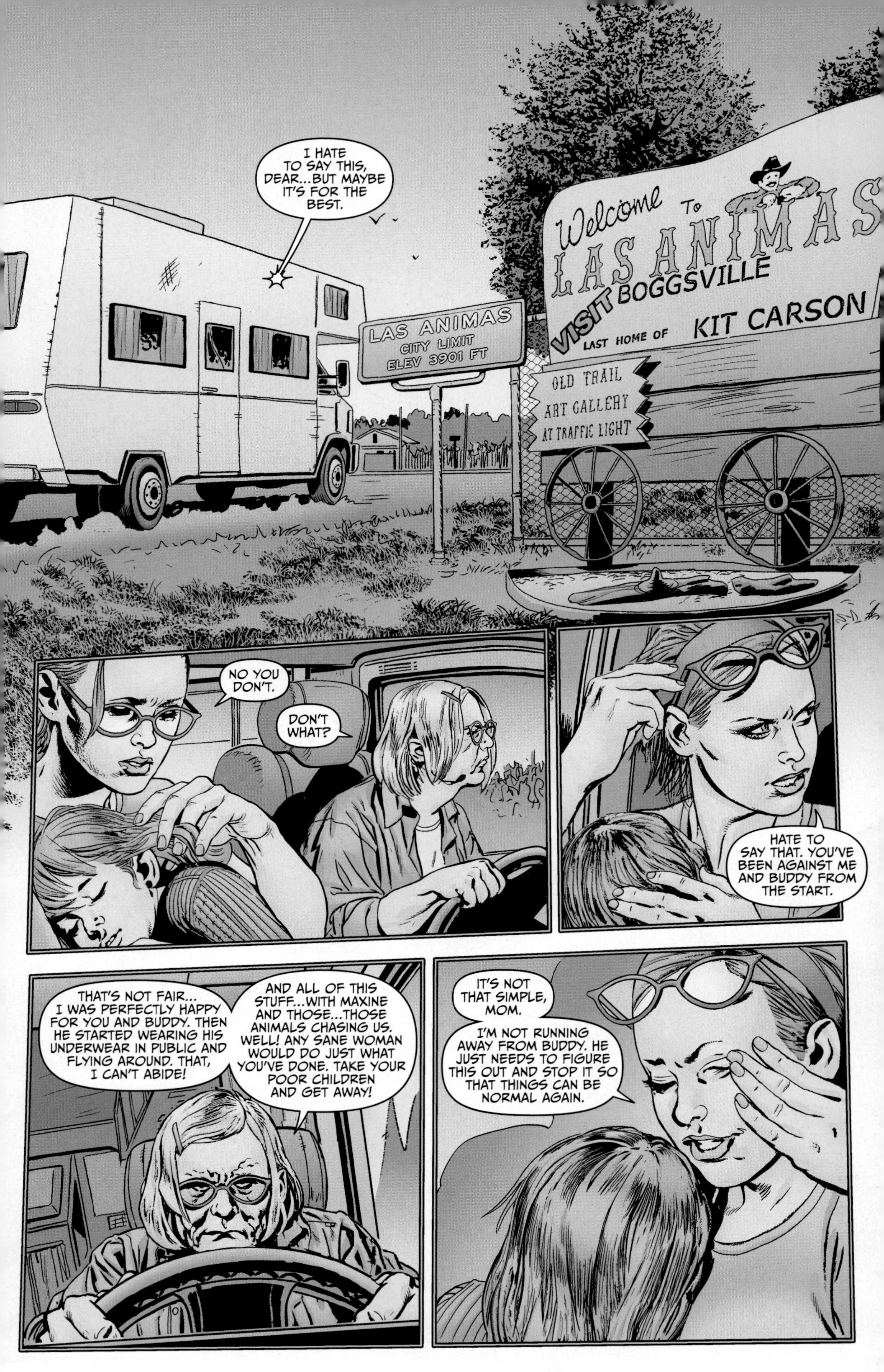
I HATE TO SAY THIS, DEAR...BUT MAYBE IT'S FOR THE BEST.
LAS ANIMAS CITY LIMIT ELEV 3901 FT
Welcome To LAS ANIMAS
VISIT BOGGSVILLE
LAST HOME OF KIT CARSON
OLD TRAIL ART GALLERY AT TRAFFIC LIGHT
NO YOU DON'T.
DON'T WHAT?
HATE TO SAY THAT. YOU'VE BEEN AGAINST ME AND BUDDY FROM THE START.
THAT'S NOT FAIR... I WAS PERFECTLY HAPPY FOR YOU AND BUDDY. THEN HE STARTED WEARING HIS UNDERWEAR IN PUBLIC AND FLYING AROUND. THAT, I CAN'T ABIDE!
AND ALL OF THIS STUFF...WITH MAXINE AND THOSE...THOSE ANIMALS CHASING US. WELL! ANY SANE WOMAN WOULD DO JUST WHAT YOU'VE DONE. TAKE YOUR POOR CHILDREN AND GET AWAY!
IT'S NOT THAT SIMPLE, MOM.
I'M NOT RUNNING AWAY FROM BUDDY. HE JUST NEEDS TO FIGURE THIS OUT AND STOP IT SO THAT THINGS CAN BE NORMAL AGAIN.

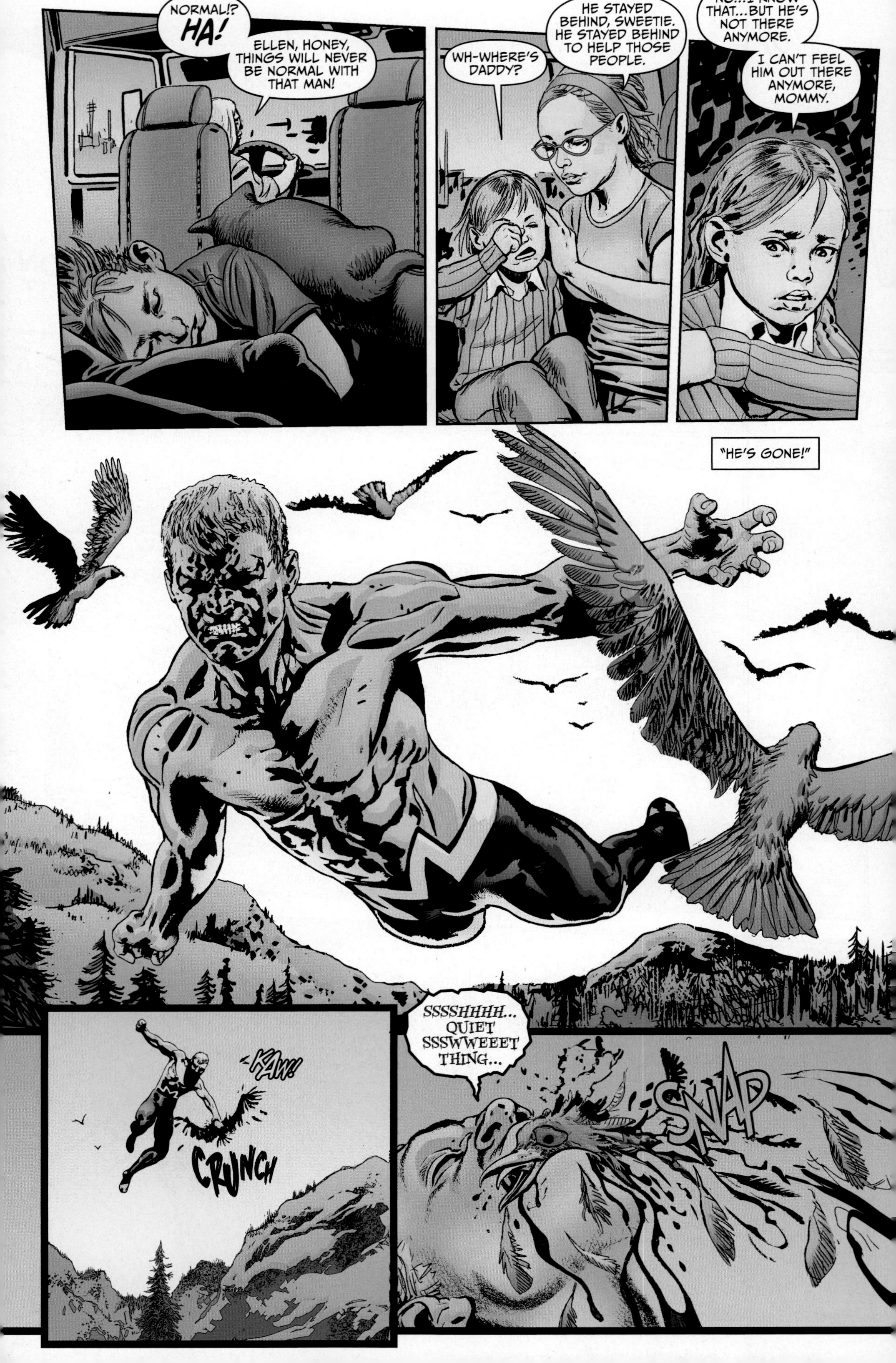

NORMAL!? HA!
ELLEN, HONEY, THINGS WILL NEVER BE NORMAL WITH THAT MAN!
WH-WHERE'S DADDY?
HE STAYED BEHIND, SWEETIE. HE STAYED BEHIND TO HELP THOSE PEOPLE.
NO...I KNOW THAT...BUT HE'S NOT THERE ANYMORE.
I CAN'T FEEL HIM OUT THERE ANYMORE, MOMMY.
"HE'S GONE!"
KAW!
CRUNCH
SSSSHHHH... QUIET SSSWWEEET THING...
SNAP

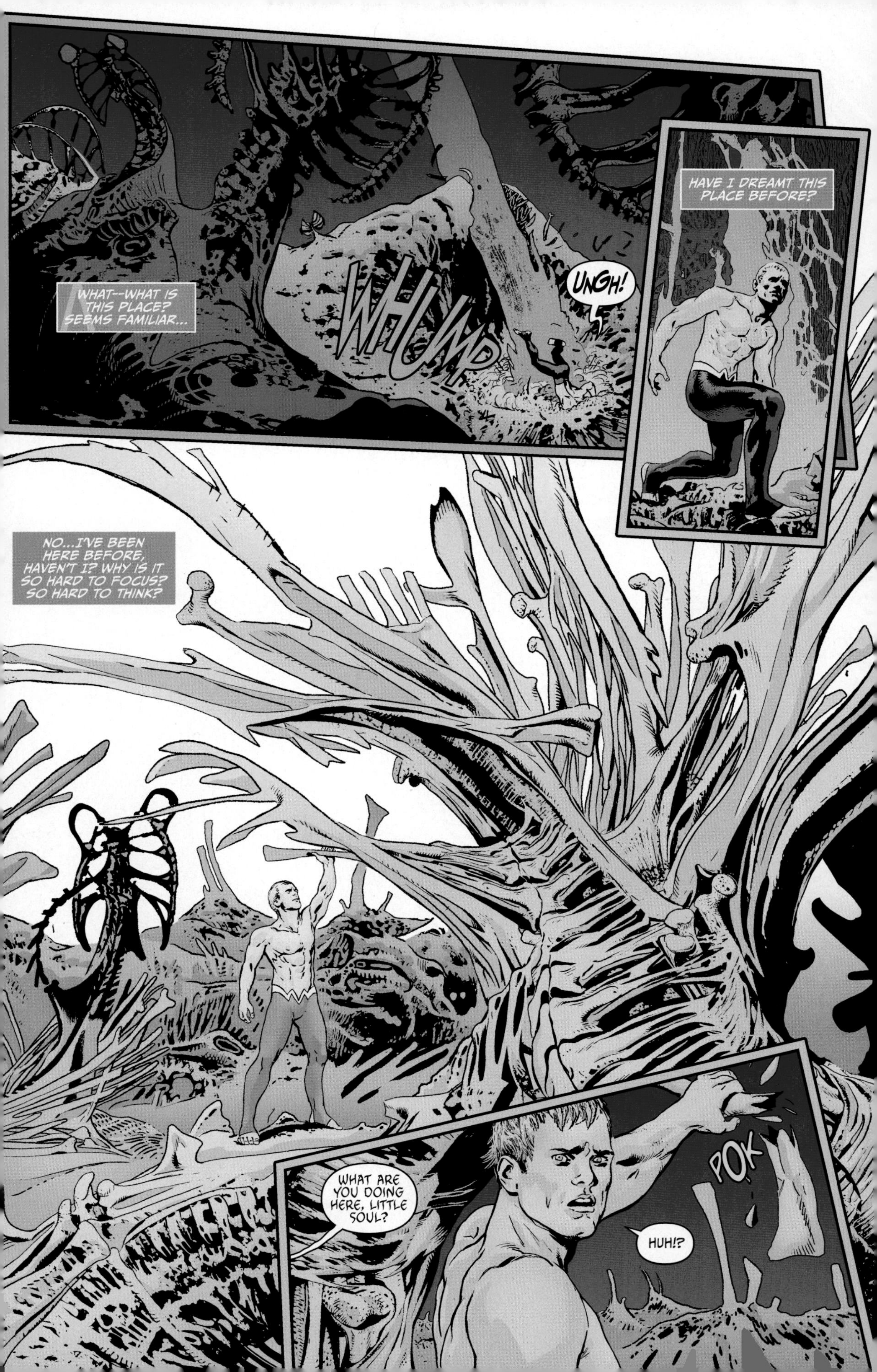
WHAT--WHAT IS THIS PLACE? SEEMS FAMILIAR...
WHUMP
UNGH!
HAVE I DREAMT THIS PLACE BEFORE?
NO...I'VE BEEN HERE BEFORE, HAVEN'T I? WHY IS IT SO HARD TO FOCUS? SO HARD TO THINK?
WHAT ARE YOU DOING HERE, LITTLE SOUL?
POK
HUH!?

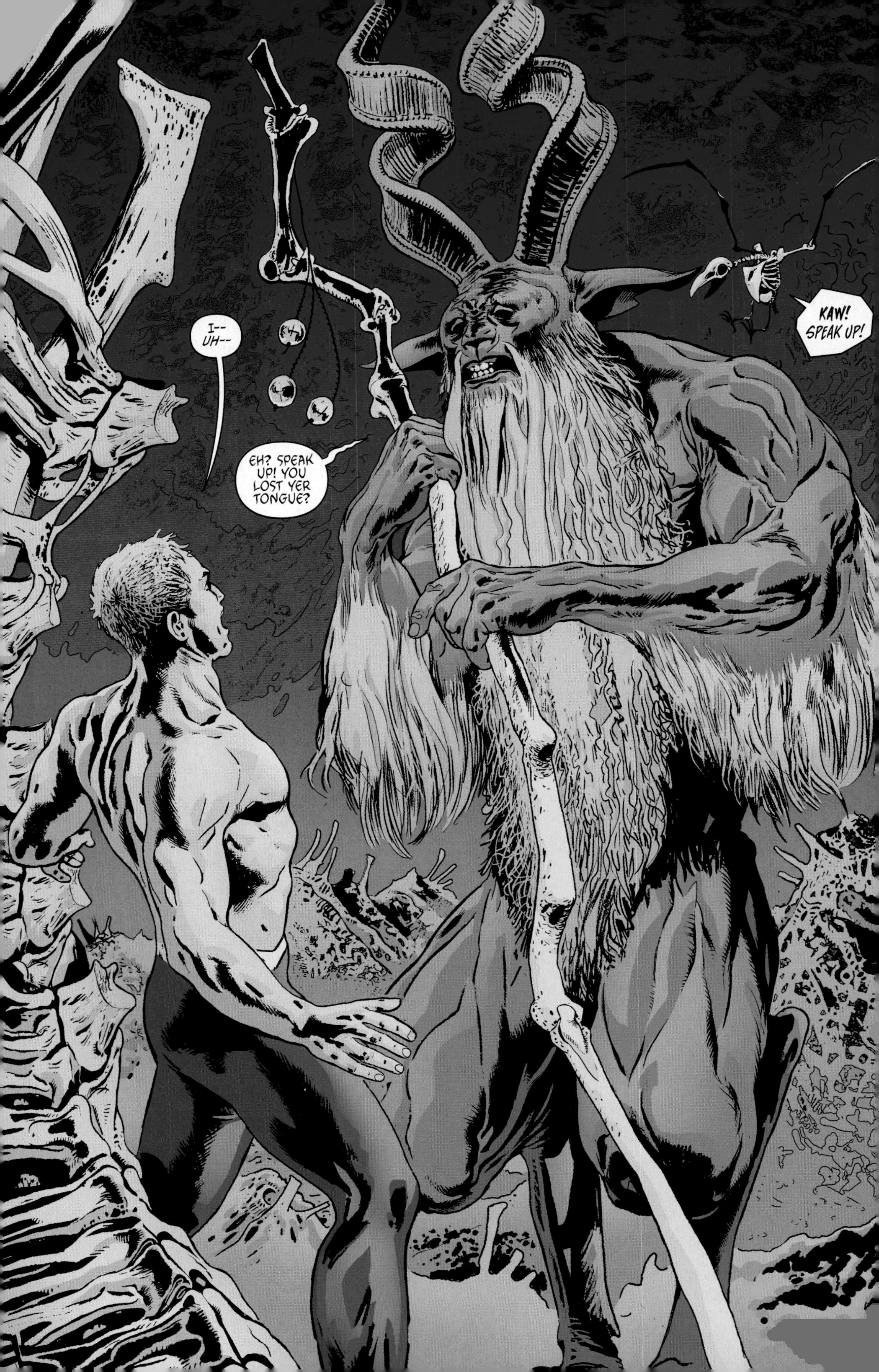
I-- UH--
EH? SPEAK UP! YOU LOST YER TONGUE?
KAW! SPEAK UP!

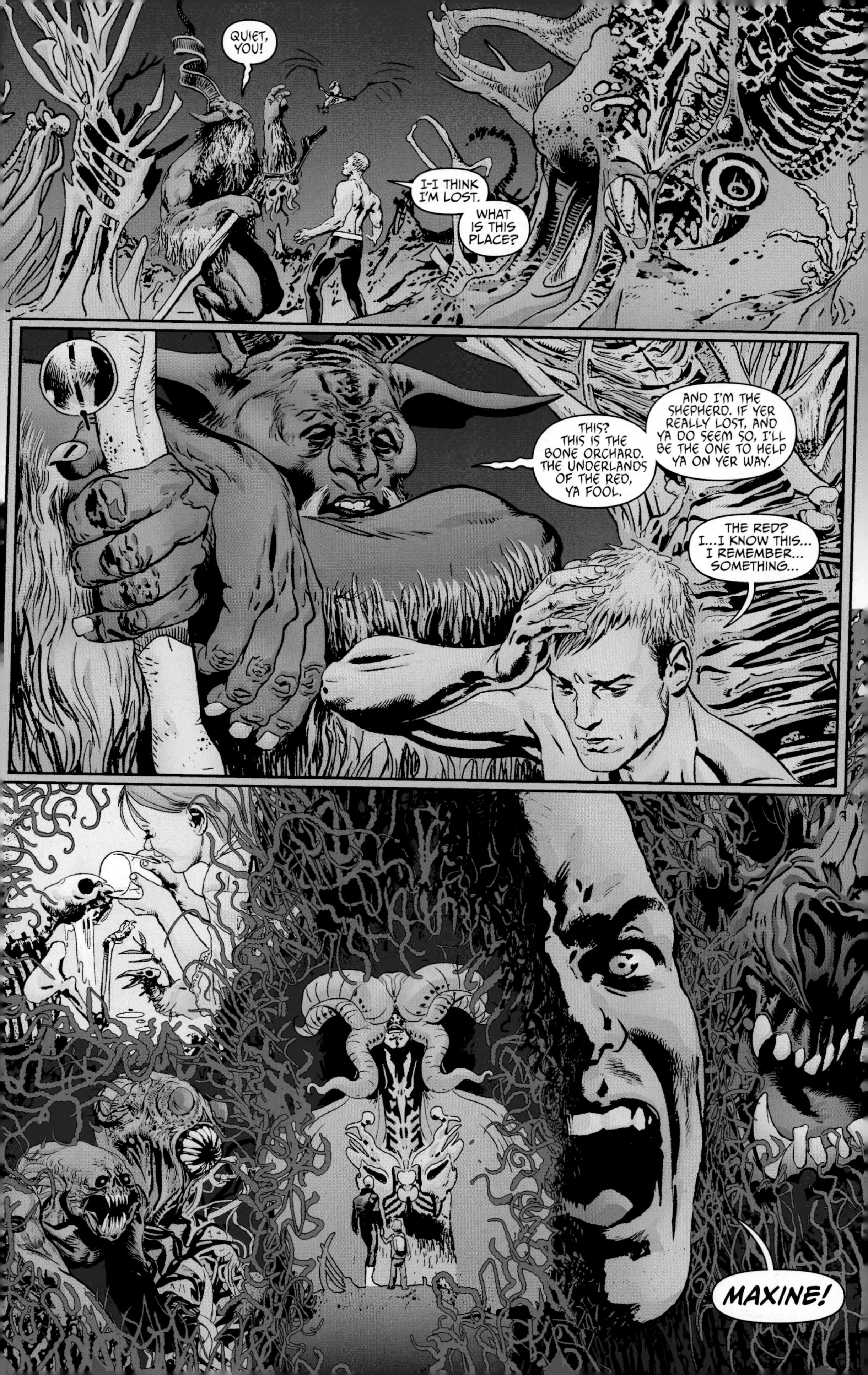
QUIET, YOU!
I-I THINK I'M LOST.
WHAT IS THIS PLACE?
THIS? THIS IS THE BONE ORCHARD. THE UNDERLANDS OF THE RED, YA FOOL.
AND I'M THE SHEPHERD. IF YER REALLY LOST, AND YA DO SEEM SO, I'LL BE THE ONE TO HELP YA ON YER WAY.
THE RED? I...I KNOW THIS... I REMEMBER... SOMETHING...
MAXINE!

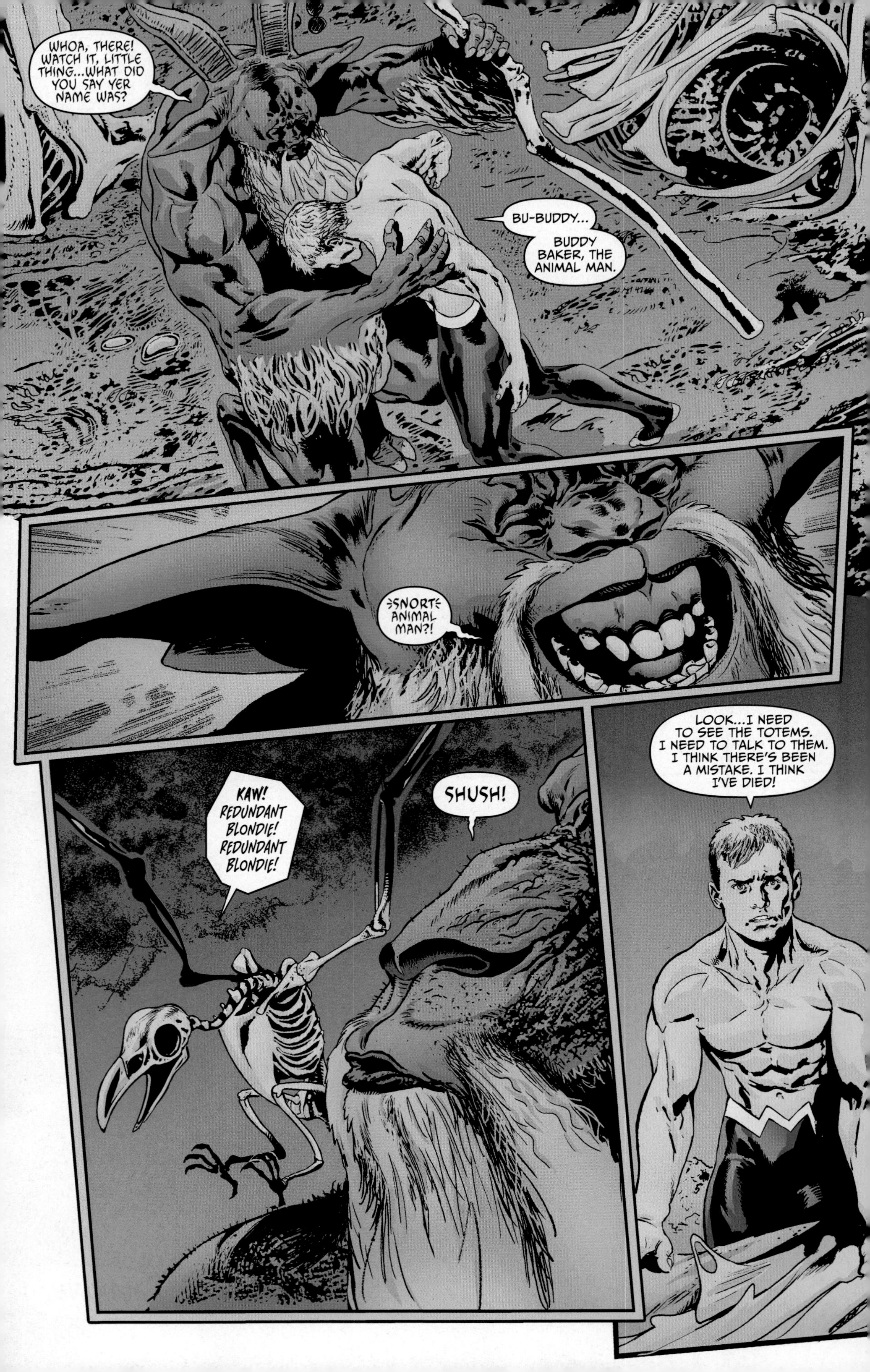
WHOA, THERE! WATCH IT, LITTLE THING...WHAT DID YOU SAY YER NAME WAS?
BU-BUDDY...
BUDDY BAKER, THE ANIMAL MAN.
SNORT ANIMAL MAN?!
LOOK...I NEED TO SEE THE TOTEMS. I NEED TO TALK TO THEM. I THINK THERE'S BEEN A MISTAKE. I THINK I'VE DIED!
KAW! REDUNDANT BLONDIE! REDUNDANT BLONDIE!
SHUSH!

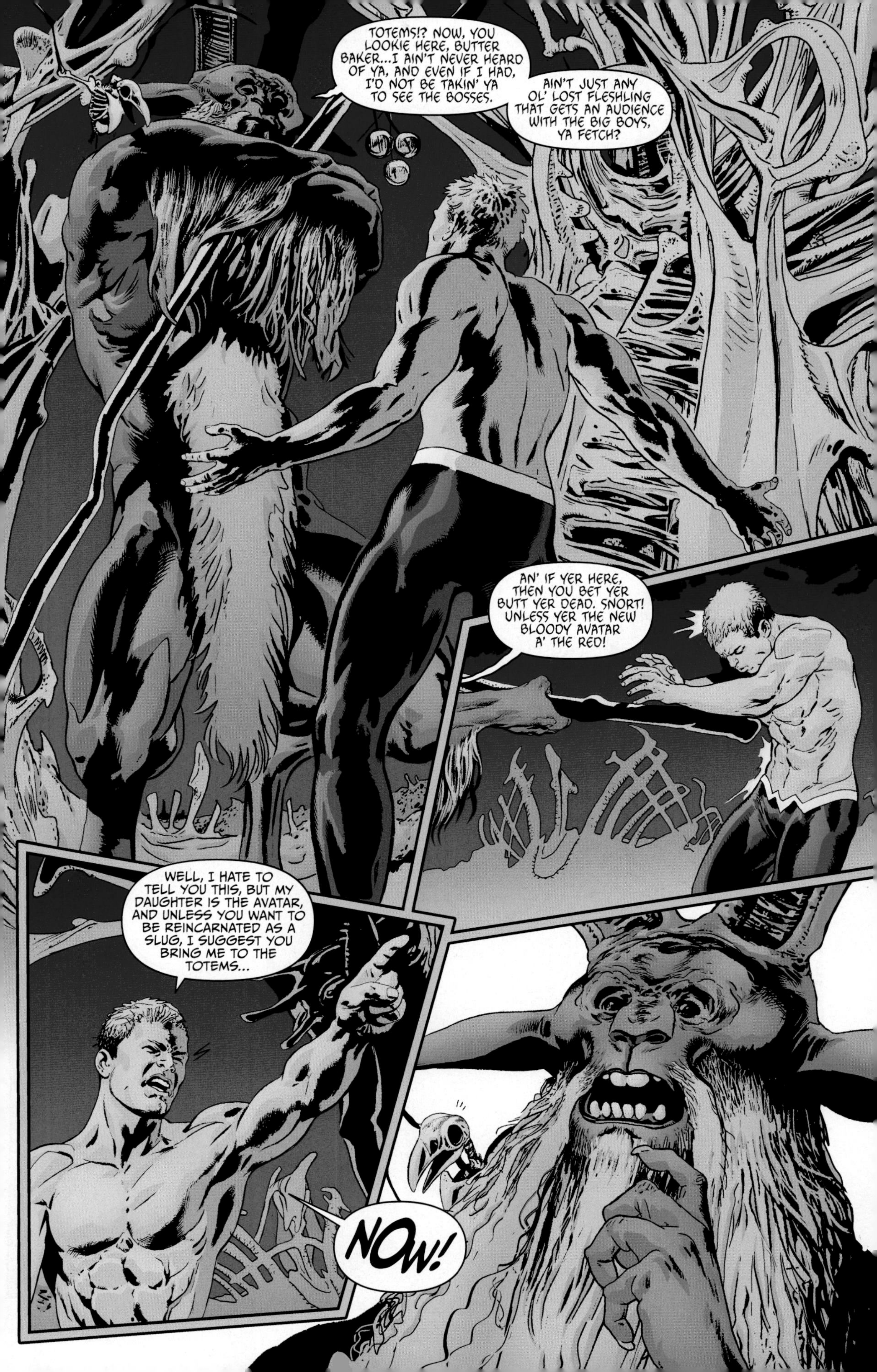
TOTEMS!? NOW, YOU LOOKIE HERE, BUTTER BAKER...I AIN'T NEVER HEARD OF YA, AND EVEN IF I HAD, I'D NOT BE TAKIN' YA TO SEE THE BOSSES.
AIN'T JUST ANY OL' LOST FLESHLING THAT GETS AN AUDIENCE WITH THE BIG BOYS, YA FETCH?
AN' IF YER HERE, THEN YOU BET YER BUTT YER DEAD. SNORT! UNLESS YER THE NEW BLOODY AVATAR A' THE RED!
WELL, I HATE TO TELL YOU THIS, BUT MY DAUGHTER IS THE AVATAR, AND UNLESS YOU WANT TO BE REINCARNATED AS A SLUG, I SUGGEST YOU BRING ME TO THE TOTEMS...
NOW!

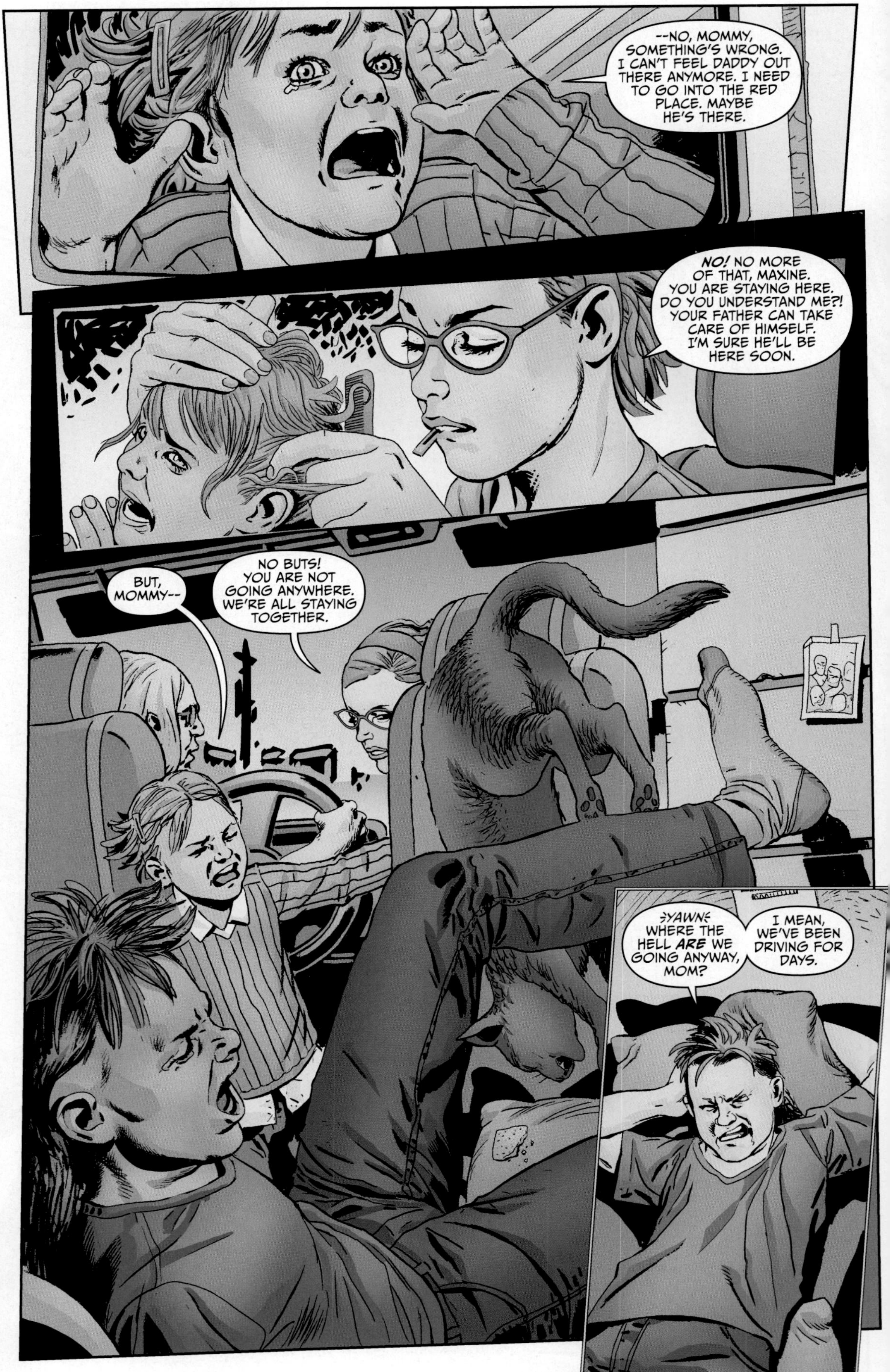
--NO, MOMMY, SOMETHING'S WRONG. I CAN'T FEEL DADDY OUT THERE ANYMORE. I NEED TO GO INTO THE RED PLACE. MAYBE HE'S THERE.
NO! NO MORE OF THAT, MAXINE. YOU ARE STAYING HERE. DO YOU UNDERSTAND ME?! YOUR FATHER CAN TAKE CARE OF HIMSELF. I'M SURE HE'LL BE HERE SOON.
BUT, MOMMY--
NO BUTS! YOU ARE NOT GOING ANYWHERE. WE'RE ALL STAYING TOGETHER.
YAWN WHERE THE HELL ARE WE GOING ANYWAY, MOM?
I MEAN, WE'VE BEEN DRIVING FOR DAYS.

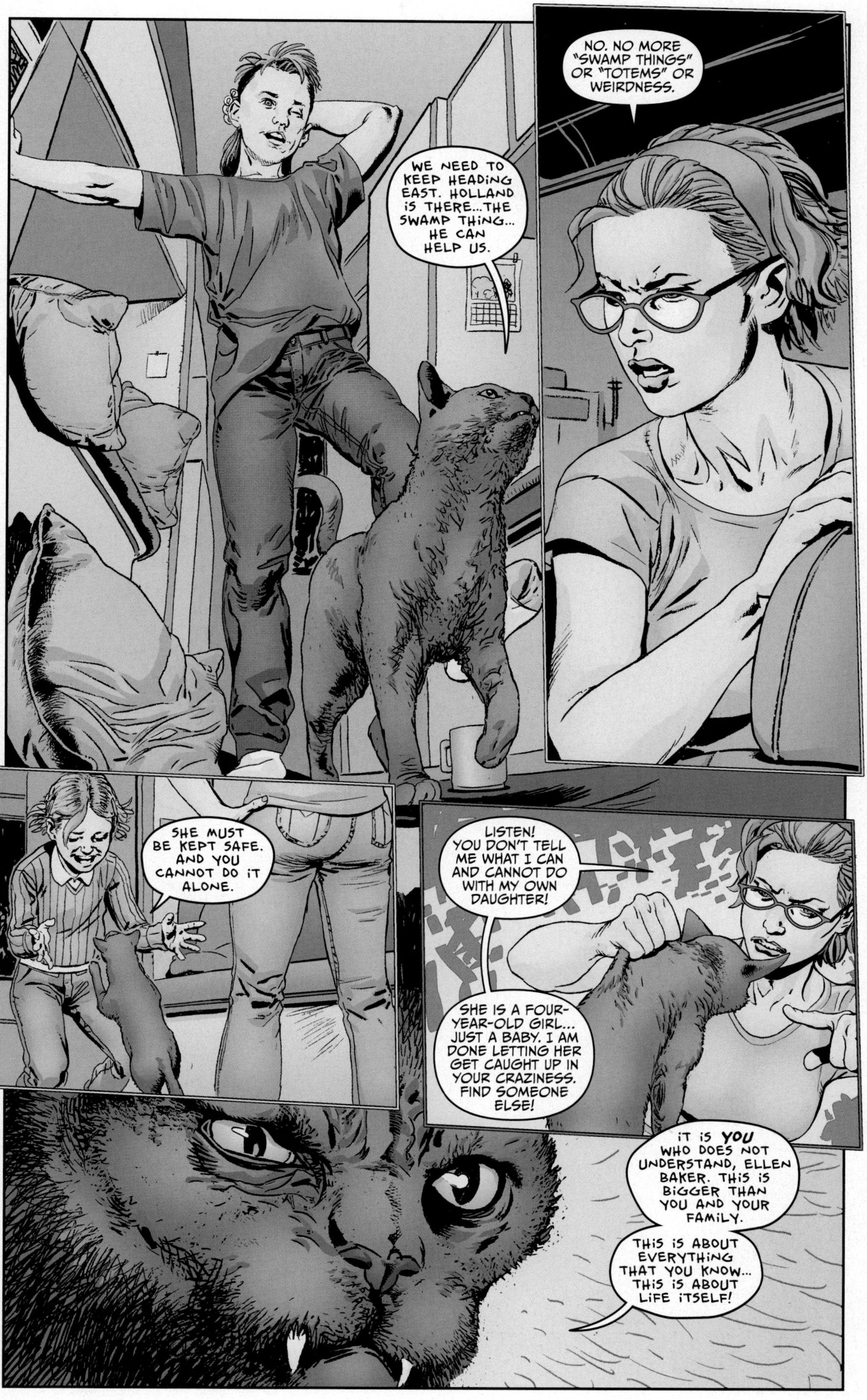
WE NEED TO KEEP HEADING EAST. HOLLAND IS THERE...THE SWAMP THING... HE CAN HELP US.
NO. NO MORE "SWAMP THINGS" OR "TOTEMS" OR WEIRDNESS.
SHE MUST BE KEPT SAFE. AND YOU CANNOT DO IT ALONE.
LISTEN! YOU DON'T TELL ME WHAT I CAN AND CANNOT DO WITH MY OWN DAUGHTER!
SHE IS A FOUR-YEAR-OLD GIRL... JUST A BABY. I AM DONE LETTING HER GET CAUGHT UP IN YOUR CRAZINESS. FIND SOMEONE ELSE!
IT IS **YOU** WHO DOES NOT UNDERSTAND, ELLEN BAKER. THIS IS BIGGER THAN YOU AND YOUR FAMILY.
THIS IS ABOUT EVERYTHING THAT YOU KNOW... THIS IS ABOUT LIFE ITSELF!

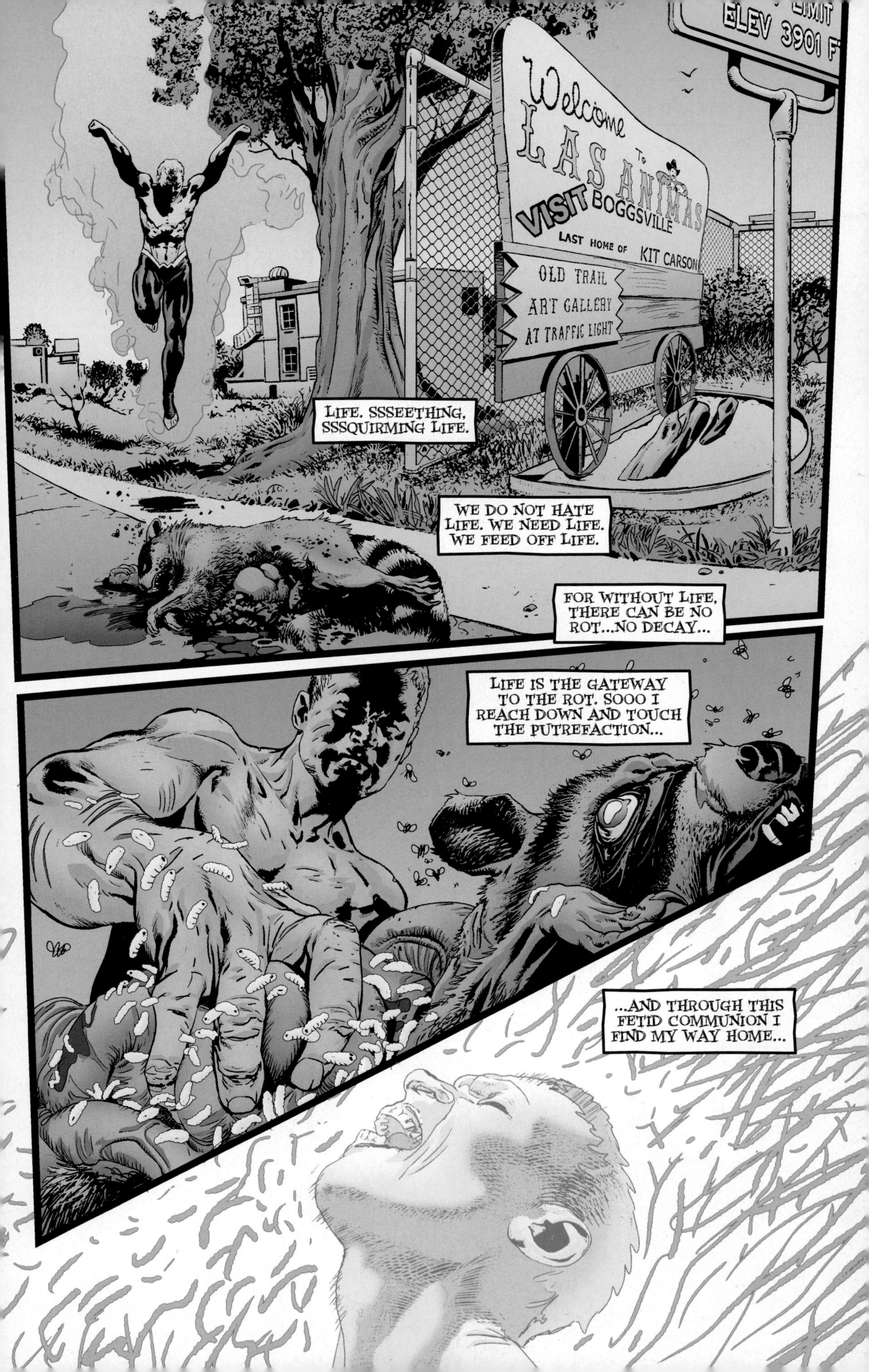
ELEV 3901 FT
Welcome To LAS ANIMAS
VISIT BOGGSVILLE
LAST HOME OF KIT CARSON
OLD TRAIL ART GALLERY AT TRAFFIC LIGHT
LIFE. SSSEETHING, SSSQUIRMING LIFE.
WE DO NOT HATE LIFE. WE NEED LIFE. WE FEED OFF LIFE.
FOR WITHOUT LIFE, THERE CAN BE NO ROT...NO DECAY...
LIFE IS THE GATEWAY TO THE ROT. SOOO I REACH DOWN AND TOUCH THE PUTREFACTION...
...AND THROUGH THIS FETID COMMUNION I FIND MY WAY HOME...

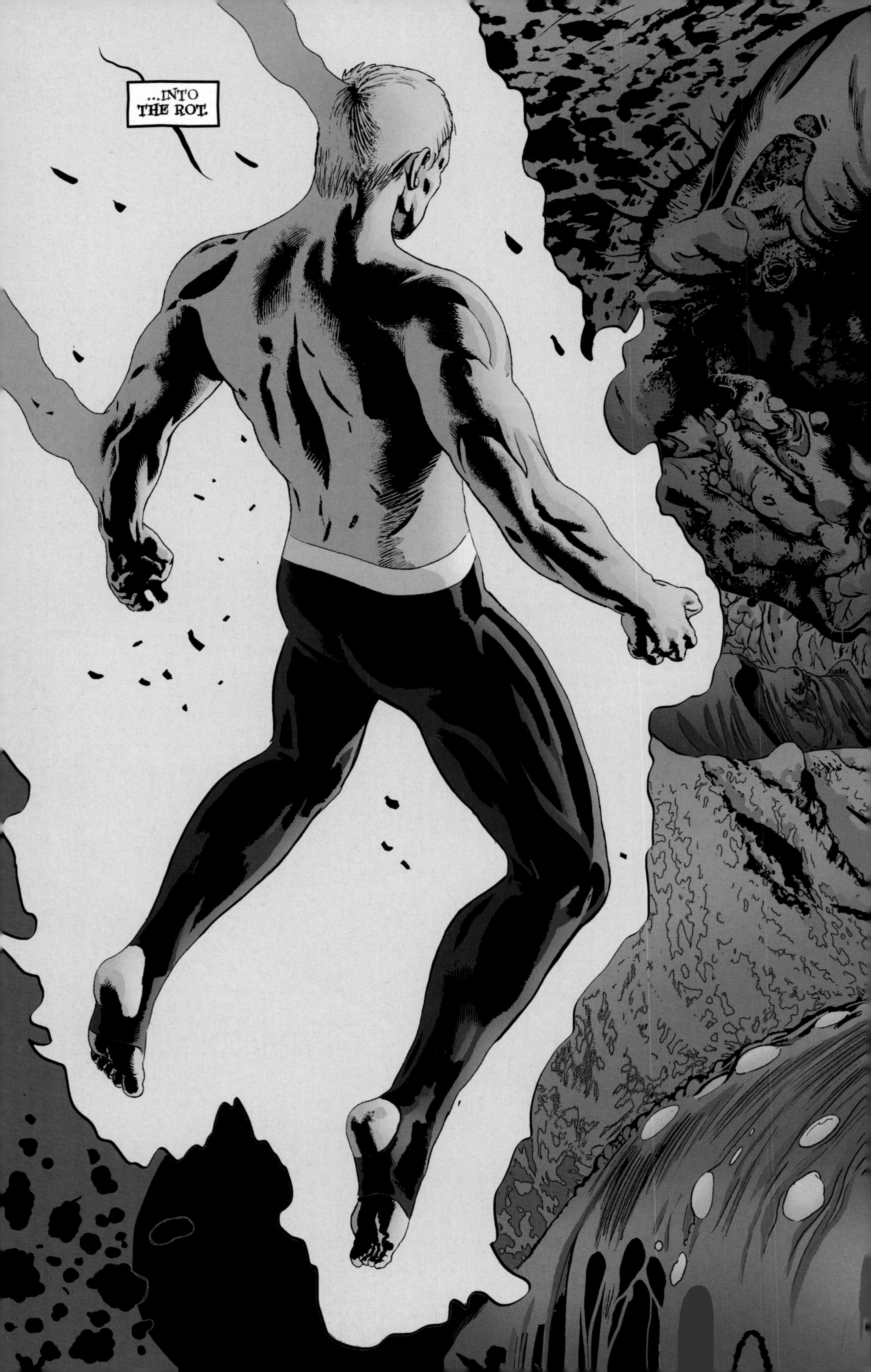
...INTO THE ROT.

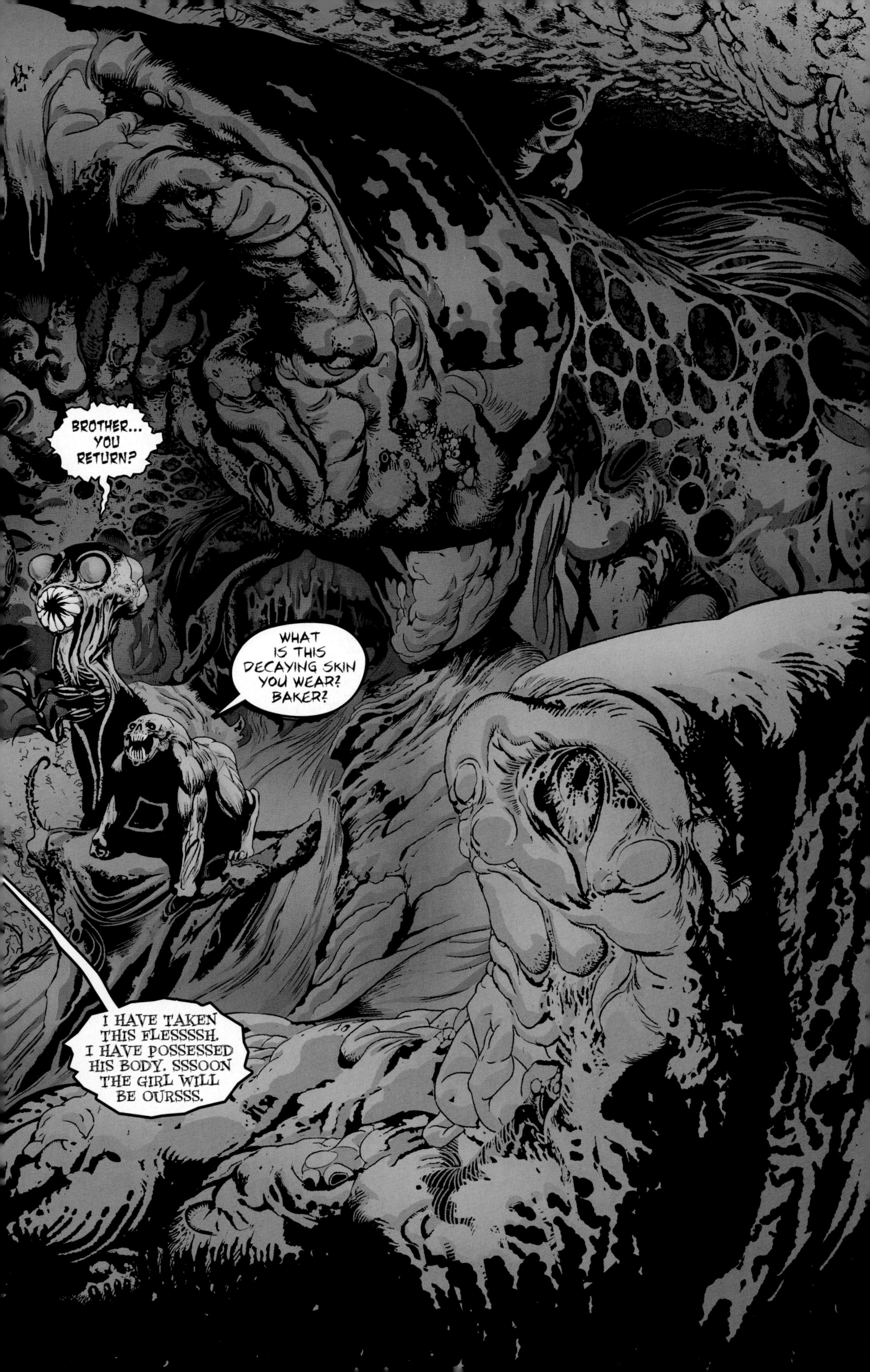
BROTHER... YOU RETURN?
WHAT IS THIS DECAYING SKIN YOU WEAR? BAKER?
I HAVE TAKEN THIS FLESSSSH. I HAVE POSSESSED HIS BODY. SSSOON THE GIRL WILL BE OURSSS.

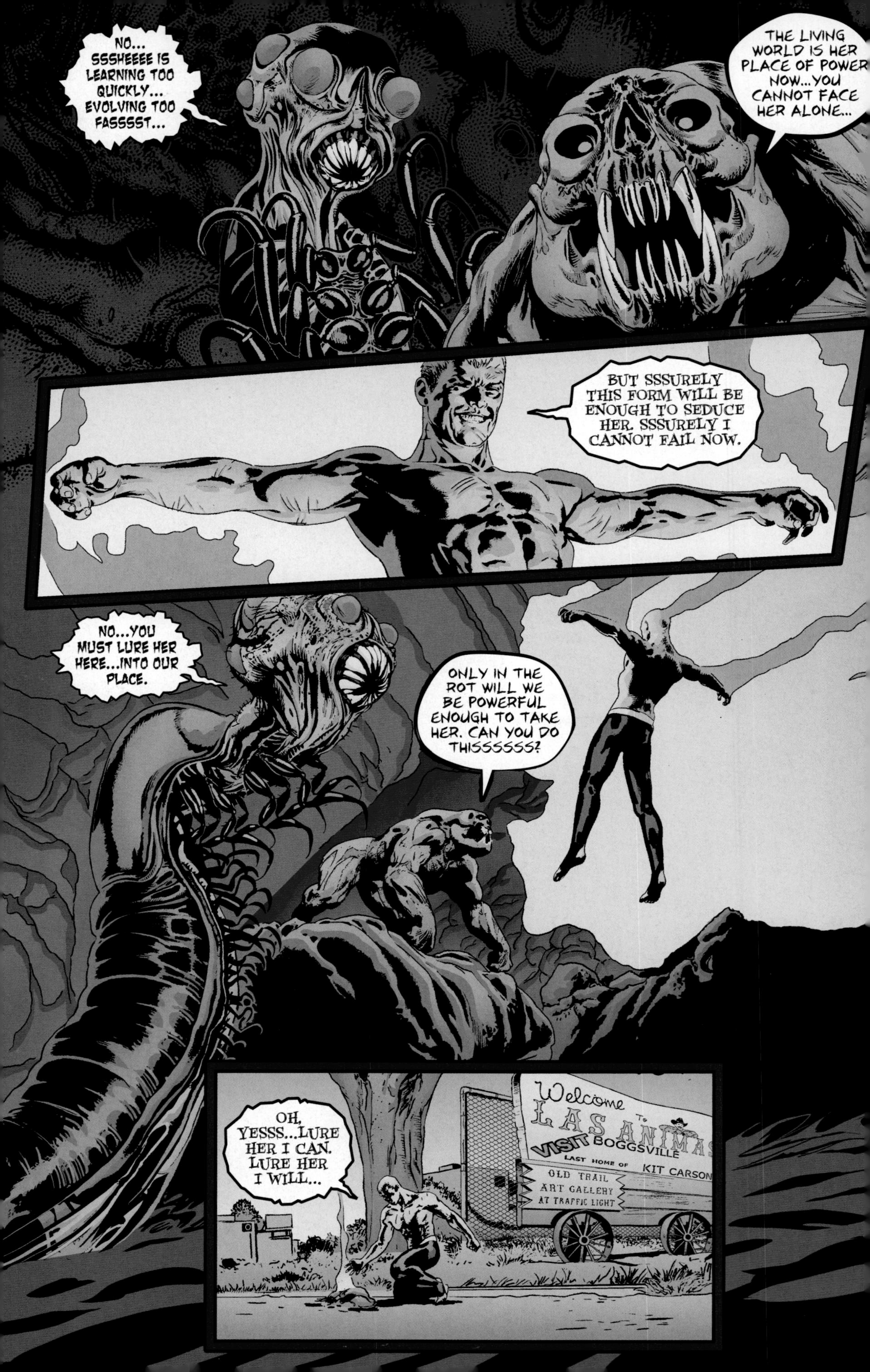
NO... SSSHEEEE IS LEARNING TOO QUICKLY... EVOLVING TOO FASSSST...
THE LIVING WORLD IS HER PLACE OF POWER NOW...YOU CANNOT FACE HER ALONE...
BUT SSSURELY THIS FORM WILL BE ENOUGH TO SEDUCE HER. SSSURELY I CANNOT FAIL NOW.
NO...YOU MUST LURE HER HERE...INTO OUR PLACE.
ONLY IN THE ROT WILL WE BE POWERFUL ENOUGH TO TAKE HER. CAN YOU DO THISSSSSS?
OH, YESSS...LURE HER I CAN. LURE HER I WILL...
Welcome To LAS ANIMAS
VISIT BOGGSVILLE
LAST HOME OF KIT CARSON
OLD TRAIL ART GALLERY AT TRAFFIC LIGHT

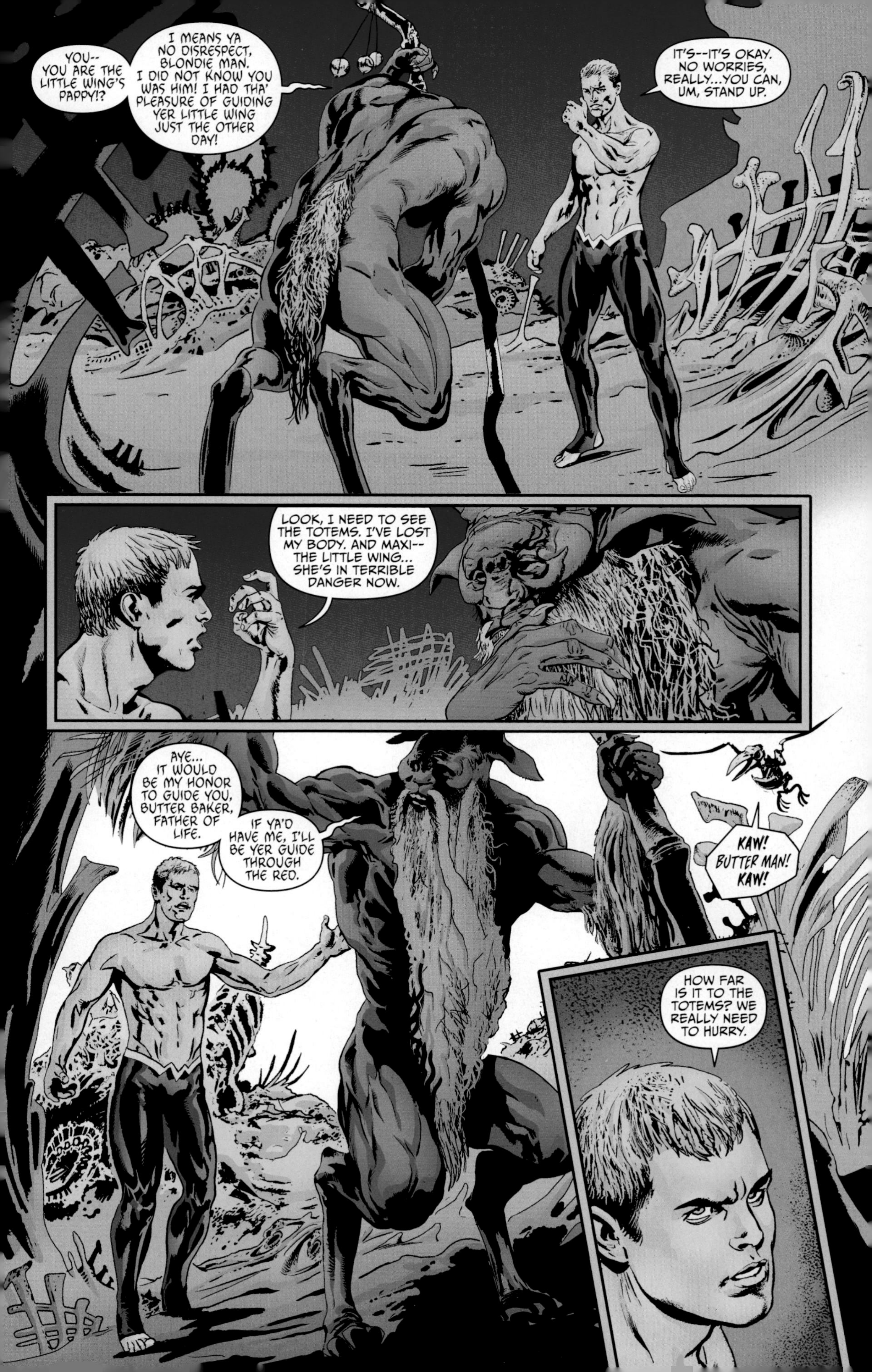
YOU-- YOU ARE THE LITTLE WING'S PAPPY!?
I MEANS YA NO DISRESPECT, BLONDIE MAN. I DID NOT KNOW YOU WAS HIM! I HAD THA' PLEASURE OF GUIDING YER LITTLE WING JUST THE OTHER DAY!
IT'S--IT'S OKAY. NO WORRIES, REALLY...YOU CAN, UM, STAND UP.
LOOK, I NEED TO SEE THE TOTEMS. I'VE LOST MY BODY. AND MAXI-- THE LITTLE WING... SHE'S IN TERRIBLE DANGER NOW.
AYE... IT WOULD BE MY HONOR TO GUIDE YOU, BUTTER BAKER, FATHER OF LIFE.
IF YA'D HAVE ME, I'LL BE YER GUIDE THROUGH THE RED.
KAW! BUTTER MAN! KAW!
HOW FAR IS IT TO THE TOTEMS? WE REALLY NEED TO HURRY.

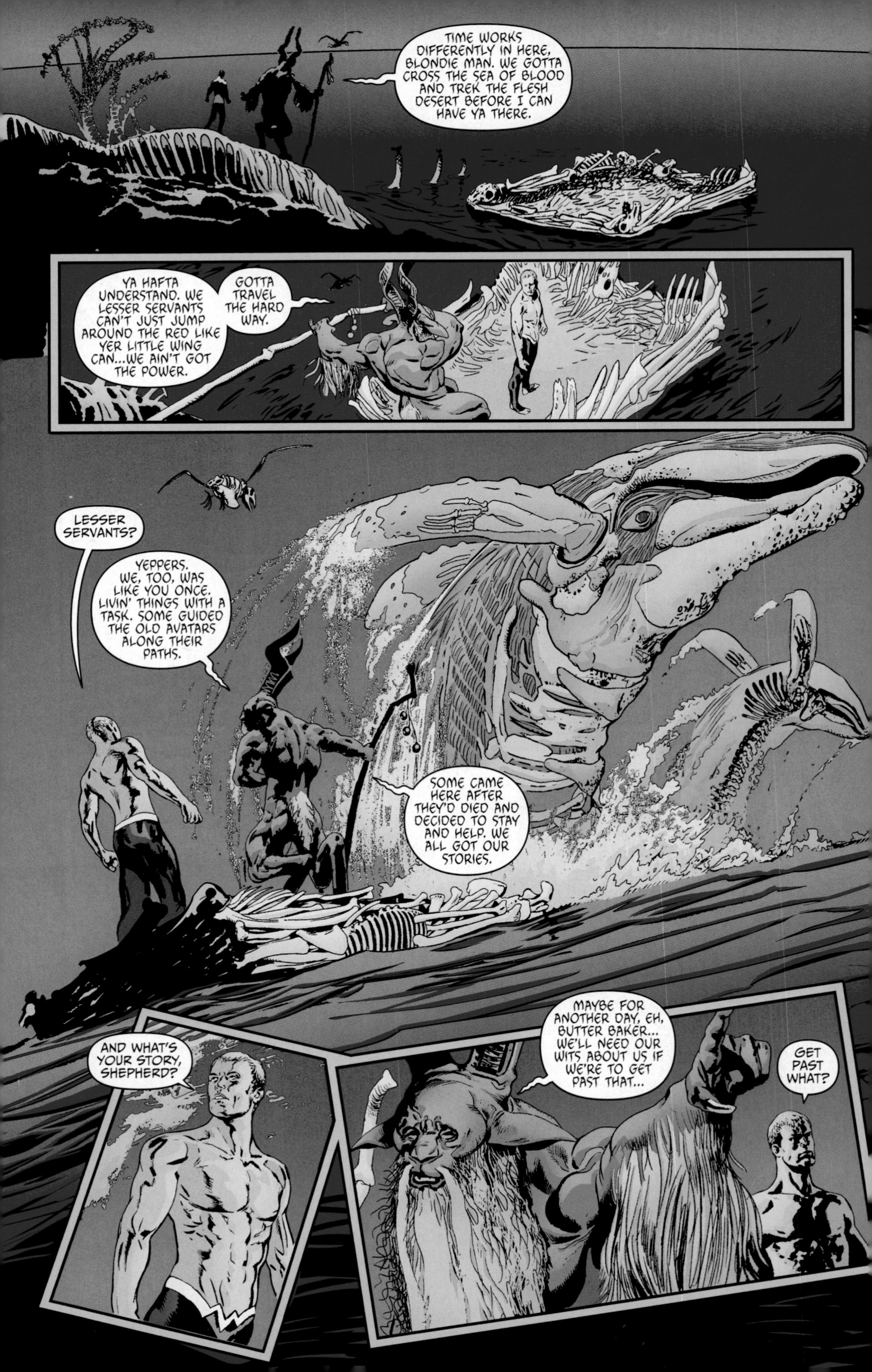
TIME WORKS DIFFERENTLY IN HERE, BLONDIE MAN. WE GOTTA CROSS THE SEA OF BLOOD AND TREK THE FLESH DESERT BEFORE I CAN HAVE YA THERE.
YA HAFTA UNDERSTAND. WE LESSER SERVANTS CAN'T JUST JUMP AROUND THE RED LIKE YER LITTLE WING CAN...WE AIN'T GOT THE POWER.
GOTTA TRAVEL THE HARD WAY.
LESSER SERVANTS?
YEPPERS. WE, TOO, WAS LIKE YOU ONCE. LIVIN' THINGS WITH A TASK. SOME GUIDED THE OLD AVATARS ALONG THEIR PATHS.
SOME CAME HERE AFTER THEY'D DIED AND DECIDED TO STAY AND HELP. WE ALL GOT OUR STORIES.
AND WHAT'S YOUR STORY, SHEPHERD?
MAYBE FOR ANOTHER DAY, EH, BUTTER BAKER... WE'LL NEED OUR WITS ABOUT US IF WE'RE TO GET PAST THAT...
GET PAST WHAT?

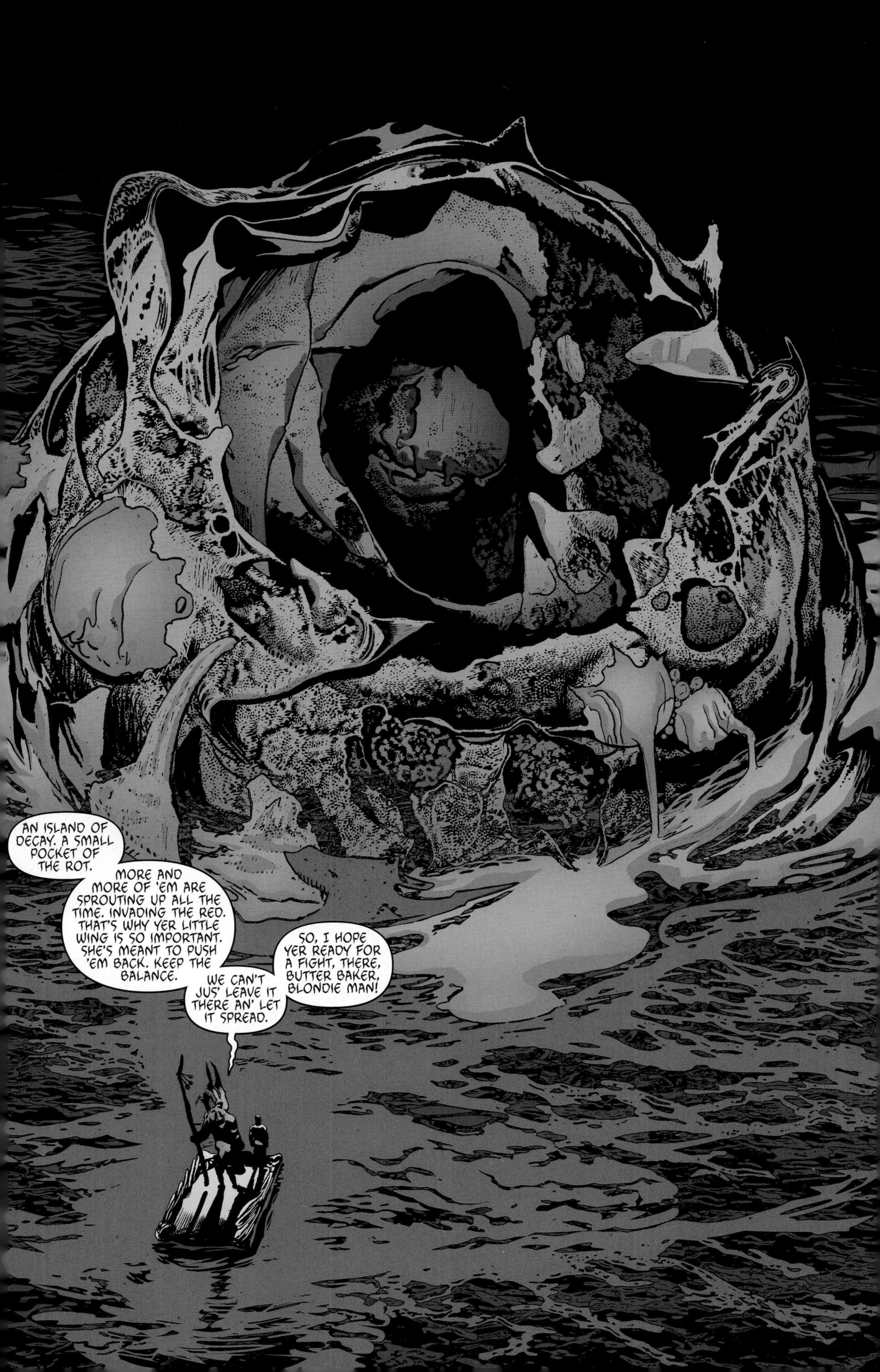
AN ISLAND OF DECAY. A SMALL POCKET OF THE ROT.
MORE AND MORE OF 'EM ARE SPROUTING UP ALL THE TIME. INVADING THE RED. THAT'S WHY YER LITTLE WING IS SO IMPORTANT. SHE'S MEANT TO PUSH 'EM BACK. KEEP THE BALANCE.
WE CAN'T JUS' LEAVE IT THERE AN' LET IT SPREAD.
SO, I HOPE YER READY FOR A FIGHT, THERE, BUTTER BAKER, BLONDIE MAN!

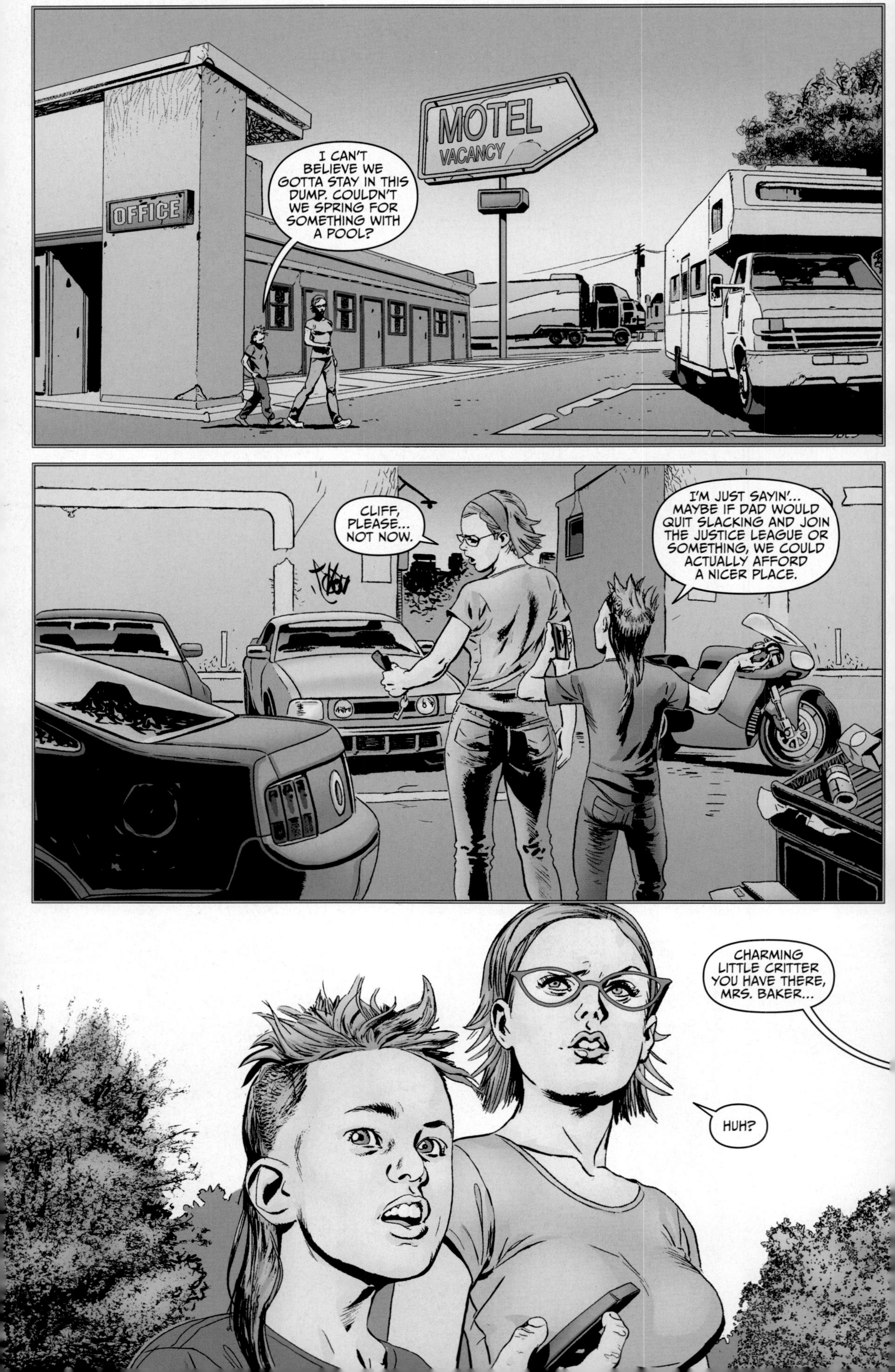
MOTEL
VACANCY
OFFICE
I CAN'T BELIEVE WE GOTTA STAY IN THIS DUMP. COULDN'T WE SPRING FOR SOMETHING WITH A POOL?
CLIFF, PLEASE... NOT NOW.
I'M JUST SAYIN'... MAYBE IF DAD WOULD QUIT SLACKING AND JOIN THE JUSTICE LEAGUE OR SOMETHING, WE COULD ACTUALLY AFFORD A NICER PLACE.
CHARMING LITTLE CRITTER YOU HAVE THERE, MRS. BAKER...
HUH?

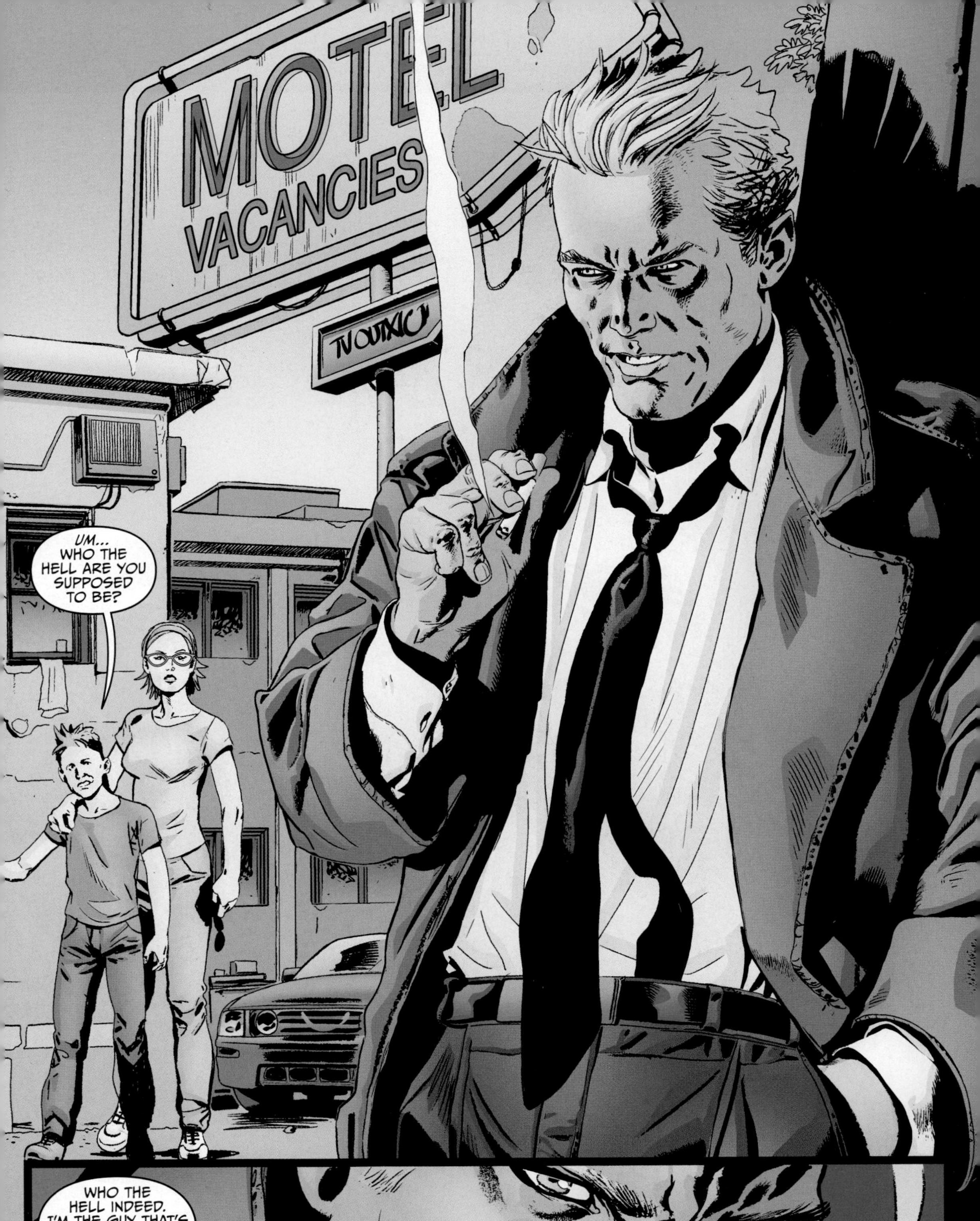
MOTEL
VACANCIES
UM... WHO THE HELL ARE YOU SUPPOSED TO BE?

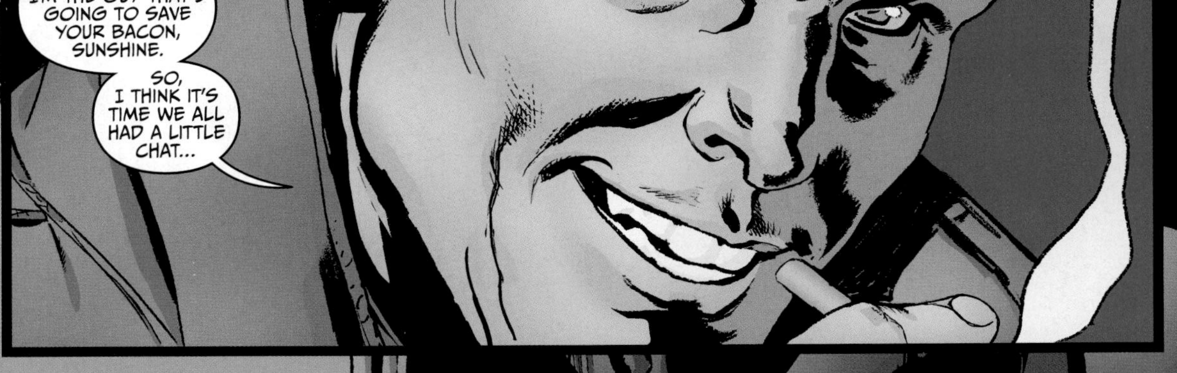
WHO THE HELL INDEED. I'M THE GUY THAT'S GOING TO SAVE YOUR BACON, SUNSHINE.
SO, I THINK IT'S TIME WE ALL HAD A LITTLE CHAT...

JEFF LEMIRE writer TIMOTHY GREEN II penciller JOSEPH SILVER inker
cover by TRAVEL FOREMAN with LOVERN KINDZIERSKI

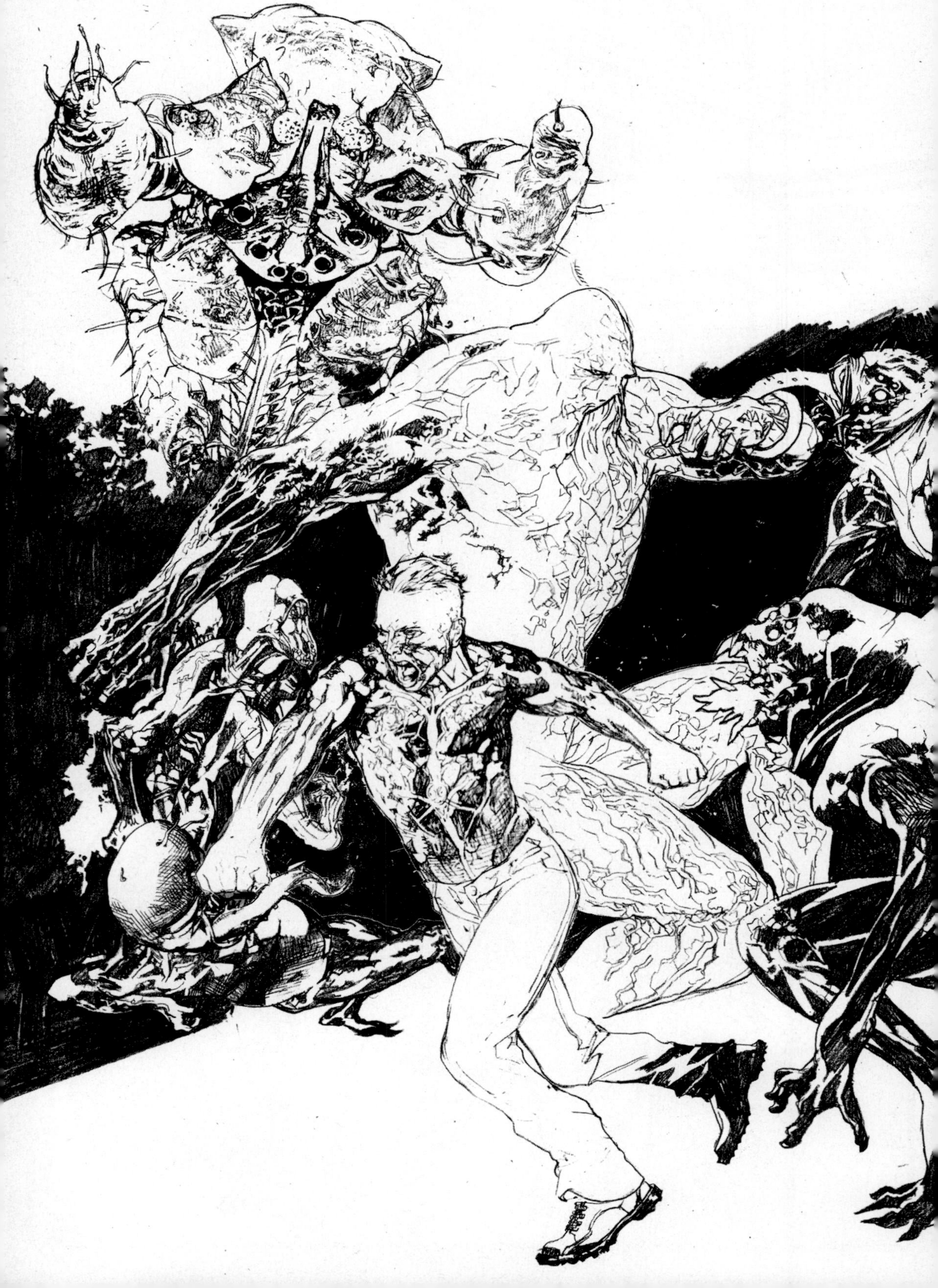

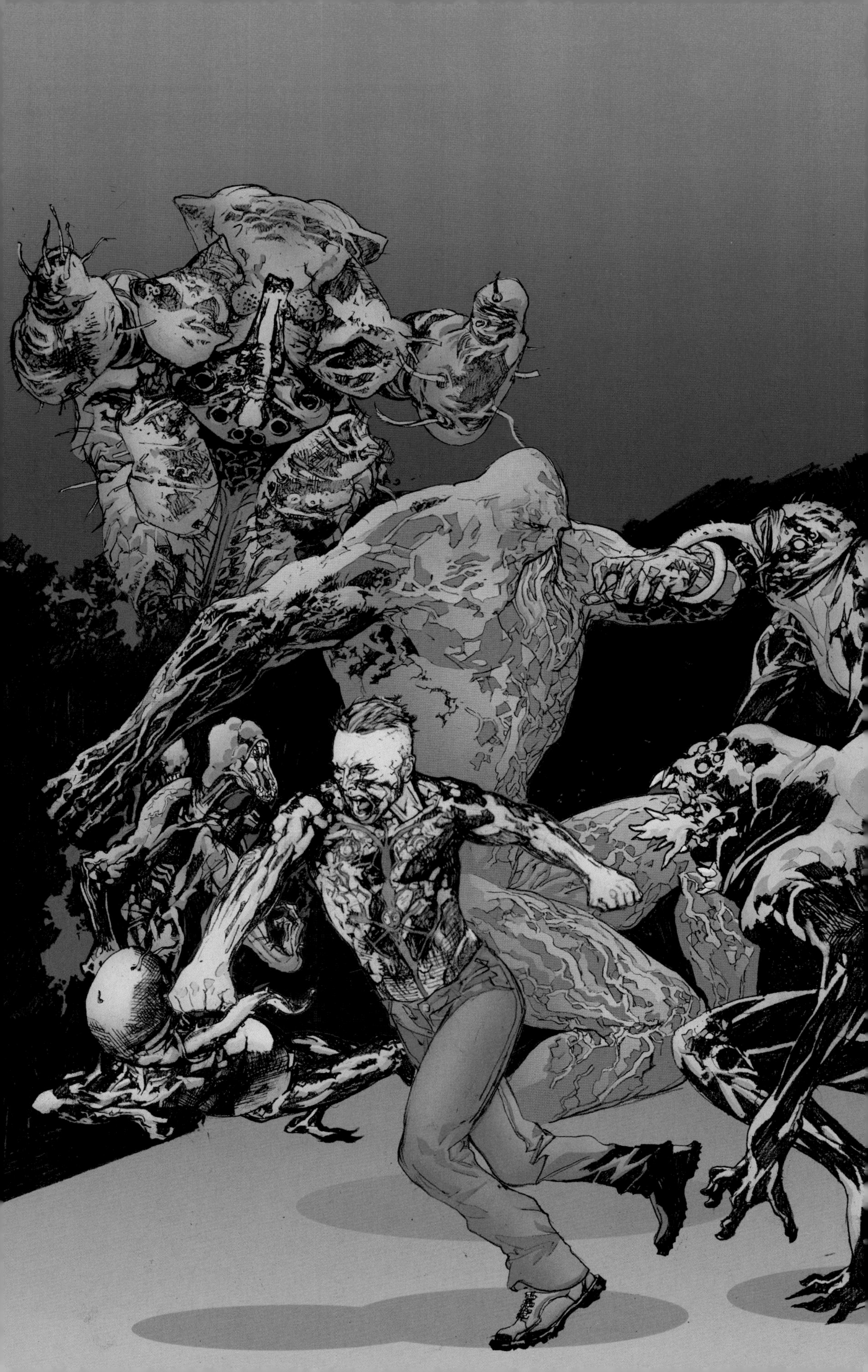

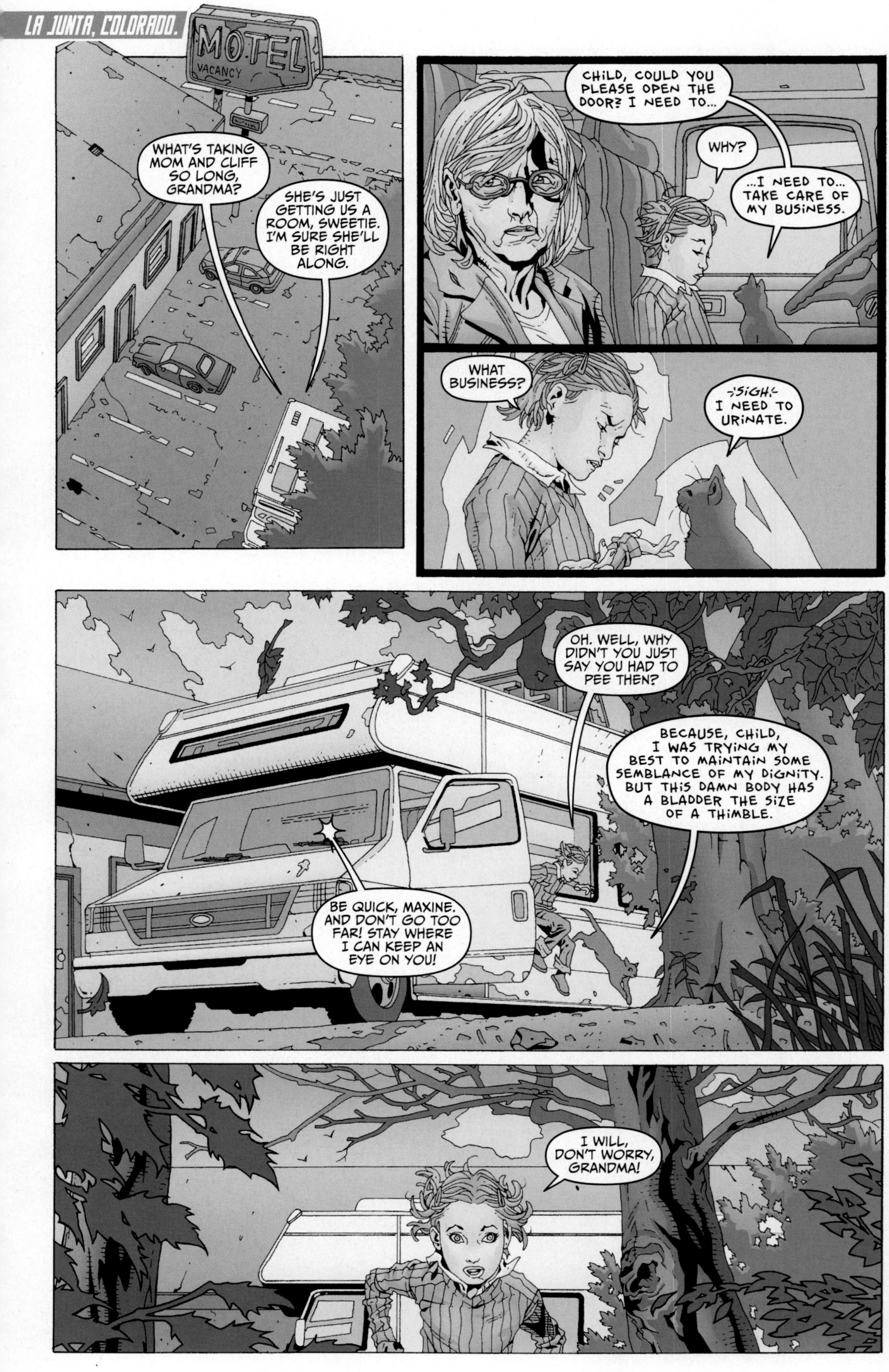
LA JUNTA, COLORADO.
MOTEL
VACANCY
WHAT'S TAKING MOM AND CLIFF SO LONG, GRANDMA?
SHE'S JUST GETTING US A ROOM, SWEETIE. I'M SURE SHE'LL BE RIGHT ALONG.
CHILD, COULD YOU PLEASE OPEN THE DOOR? I NEED TO...
WHY?
...I NEED TO... TAKE CARE OF MY BUSINESS.
WHAT BUSINESS?
-SIGH- I NEED TO URINATE.
OH. WELL, WHY DIDN'T YOU JUST SAY YOU HAD TO PEE THEN?
BECAUSE, CHILD, I WAS TRYING MY BEST TO MAINTAIN SOME SEMBLANCE OF MY DIGNITY. BUT THIS DAMN BODY HAS A BLADDER THE SIZE OF A THIMBLE.
BE QUICK, MAXINE. AND DON'T GO TOO FAR! STAY WHERE I CAN KEEP AN EYE ON YOU!
I WILL, DON'T WORRY, GRANDMA!

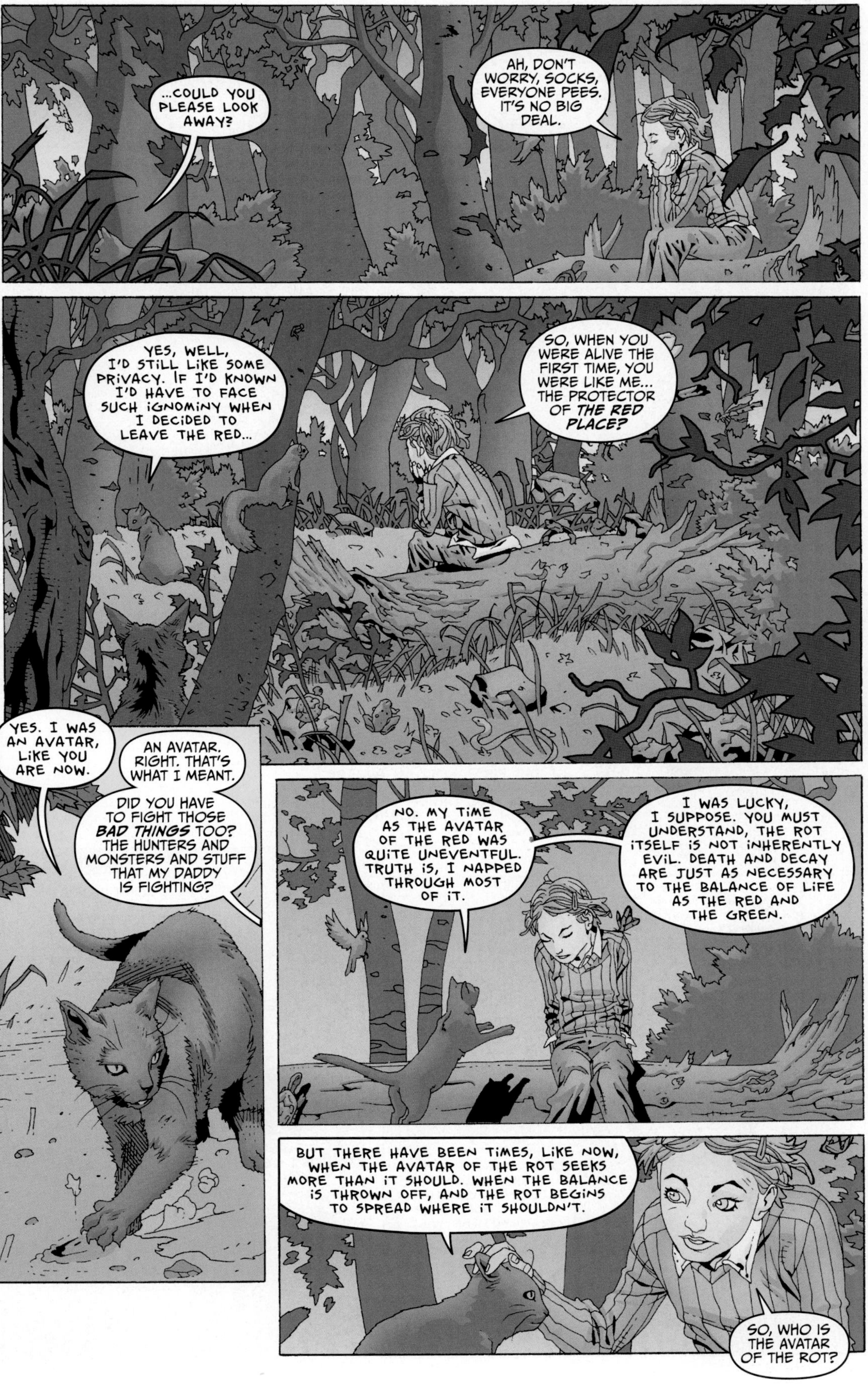
...COULD YOU PLEASE LOOK AWAY?
AH, DON'T WORRY, SOCKS, EVERYONE PEES. IT'S NO BIG DEAL.
YES, WELL, I'D STILL LIKE SOME PRIVACY. IF I'D KNOWN I'D HAVE TO FACE SUCH IGNOMINY WHEN I DECIDED TO LEAVE THE RED...
SO, WHEN YOU WERE ALIVE THE FIRST TIME, YOU WERE LIKE ME... THE PROTECTOR OF THE RED PLACE?
YES. I WAS AN AVATAR, LIKE YOU ARE NOW.
AN AVATAR. RIGHT. THAT'S WHAT I MEANT.
DID YOU HAVE TO FIGHT THOSE BAD THINGS TOO? THE HUNTERS AND MONSTERS AND STUFF THAT MY DADDY IS FIGHTING?
NO. MY TIME AS THE AVATAR OF THE RED WAS QUITE UNEVENTFUL. TRUTH IS, I NAPPED THROUGH MOST OF IT.
I WAS LUCKY, I SUPPOSE. YOU MUST UNDERSTAND, THE ROT ITSELF IS NOT INHERENTLY EVIL. DEATH AND DECAY ARE JUST AS NECESSARY TO THE BALANCE OF LIFE AS THE RED AND THE GREEN.
BUT THERE HAVE BEEN TIMES, LIKE NOW, WHEN THE AVATAR OF THE ROT SEEKS MORE THAN IT SHOULD. WHEN THE BALANCE IS THROWN OFF, AND THE ROT BEGINS TO SPREAD WHERE IT SHOULDN'T.
SO, WHO IS THE AVATAR OF THE ROT?

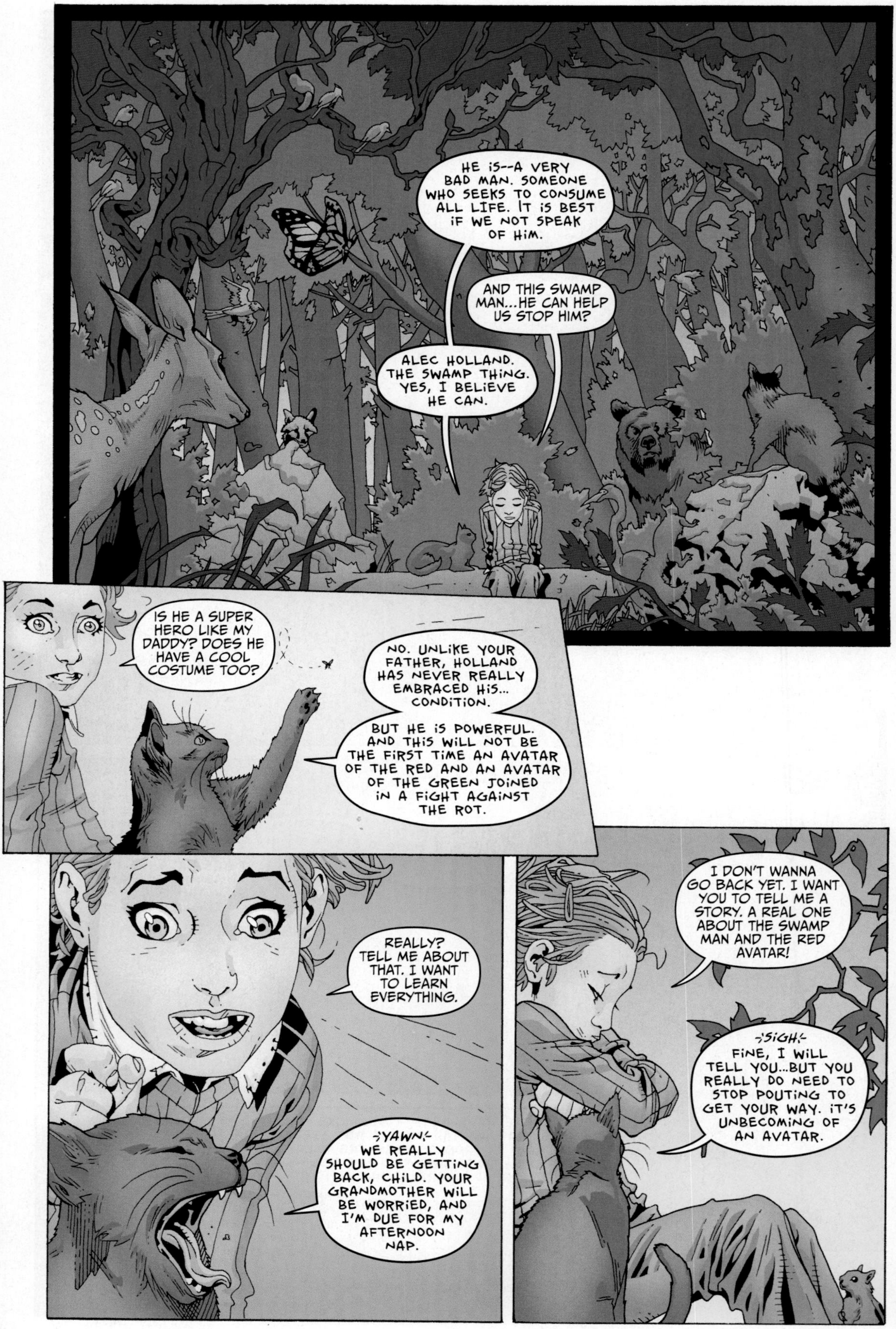
HE IS--A VERY BAD MAN. SOMEONE WHO SEEKS TO CONSUME ALL LIFE. IT IS BEST IF WE NOT SPEAK OF HIM.
AND THIS SWAMP MAN...HE CAN HELP US STOP HIM?
ALEC HOLLAND. THE SWAMP THING. YES, I BELIEVE HE CAN.
IS HE A SUPER HERO LIKE MY DADDY? DOES HE HAVE A COOL COSTUME TOO?
NO. UNLIKE YOUR FATHER, HOLLAND HAS NEVER REALLY EMBRACED HIS... CONDITION.
BUT HE IS POWERFUL. AND THIS WILL NOT BE THE FIRST TIME AN AVATAR OF THE RED AND AN AVATAR OF THE GREEN JOINED IN A FIGHT AGAINST THE ROT.
REALLY? TELL ME ABOUT THAT. I WANT TO LEARN EVERYTHING.
-YAWN-
WE REALLY SHOULD BE GETTING BACK, CHILD. YOUR GRANDMOTHER WILL BE WORRIED, AND I'M DUE FOR MY AFTERNOON NAP.
I DON'T WANNA GO BACK YET. I WANT YOU TO TELL ME A STORY. A REAL ONE ABOUT THE SWAMP MAN AND THE RED AVATAR!
-SIGH-
FINE, I WILL TELL YOU...BUT YOU REALLY DO NEED TO STOP POUTING TO GET YOUR WAY. IT'S UNBECOMING OF AN AVATAR.

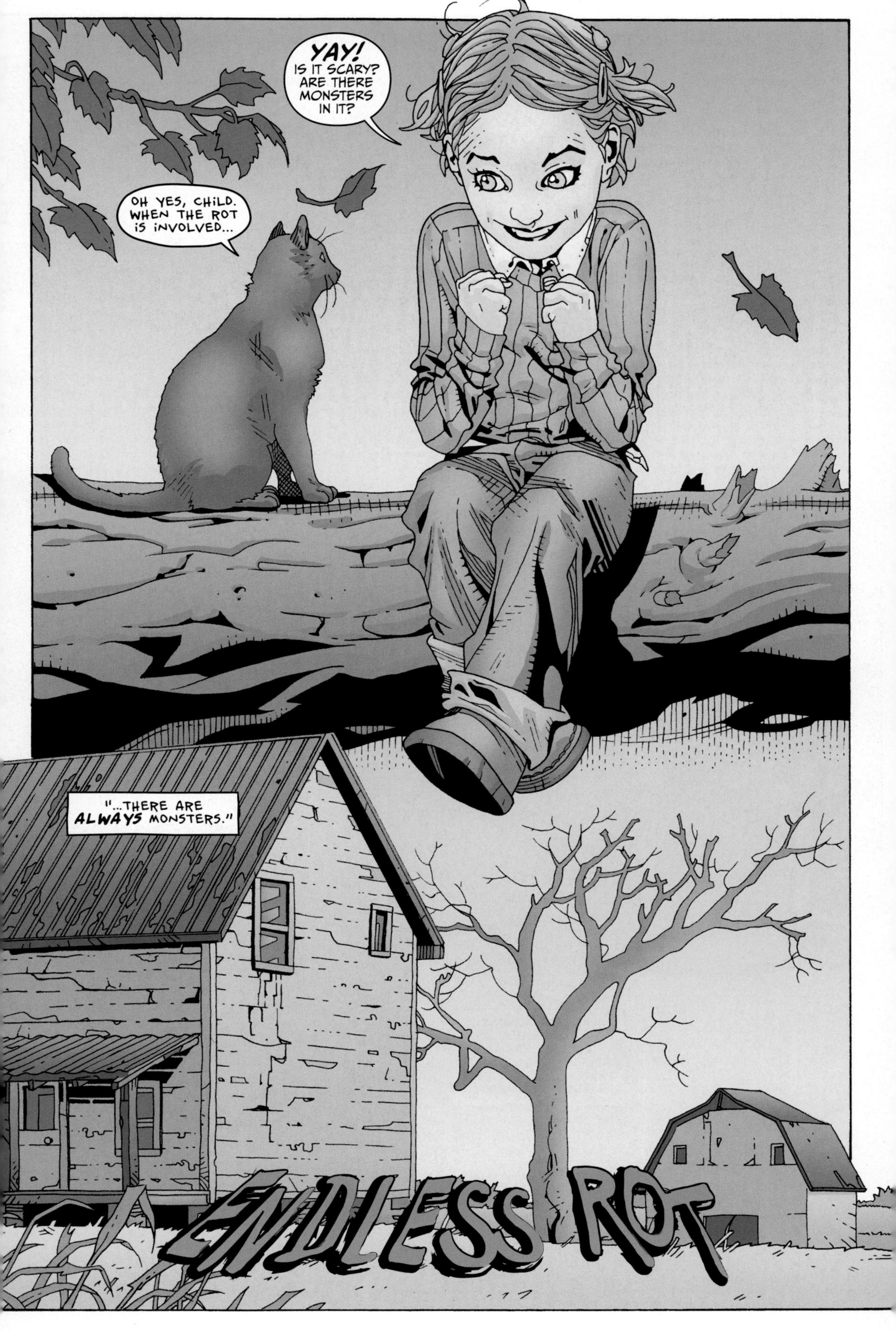
YAY! IS IT SCARY? ARE THERE MONSTERS IN IT?
OH YES, CHILD. WHEN THE ROT IS INVOLVED...
"...THERE ARE ALWAYS MONSTERS."
ENDLESS ROT

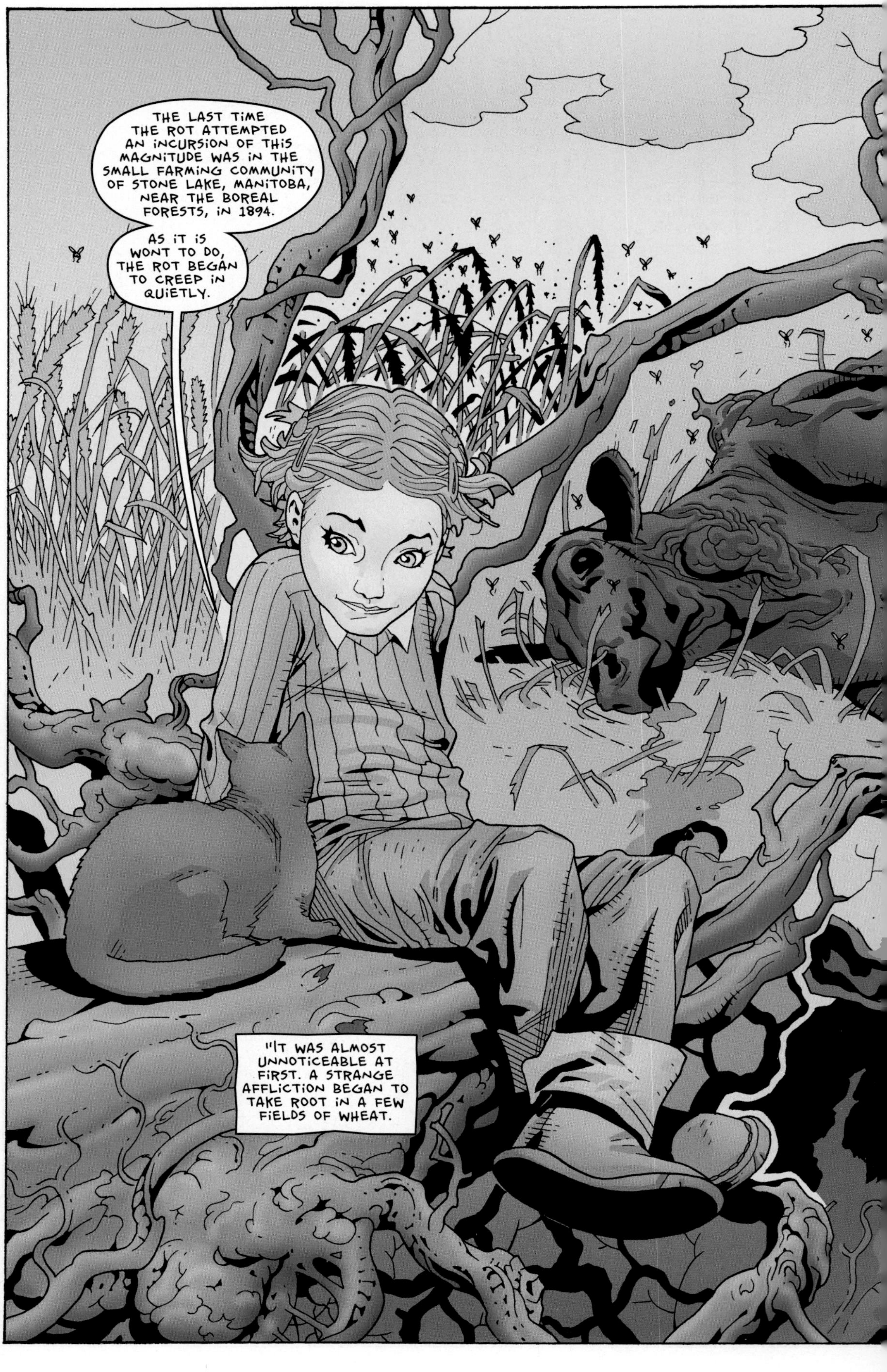
THE LAST TIME THE ROT ATTEMPTED AN INCURSION OF THIS MAGNITUDE WAS IN THE SMALL FARMING COMMUNITY OF STONE LAKE, MANITOBA, NEAR THE BOREAL FORESTS, IN 1894.
AS IT IS WONT TO DO, THE ROT BEGAN TO CREEP IN QUIETLY.
"IT WAS ALMOST UNNOTICEABLE AT FIRST. A STRANGE AFFLICTION BEGAN TO TAKE ROOT IN A FEW FIELDS OF WHEAT.

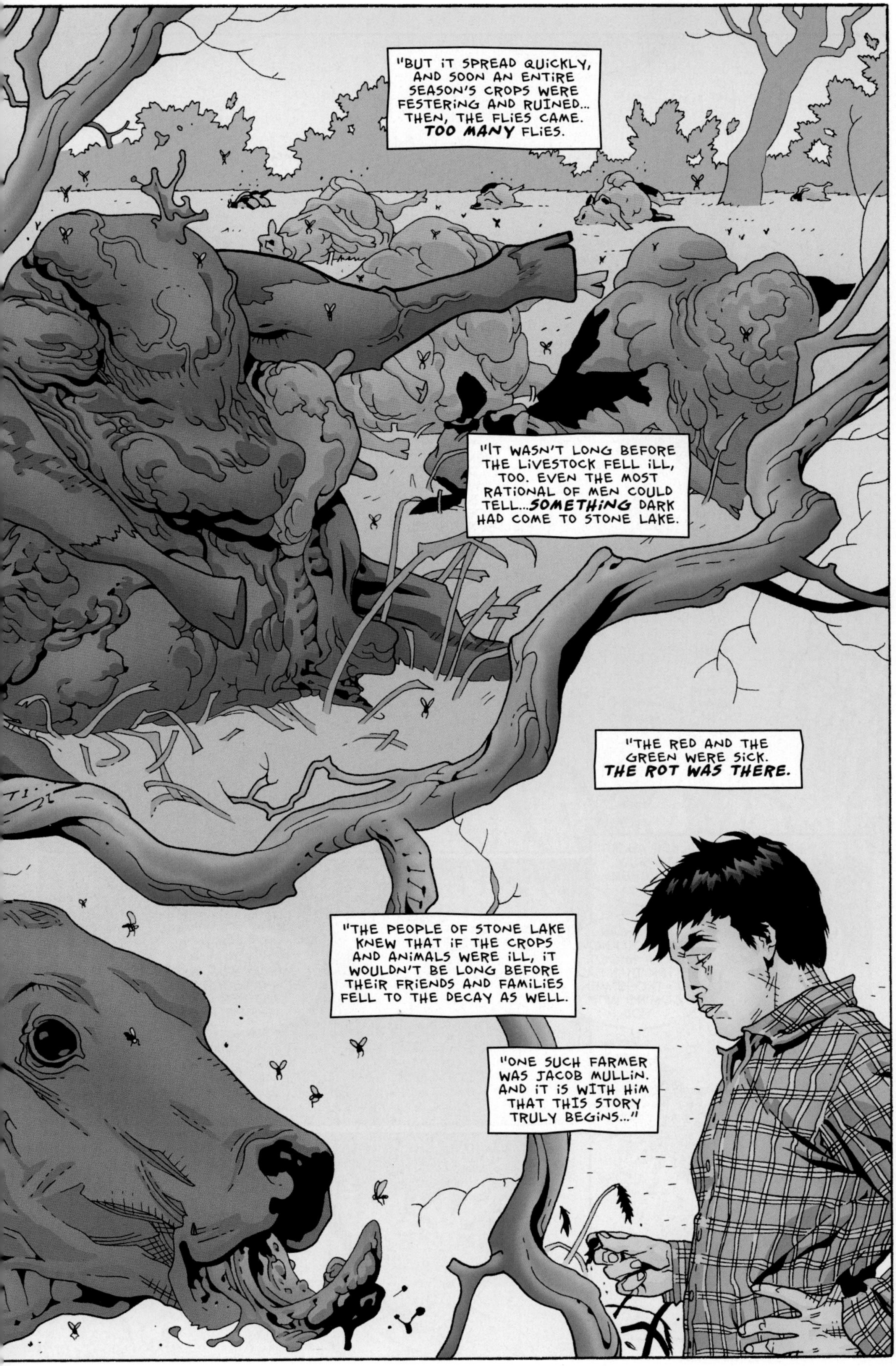
"BUT IT SPREAD QUICKLY, AND SOON AN ENTIRE SEASON'S CROPS WERE FESTERING AND RUINED... THEN, THE FLIES CAME. TOO MANY FLIES.
"IT WASN'T LONG BEFORE THE LIVESTOCK FELL ILL, TOO. EVEN THE MOST RATIONAL OF MEN COULD TELL...SOMETHING DARK HAD COME TO STONE LAKE.
"THE RED AND THE GREEN WERE SICK. THE ROT WAS THERE.
"THE PEOPLE OF STONE LAKE KNEW THAT IF THE CROPS AND ANIMALS WERE ILL, IT WOULDN'T BE LONG BEFORE THEIR FRIENDS AND FAMILIES FELL TO THE DECAY AS WELL.
"ONE SUCH FARMER WAS JACOB MULLIN. AND IT IS WITH HIM THAT THIS STORY TRULY BEGINS..."

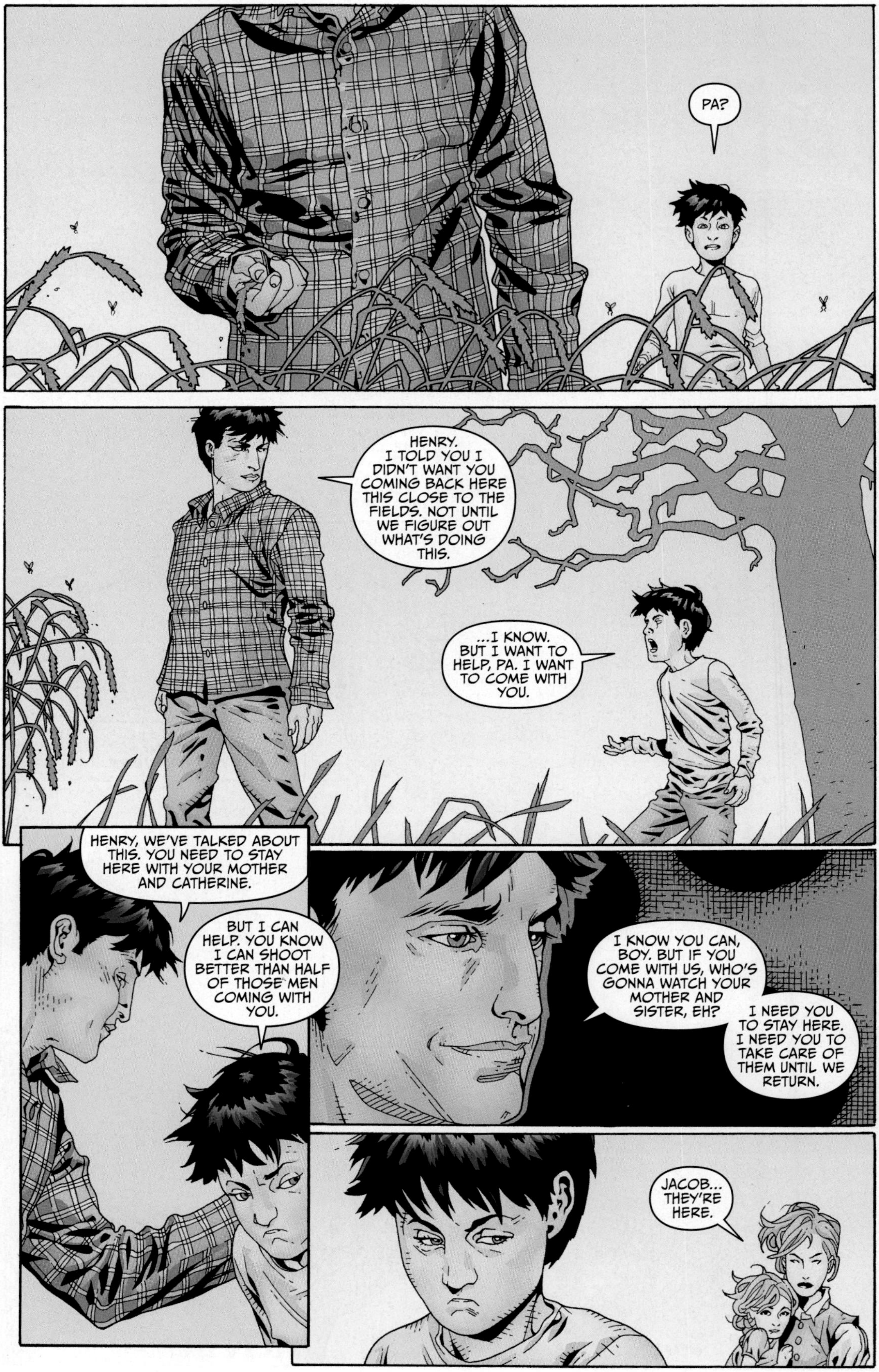
PA?
HENRY. I TOLD YOU I DIDN'T WANT YOU COMING BACK HERE THIS CLOSE TO THE FIELDS. NOT UNTIL WE FIGURE OUT WHAT'S DOING THIS.
...I KNOW. BUT I WANT TO HELP, PA. I WANT TO COME WITH YOU.
HENRY, WE'VE TALKED ABOUT THIS. YOU NEED TO STAY HERE WITH YOUR MOTHER AND CATHERINE.
BUT I CAN HELP. YOU KNOW I CAN SHOOT BETTER THAN HALF OF THOSE MEN COMING WITH YOU.
I KNOW YOU CAN, BOY. BUT IF YOU COME WITH US, WHO'S GONNA WATCH YOUR MOTHER AND SISTER, EH?
I NEED YOU TO STAY HERE. I NEED YOU TO TAKE CARE OF THEM UNTIL WE RETURN.
JACOB... THEY'RE HERE.

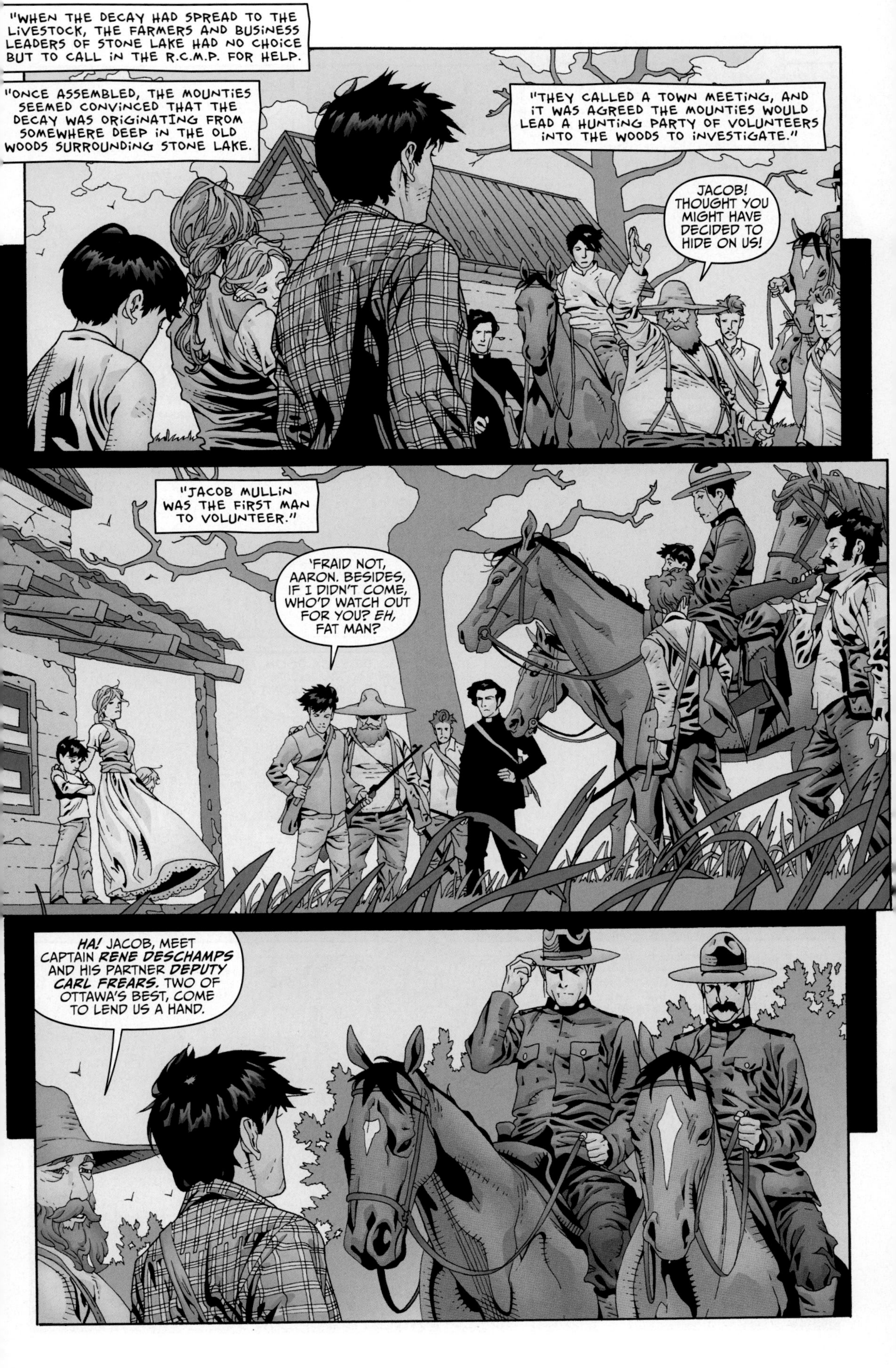
"WHEN THE DECAY HAD SPREAD TO THE LIVESTOCK, THE FARMERS AND BUSINESS LEADERS OF STONE LAKE HAD NO CHOICE BUT TO CALL IN THE R.C.M.P. FOR HELP.
"ONCE ASSEMBLED, THE MOUNTIES SEEMED CONVINCED THAT THE DECAY WAS ORIGINATING FROM SOMEWHERE DEEP IN THE OLD WOODS SURROUNDING STONE LAKE.
"THEY CALLED A TOWN MEETING, AND IT WAS AGREED THE MOUNTIES WOULD LEAD A HUNTING PARTY OF VOLUNTEERS INTO THE WOODS TO INVESTIGATE."
JACOB! THOUGHT YOU MIGHT HAVE DECIDED TO HIDE ON US!
"JACOB MULLIN WAS THE FIRST MAN TO VOLUNTEER."
'FRAID NOT, AARON. BESIDES, IF I DIDN'T COME, WHO'D WATCH OUT FOR YOU? EH, FAT MAN?
HA! JACOB, MEET CAPTAIN RENE DESCHAMPS AND HIS PARTNER DEPUTY CARL FREARS. TWO OF OTTAWA'S BEST, COME TO LEND US A HAND.

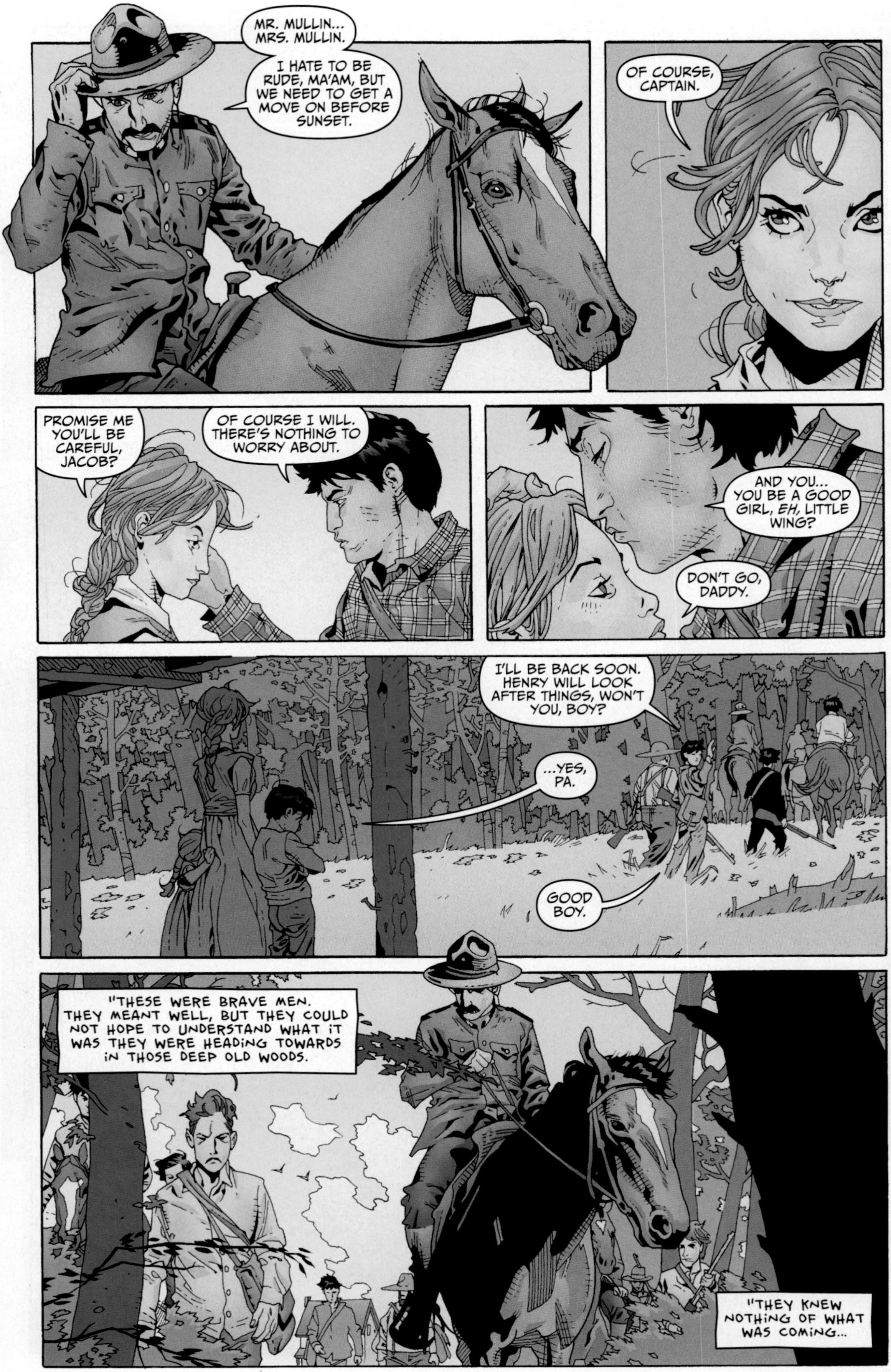
MR. MULLIN... MRS. MULLIN.
I HATE TO BE RUDE, MA'AM, BUT WE NEED TO GET A MOVE ON BEFORE SUNSET.
OF COURSE, CAPTAIN.
PROMISE ME YOU'LL BE CAREFUL, JACOB?
OF COURSE I WILL. THERE'S NOTHING TO WORRY ABOUT.
AND YOU... YOU BE A GOOD GIRL, *EH*, LITTLE WING?
DON'T GO, DADDY.
I'LL BE BACK SOON. HENRY WILL LOOK AFTER THINGS, WON'T YOU, BOY?
...YES, PA.
GOOD BOY.
"THESE WERE BRAVE MEN. THEY MEANT WELL, BUT THEY COULD NOT HOPE TO UNDERSTAND WHAT IT WAS THEY WERE HEADING TOWARDS IN THOSE DEEP OLD WOODS.
"THEY KNEW NOTHING OF WHAT WAS COMING...

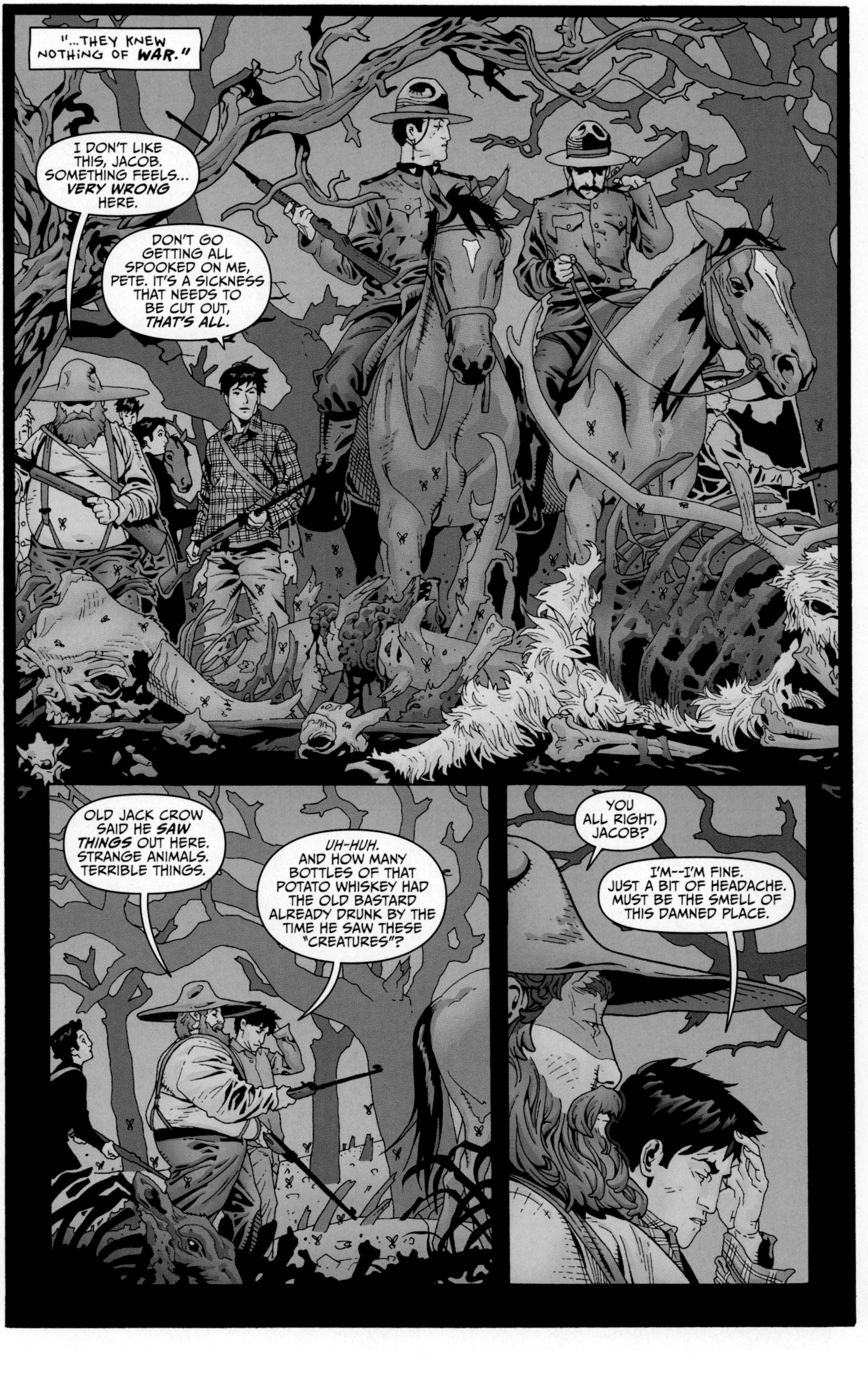
"...THEY KNEW NOTHING OF WAR."
I DON'T LIKE THIS, JACOB. SOMETHING FEELS... VERY WRONG HERE.
DON'T GO GETTING ALL SPOOKED ON ME, PETE. IT'S A SICKNESS THAT NEEDS TO BE CUT OUT, THAT'S ALL.
OLD JACK CROW SAID HE SAW THINGS OUT HERE. STRANGE ANIMALS. TERRIBLE THINGS.
UH-HUH. AND HOW MANY BOTTLES OF THAT POTATO WHISKEY HAD THE OLD BASTARD ALREADY DRUNK BY THE TIME HE SAW THESE "CREATURES"?
YOU ALL RIGHT, JACOB?
I'M--I'M FINE. JUST A BIT OF HEADACHE. MUST BE THE SMELL OF THIS DAMNED PLACE.

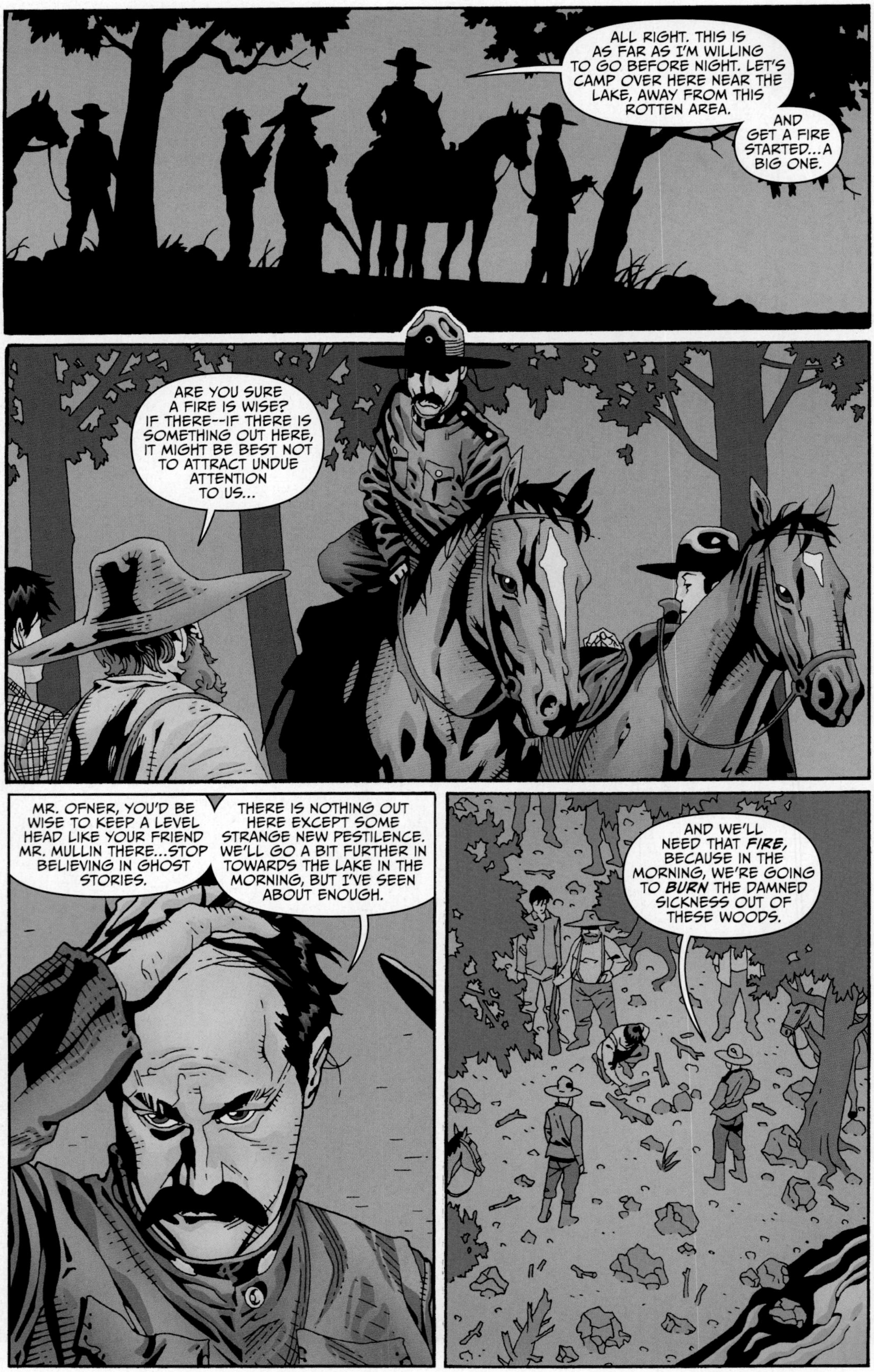
ALL RIGHT. THIS IS AS FAR AS I'M WILLING TO GO BEFORE NIGHT. LET'S CAMP OVER HERE NEAR THE LAKE, AWAY FROM THIS ROTTEN AREA.
AND GET A FIRE STARTED...A BIG ONE.
ARE YOU SURE A FIRE IS WISE? IF THERE--IF THERE IS SOMETHING OUT HERE, IT MIGHT BE BEST NOT TO ATTRACT UNDUE ATTENTION TO US...
MR. OFNER, YOU'D BE WISE TO KEEP A LEVEL HEAD LIKE YOUR FRIEND MR. MULLIN THERE...STOP BELIEVING IN GHOST STORIES.
THERE IS NOTHING OUT HERE EXCEPT SOME STRANGE NEW PESTILENCE. WE'LL GO A BIT FURTHER IN TOWARDS THE LAKE IN THE MORNING, BUT I'VE SEEN ABOUT ENOUGH.
AND WE'LL NEED THAT *FIRE,* BECAUSE IN THE MORNING, WE'RE GOING TO *BURN* THE DAMNED SICKNESS OUT OF THESE WOODS.

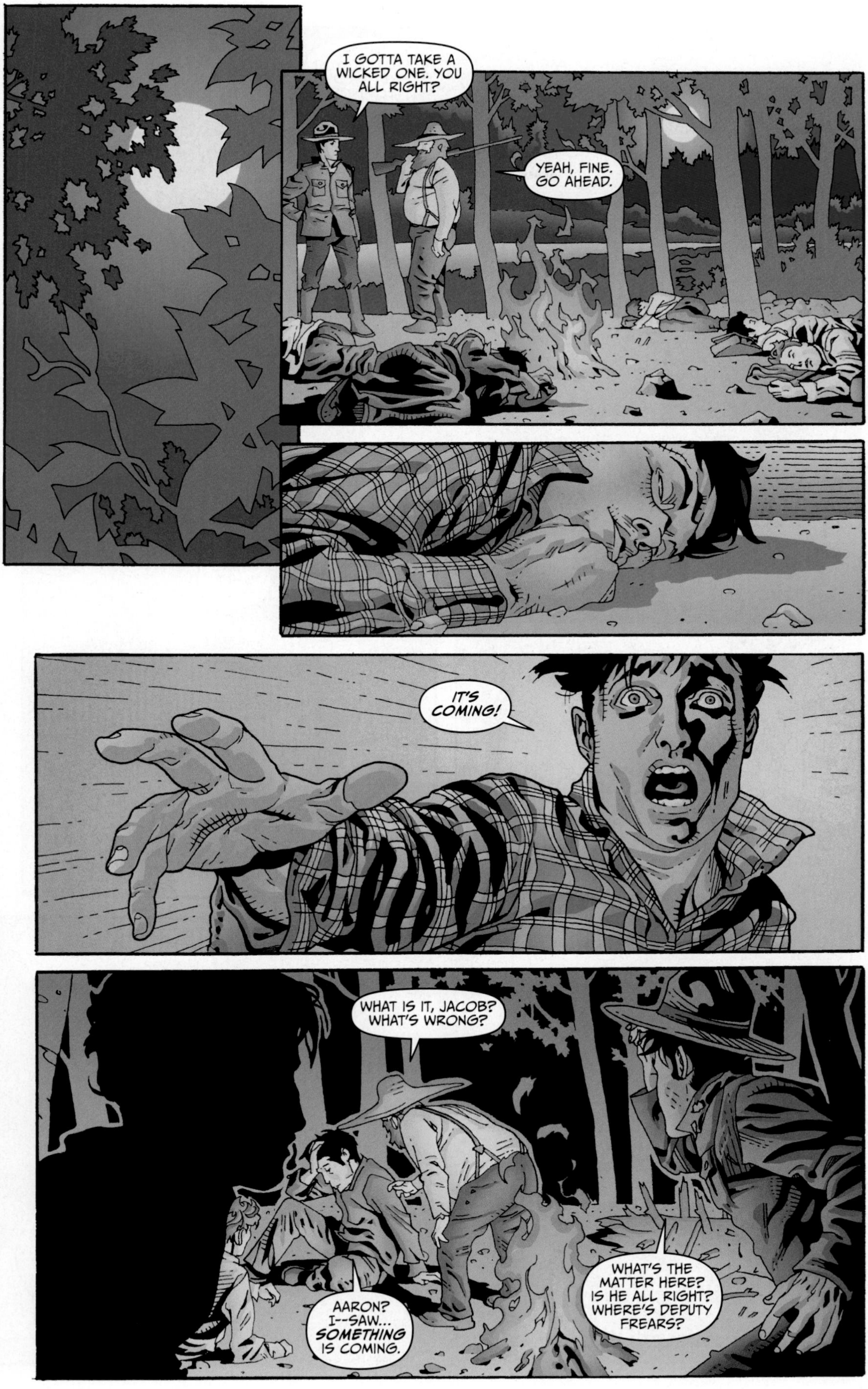
I GOTTA TAKE A WICKED ONE. YOU ALL RIGHT?
YEAH, FINE. GO AHEAD.
IT'S COMING!
WHAT IS IT, JACOB? WHAT'S WRONG?
AARON? I--SAW... SOMETHING IS COMING.
WHAT'S THE MATTER HERE? IS HE ALL RIGHT? WHERE'S DEPUTY FREARS?

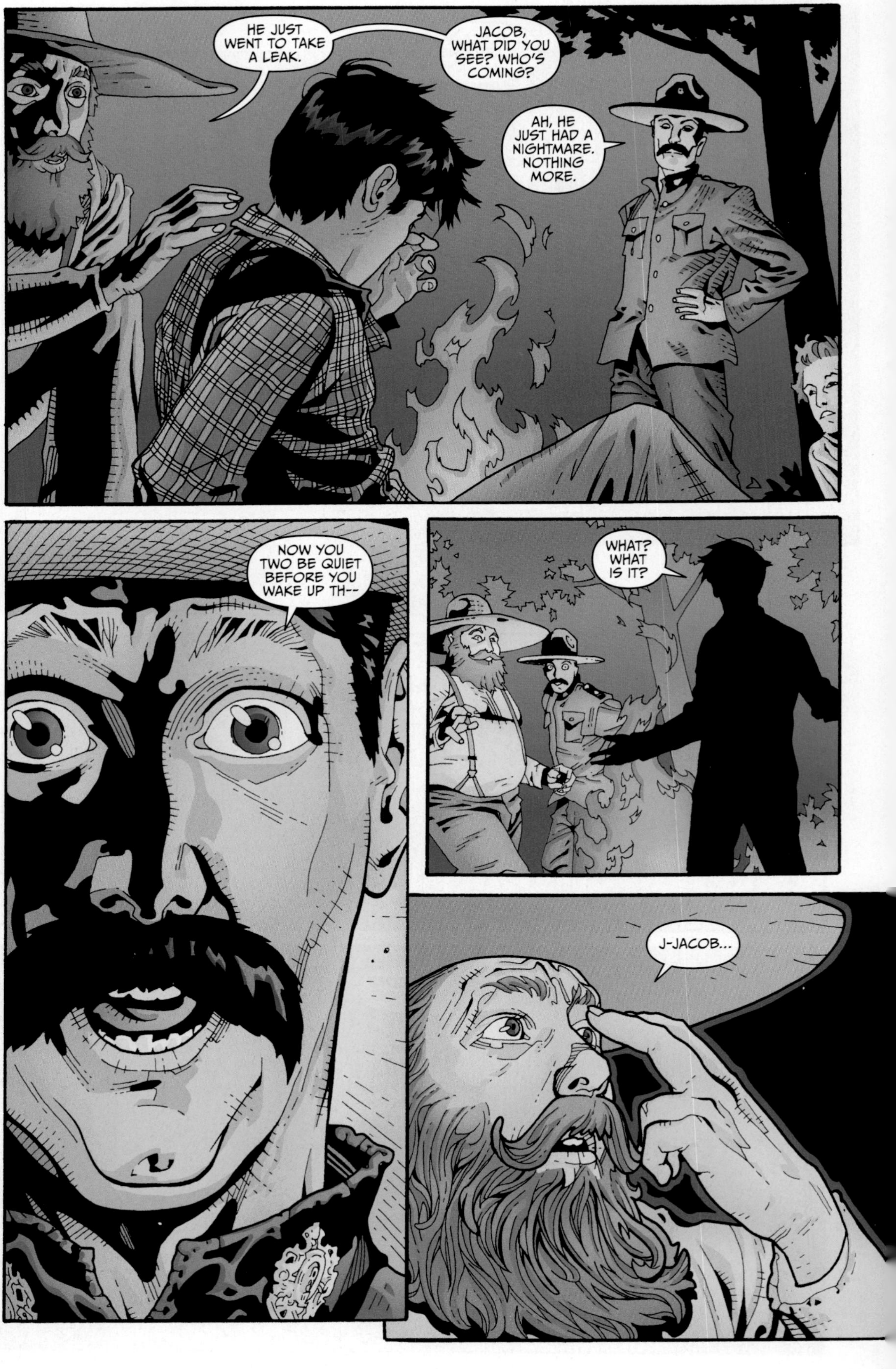

HE JUST WENT TO TAKE A LEAK.
JACOB, WHAT DID YOU SEE? WHO'S COMING?
AH, HE JUST HAD A NIGHTMARE. NOTHING MORE.
NOW YOU TWO BE QUIET BEFORE YOU WAKE UP TH--
WHAT? WHAT IS IT?
J-JACOB...

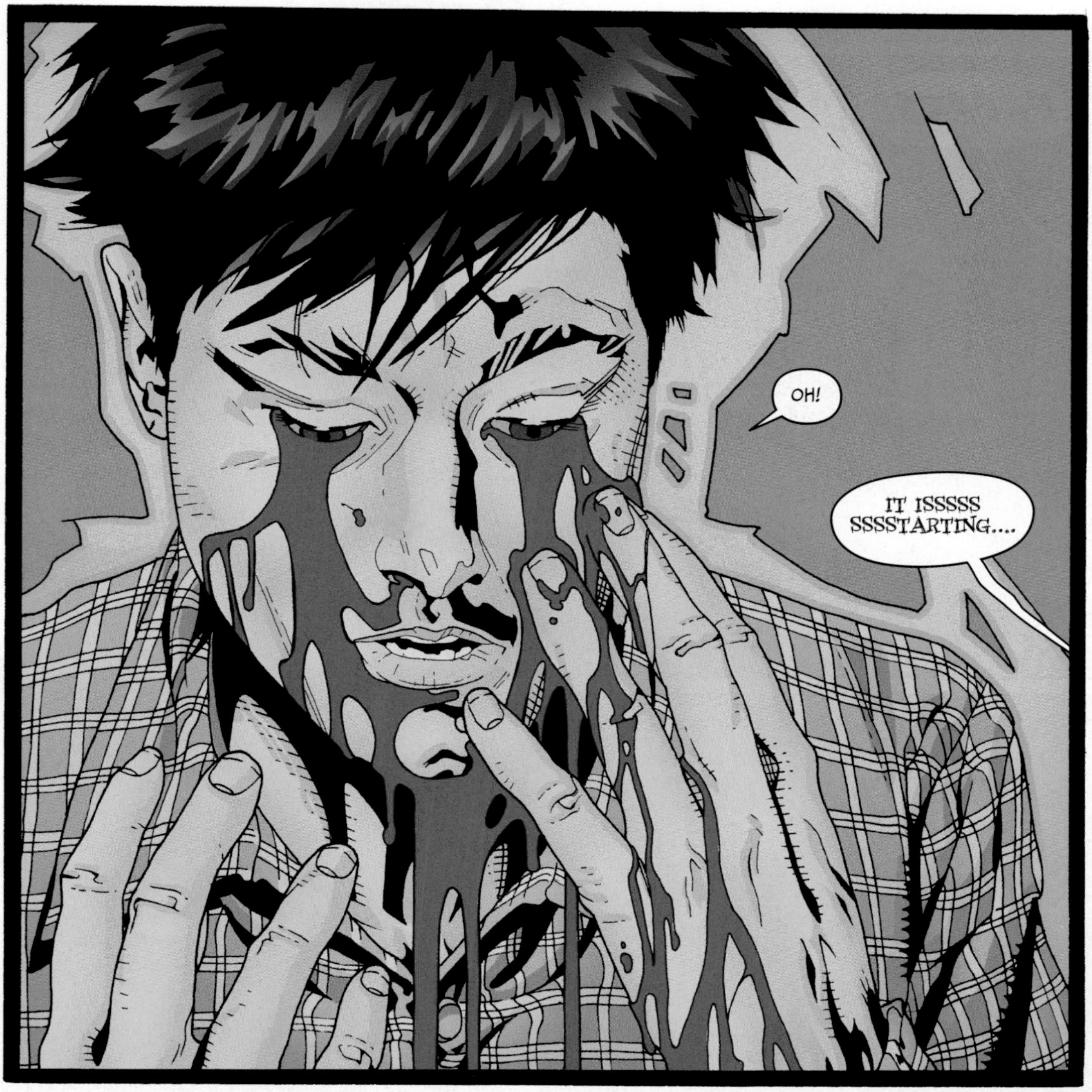
OH!
IT ISSSSS SSSSTARTING....

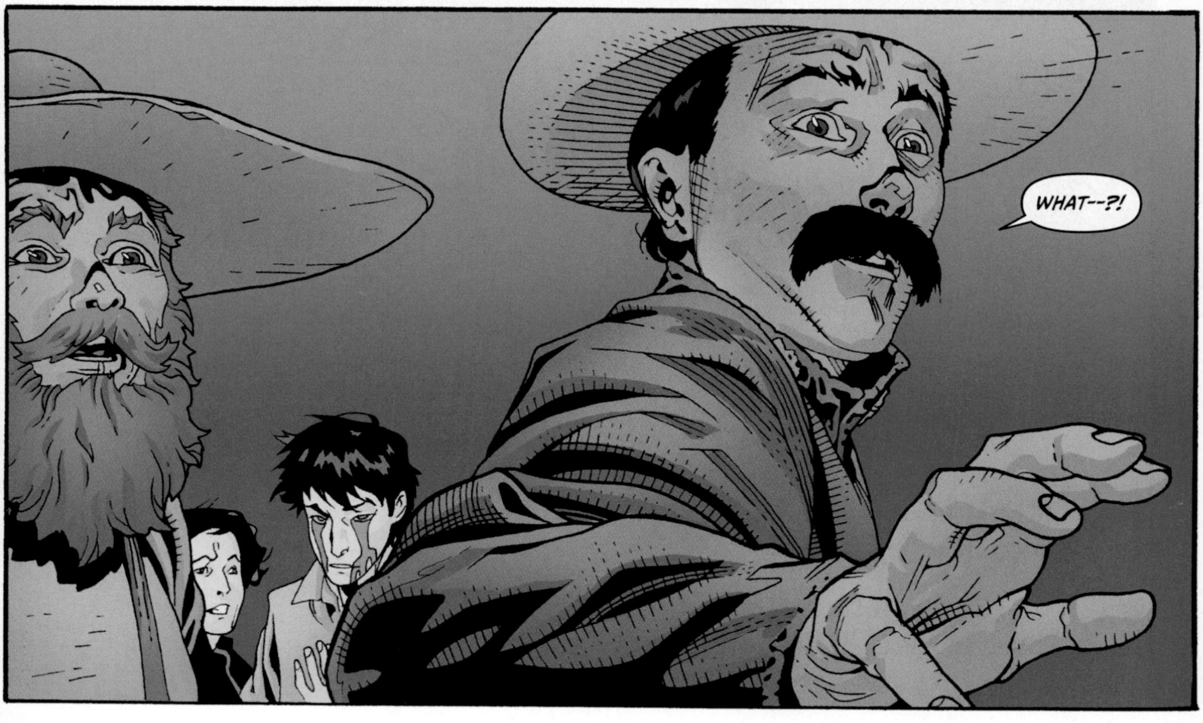
WHAT--?!

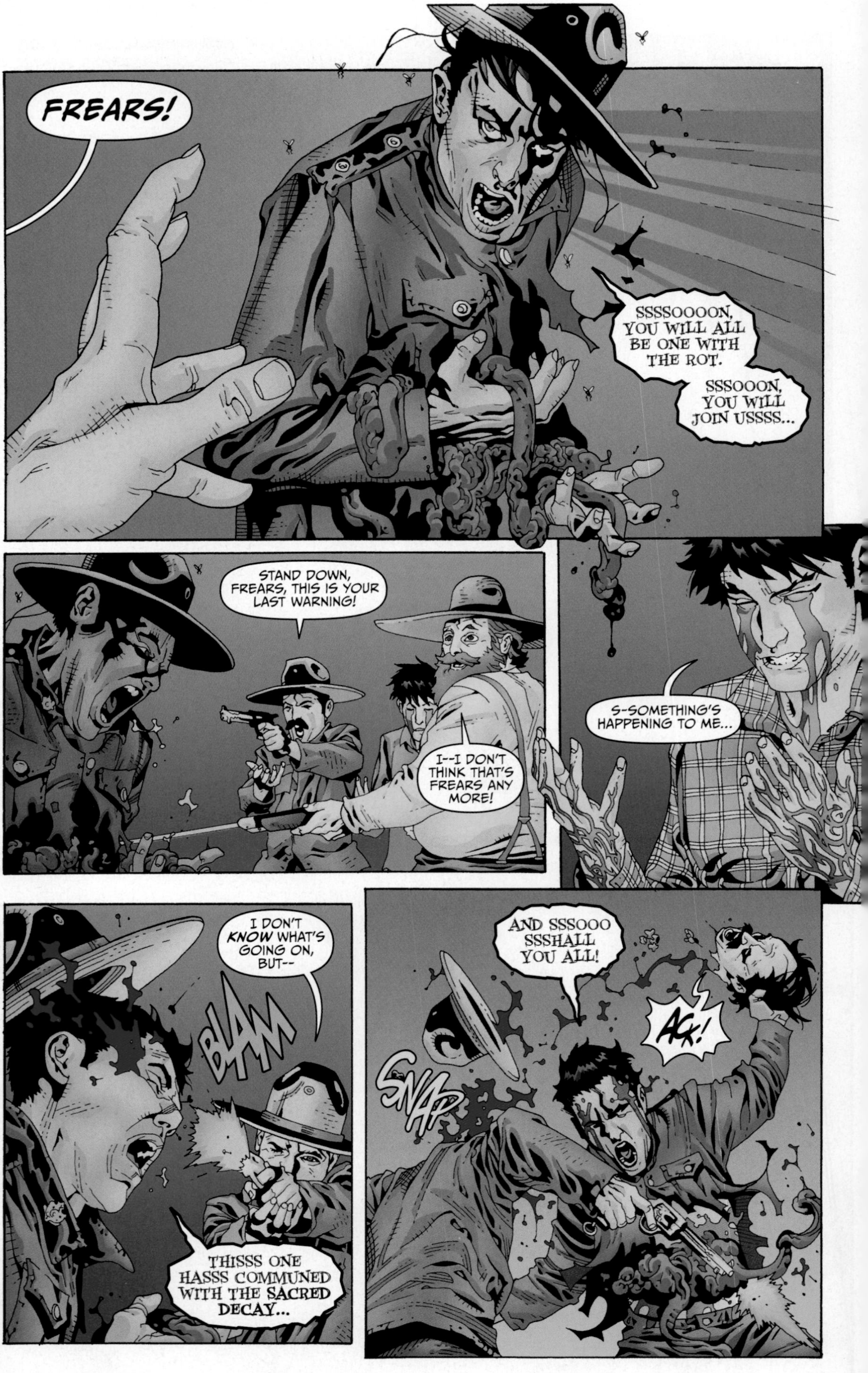
FREARS!
SSSSOOOON, YOU WILL ALL BE ONE WITH THE ROT.
SSSOOON, YOU WILL JOIN USSSS...
STAND DOWN, FREARS, THIS IS YOUR LAST WARNING!
I--I DON'T THINK THAT'S FREARS ANY MORE!
S-SOMETHING'S HAPPENING TO ME...
I DON'T KNOW WHAT'S GOING ON, BUT--
BLAM
THISSS ONE HASSS COMMUNED WITH THE SACRED DECAY...
AND SSSOOO SSSHALL YOU ALL!
ACK!
SNAP

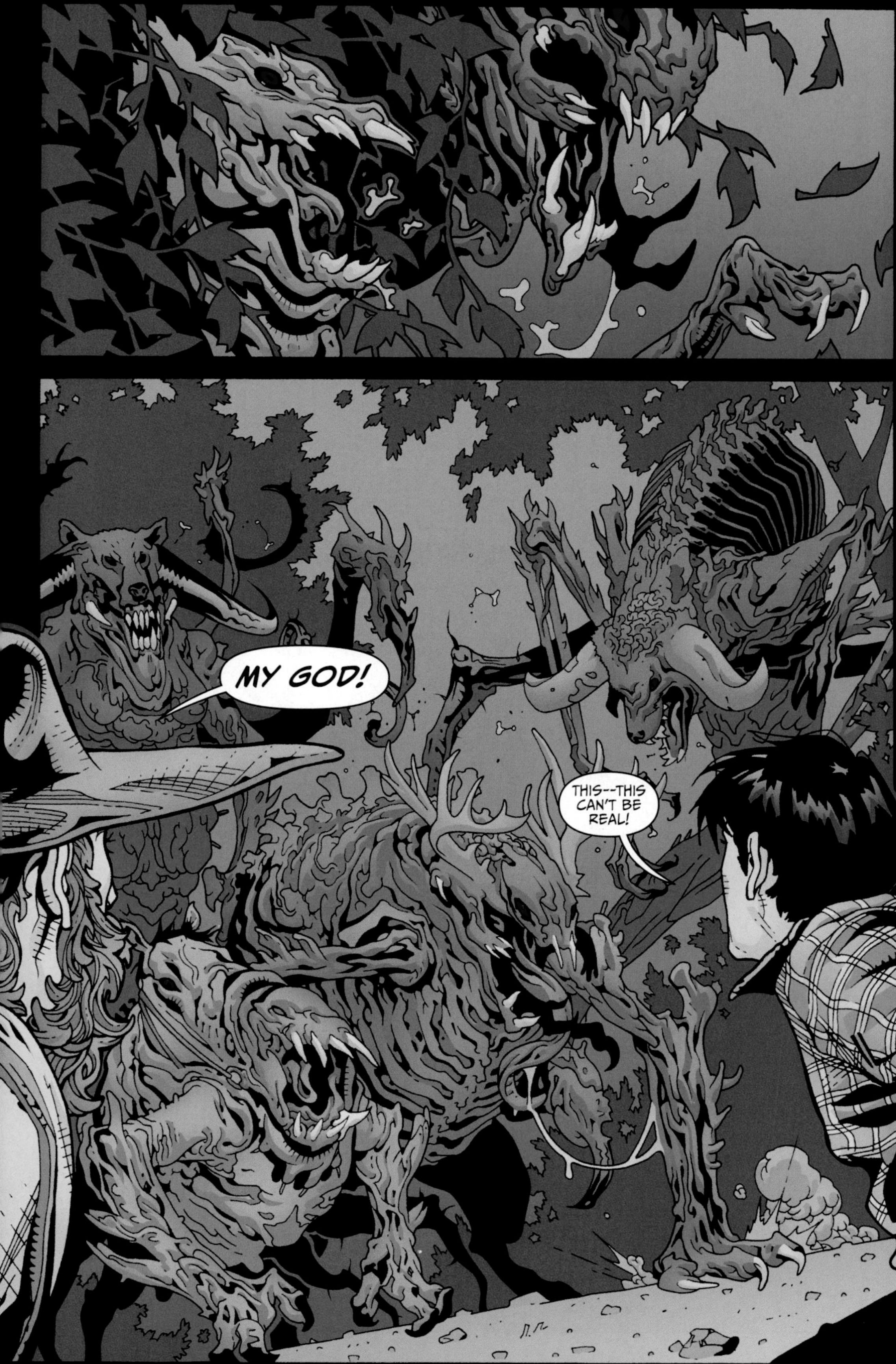
MY GOD!
THIS--THIS CAN'T BE REAL!

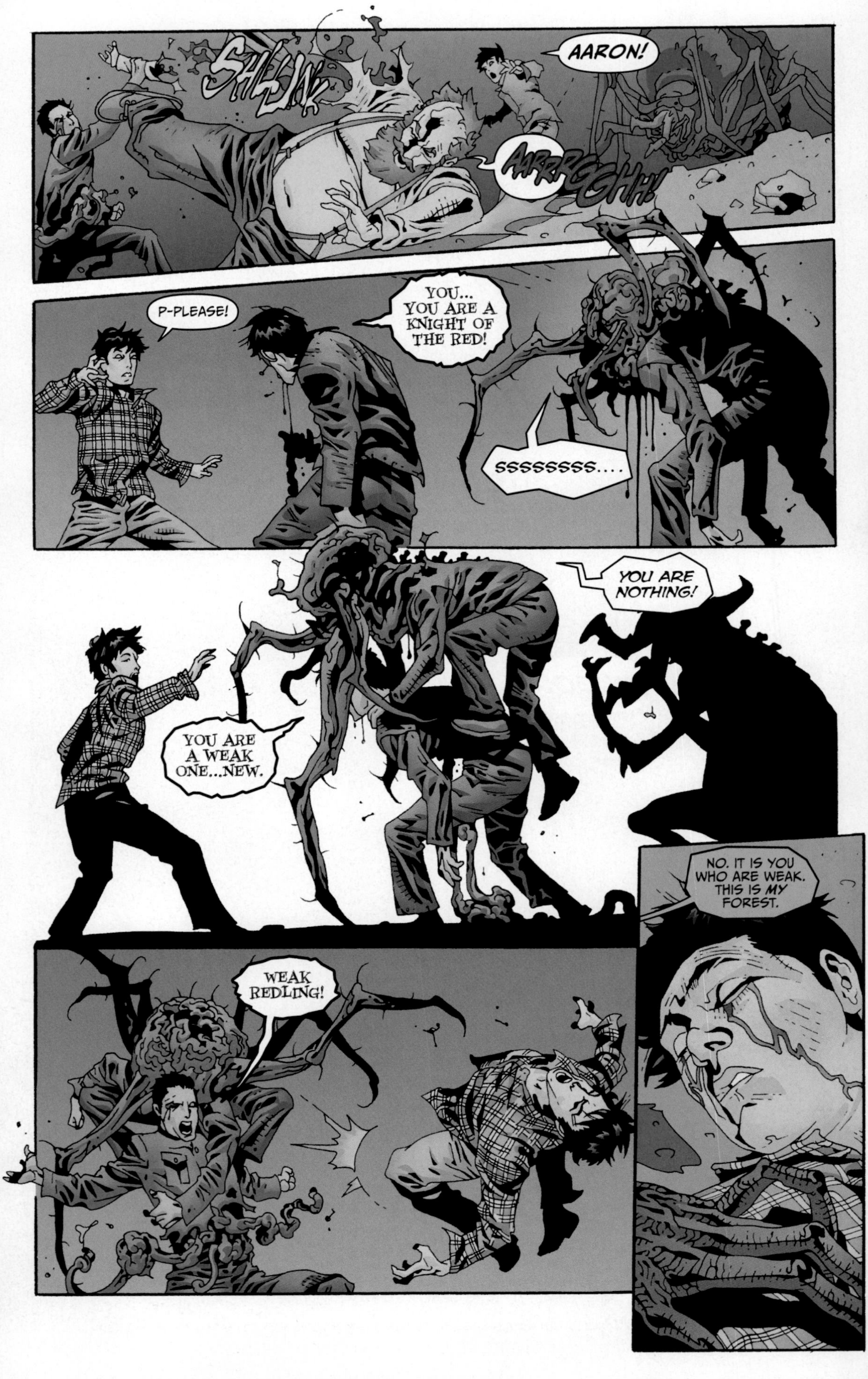
SHLUNK!
AARON!
AARRRGGHH!
P-PLEASE!
YOU... YOU ARE A KNIGHT OF THE RED!
SSSSSSSS....
YOU ARE NOTHING!
YOU ARE A WEAK ONE...NEW.
NO. IT IS YOU WHO ARE WEAK. THIS IS MY FOREST.
WEAK REDLING!

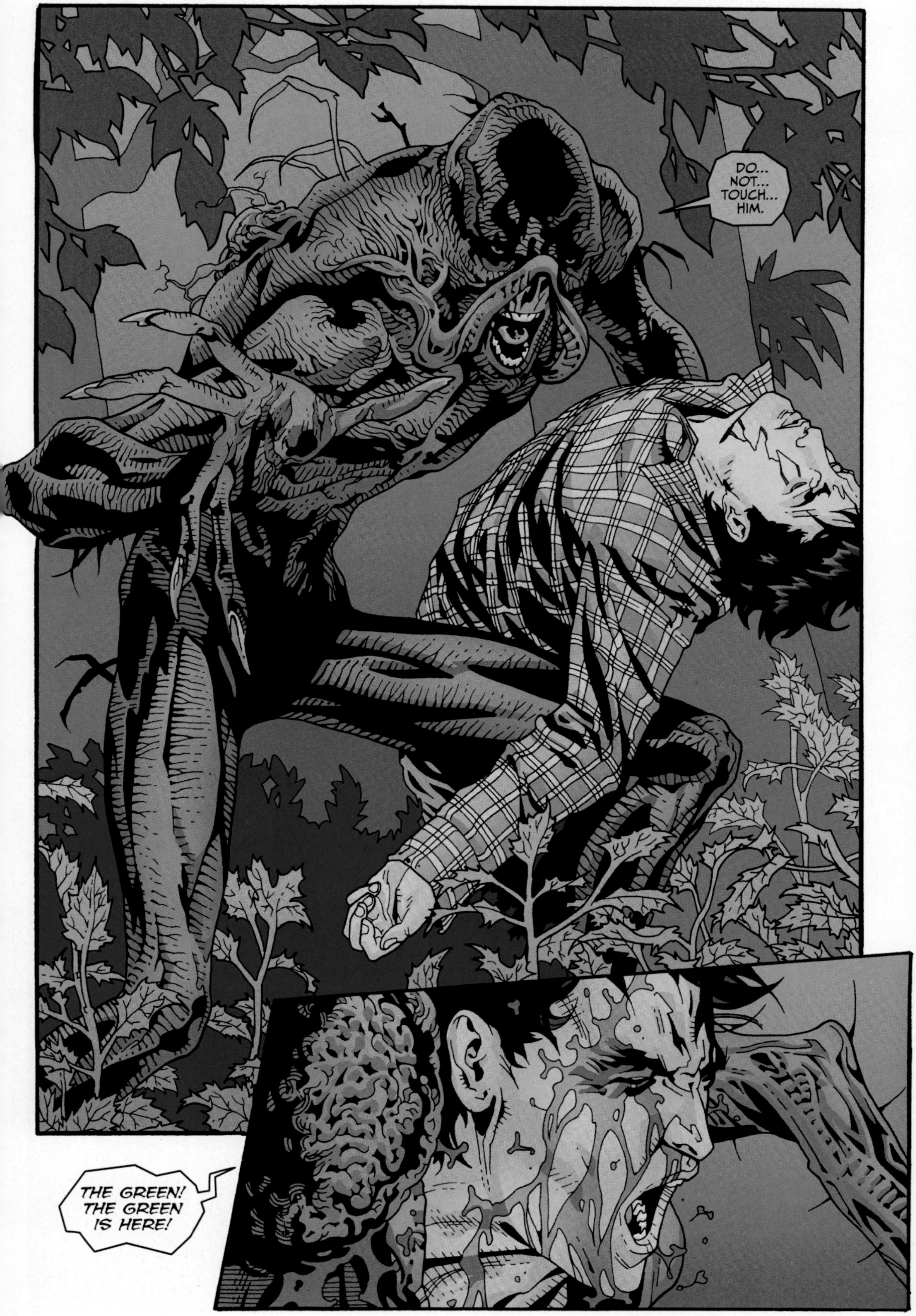
DO... NOT... TOUCH... HIM.
THE GREEN! THE GREEN IS HERE!

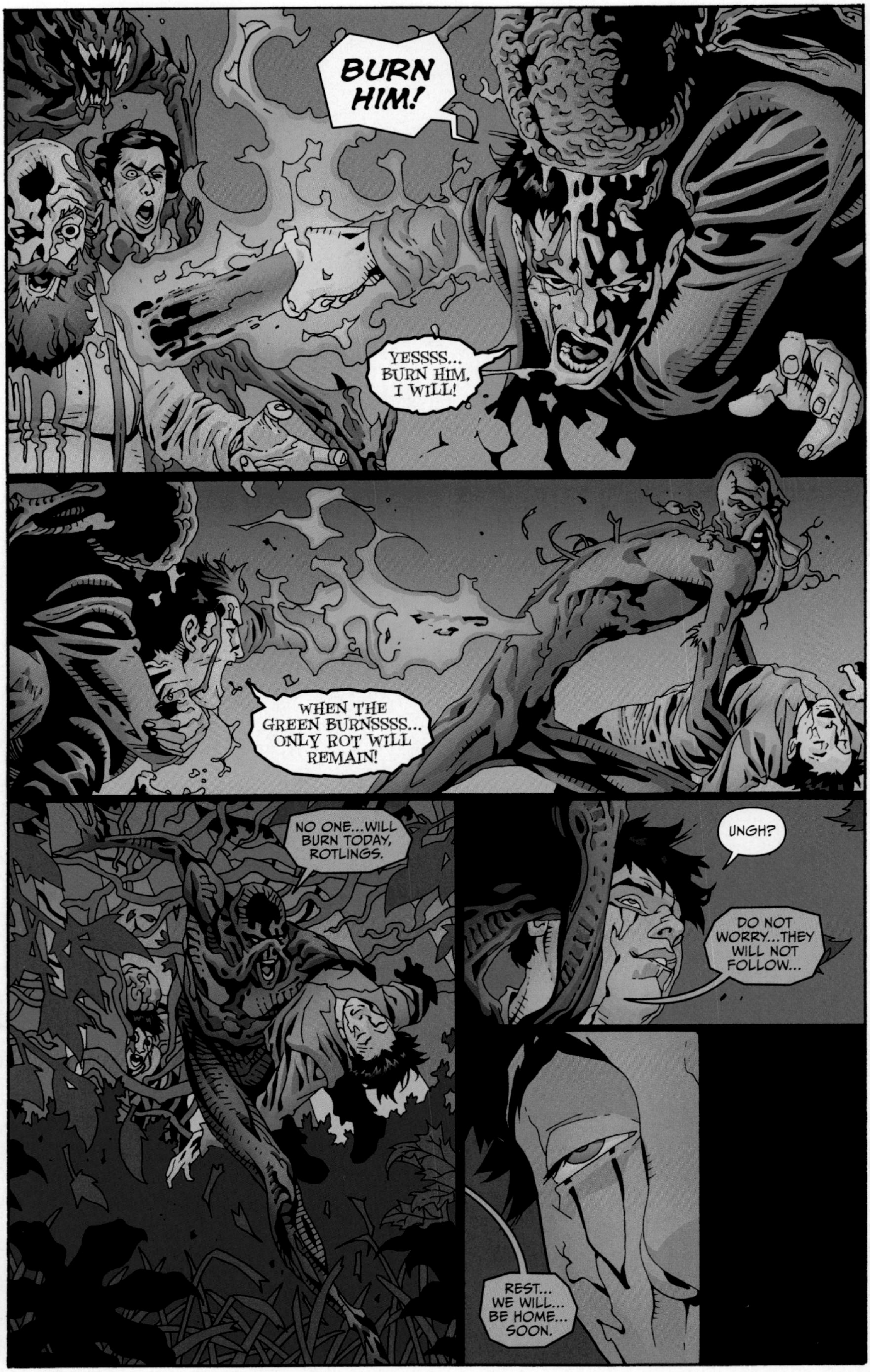
BURN HIM!
YESSSS... BURN HIM, I WILL!
WHEN THE GREEN BURNSSSS... ONLY ROT WILL REMAIN!
NO ONE...WILL BURN TODAY, ROTLINGS.
UNGH?
DO NOT WORRY...THEY WILL NOT FOLLOW...
REST... WE WILL... BE HOME... SOON.

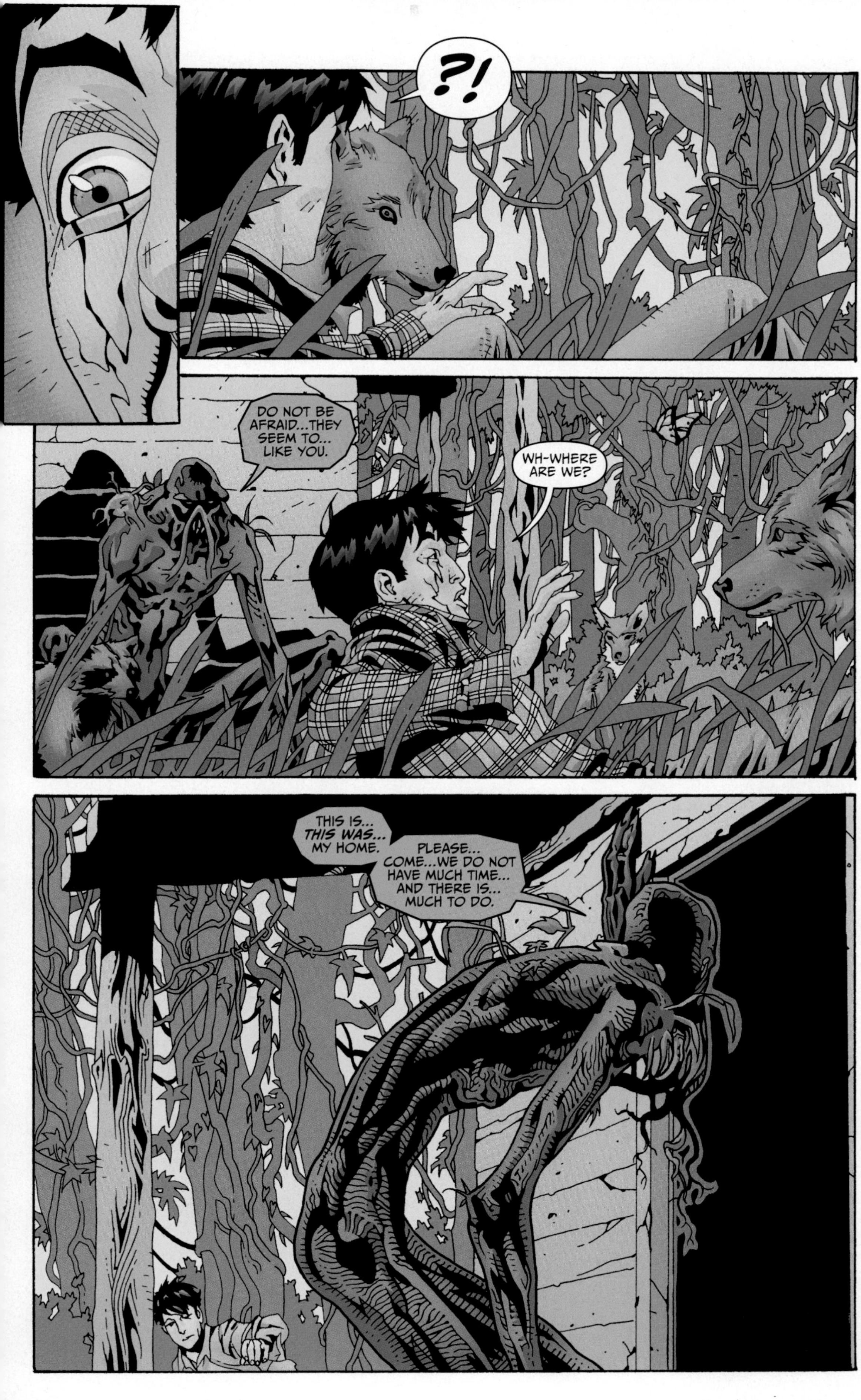
?!
DO NOT BE AFRAID...THEY SEEM TO... LIKE YOU.
WH-WHERE ARE WE?
THIS IS... *THIS WAS...* MY HOME.
PLEASE... COME...WE DO NOT HAVE MUCH TIME... AND THERE IS... MUCH TO DO.

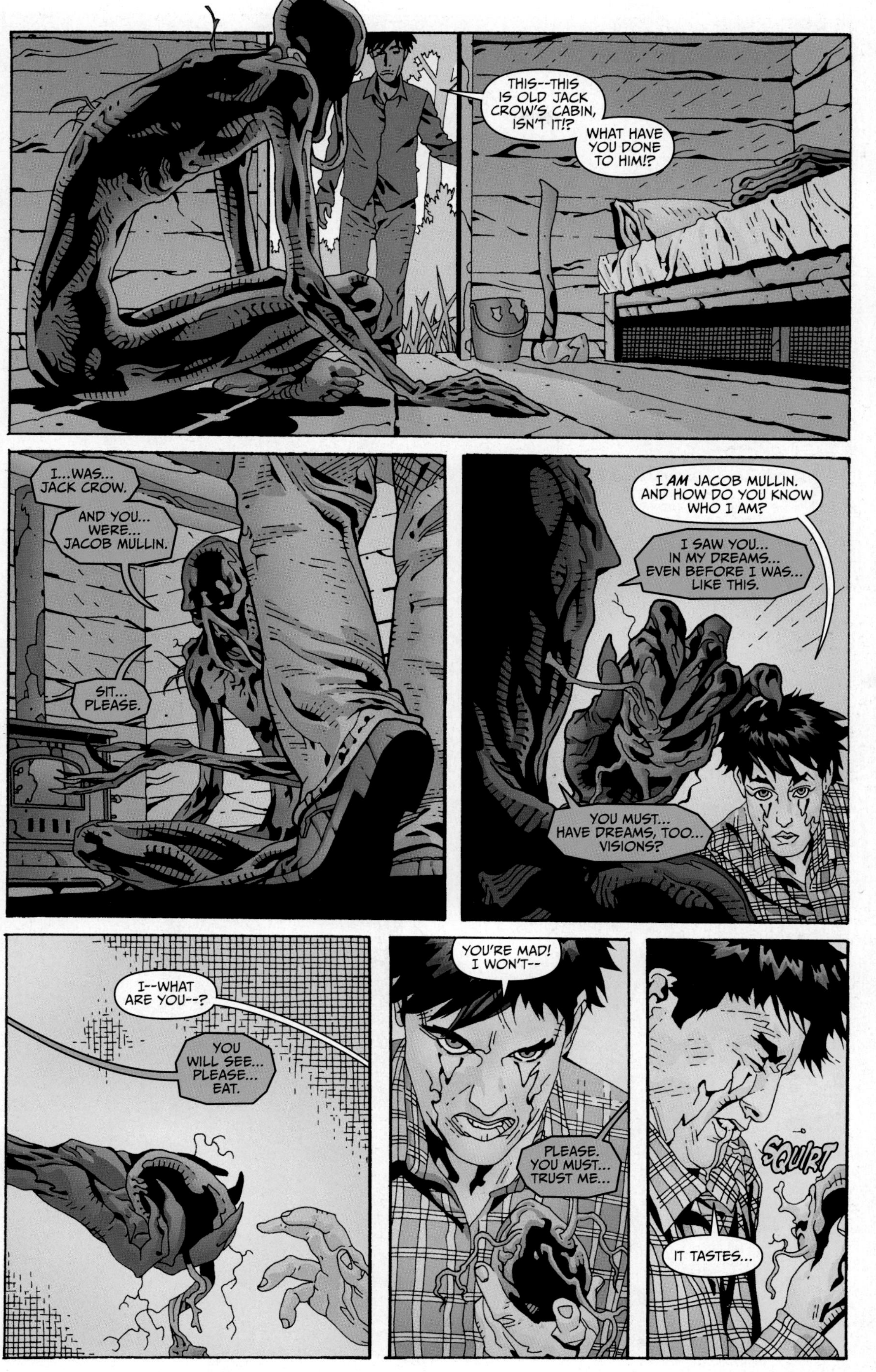
THIS--THIS IS OLD JACK CROW'S CABIN, ISN'T IT!?
WHAT HAVE YOU DONE TO HIM!?
I...WAS... JACK CROW.
AND YOU... WERE... JACOB MULLIN.
SIT... PLEASE.
I AM JACOB MULLIN. AND HOW DO YOU KNOW WHO I AM?
I SAW YOU... IN MY DREAMS... EVEN BEFORE I WAS... LIKE THIS.
YOU MUST... HAVE DREAMS, TOO... VISIONS?
I--WHAT ARE YOU--?
YOU WILL SEE... PLEASE... EAT.
YOU'RE MAD! I WON'T--
PLEASE. YOU MUST... TRUST ME...
SQUIRT
IT TASTES...

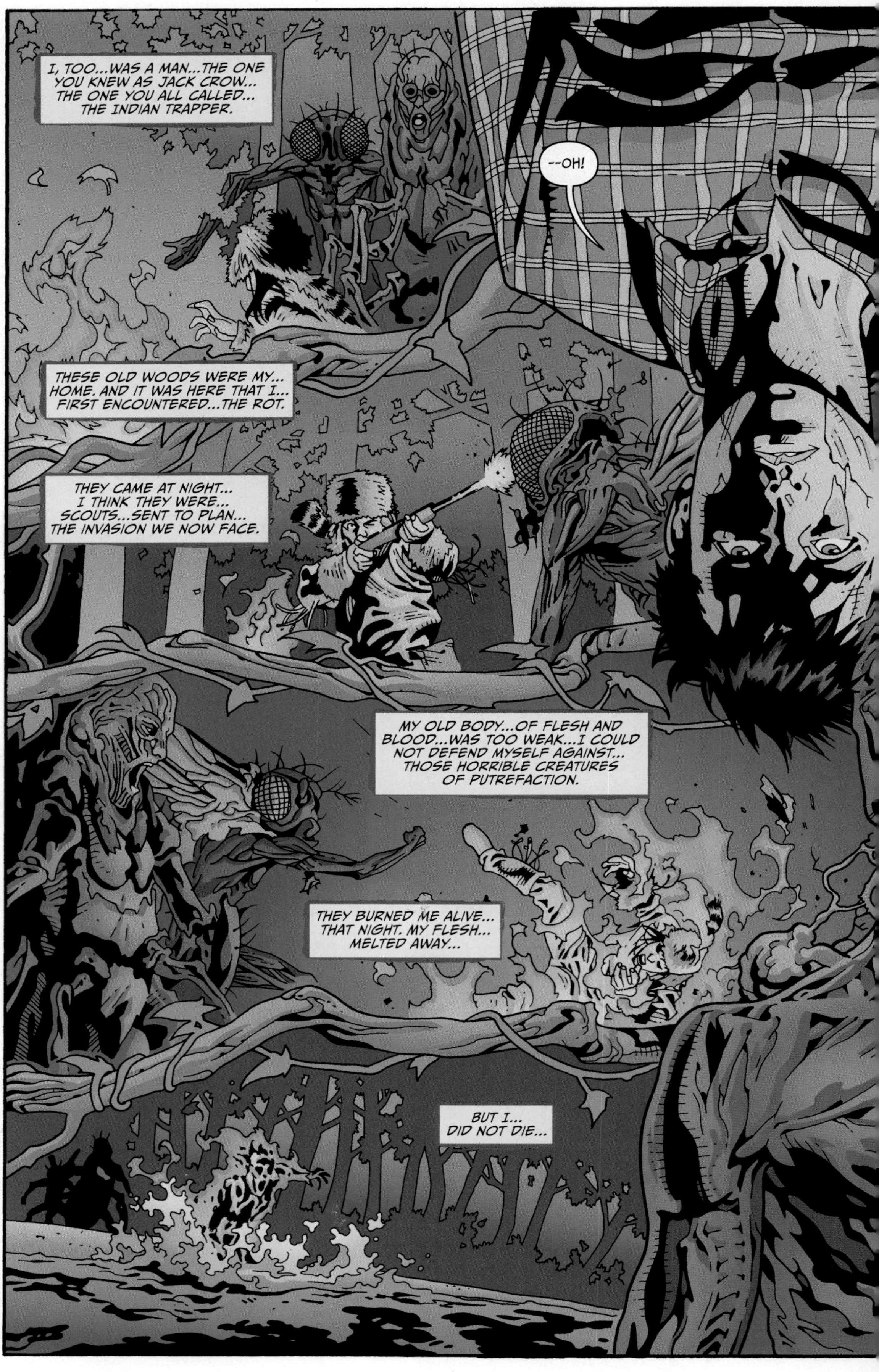
I, TOO...WAS A MAN...THE ONE YOU KNEW AS JACK CROW... THE ONE YOU ALL CALLED... THE INDIAN TRAPPER.
--OH!
THESE OLD WOODS WERE MY... HOME. AND IT WAS HERE THAT I... FIRST ENCOUNTERED...THE ROT.
THEY CAME AT NIGHT... I THINK THEY WERE... SCOUTS...SENT TO PLAN... THE INVASION WE NOW FACE.
MY OLD BODY...OF FLESH AND BLOOD...WAS TOO WEAK...I COULD NOT DEFEND MYSELF AGAINST... THOSE HORRIBLE CREATURES OF PUTREFACTION.
THEY BURNED ME ALIVE... THAT NIGHT. MY FLESH... MELTED AWAY...
BUT I... DID NOT DIE...

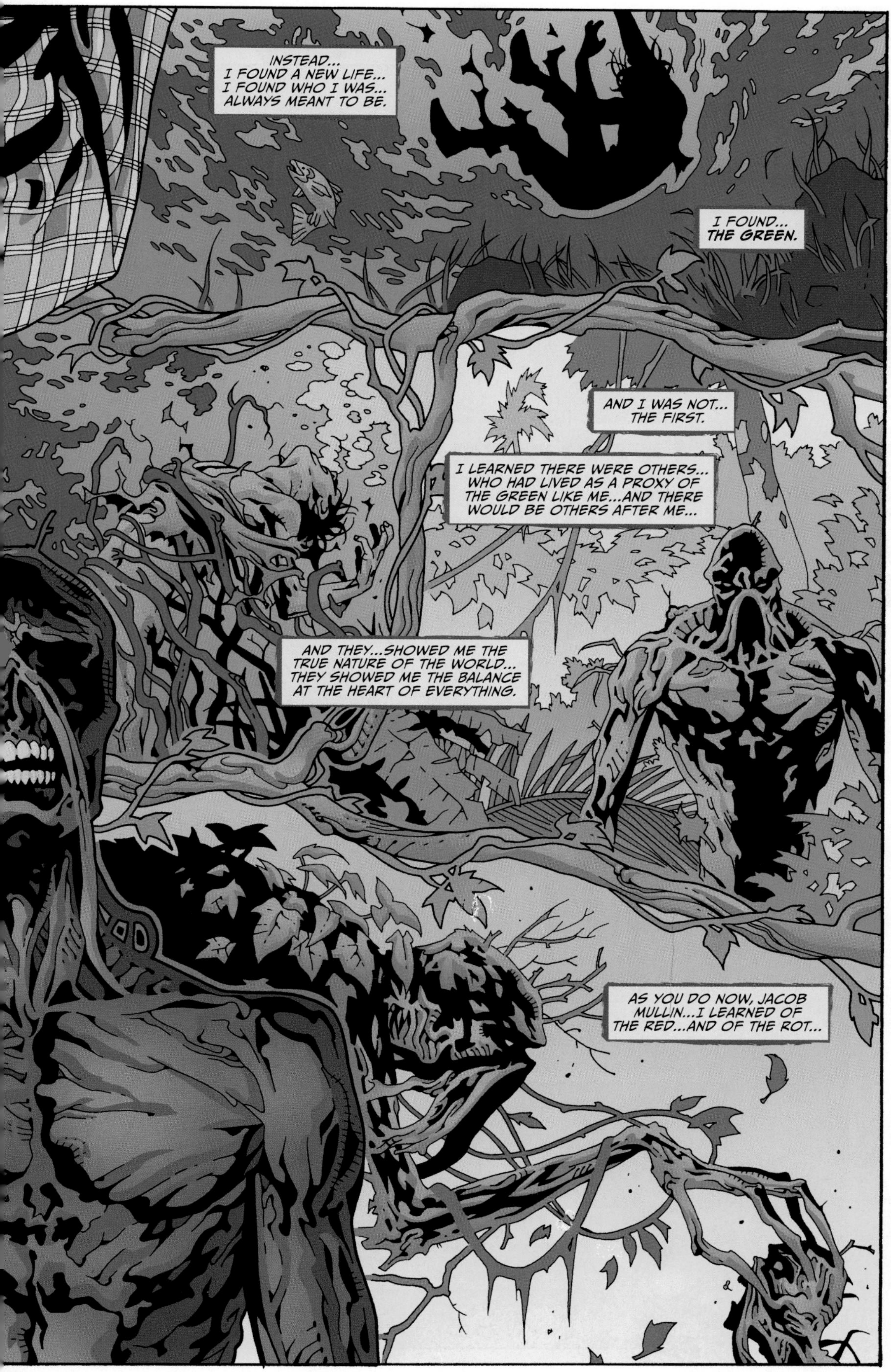
INSTEAD... I FOUND A NEW LIFE... I FOUND WHO I WAS... ALWAYS MEANT TO BE.
I FOUND... THE GREEN.
AND I WAS NOT... THE FIRST.
I LEARNED THERE WERE OTHERS... WHO HAD LIVED AS A PROXY OF THE GREEN LIKE ME...AND THERE WOULD BE OTHERS AFTER ME...
AND THEY...SHOWED ME THE TRUE NATURE OF THE WORLD... THEY SHOWED ME THE BALANCE AT THE HEART OF EVERYTHING.
AS YOU DO NOW, JACOB MULLIN...I LEARNED OF THE RED...AND OF THE ROT...

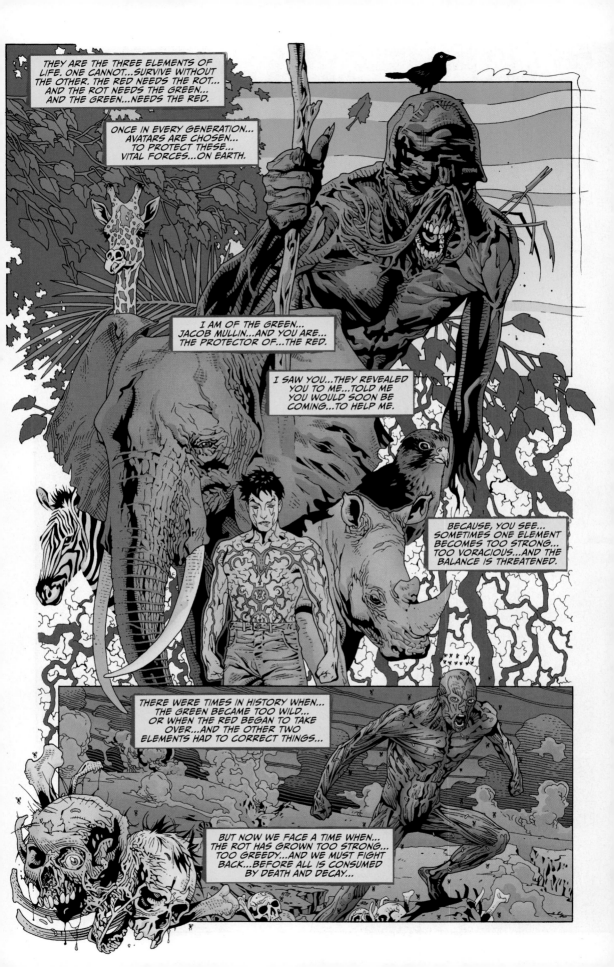

THEY ARE THE THREE ELEMENTS OF LIFE. ONE CANNOT...SURVIVE WITHOUT THE OTHER. THE RED NEEDS THE ROT... AND THE ROT NEEDS THE GREEN... AND THE GREEN...NEEDS THE RED.

ONCE IN EVERY GENERATION... AVATARS ARE CHOSEN... TO PROTECT THESE... VITAL FORCES...ON EARTH.

I AM OF THE GREEN... JACOB MULLIN...AND YOU ARE... THE PROTECTOR OF...THE RED.

I SAW YOU...THEY REVEALED YOU TO ME...TOLD ME YOU WOULD SOON BE COMING...TO HELP ME.

BECAUSE, YOU SEE... SOMETIMES ONE ELEMENT BECOMES TOO STRONG... TOO VORACIOUS...AND THE BALANCE IS THREATENED.

THERE WERE TIMES IN HISTORY WHEN... THE GREEN BECAME TOO WILD... OR WHEN THE RED BEGAN TO TAKE OVER...AND THE OTHER TWO ELEMENTS HAD TO CORRECT THINGS...

BUT NOW WE FACE A TIME WHEN... THE ROT HAS GROWN TOO STRONG... TOO GREEDY...AND WE MUST FIGHT BACK...BEFORE ALL IS CONSUMED BY DEATH AND DECAY...

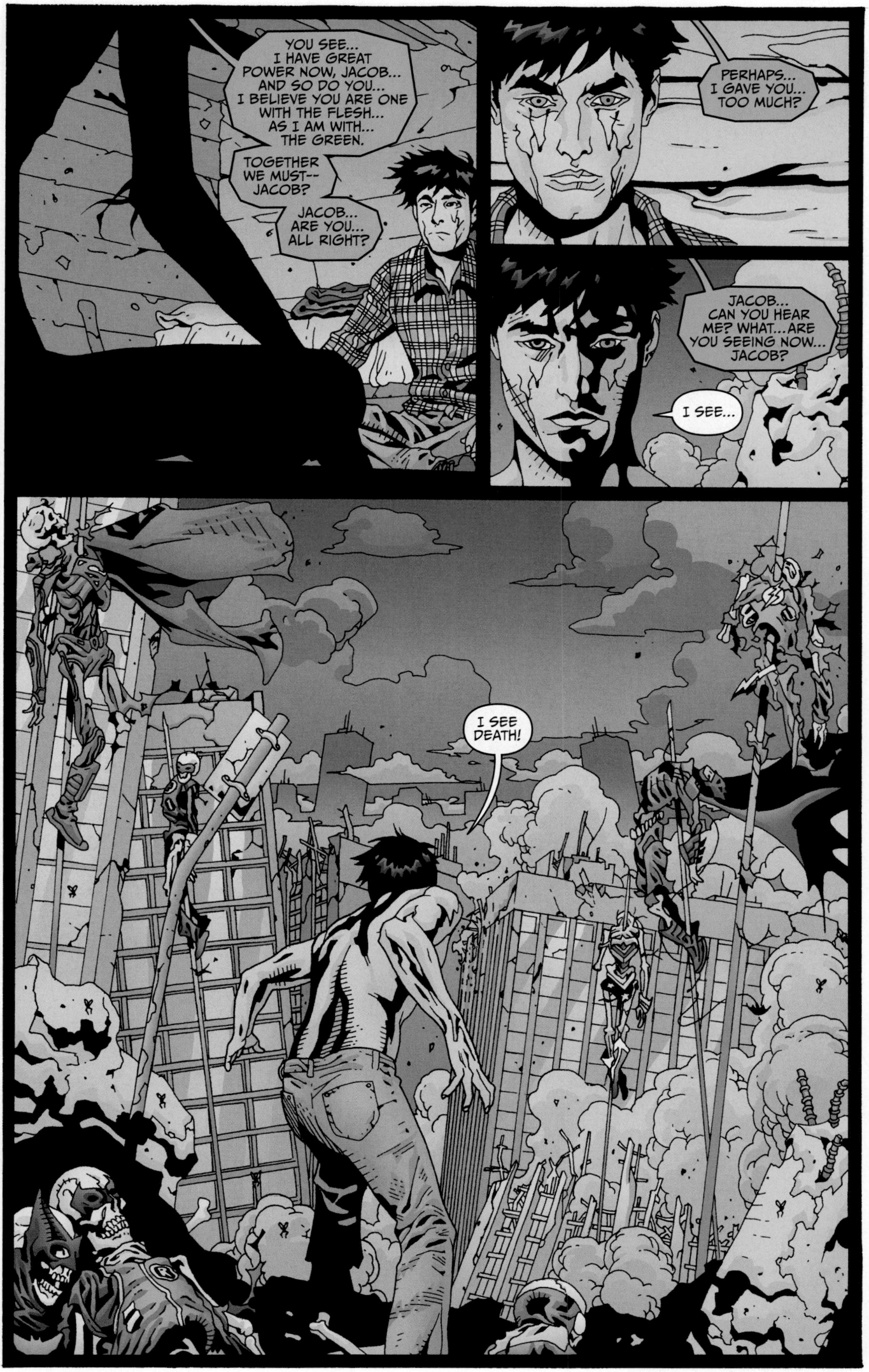
YOU SEE... I HAVE GREAT POWER NOW, JACOB... AND SO DO YOU... I BELIEVE YOU ARE ONE WITH THE FLESH... AS I AM WITH... THE GREEN.
TOGETHER WE MUST-- JACOB?
JACOB... ARE YOU... ALL RIGHT?
PERHAPS... I GAVE YOU... TOO MUCH?
JACOB... CAN YOU HEAR ME? WHAT...ARE YOU SEEING NOW... JACOB?
I SEE...
I SEE DEATH!

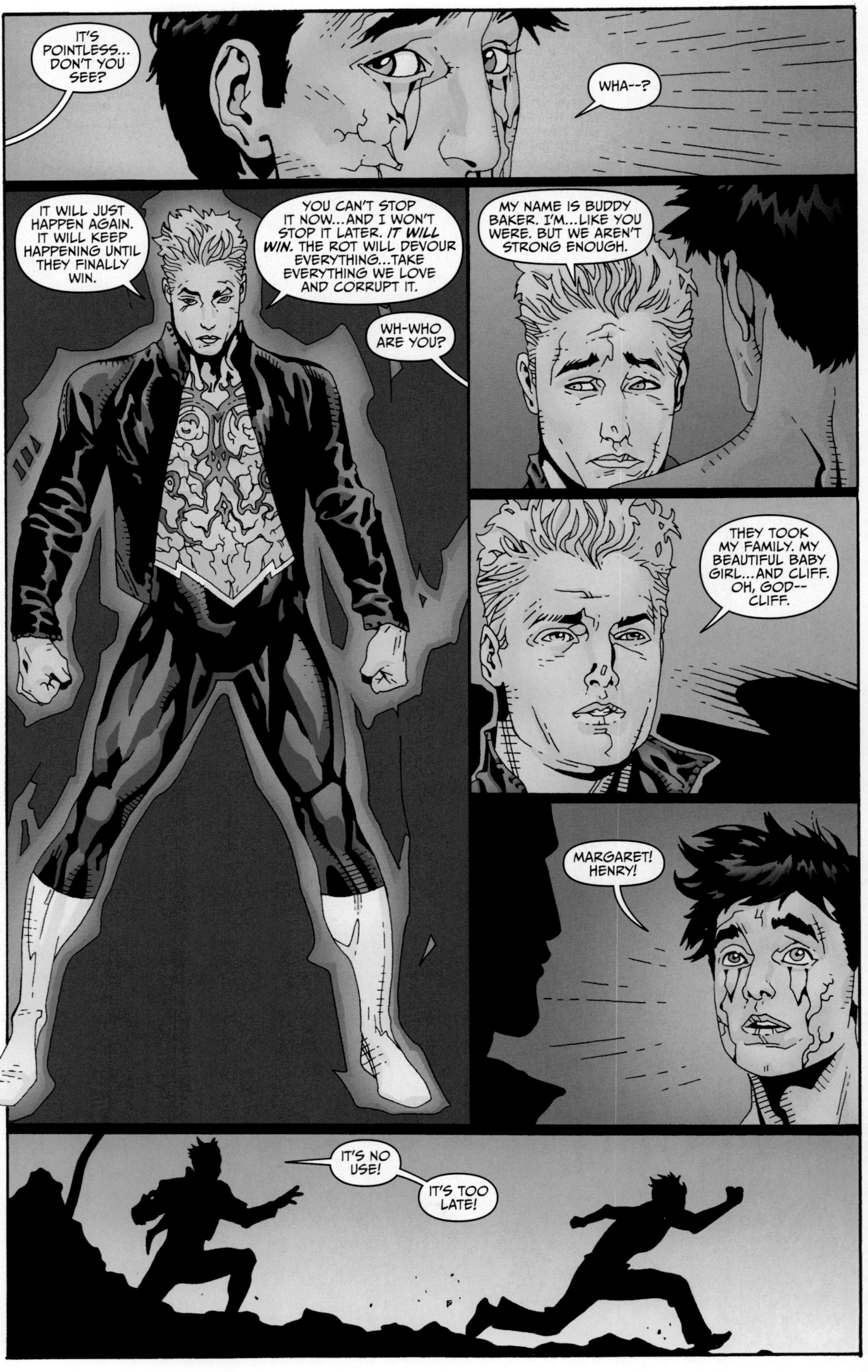
IT'S POINTLESS... DON'T YOU SEE?
WHA--?
IT WILL JUST HAPPEN AGAIN. IT WILL KEEP HAPPENING UNTIL THEY FINALLY WIN.
YOU CAN'T STOP IT NOW...AND I WON'T STOP IT LATER. IT WILL WIN. THE ROT WILL DEVOUR EVERYTHING...TAKE EVERYTHING WE LOVE AND CORRUPT IT.
WH-WHO ARE YOU?
MY NAME IS BUDDY BAKER. I'M...LIKE YOU WERE. BUT WE AREN'T STRONG ENOUGH.
THEY TOOK MY FAMILY. MY BEAUTIFUL BABY GIRL...AND CLIFF. OH, GOD-- CLIFF.
MARGARET! HENRY!
IT'S NO USE!
IT'S TOO LATE!

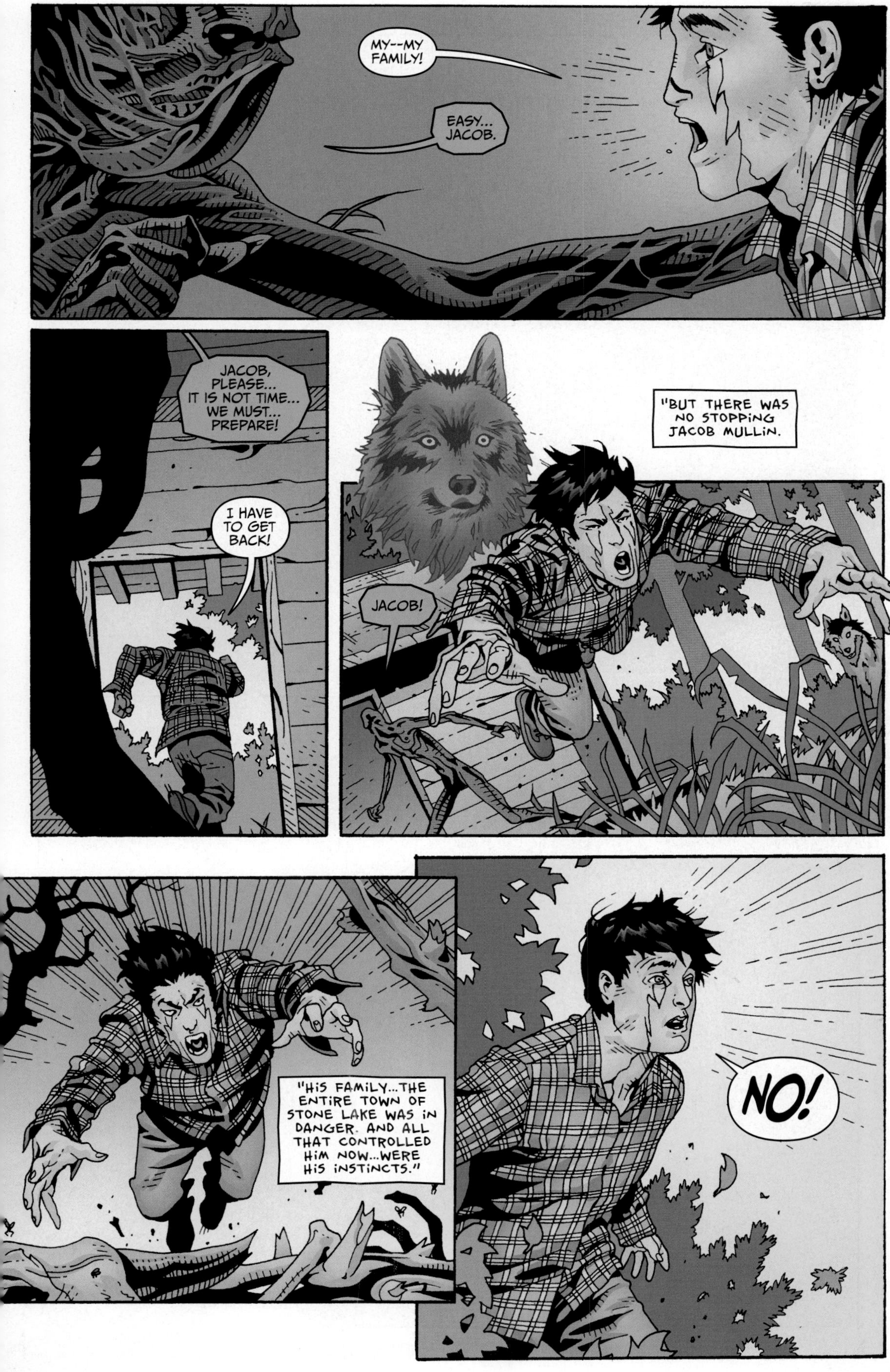
MY--MY FAMILY!
EASY... JACOB.
JACOB, PLEASE... IT IS NOT TIME... WE MUST... PREPARE!
I HAVE TO GET BACK!
"BUT THERE WAS NO STOPPING JACOB MULLIN.
JACOB!
"HIS FAMILY...THE ENTIRE TOWN OF STONE LAKE WAS IN DANGER. AND ALL THAT CONTROLLED HIM NOW...WERE HIS INSTINCTS."
NO!

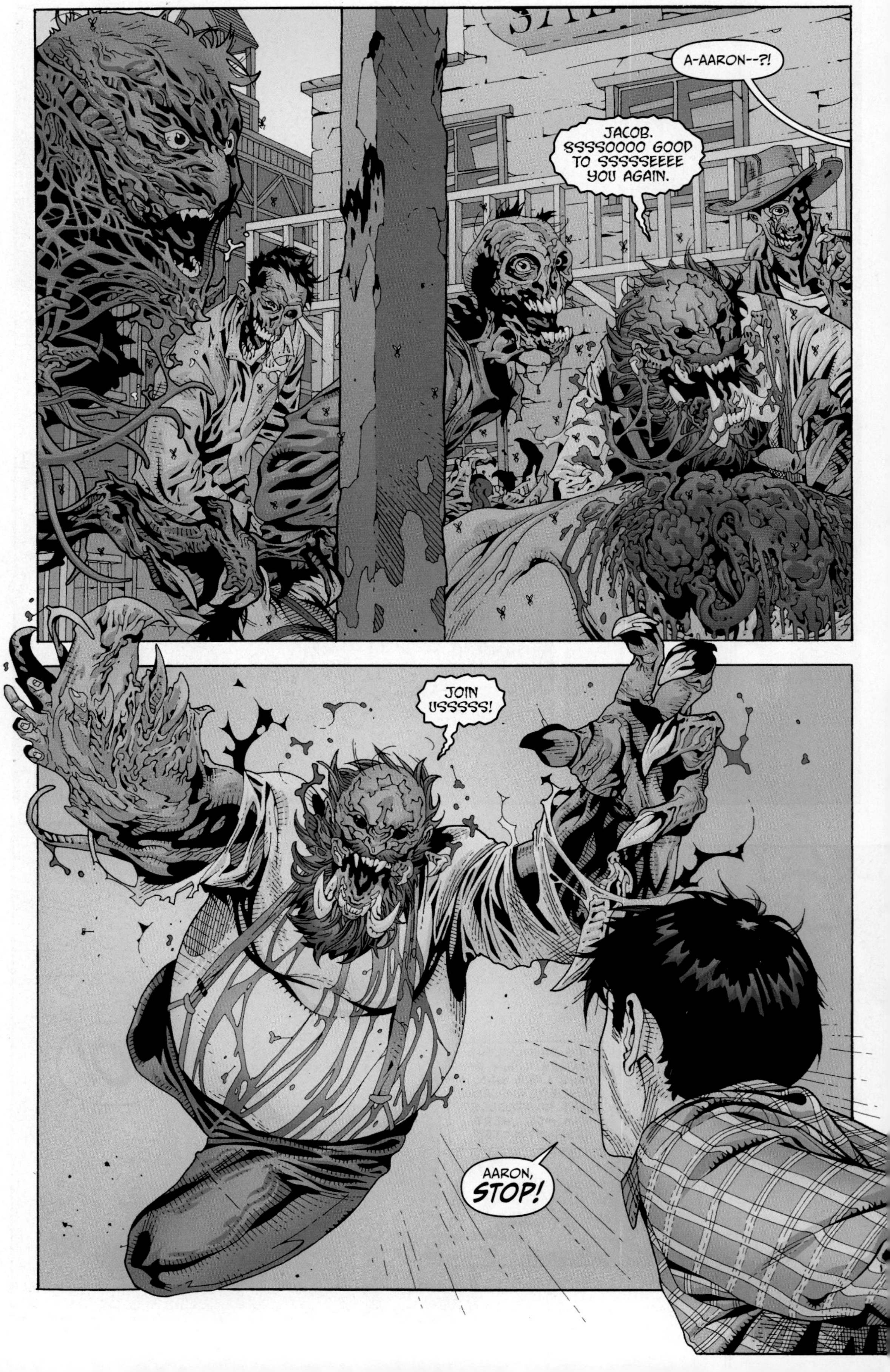
A-AARON--?!
JACOB. SSSSOOOO GOOD TO SSSSSEEEE YOU AGAIN.
JOIN USSSSS!
AARON, STOP!

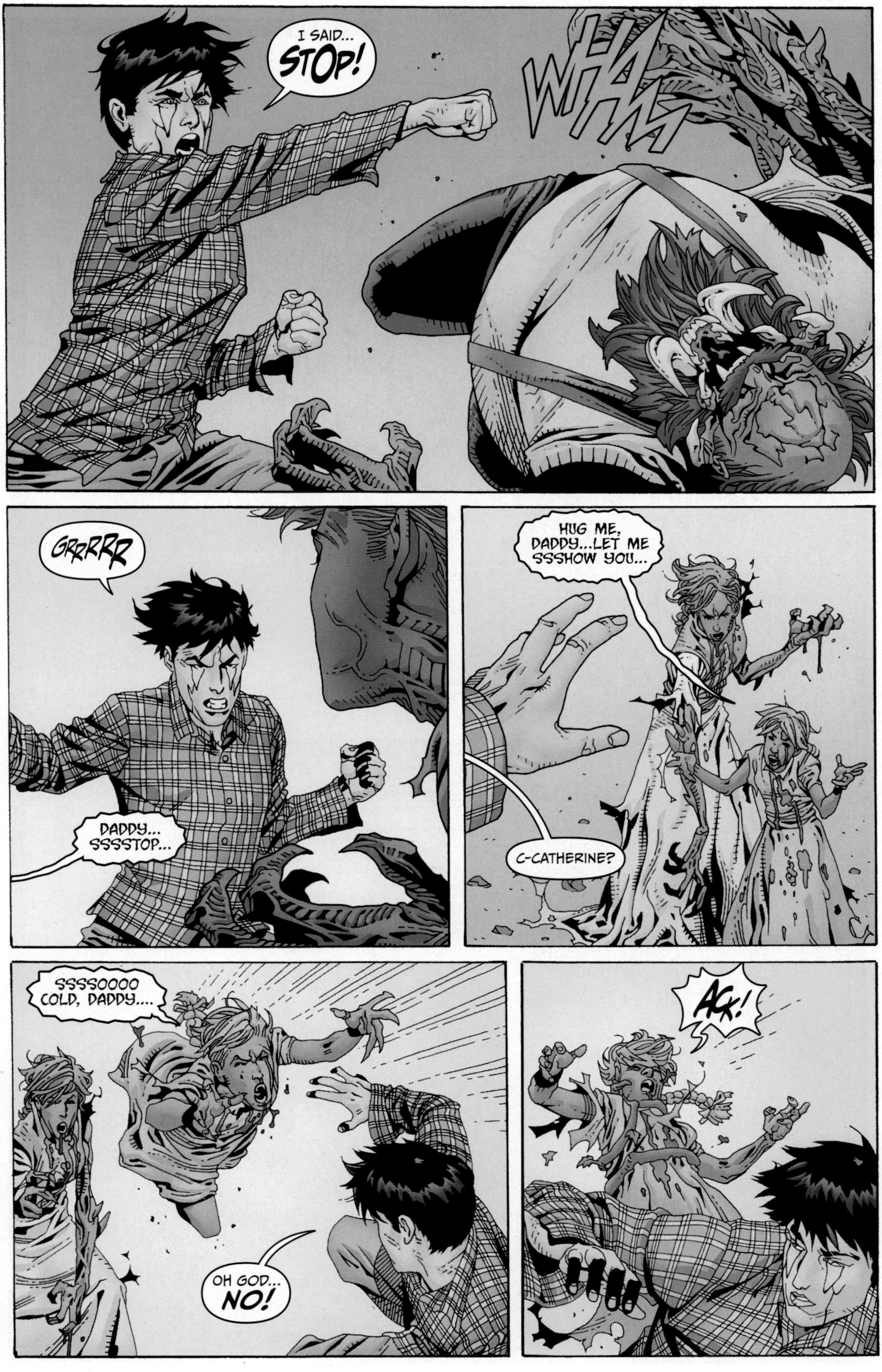
I SAID...
STOP!
WHAM
GRRRRR
DADDY...
SSSSTOP...
HUG ME, DADDY...LET ME SSSHOW YOU...
C-CATHERINE?
SSSSOOOO COLD, DADDY....
OH GOD...
NO!
ACK!

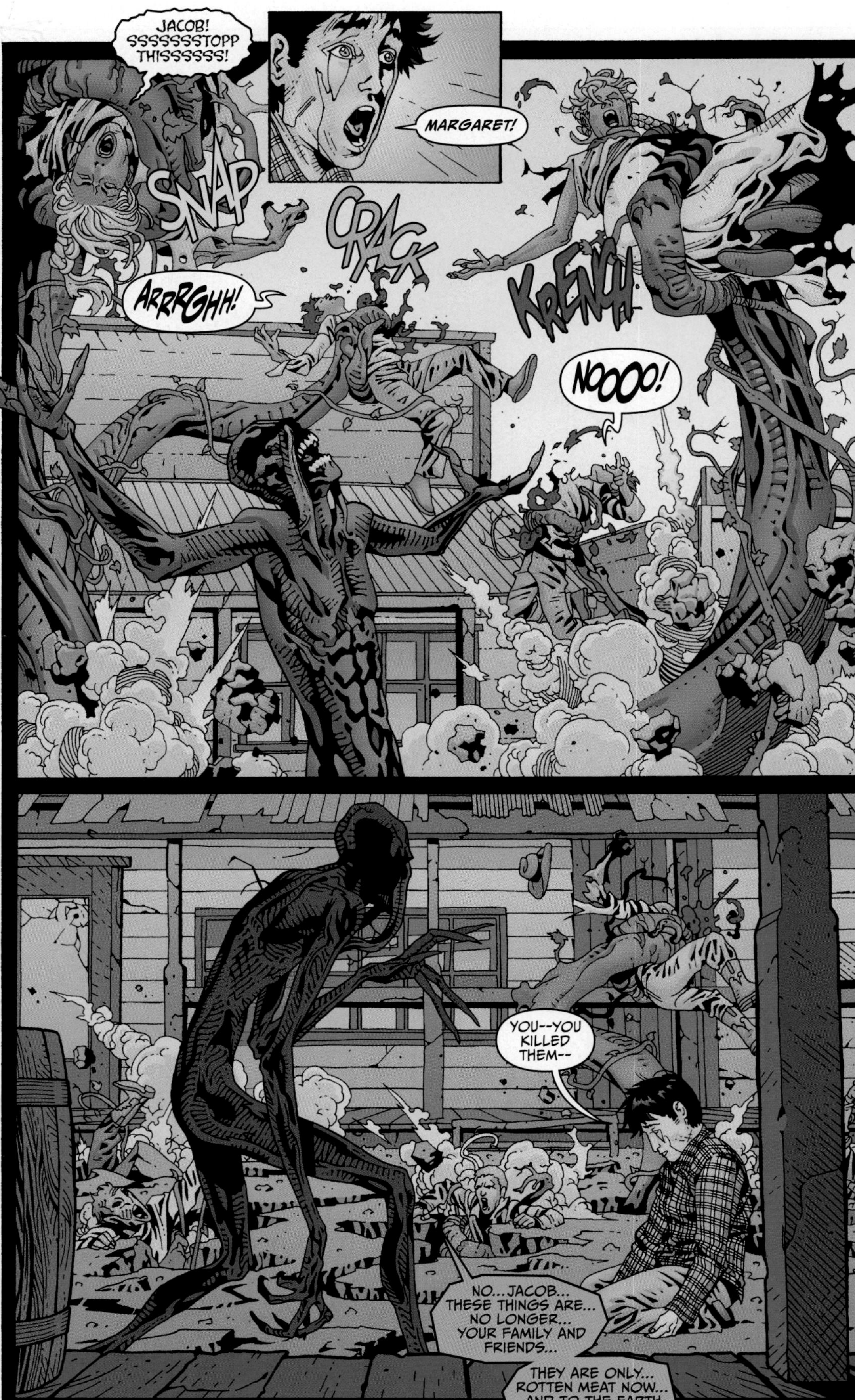
JACOB! SSSSSSSTOPP THISSSSSS!
MARGARET!
SNAP
CRACK
ARRRGHH!
KRENCH
NOOOO!
YOU--YOU KILLED THEM--
NO...JACOB... THESE THINGS ARE... NO LONGER... YOUR FAMILY AND FRIENDS...
THEY ARE ONLY... ROTTEN MEAT NOW... AND TO THE EARTH THEY RETURN.

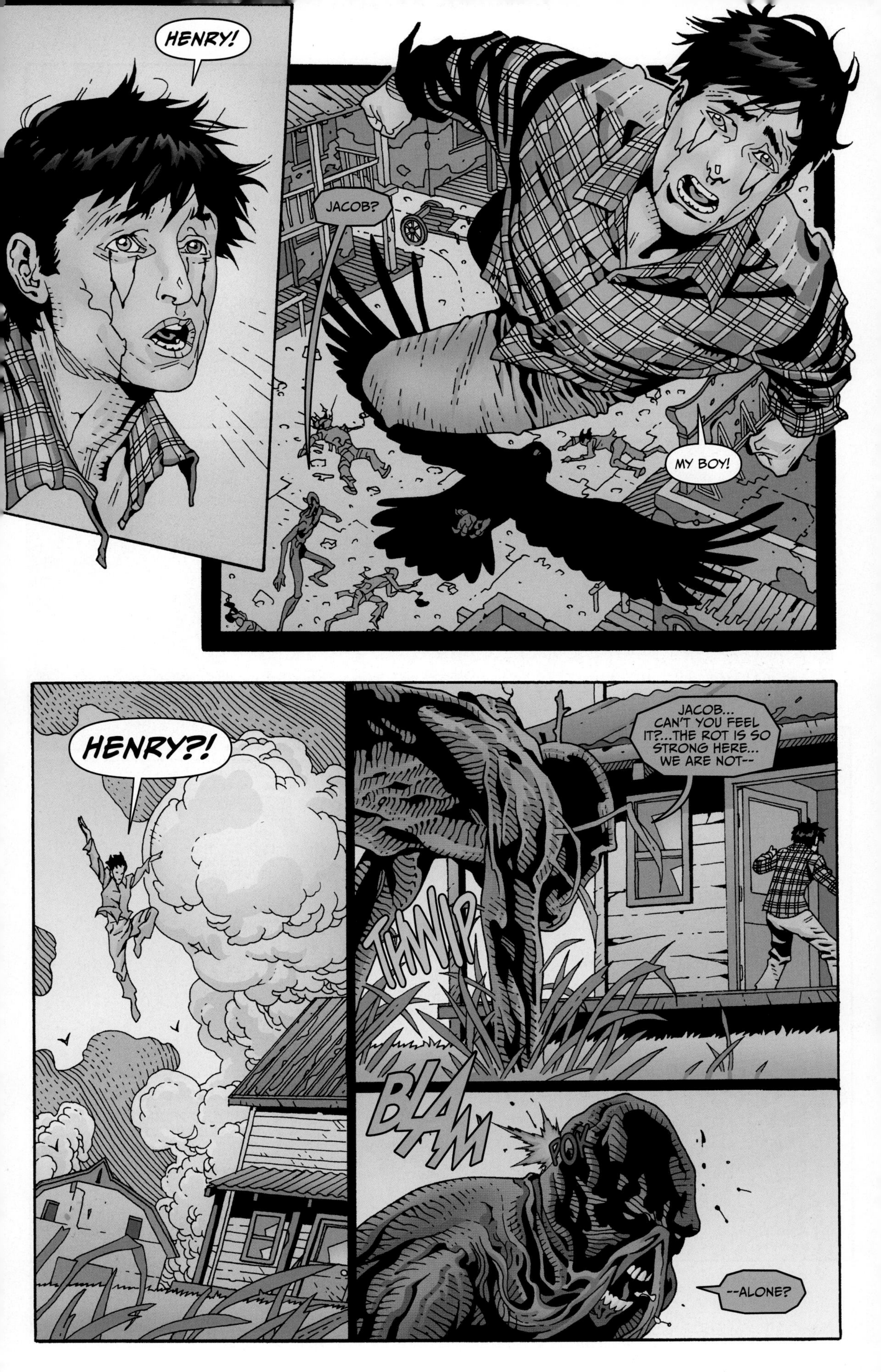
HENRY!
JACOB?
MY BOY!
HENRY?!
JACOB... CAN'T YOU FEEL IT?...THE ROT IS SO STRONG HERE... WE ARE NOT--
TWIP
BLAM
POK
--ALONE?

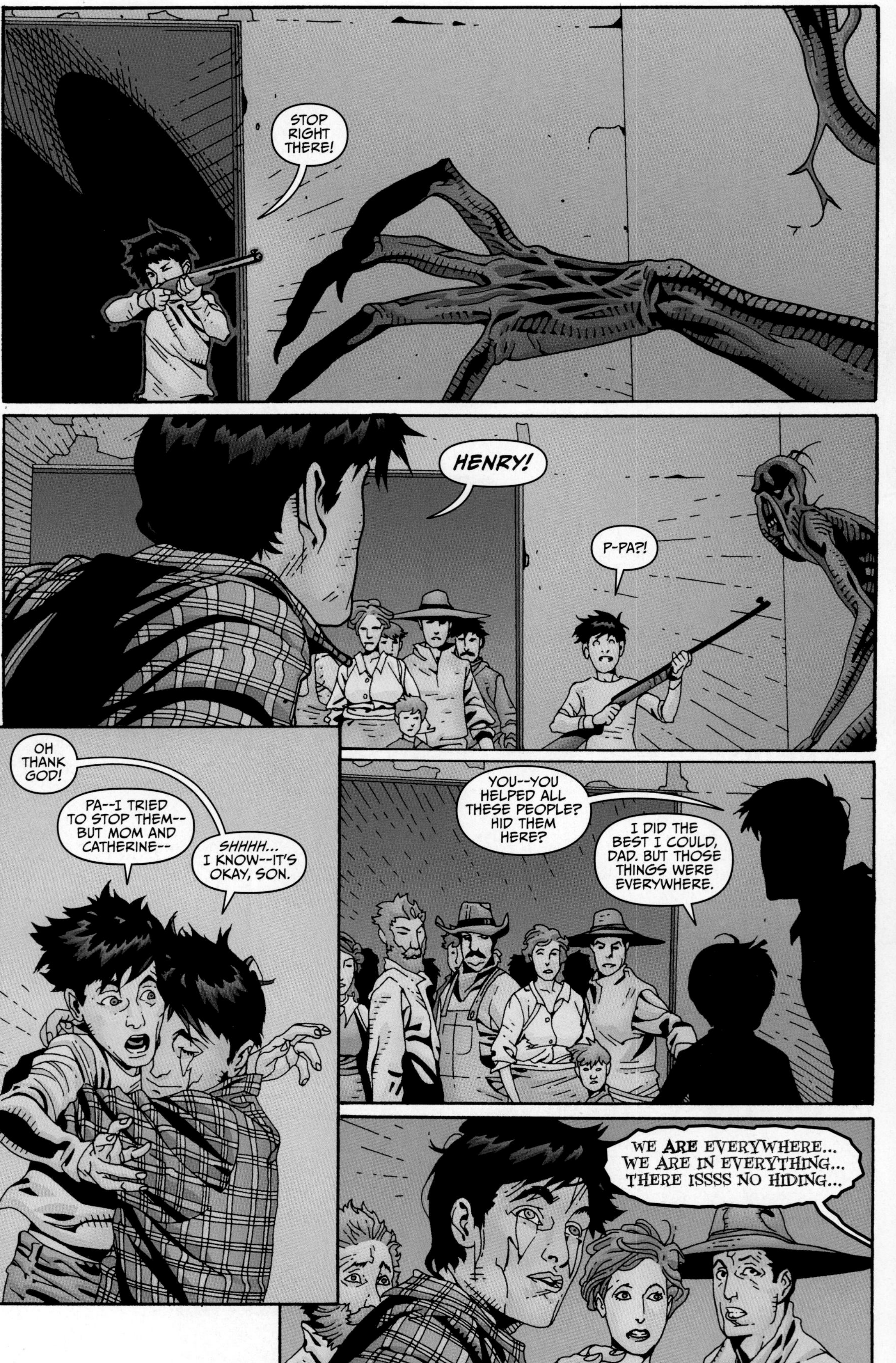
STOP RIGHT THERE!
HENRY!
P-PA?!
OH THANK GOD!
PA--I TRIED TO STOP THEM--BUT MOM AND CATHERINE--
SHHHH... I KNOW--IT'S OKAY, SON.
YOU--YOU HELPED ALL THESE PEOPLE? HID THEM HERE?
I DID THE BEST I COULD, DAD. BUT THOSE THINGS WERE EVERYWHERE.
WE ARE EVERYWHERE... WE ARE IN EVERYTHING... THERE ISSSS NO HIDING...

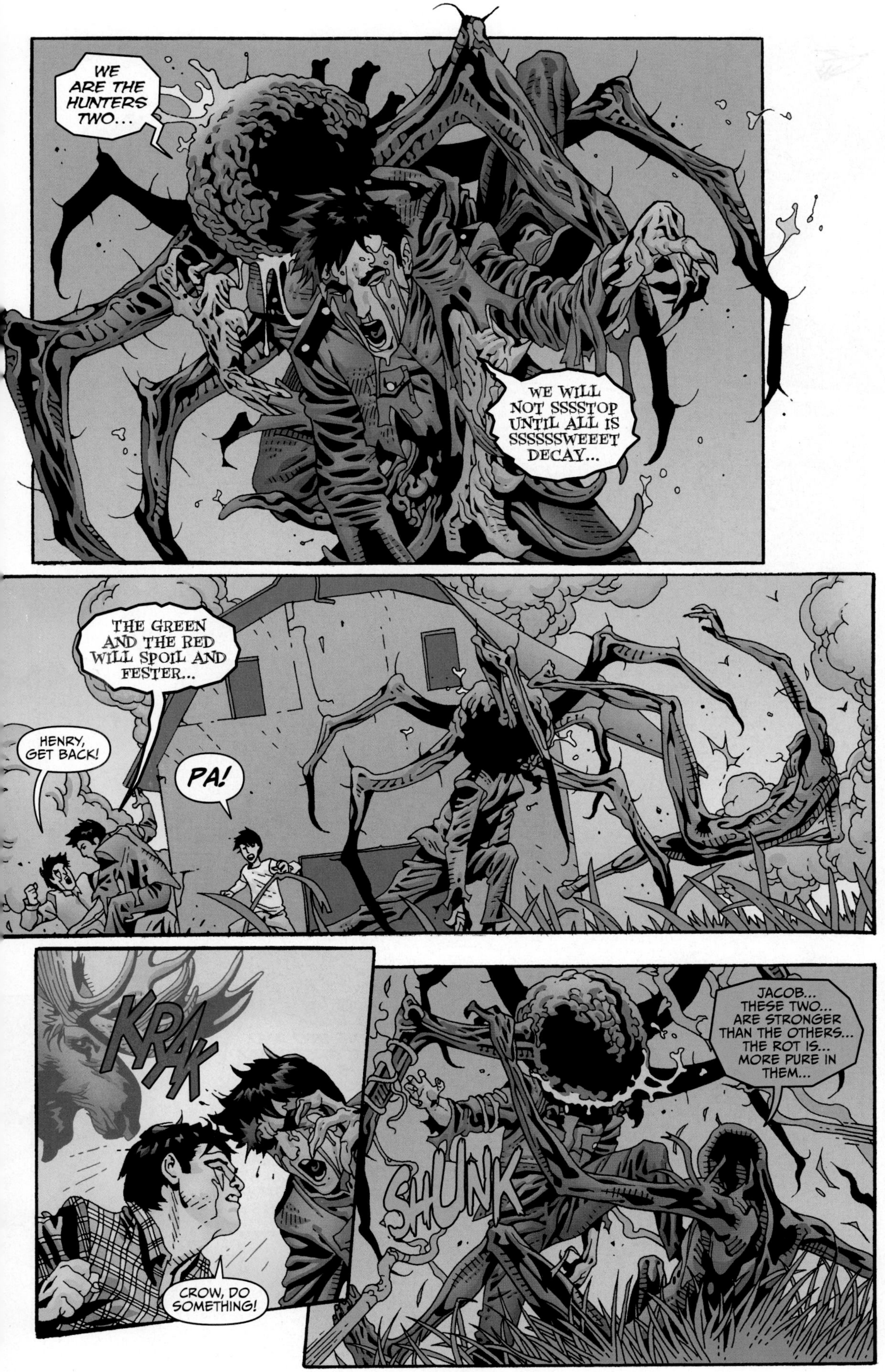
WE ARE THE HUNTERS TWO...
WE WILL NOT SSSSTOP UNTIL ALL IS SSSSSWEEET DECAY...
THE GREEN AND THE RED WILL SPOIL AND FESTER...
HENRY, GET BACK!
PA!
KRAK
CROW, DO SOMETHING!
SHUNK
JACOB... THESE TWO... ARE STRONGER THAN THE OTHERS... THE ROT IS... MORE PURE IN THEM...

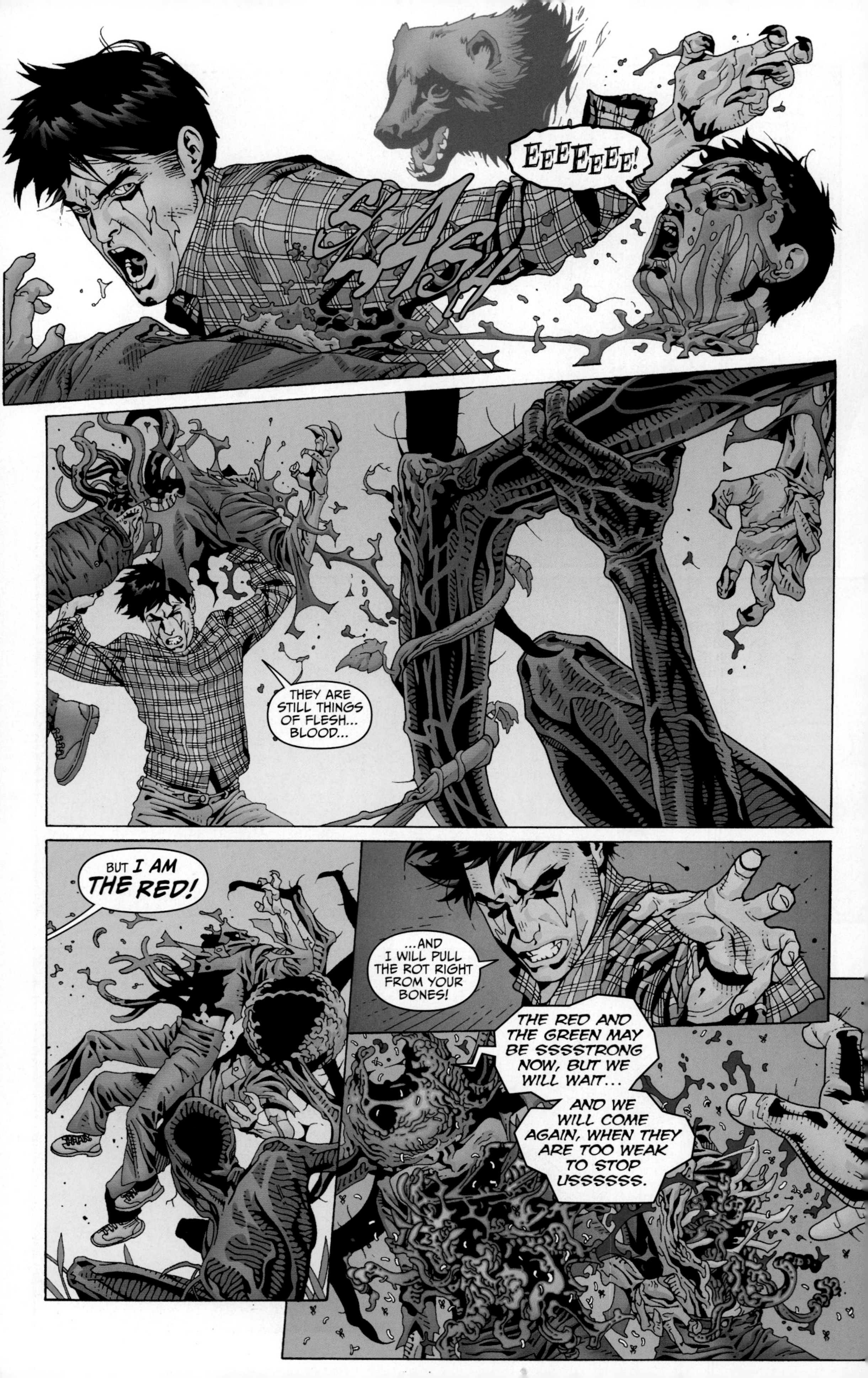
EEEEEEE!
SHASH
THEY ARE STILL THINGS OF FLESH... BLOOD...
BUT I AM THE RED!
...AND I WILL PULL THE ROT RIGHT FROM YOUR BONES!
THE RED AND THE GREEN MAY BE SSSSTRONG NOW, BUT WE WILL WAIT...
AND WE WILL COME AGAIN, WHEN THEY ARE TOO WEAK TO STOP USSSSSS.

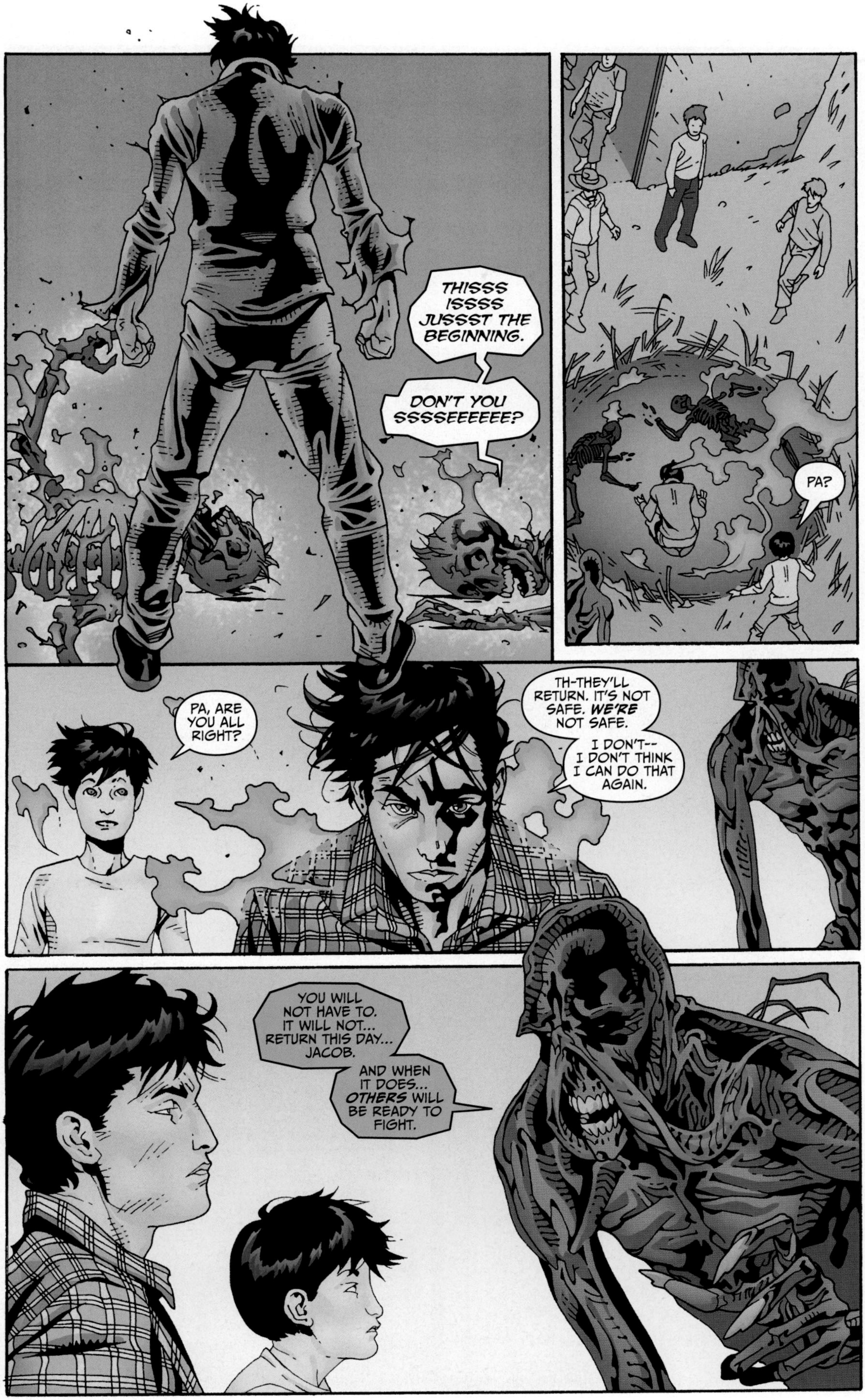
THISSS ISSSS JUSSST THE BEGINNING.
DON'T YOU SSSSEEEEEE?
PA?
PA, ARE YOU ALL RIGHT?
TH-THEY'LL RETURN. IT'S NOT SAFE. WE'RE NOT SAFE.
I DON'T-- I DON'T THINK I CAN DO THAT AGAIN.
YOU WILL NOT HAVE TO. IT WILL NOT... RETURN THIS DAY... JACOB.
AND WHEN IT DOES... OTHERS WILL BE READY TO FIGHT.

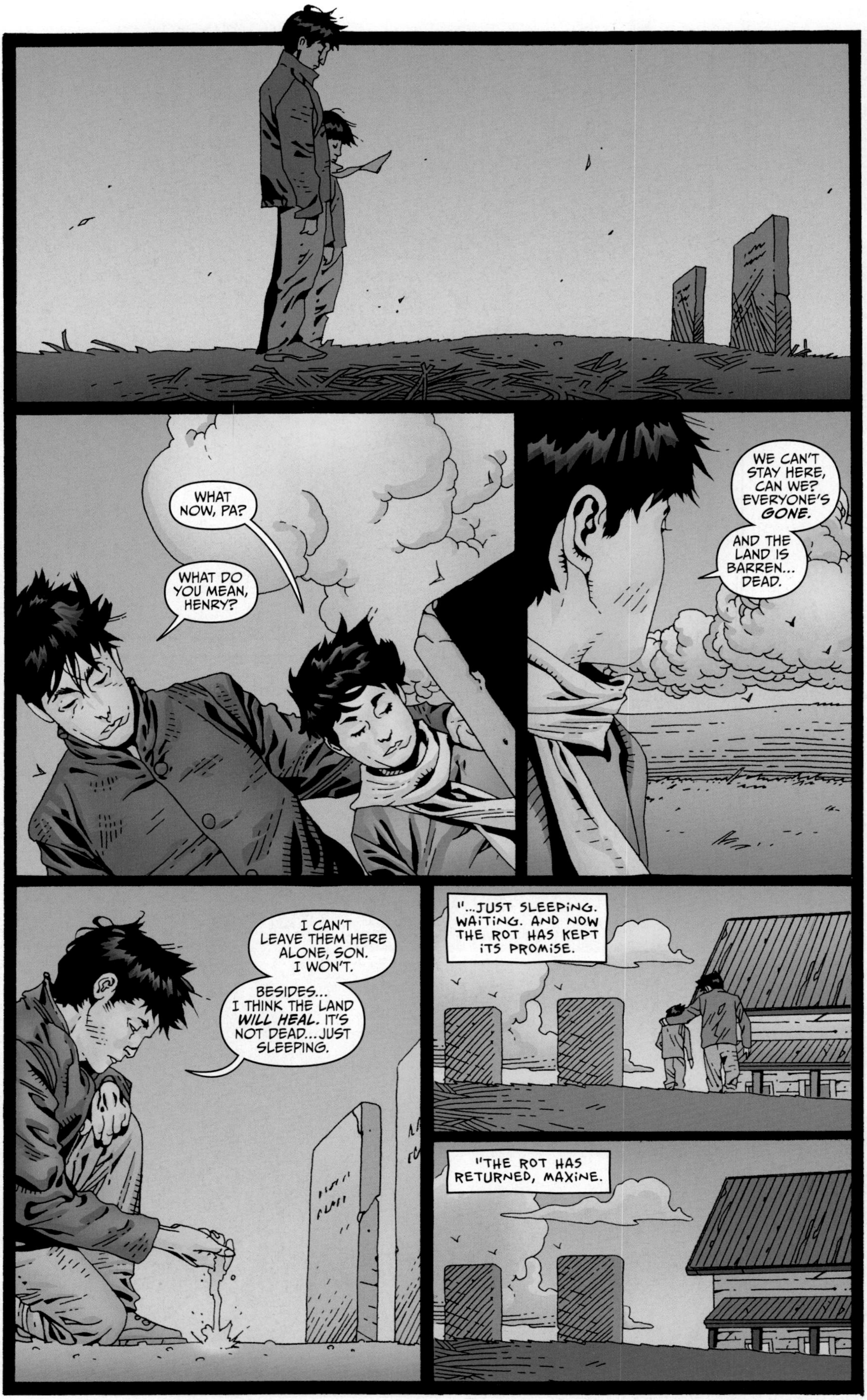
WHAT NOW, PA?
WHAT DO YOU MEAN, HENRY?
WE CAN'T STAY HERE, CAN WE? EVERYONE'S GONE.
AND THE LAND IS BARREN... DEAD.
I CAN'T LEAVE THEM HERE ALONE, SON. I WON'T.
BESIDES... I THINK THE LAND WILL HEAL. IT'S NOT DEAD...JUST SLEEPING.
"...JUST SLEEPING. WAITING. AND NOW THE ROT HAS KEPT ITS PROMISE.
"THE ROT HAS RETURNED, MAXINE.

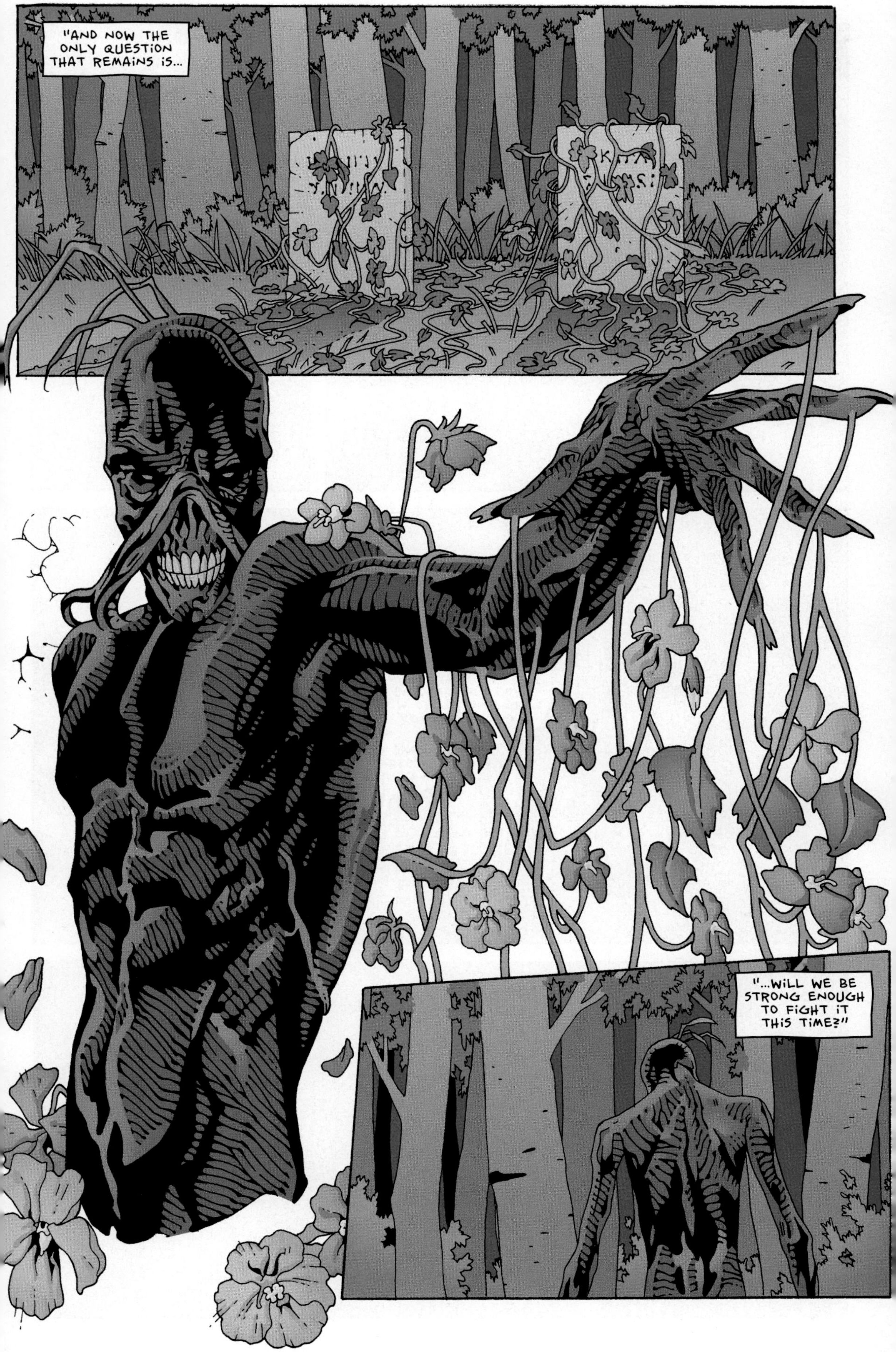
"AND NOW THE ONLY QUESTION THAT REMAINS IS...
"...WILL WE BE STRONG ENOUGH TO FIGHT IT THIS TIME?"

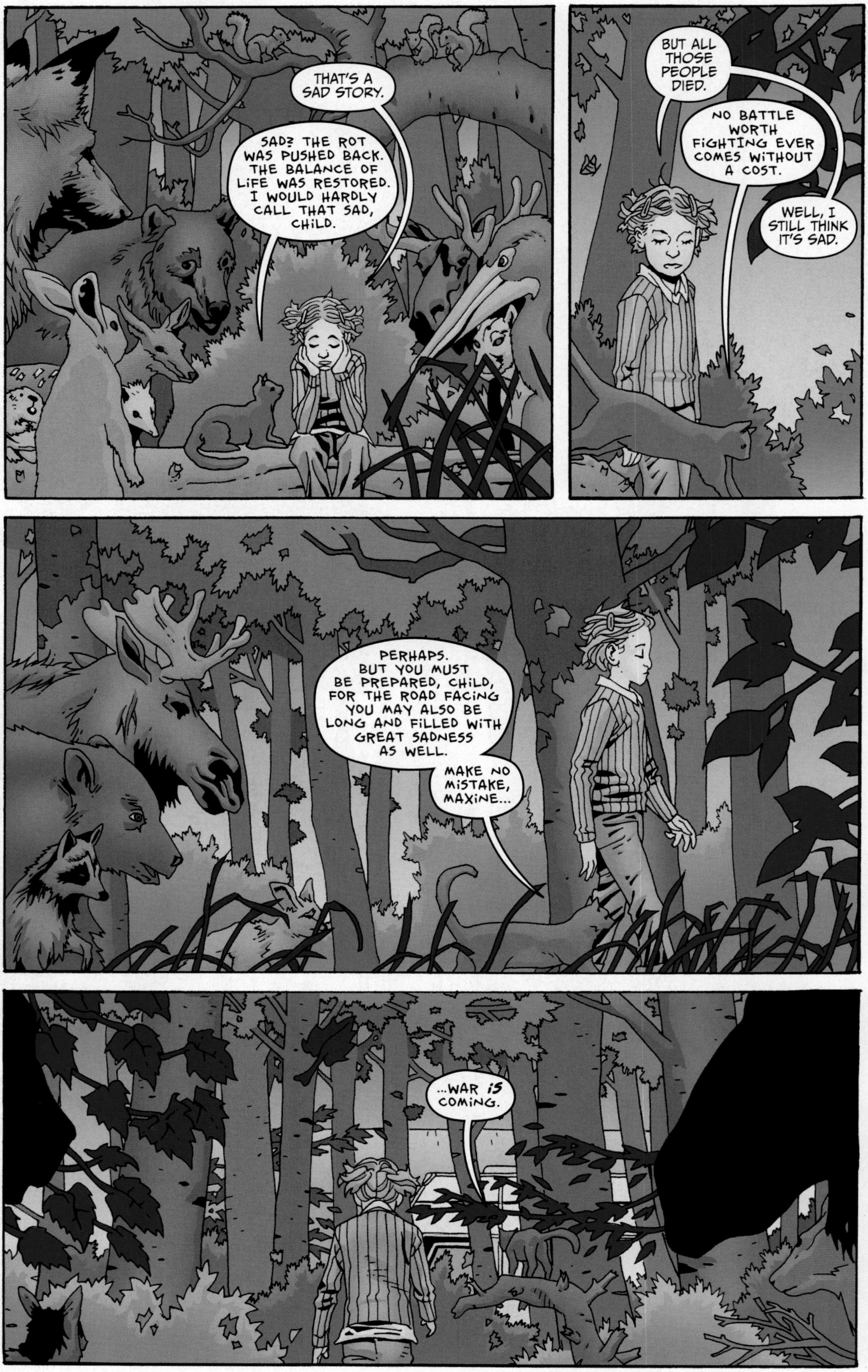
THAT'S A SAD STORY.
SAD? THE ROT WAS PUSHED BACK. THE BALANCE OF LIFE WAS RESTORED. I WOULD HARDLY CALL THAT SAD, CHILD.
BUT ALL THOSE PEOPLE DIED.
NO BATTLE WORTH FIGHTING EVER COMES WITHOUT A COST.
WELL, I STILL THINK IT'S SAD.
PERHAPS. BUT YOU MUST BE PREPARED, CHILD, FOR THE ROAD FACING YOU MAY ALSO BE LONG AND FILLED WITH GREAT SADNESS AS WELL.
MAKE NO MISTAKE, MAXINE...
...WAR IS COMING.

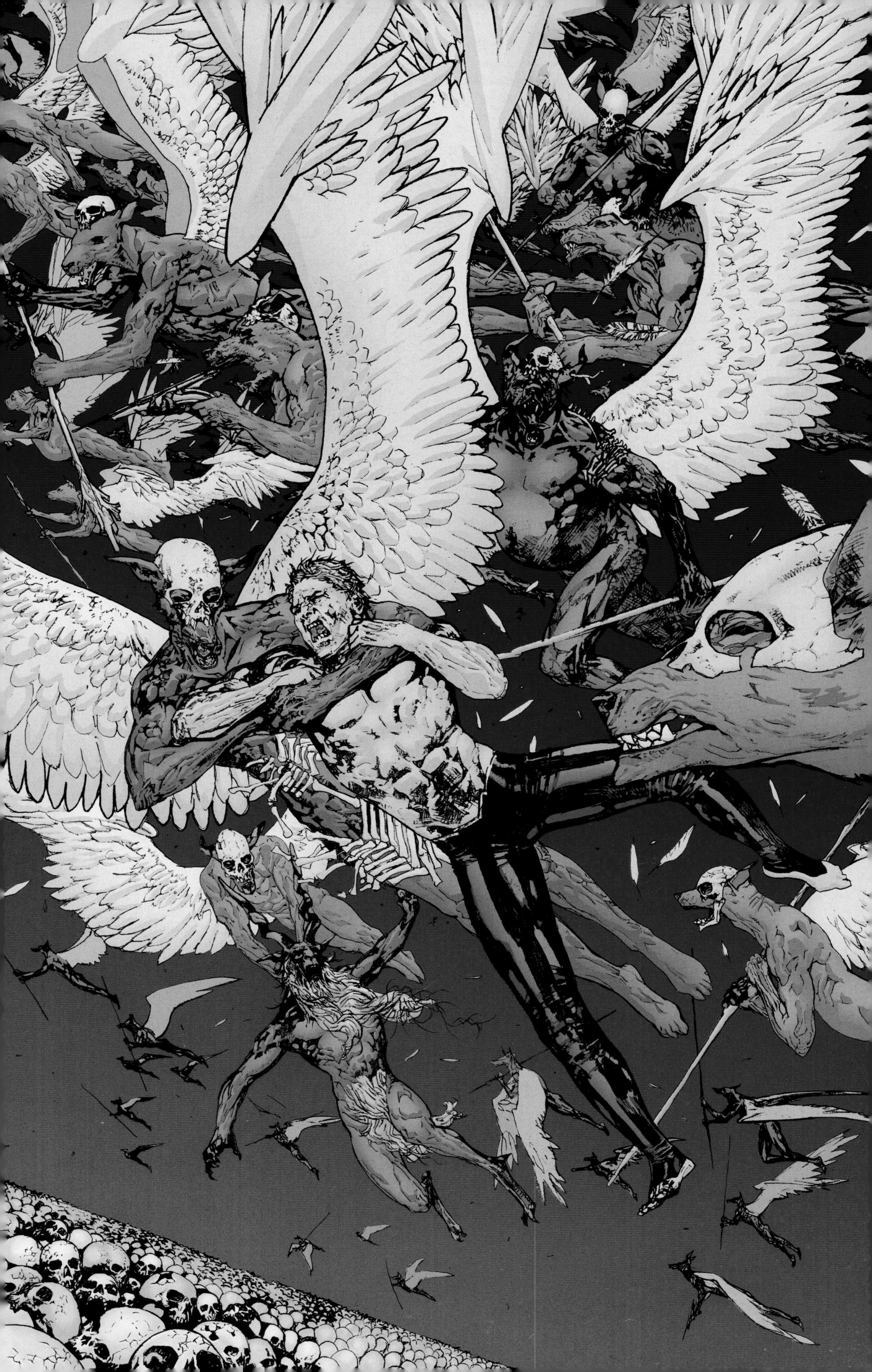

JEFF LEMIRE writer **STEVE PUGH** artist
cover by **TRAVEL FOREMAN** with **LOVERN KINDZIERSKI**

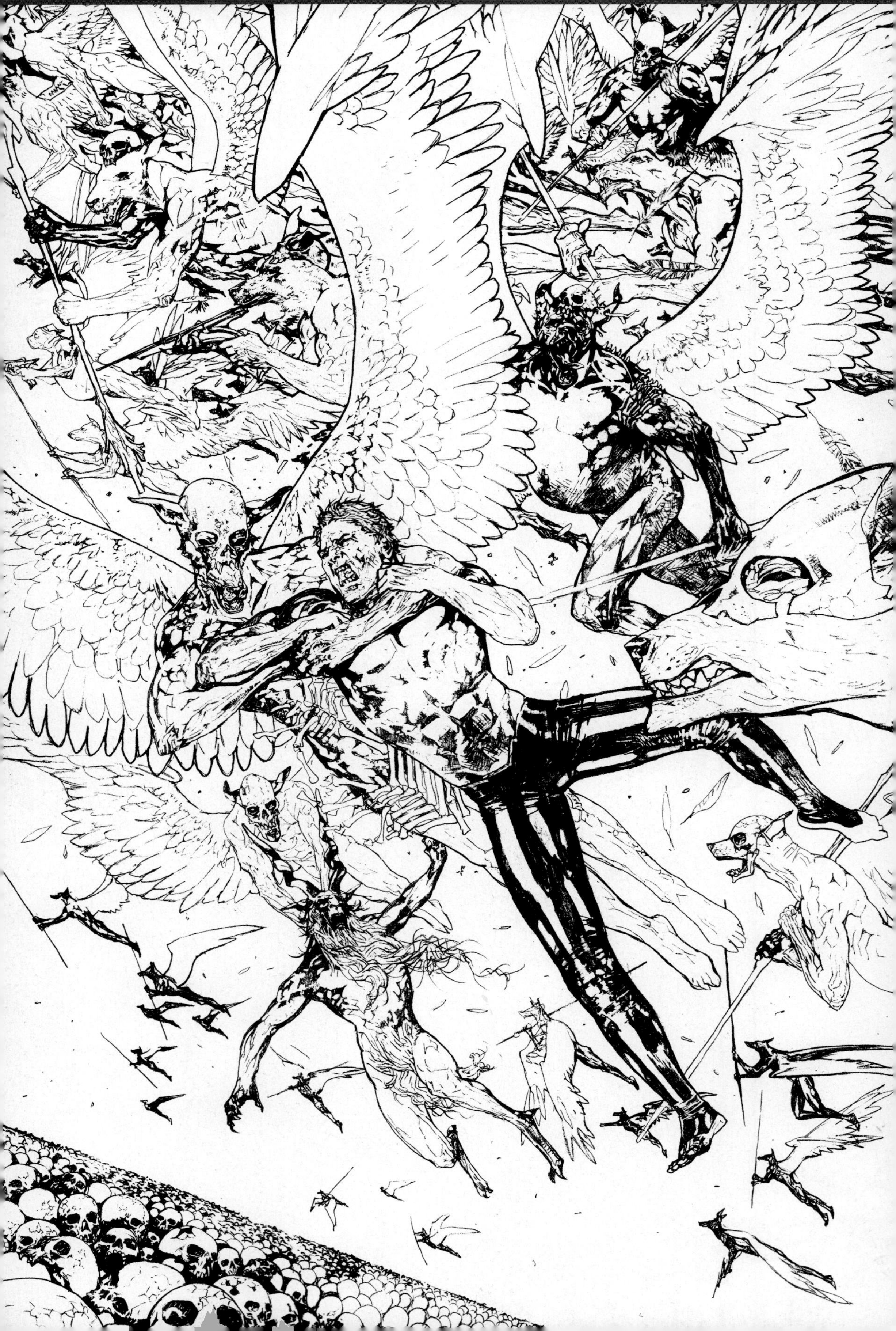

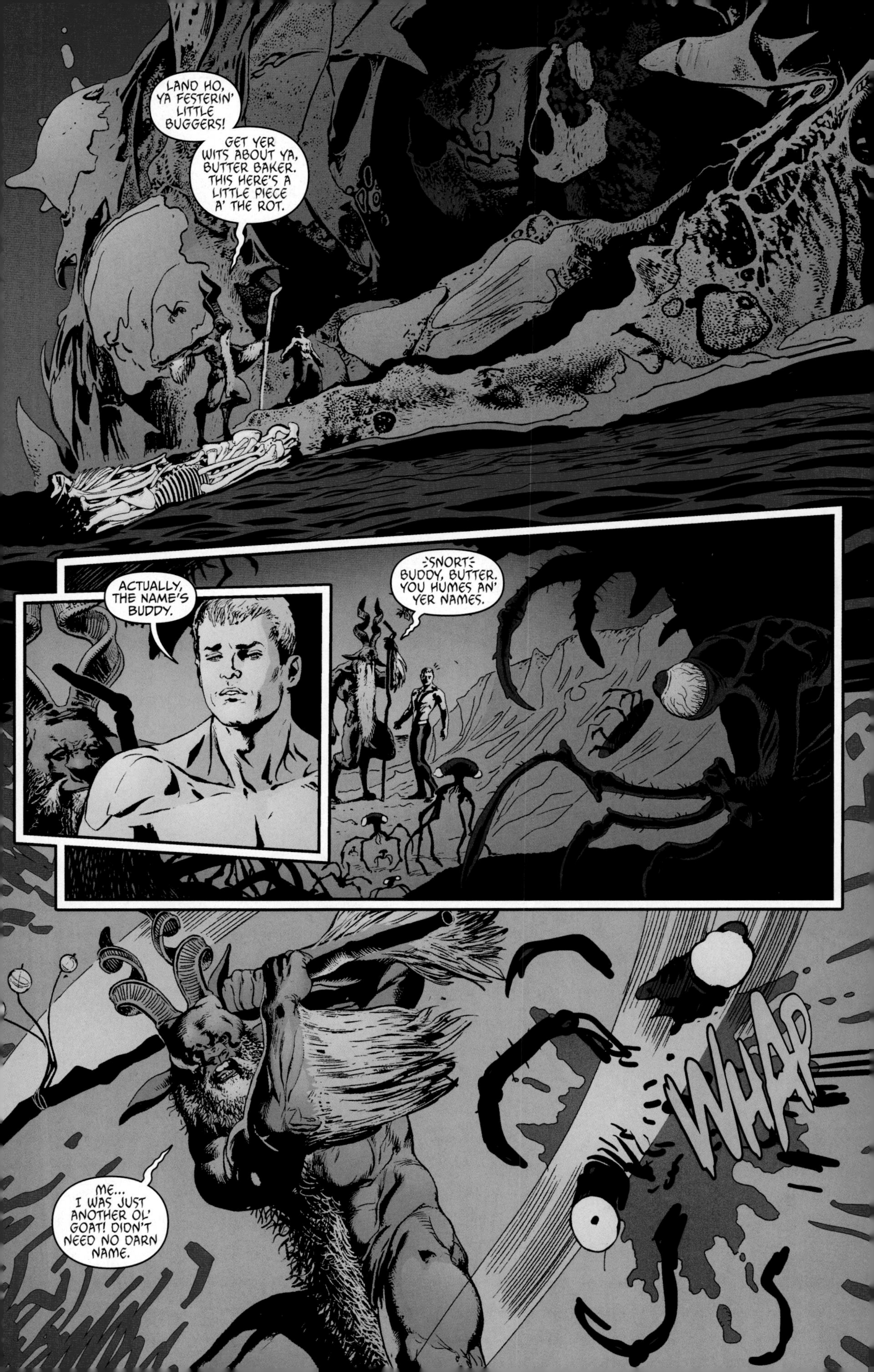
LAND HO, YA FESTERIN' LITTLE BUGGERS!
GET YER WITS ABOUT YA, BUTTER BAKER. THIS HERE'S A LITTLE PIECE A' THE ROT.
ACTUALLY, THE NAME'S BUDDY.
-SNORT- BUDDY, BUTTER. YOU HUMES AN' YER NAMES.
WHAP
ME... I WAS JUST ANOTHER OL' GOAT! DIDN'T NEED NO DARN NAME.

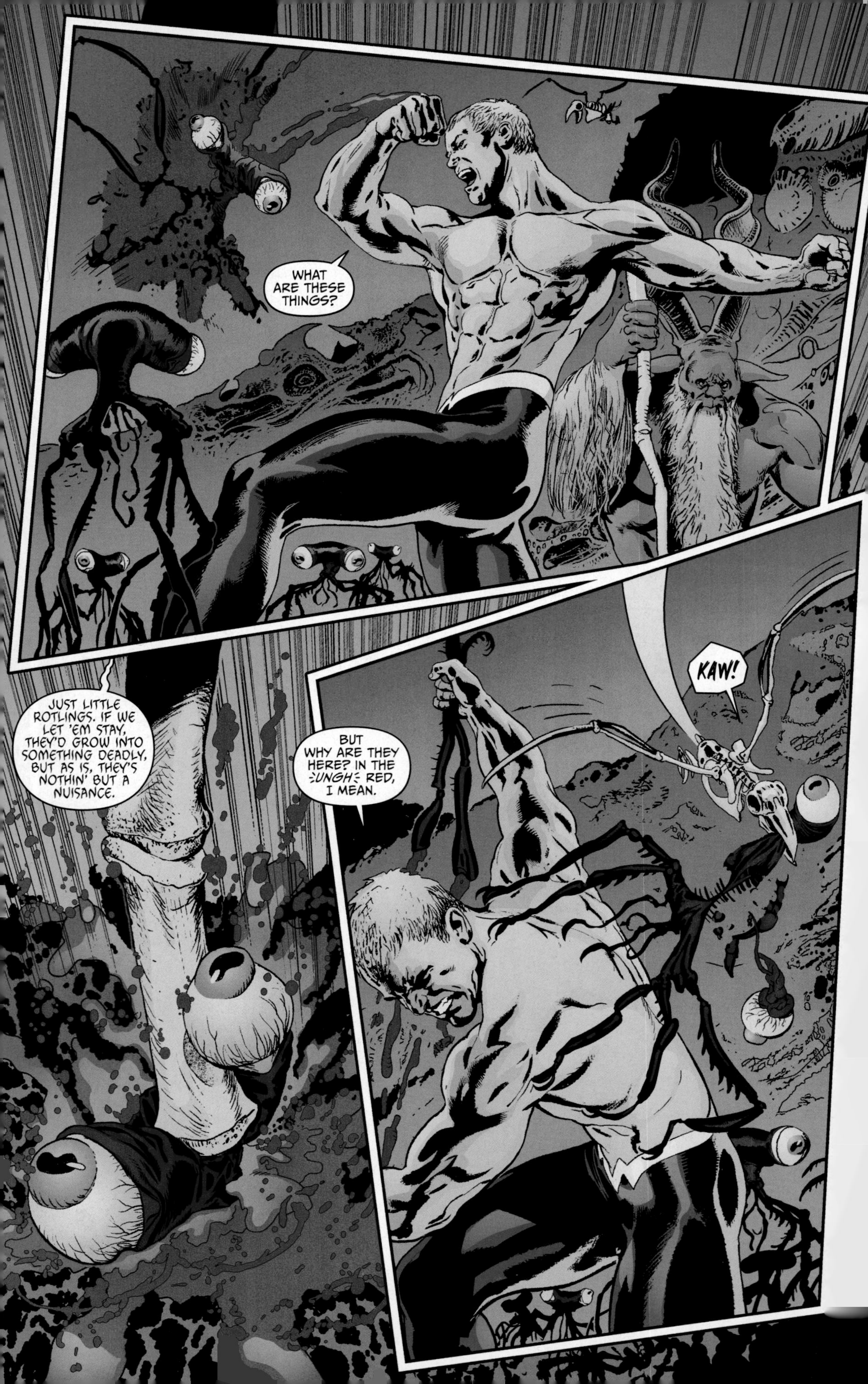
WHAT ARE THESE THINGS?
JUST LITTLE ROTLINGS. IF WE LET 'EM STAY, THEY'D GROW INTO SOMETHING DEADLY, BUT AS IS, THEY'S NOTHIN' BUT A NUISANCE.
BUT WHY ARE THEY HERE? IN THE UNGH RED, I MEAN.
KAW!

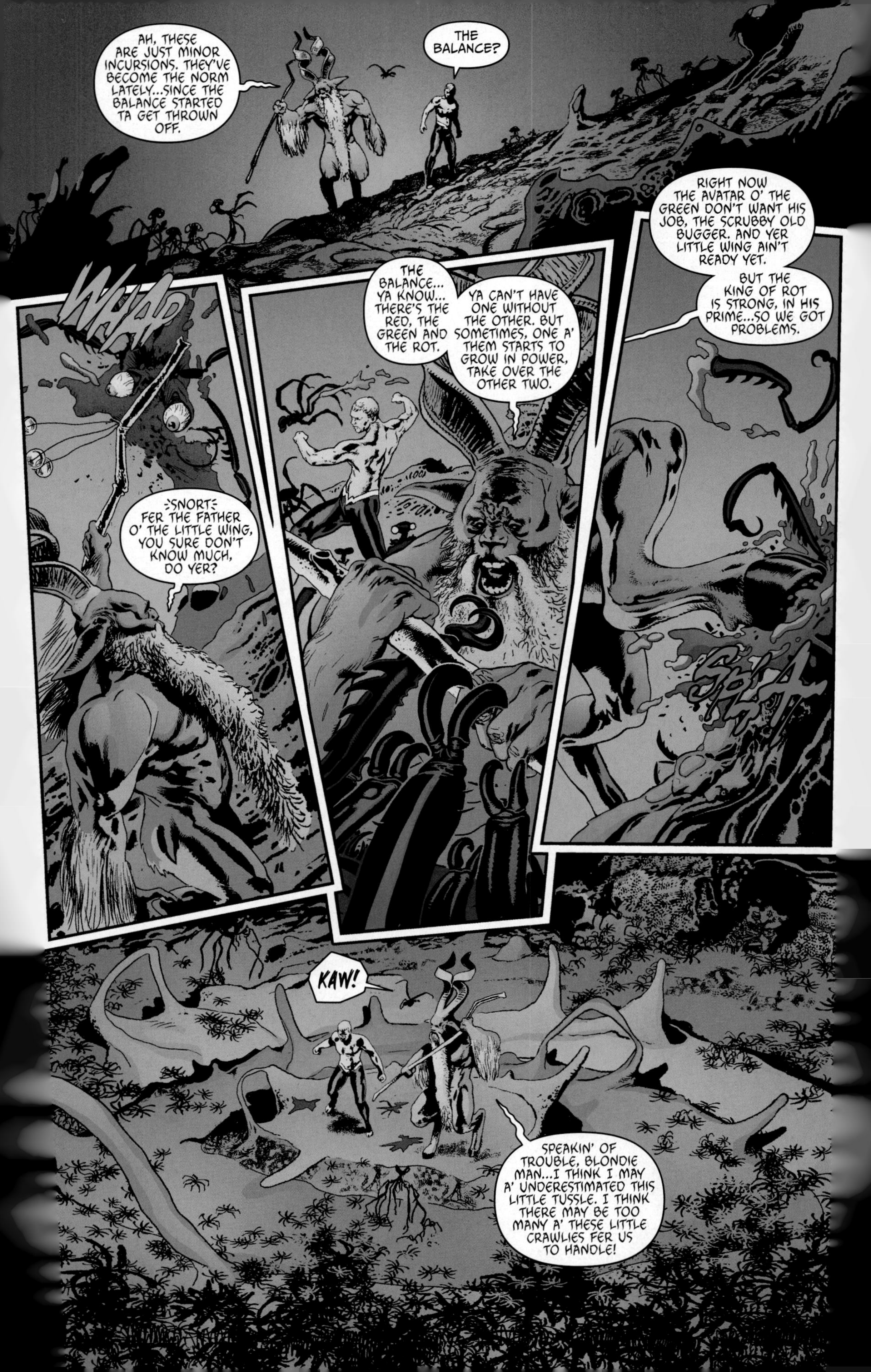
AH, THESE ARE JUST MINOR INCURSIONS. THEY'VE BECOME THE NORM LATELY...SINCE THE BALANCE STARTED TA GET THROWN OFF.
THE BALANCE?
WHAP
SNORT FER THE FATHER O' THE LITTLE WING, YOU SURE DON'T KNOW MUCH, DO YER?
THE BALANCE... YA KNOW... THERE'S THE RED, THE GREEN AND THE ROT.
YA CAN'T HAVE ONE WITHOUT THE OTHER. BUT SOMETIMES, ONE A' THEM STARTS TO GROW IN POWER, TAKE OVER THE OTHER TWO.
RIGHT NOW THE AVATAR O' THE GREEN DON'T WANT HIS JOB, THE SCRUBBY OLD BUGGER. AND YER LITTLE WING AIN'T READY YET.
BUT THE KING OF ROT IS STRONG, IN HIS PRIME...SO WE GOT PROBLEMS.
SPLA
KAW!
SPEAKIN' OF TROUBLE, BLONDIE MAN...I THINK I MAY A' UNDERESTIMATED THIS LITTLE TUSSLE. I THINK THERE MAY BE TOO MANY A' THESE LITTLE CRAWLIES FER US TO HANDLE!

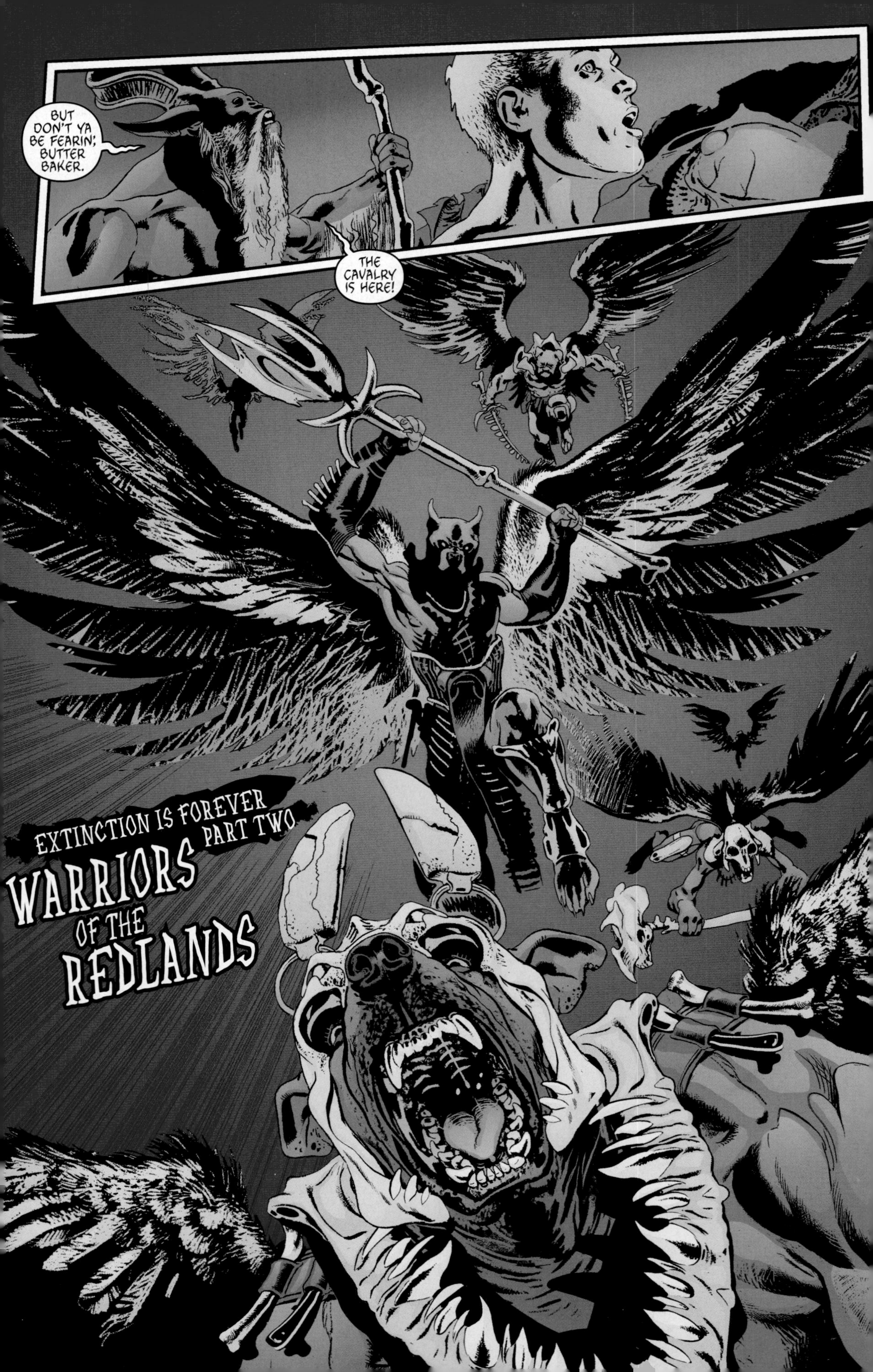
BUT DON'T YA BE FEARIN', BUTTER BAKER.
THE CAVALRY IS HERE!
EXTINCTION IS FOREVER PART TWO
WARRIORS OF THE REDLANDS

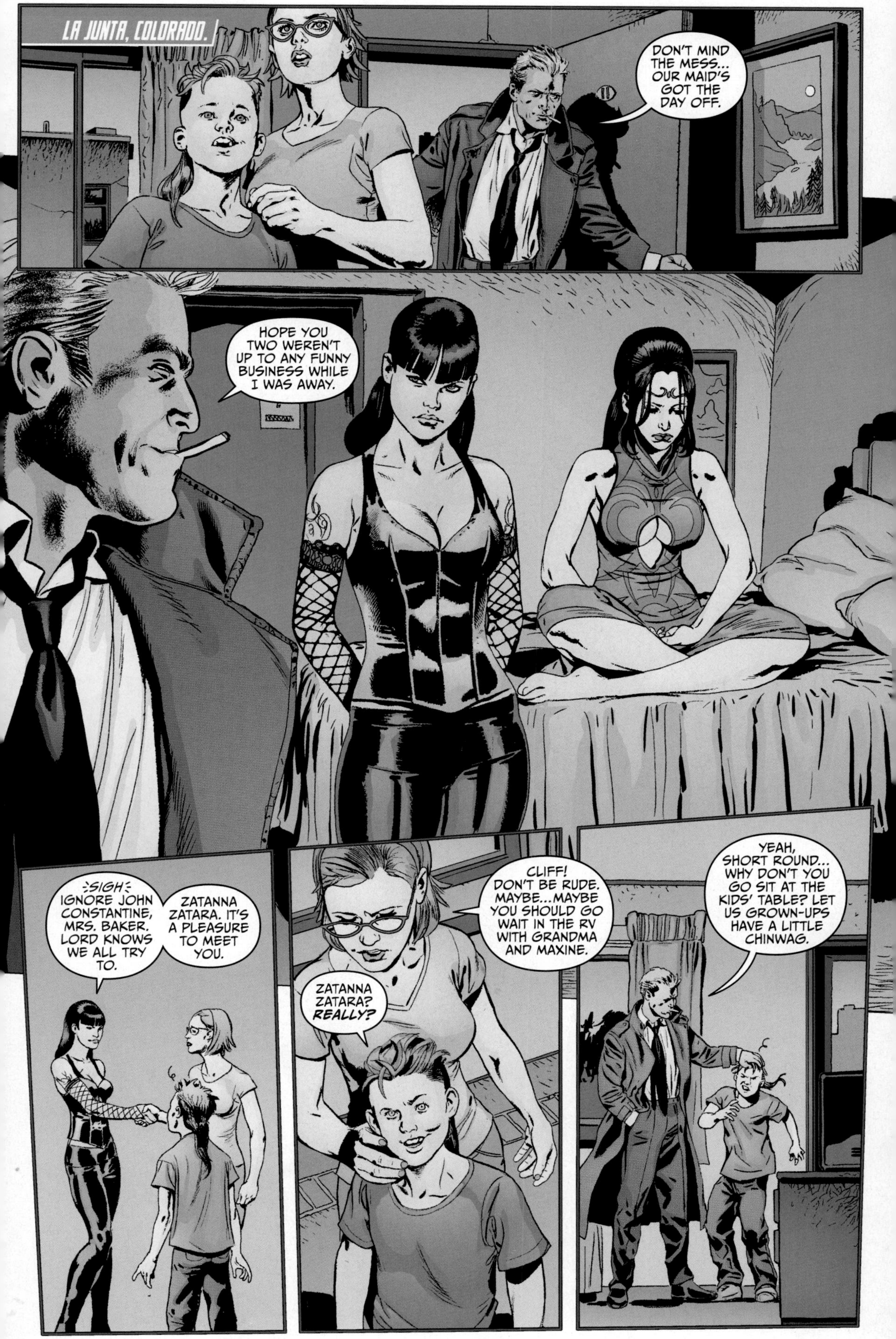
LA JUNTA, COLORADO.
DON'T MIND THE MESS... OUR MAID'S GOT THE DAY OFF.
HOPE YOU TWO WEREN'T UP TO ANY FUNNY BUSINESS WHILE I WAS AWAY.
SIGH
IGNORE JOHN CONSTANTINE, MRS. BAKER. LORD KNOWS WE ALL TRY TO.
ZATANNA ZATARA. IT'S A PLEASURE TO MEET YOU.
ZATANNA ZATARA? REALLY?
CLIFF! DON'T BE RUDE. MAYBE...MAYBE YOU SHOULD GO WAIT IN THE RV WITH GRANDMA AND MAXINE.
YEAH, SHORT ROUND... WHY DON'T YOU GO SIT AT THE KIDS' TABLE? LET US GROWN-UPS HAVE A LITTLE CHINWAG.

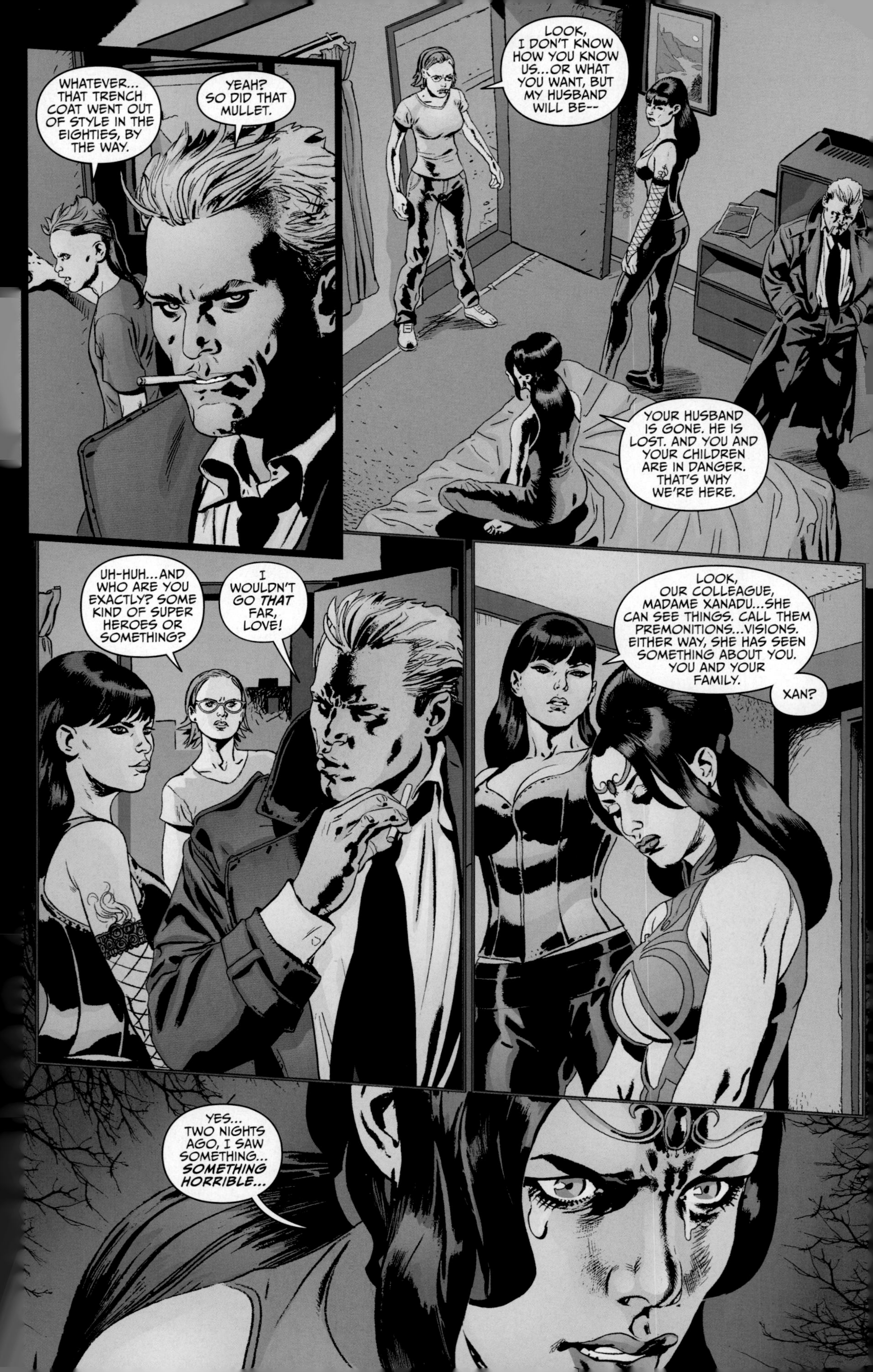
WHATEVER... THAT TRENCH COAT WENT OUT OF STYLE IN THE EIGHTIES, BY THE WAY.
YEAH? SO DID THAT MULLET.
LOOK, I DON'T KNOW HOW YOU KNOW US...OR WHAT YOU WANT, BUT MY HUSBAND WILL BE--
YOUR HUSBAND IS GONE. HE IS LOST. AND YOU AND YOUR CHILDREN ARE IN DANGER. THAT'S WHY WE'RE HERE.
UH-HUH...AND WHO ARE YOU EXACTLY? SOME KIND OF SUPER HEROES OR SOMETHING?
I WOULDN'T GO *THAT* FAR, LOVE!
LOOK, OUR COLLEAGUE, MADAME XANADU...SHE CAN SEE THINGS. CALL THEM PREMONITIONS...VISIONS. EITHER WAY, SHE HAS SEEN SOMETHING ABOUT YOU. YOU AND YOUR FAMILY.
XAN?
YES... TWO NIGHTS AGO, I SAW SOMETHING... ***SOMETHING HORRIBLE...***

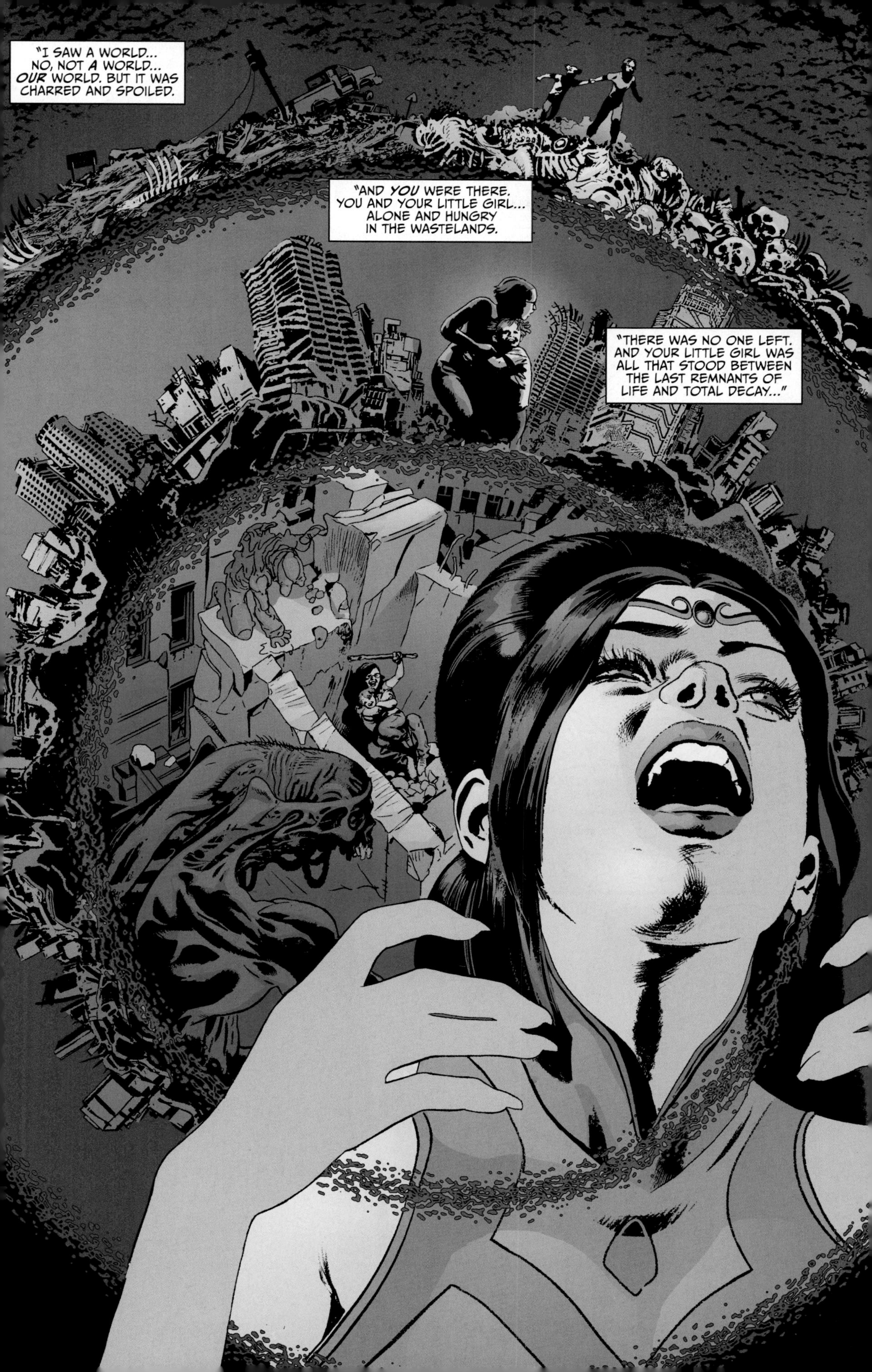
"I SAW A WORLD... NO, NOT *A* WORLD... *OUR* WORLD. BUT IT WAS CHARRED AND SPOILED.
"AND *YOU* WERE THERE. YOU AND YOUR LITTLE GIRL... ALONE AND HUNGRY IN THE WASTELANDS.
"THERE WAS NO ONE LEFT. AND YOUR LITTLE GIRL WAS ALL THAT STOOD BETWEEN THE LAST REMNANTS OF LIFE AND TOTAL DECAY..."

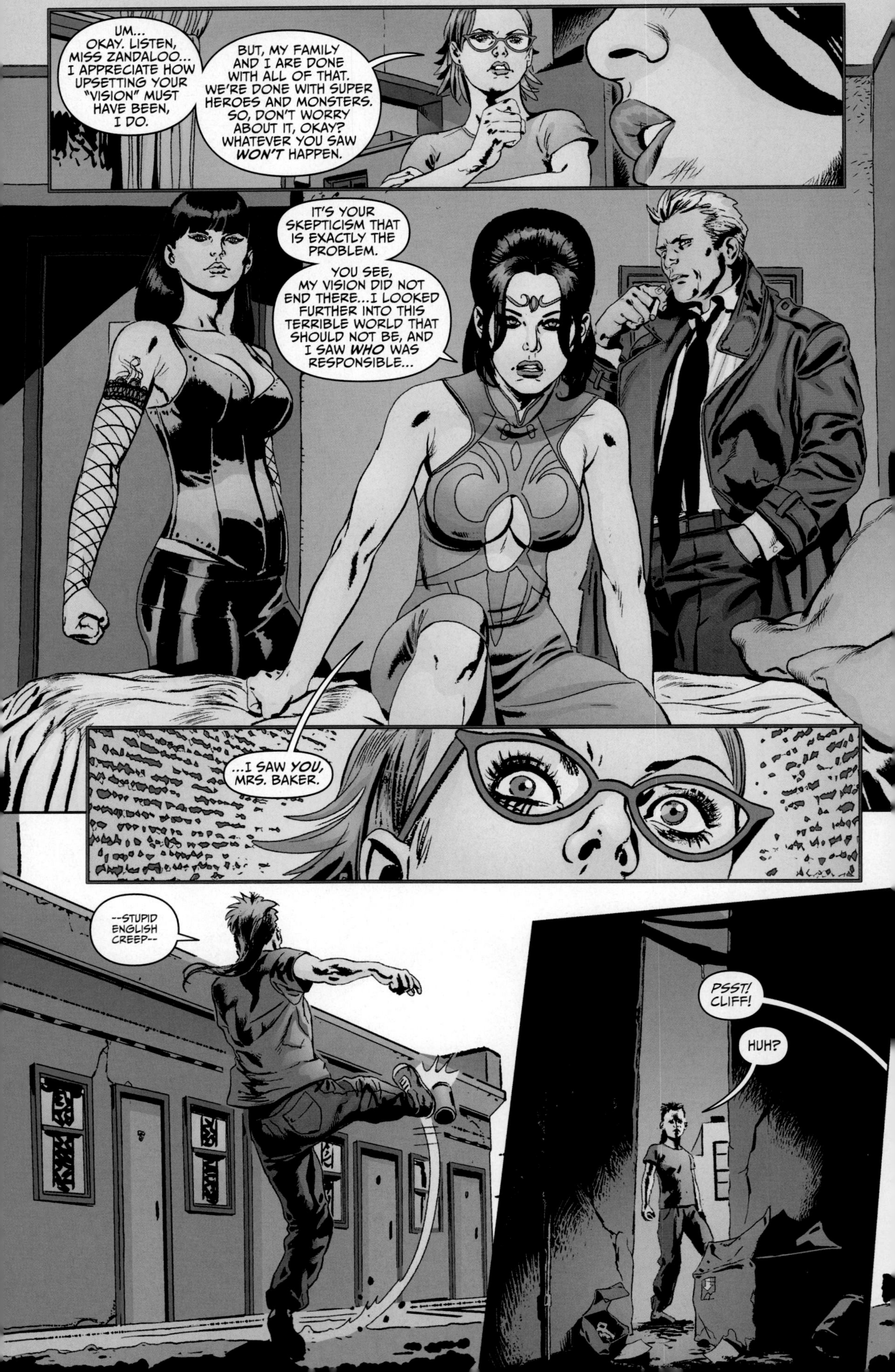
UM... OKAY. LISTEN, MISS ZANDALOO... I APPRECIATE HOW UPSETTING YOUR "VISION" MUST HAVE BEEN, I DO.
BUT, MY FAMILY AND I ARE DONE WITH ALL OF THAT. WE'RE DONE WITH SUPER HEROES AND MONSTERS. SO, DON'T WORRY ABOUT IT, OKAY? WHATEVER YOU SAW WON'T HAPPEN.
IT'S YOUR SKEPTICISM THAT IS EXACTLY THE PROBLEM.
YOU SEE, MY VISION DID NOT END THERE...I LOOKED FURTHER INTO THIS TERRIBLE WORLD THAT SHOULD NOT BE, AND I SAW WHO WAS RESPONSIBLE...
...I SAW YOU, MRS. BAKER.
--STUPID ENGLISH CREEP--
PSST! CLIFF!
HUH?

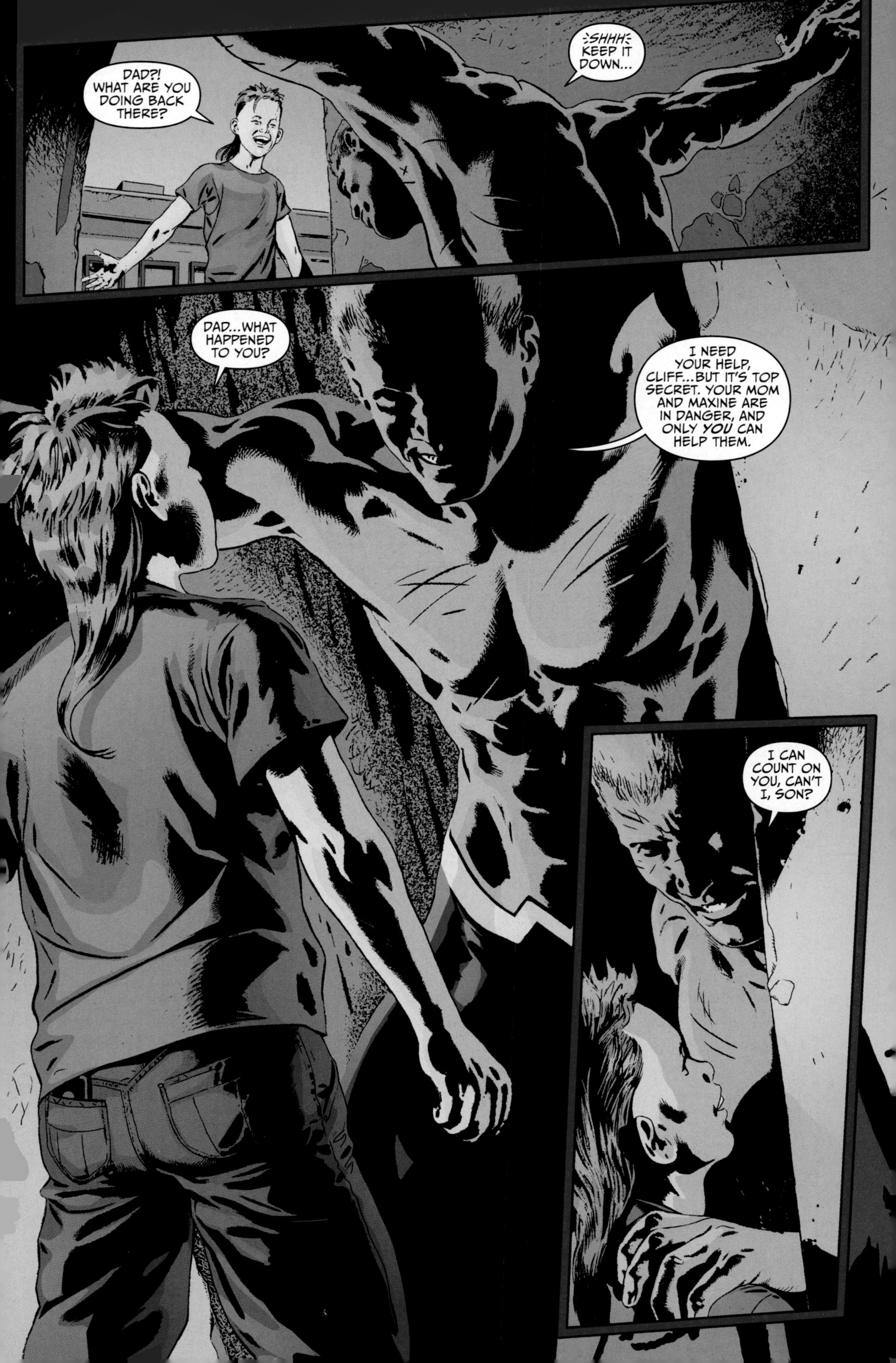
DAD?! WHAT ARE YOU DOING BACK THERE?
SHHH KEEP IT DOWN...
DAD...WHAT HAPPENED TO YOU?
I NEED YOUR HELP, CLIFF...BUT IT'S TOP SECRET. YOUR MOM AND MAXINE ARE IN DANGER, AND ONLY *YOU* CAN HELP THEM.
I CAN COUNT ON YOU, CAN'T I, SON?

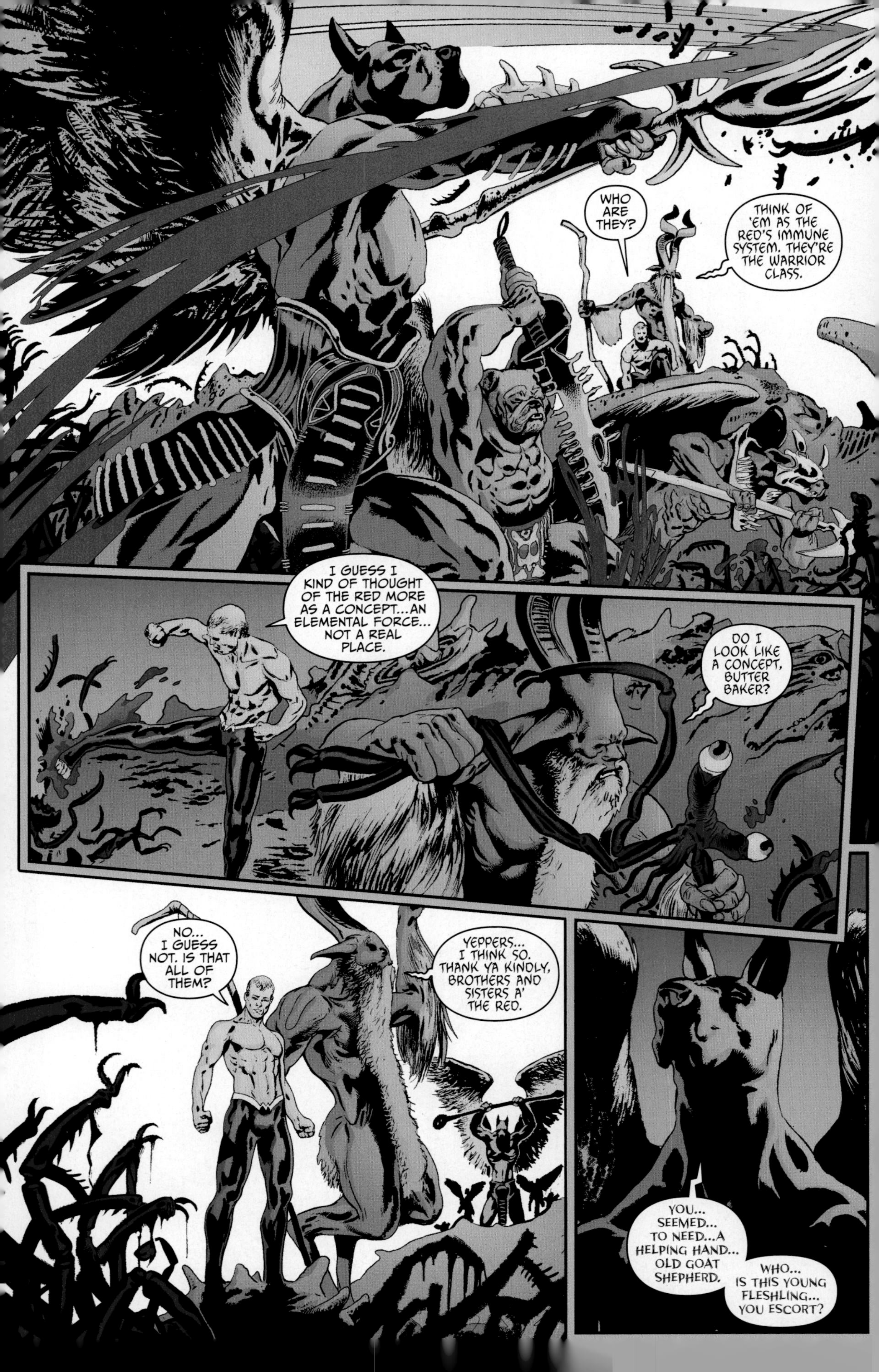
WHO ARE THEY?
THINK OF 'EM AS THE RED'S IMMUNE SYSTEM. THEY'RE THE WARRIOR CLASS.
I GUESS I KIND OF THOUGHT OF THE RED MORE AS A CONCEPT...AN ELEMENTAL FORCE... NOT A REAL PLACE.
DO I LOOK LIKE A CONCEPT, BUTTER BAKER?
NO... I GUESS NOT. IS THAT ALL OF THEM?
YEPPERS... I THINK SO. THANK YA KINDLY, BROTHERS AND SISTERS A' THE RED.
YOU... SEEMED... TO NEED...A HELPING HAND... OLD GOAT SHEPHERD.
WHO... IS THIS YOUNG FLESHLING... YOU ESCORT?

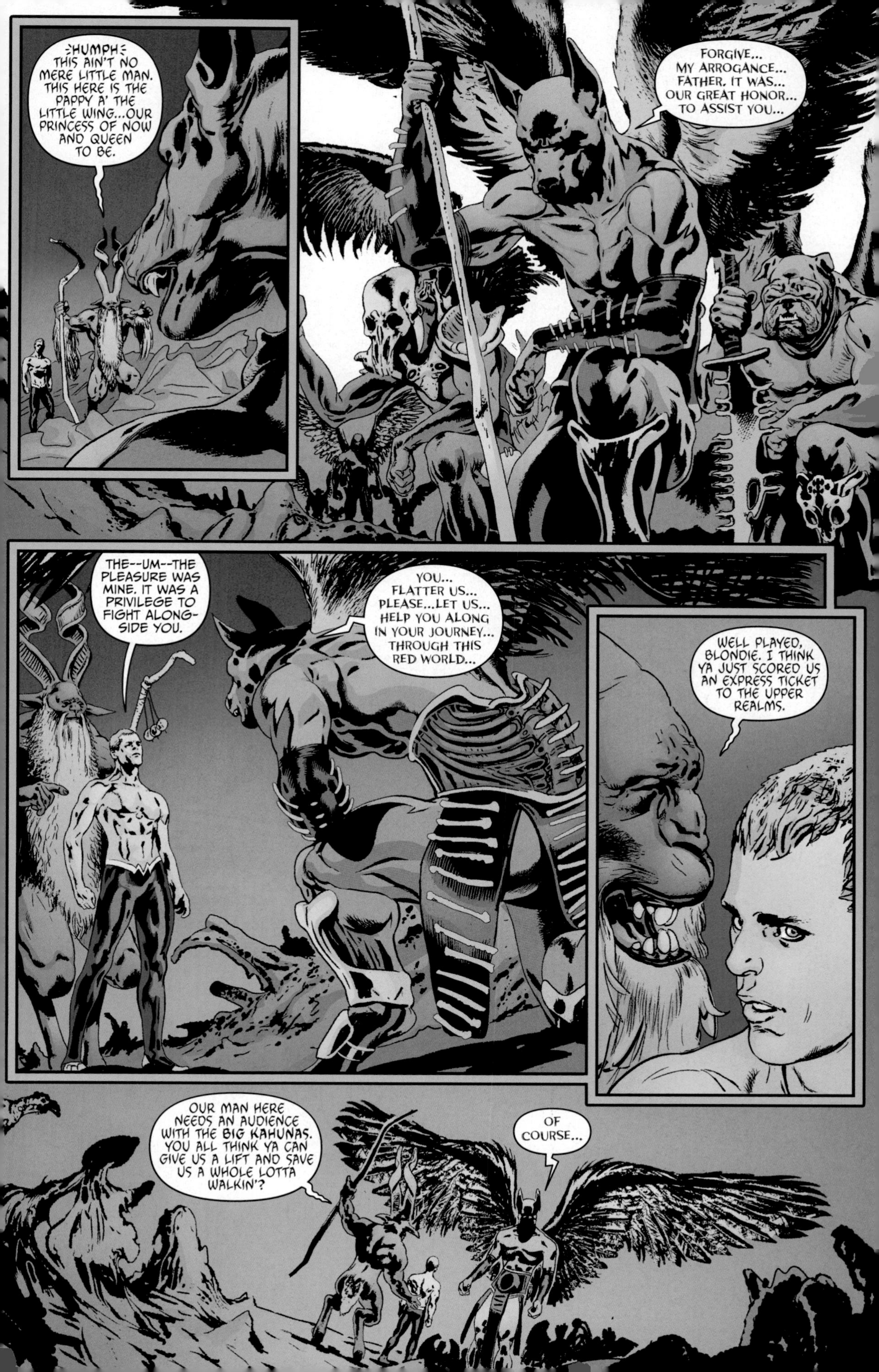

HUMPH
THIS AIN'T NO MERE LITTLE MAN. THIS HERE IS THE PAPPY A' THE LITTLE WING...OUR PRINCESS OF NOW AND QUEEN TO BE.
FORGIVE... MY ARROGANCE... FATHER. IT WAS... OUR GREAT HONOR... TO ASSIST YOU...
THE--UM--THE PLEASURE WAS MINE. IT WAS A PRIVILEGE TO FIGHT ALONG-SIDE YOU.
YOU... FLATTER US... PLEASE...LET US... HELP YOU ALONG IN YOUR JOURNEY... THROUGH THIS RED WORLD...
WELL PLAYED, BLONDIE. I THINK YA JUST SCORED US AN EXPRESS TICKET TO THE UPPER REALMS.
OUR MAN HERE NEEDS AN AUDIENCE WITH THE BIG KAHUNAS. YOU ALL THINK YA CAN GIVE US A LIFT AND SAVE US A WHOLE LOTTA WALKIN'?
OF COURSE...

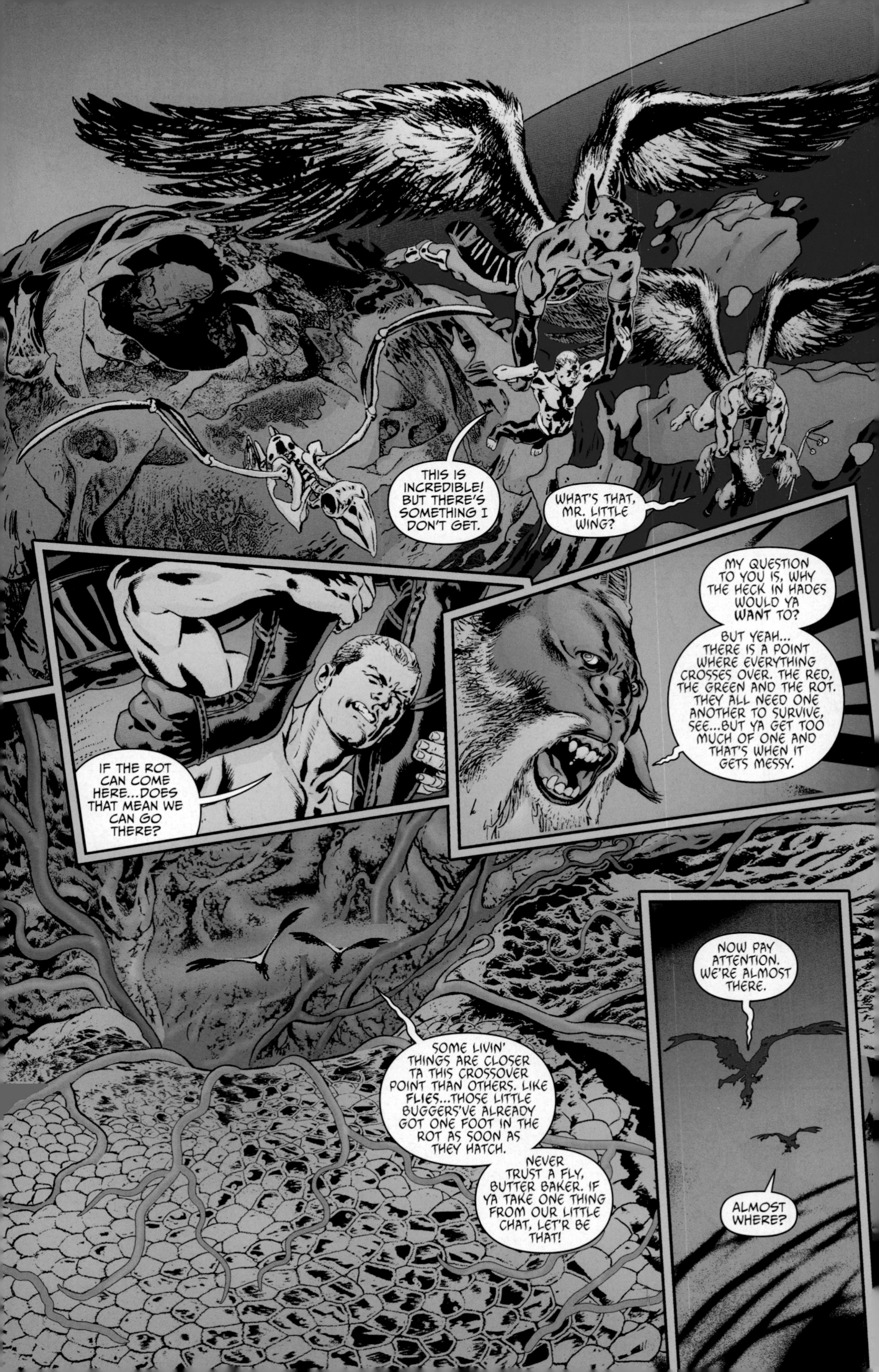
THIS IS INCREDIBLE! BUT THERE'S SOMETHING I DON'T GET.
WHAT'S THAT, MR. LITTLE WING?
IF THE ROT CAN COME HERE...DOES THAT MEAN WE CAN GO THERE?
MY QUESTION TO YOU IS, WHY THE HECK IN HADES WOULD YA WANT TO?
BUT YEAH... THERE IS A POINT WHERE EVERYTHING CROSSES OVER. THE RED, THE GREEN AND THE ROT. THEY ALL NEED ONE ANOTHER TO SURVIVE, SEE...BUT YA GET TOO MUCH OF ONE AND THAT'S WHEN IT GETS MESSY.
SOME LIVIN' THINGS ARE CLOSER TA THIS CROSSOVER POINT THAN OTHERS. LIKE FLIES...THOSE LITTLE BUGGERS'VE ALREADY GOT ONE FOOT IN THE ROT AS SOON AS THEY HATCH.
NEVER TRUST A FLY, BUTTER BAKER. IF YA TAKE ONE THING FROM OUR LITTLE CHAT, LET'R BE THAT!
NOW PAY ATTENTION. WE'RE ALMOST THERE.
ALMOST WHERE?

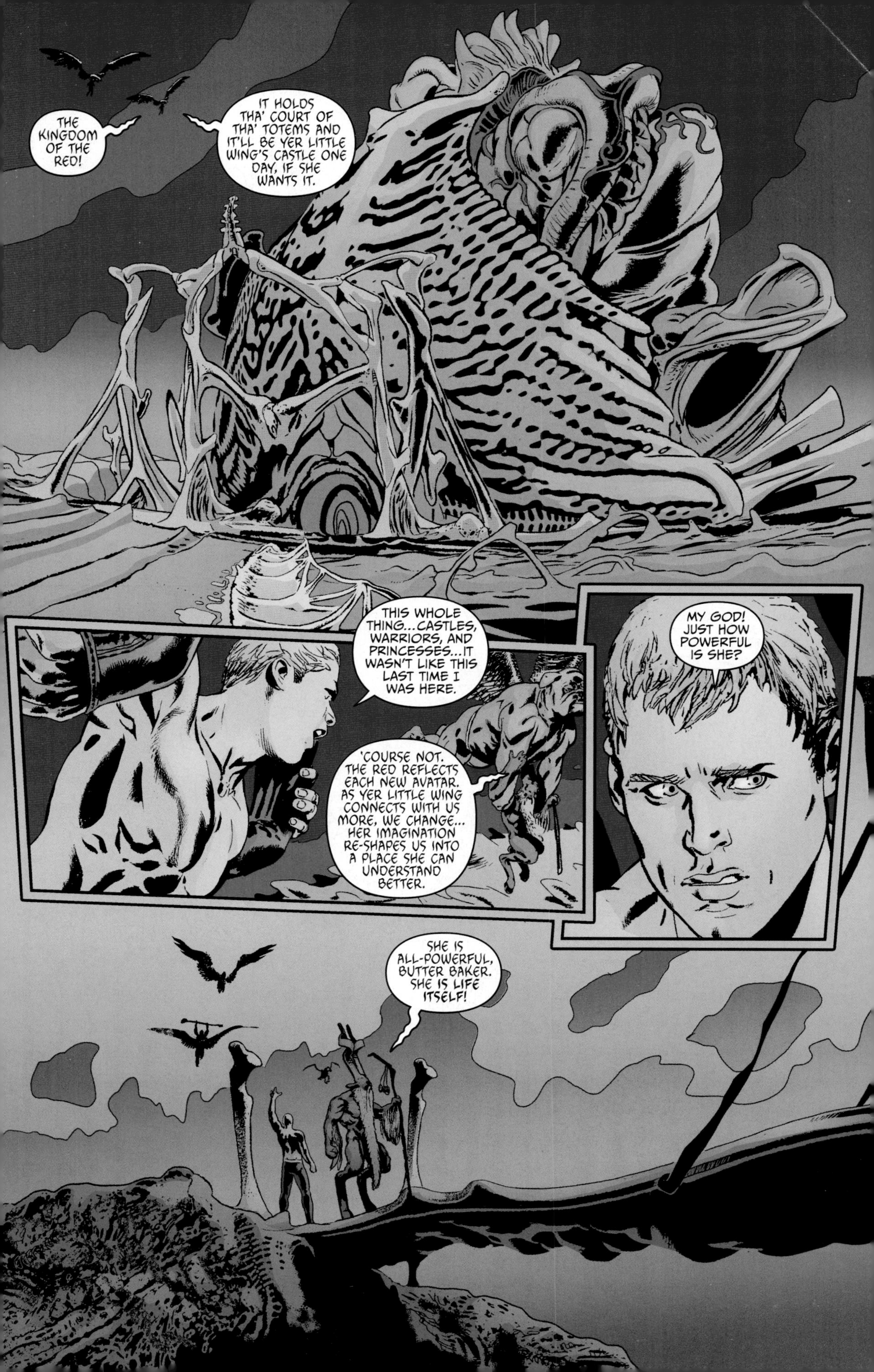
THE KINGDOM OF THE RED!
IT HOLDS THA' COURT OF THA' TOTEMS AND IT'LL BE YER LITTLE WING'S CASTLE ONE DAY, IF SHE WANTS IT.
THIS WHOLE THING...CASTLES, WARRIORS, AND PRINCESSES...IT WASN'T LIKE THIS LAST TIME I WAS HERE.
'COURSE NOT. THE RED REFLECTS EACH NEW AVATAR. AS YER LITTLE WING CONNECTS WITH US MORE, WE CHANGE... HER IMAGINATION RE-SHAPES US INTO A PLACE SHE CAN UNDERSTAND BETTER.
MY GOD! JUST HOW POWERFUL IS SHE?
SHE IS ALL-POWERFUL, BUTTER BAKER. SHE IS LIFE ITSELF!

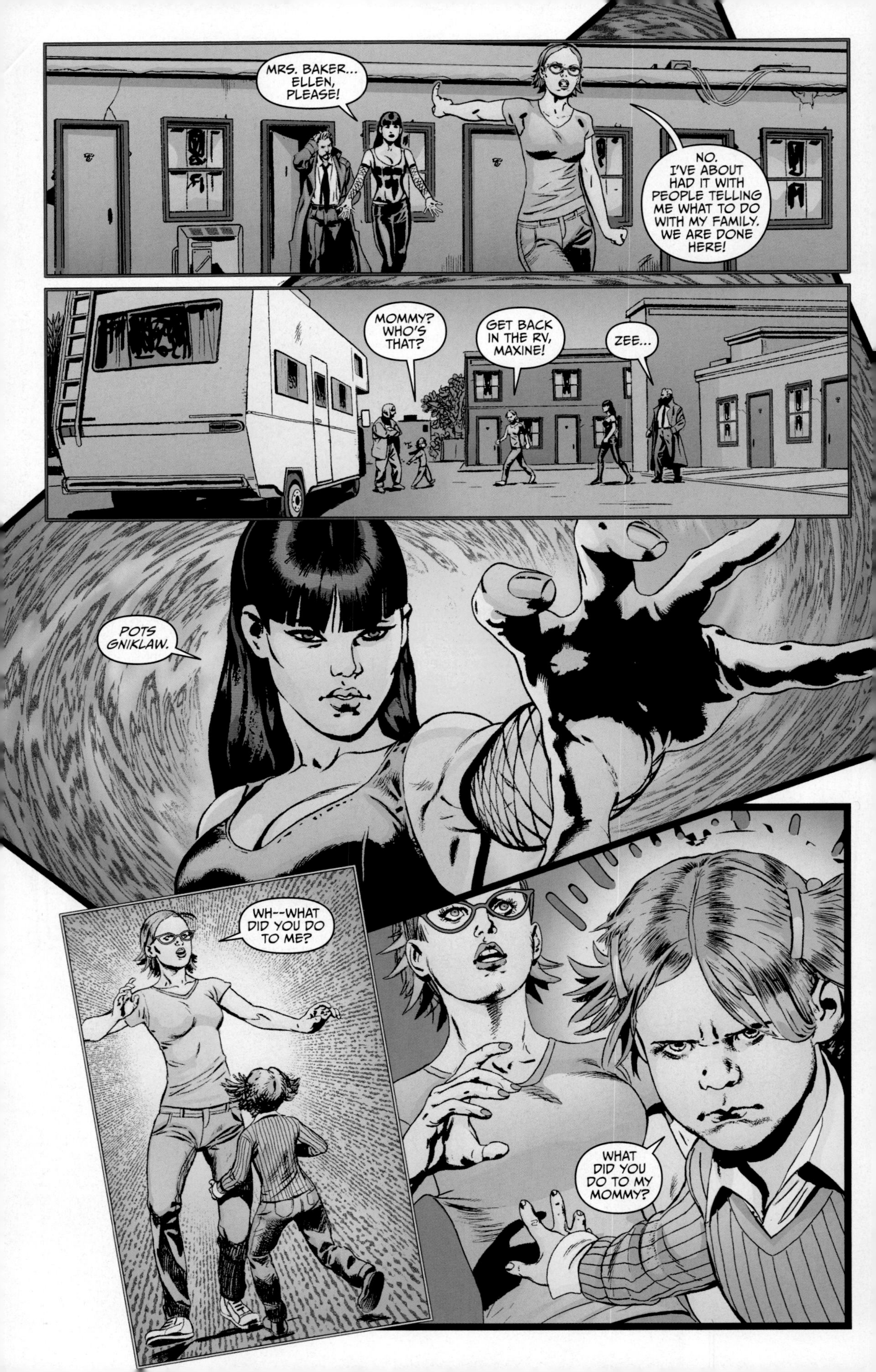
MRS. BAKER... ELLEN, PLEASE!
NO. I'VE ABOUT HAD IT WITH PEOPLE TELLING ME WHAT TO DO WITH MY FAMILY. WE ARE DONE HERE!
MOMMY? WHO'S THAT?
GET BACK IN THE RV, MAXINE!
ZEE...
POTS GNIKLAW.
WH--WHAT DID YOU DO TO ME?
WHAT DID YOU DO TO MY MOMMY?

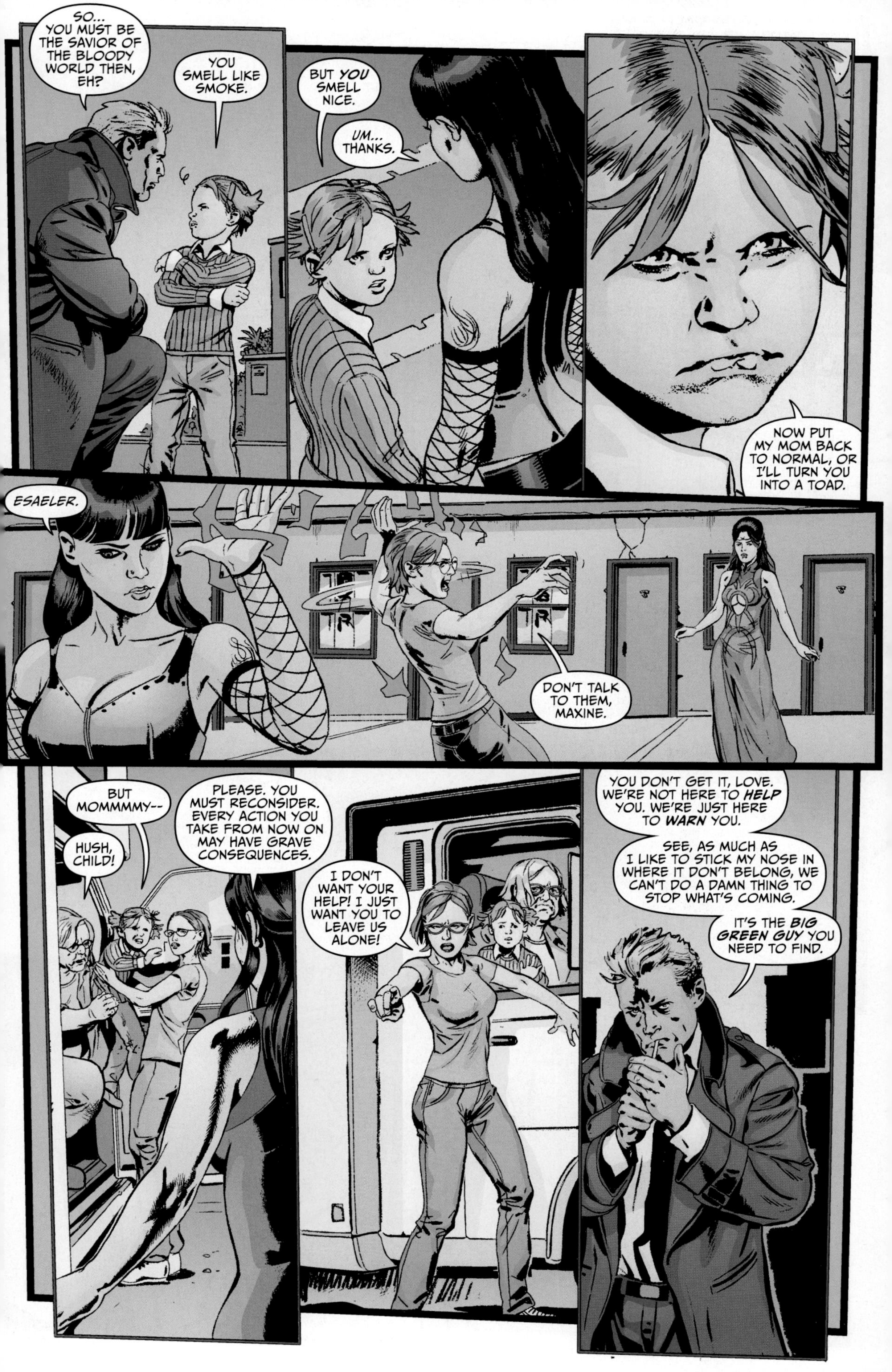
SO... YOU MUST BE THE SAVIOR OF THE BLOODY WORLD THEN, EH?
YOU SMELL LIKE SMOKE.
BUT *YOU* SMELL NICE.
UM... THANKS.
NOW PUT MY MOM BACK TO NORMAL, OR I'LL TURN YOU INTO A TOAD.
ESAELER.
DON'T TALK TO THEM, MAXINE.
BUT MOMMMMY--
HUSH, CHILD!
PLEASE. YOU MUST RECONSIDER. EVERY ACTION YOU TAKE FROM NOW ON MAY HAVE GRAVE CONSEQUENCES.
I DON'T WANT YOUR HELP! I JUST WANT YOU TO LEAVE US ALONE!
YOU DON'T GET IT, LOVE. WE'RE NOT HERE TO ***HELP*** YOU. WE'RE JUST HERE TO ***WARN*** YOU.
SEE, AS MUCH AS I LIKE TO STICK MY NOSE IN WHERE IT DON'T BELONG, WE CAN'T DO A DAMN THING TO STOP WHAT'S COMING.
IT'S THE ***BIG GREEN GUY*** YOU NEED TO FIND.

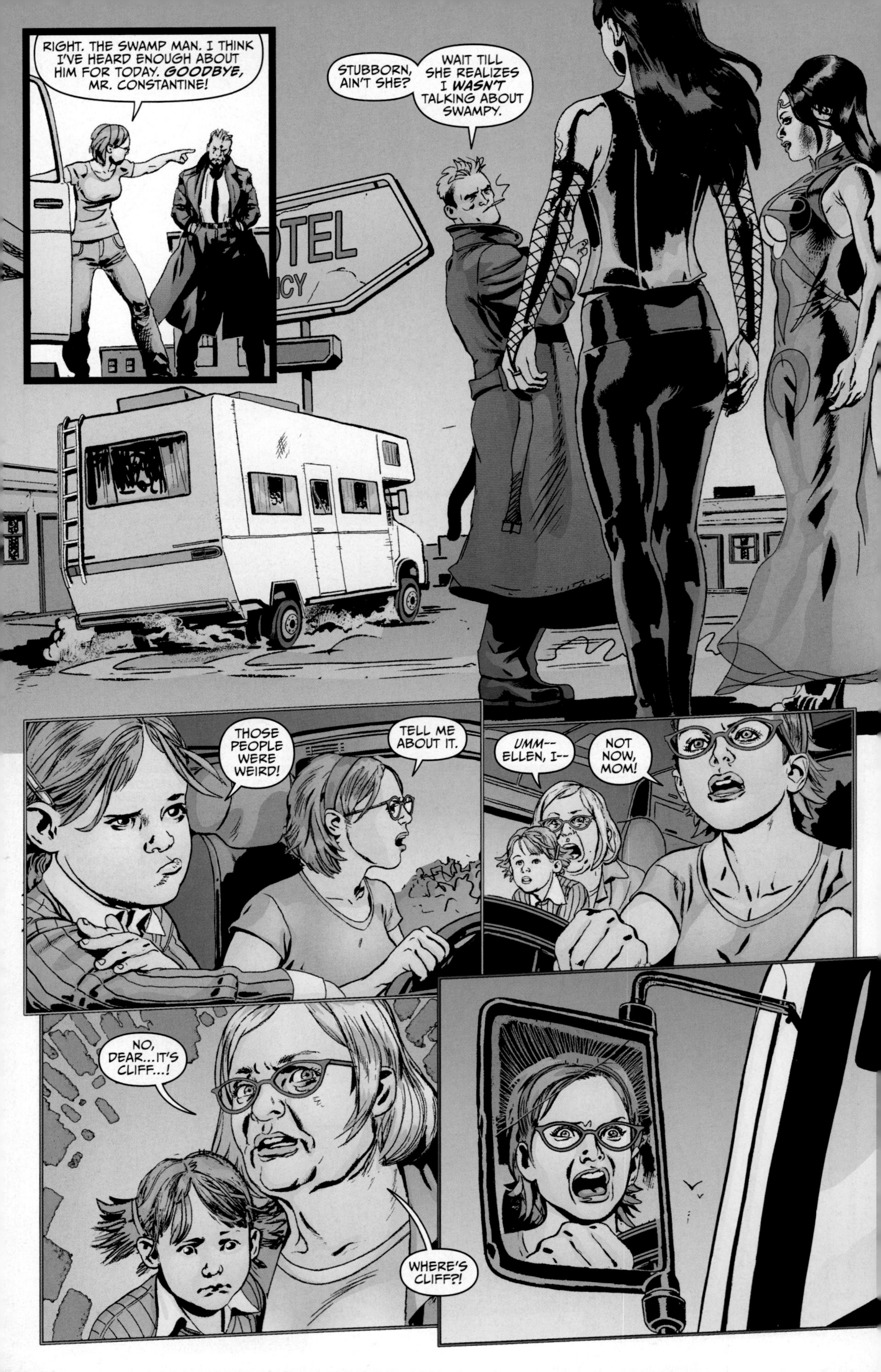
RIGHT. THE SWAMP MAN. I THINK I'VE HEARD ENOUGH ABOUT HIM FOR TODAY. *GOODBYE,* MR. CONSTANTINE!
STUBBORN, AIN'T SHE?
WAIT TILL SHE REALIZES I *WASN'T* TALKING ABOUT SWAMPY.
TEL
THOSE PEOPLE WERE WEIRD!
TELL ME ABOUT IT.
UMM-- ELLEN, I--
NOT NOW, MOM!
NO, DEAR...IT'S CLIFF...!
WHERE'S CLIFF?!

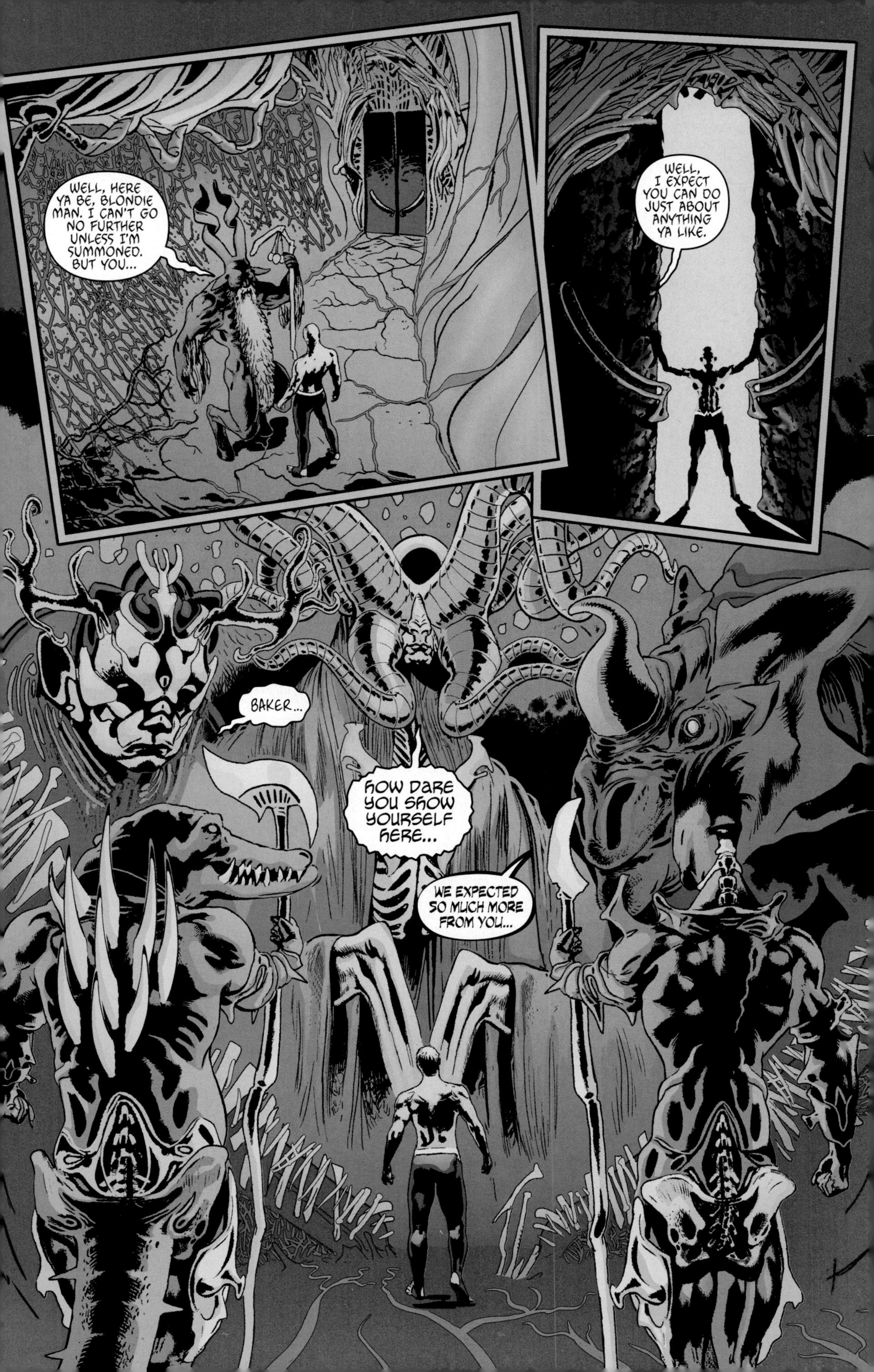
WELL, HERE YA BE, BLONDIE MAN. I CAN'T GO NO FURTHER UNLESS I'M SUMMONED. BUT YOU...
WELL, I EXPECT YOU CAN DO JUST ABOUT ANYTHING YA LIKE.
BAKER...
HOW DARE YOU SHOW YOURSELF HERE...
WE EXPECTED SO MUCH MORE FROM YOU...

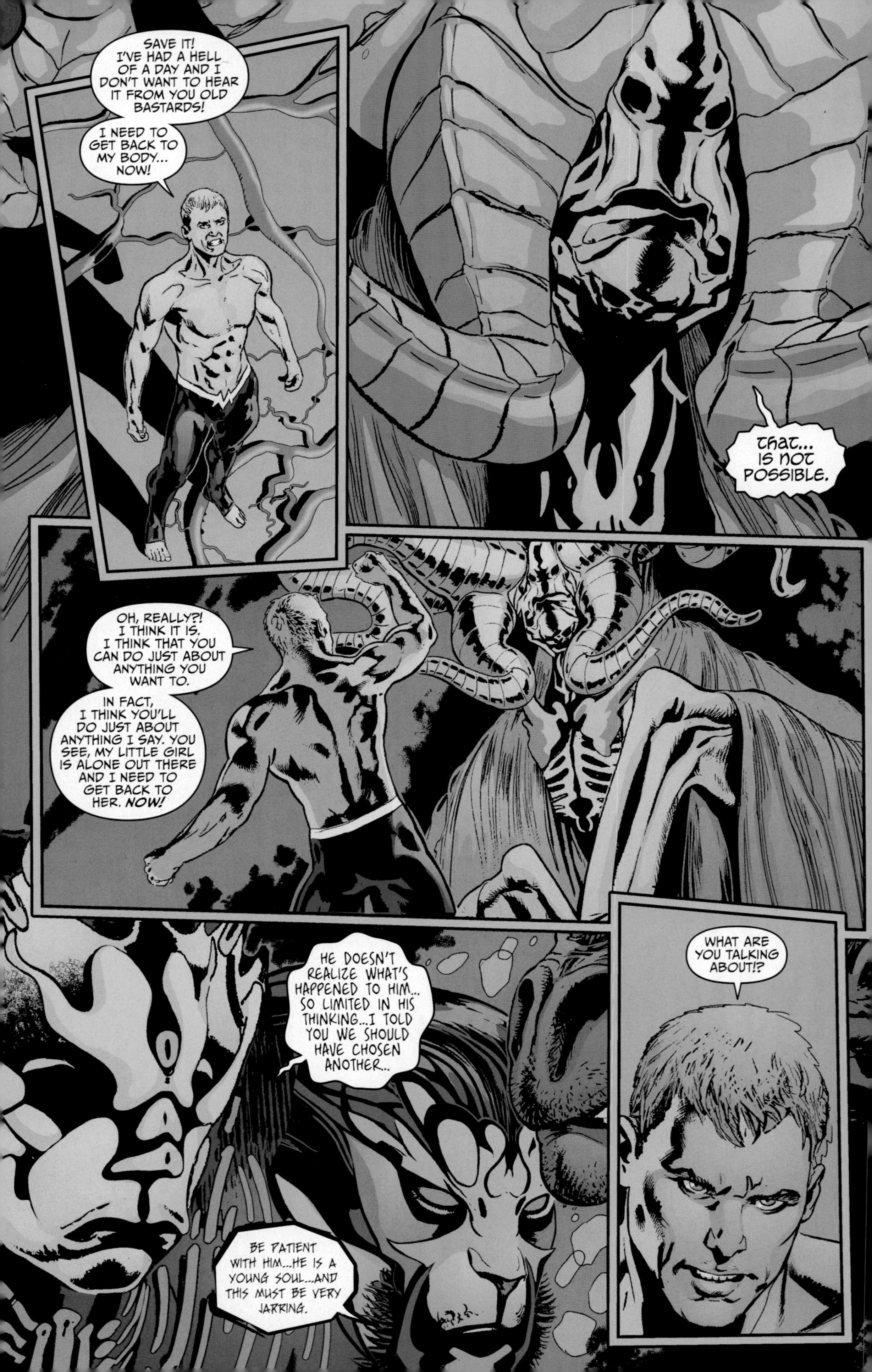
SAVE IT! I'VE HAD A HELL OF A DAY AND I DON'T WANT TO HEAR IT FROM YOU OLD BASTARDS!
I NEED TO GET BACK TO MY BODY... NOW!
THAT... IS NOT POSSIBLE.
OH, REALLY?! I THINK IT IS. I THINK THAT YOU CAN DO JUST ABOUT ANYTHING YOU WANT TO.
IN FACT, I THINK YOU'LL DO JUST ABOUT ANYTHING I SAY. YOU SEE, MY LITTLE GIRL IS ALONE OUT THERE AND I NEED TO GET BACK TO HER. NOW!
HE DOESN'T REALIZE WHAT'S HAPPENED TO HIM... SO LIMITED IN HIS THINKING...I TOLD YOU WE SHOULD HAVE CHOSEN ANOTHER...
WHAT ARE YOU TALKING ABOUT!?
BE PATIENT WITH HIM...HE IS A YOUNG SOUL...AND THIS MUST BE VERY JARRING.

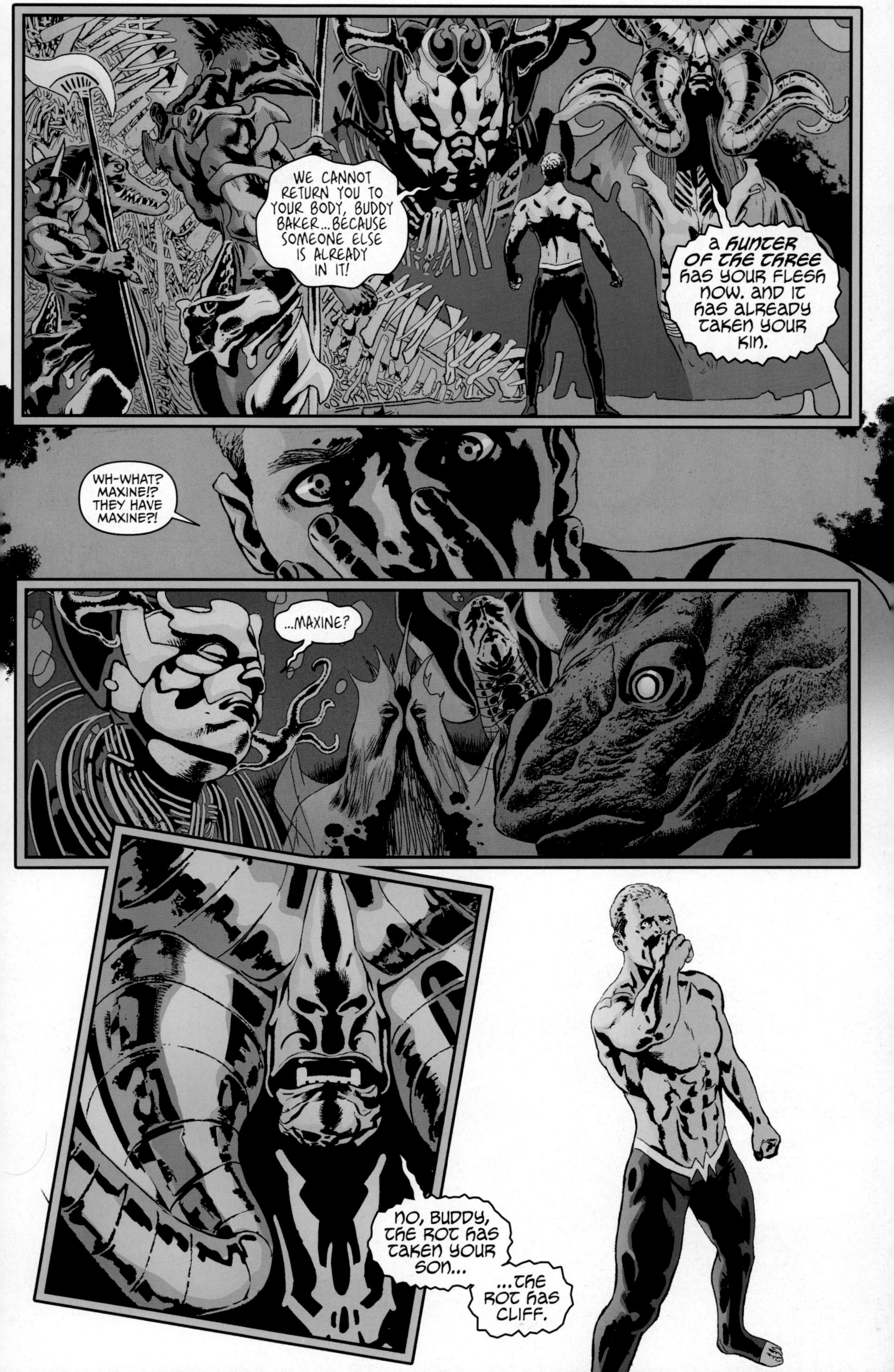
WE CANNOT RETURN YOU TO YOUR BODY, BUDDY BAKER...BECAUSE SOMEONE ELSE IS ALREADY IN IT!
A HUNTER OF THE THREE HAS YOUR FLESH NOW. AND IT HAS ALREADY TAKEN YOUR KIN.
WH-WHAT? MAXINE!? THEY HAVE MAXINE?!
...MAXINE?
NO, BUDDY, THE ROT HAS TAKEN YOUR SON...
...THE ROT HAS CLIFF.

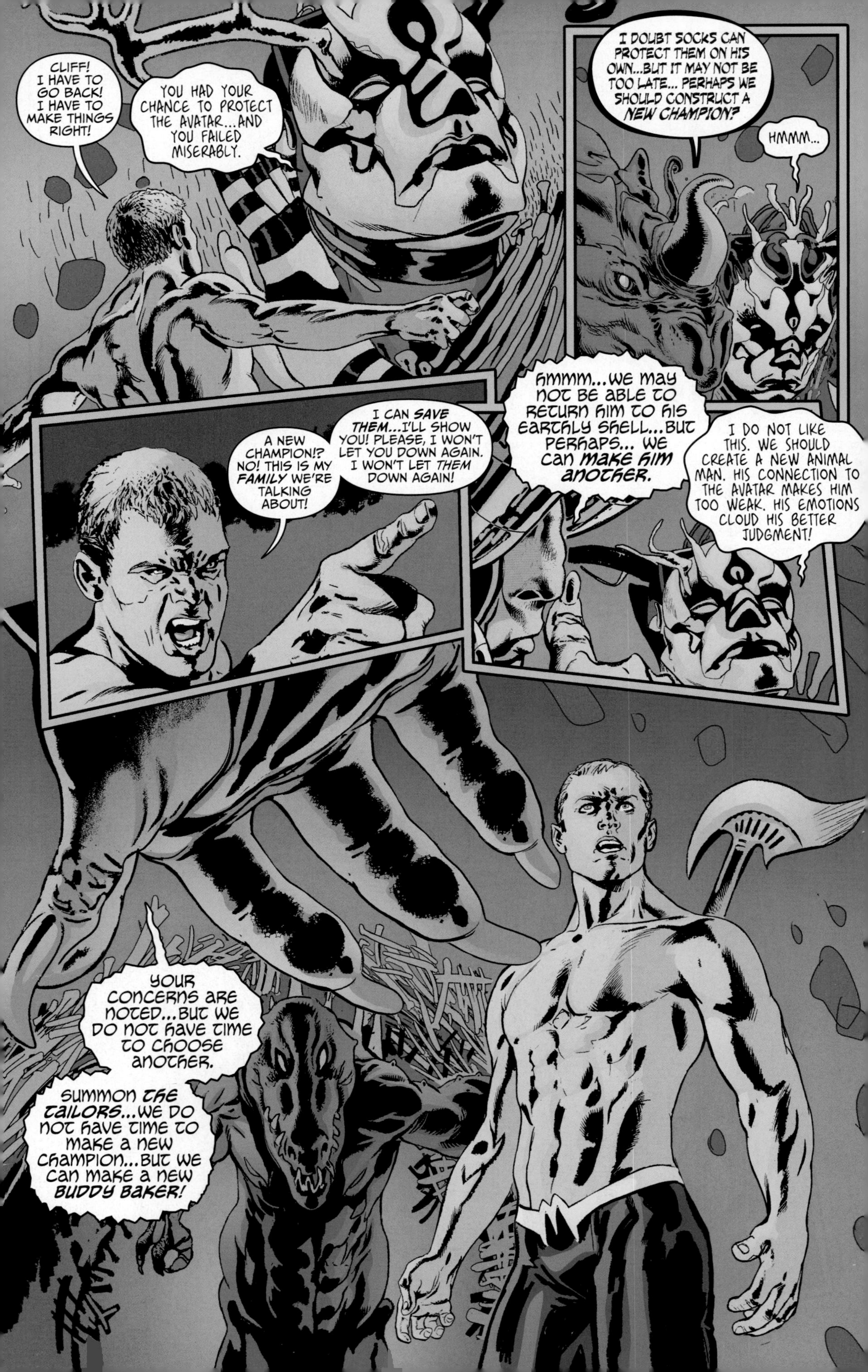
CLIFF! I HAVE TO GO BACK! I HAVE TO MAKE THINGS RIGHT!
YOU HAD YOUR CHANCE TO PROTECT THE AVATAR...AND YOU FAILED MISERABLY.
I DOUBT SOCKS CAN PROTECT THEM ON HIS OWN...BUT IT MAY NOT BE TOO LATE... PERHAPS WE SHOULD CONSTRUCT A NEW CHAMPION?
HMMM...
A NEW CHAMPION!? NO! THIS IS MY FAMILY WE'RE TALKING ABOUT!
I CAN SAVE THEM...I'LL SHOW YOU! PLEASE, I WON'T LET YOU DOWN AGAIN. I WON'T LET THEM DOWN AGAIN!
HMMM...WE MAY NOT BE ABLE TO RETURN HIM TO HIS EARTHLY SHELL...BUT PERHAPS... WE CAN MAKE HIM ANOTHER.
I DO NOT LIKE THIS. WE SHOULD CREATE A NEW ANIMAL MAN. HIS CONNECTION TO THE AVATAR MAKES HIM TOO WEAK. HIS EMOTIONS CLOUD HIS BETTER JUDGMENT!
YOUR CONCERNS ARE NOTED...BUT WE DO NOT HAVE TIME TO CHOOSE ANOTHER.
SUMMON THE TAILORS...WE DO NOT HAVE TIME TO MAKE A NEW CHAMPION...BUT WE CAN MAKE A NEW BUDDY BAKER!

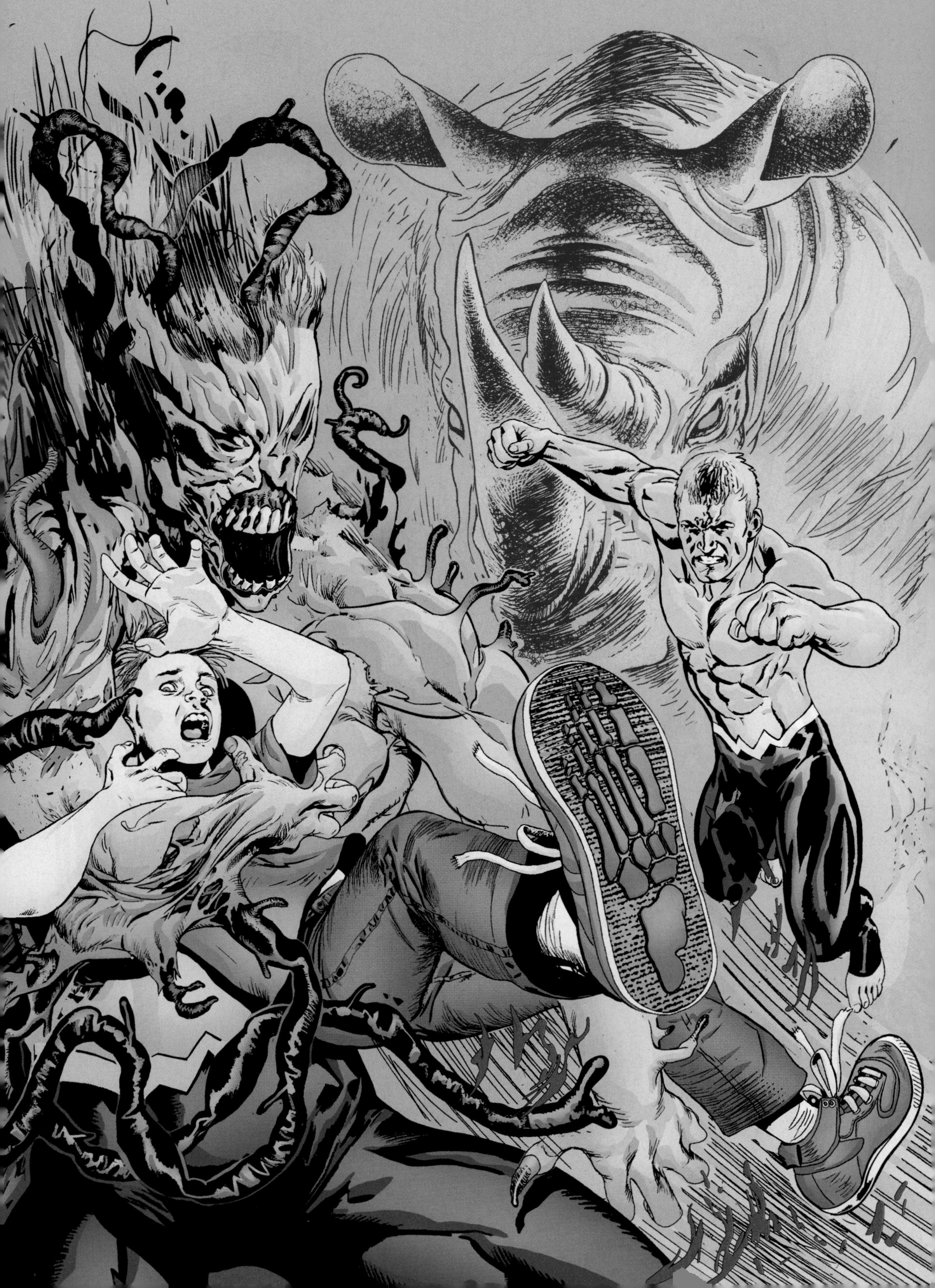

JEFF LEMIRE writer ALBERTO PONTICELLI penciller WAYNE FAUCHER inker
cover by STEVE PUGH with LOVERN KINDZIERSKI

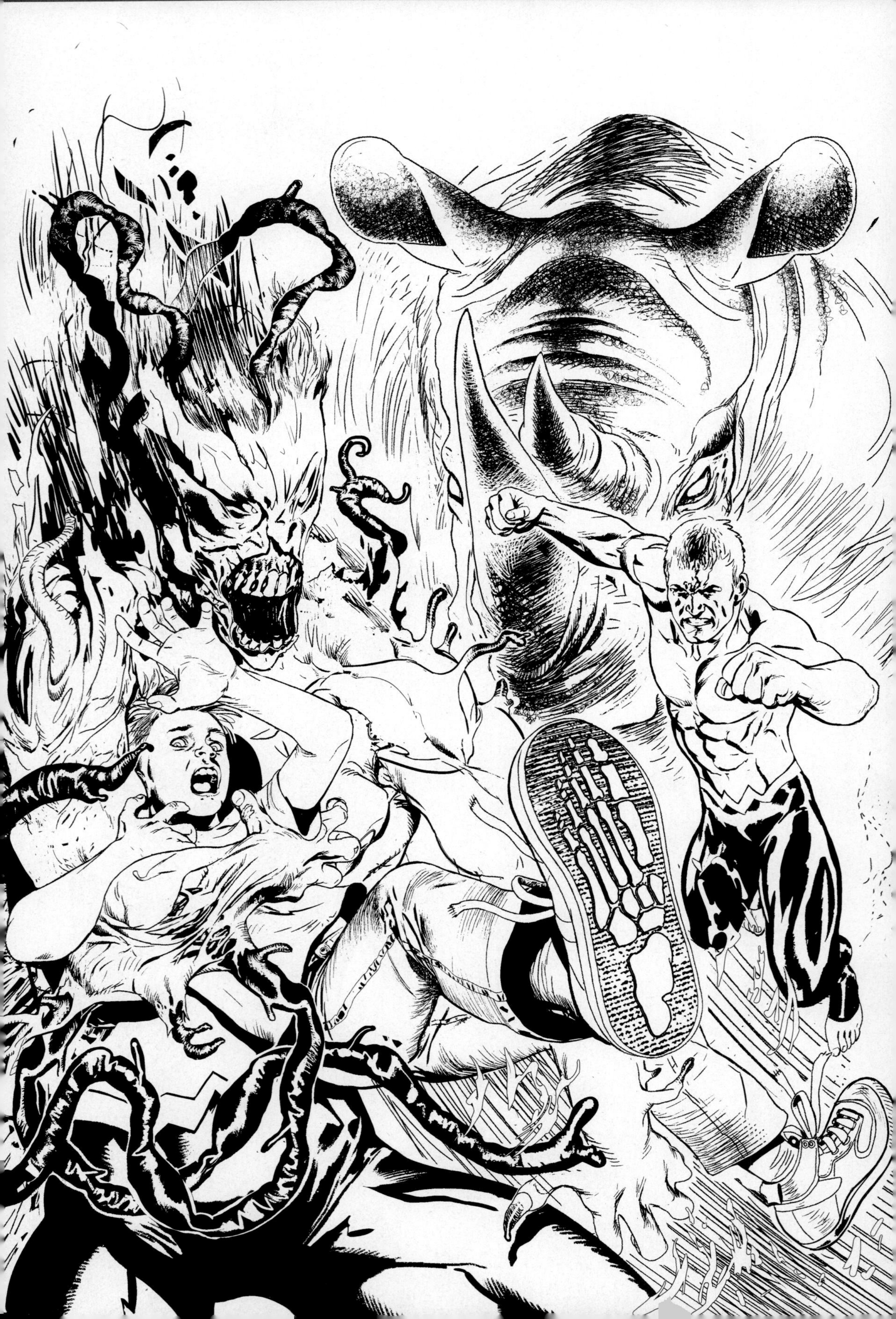

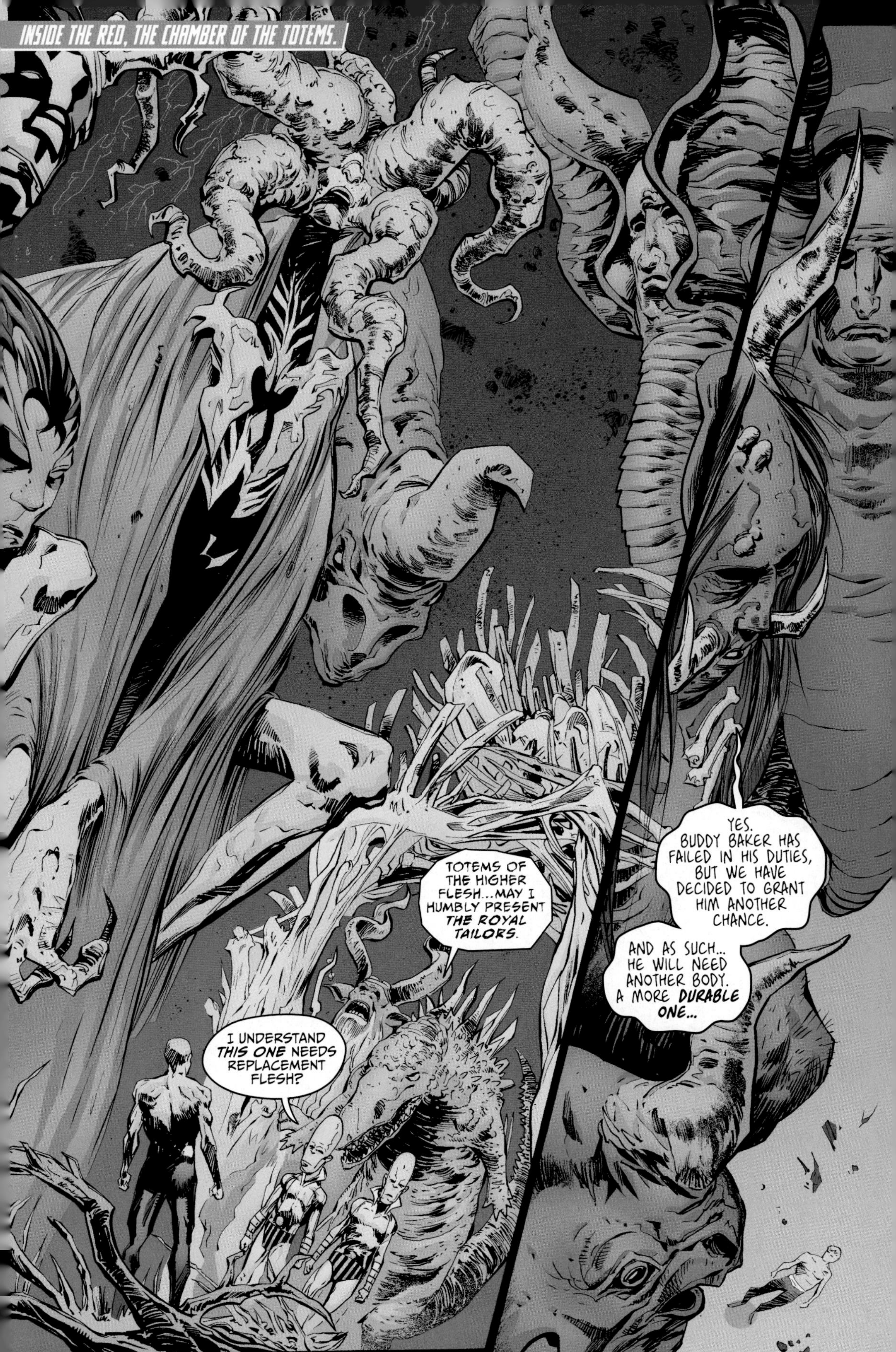
INSIDE THE RED, THE CHAMBER OF THE TOTEMS.
TOTEMS OF THE HIGHER FLESH...MAY I HUMBLY PRESENT THE ROYAL TAILORS.
I UNDERSTAND THIS ONE NEEDS REPLACEMENT FLESH?
YES. BUDDY BAKER HAS FAILED IN HIS DUTIES, BUT WE HAVE DECIDED TO GRANT HIM ANOTHER CHANCE.
AND AS SUCH... HE WILL NEED ANOTHER BODY. A MORE DURABLE ONE...

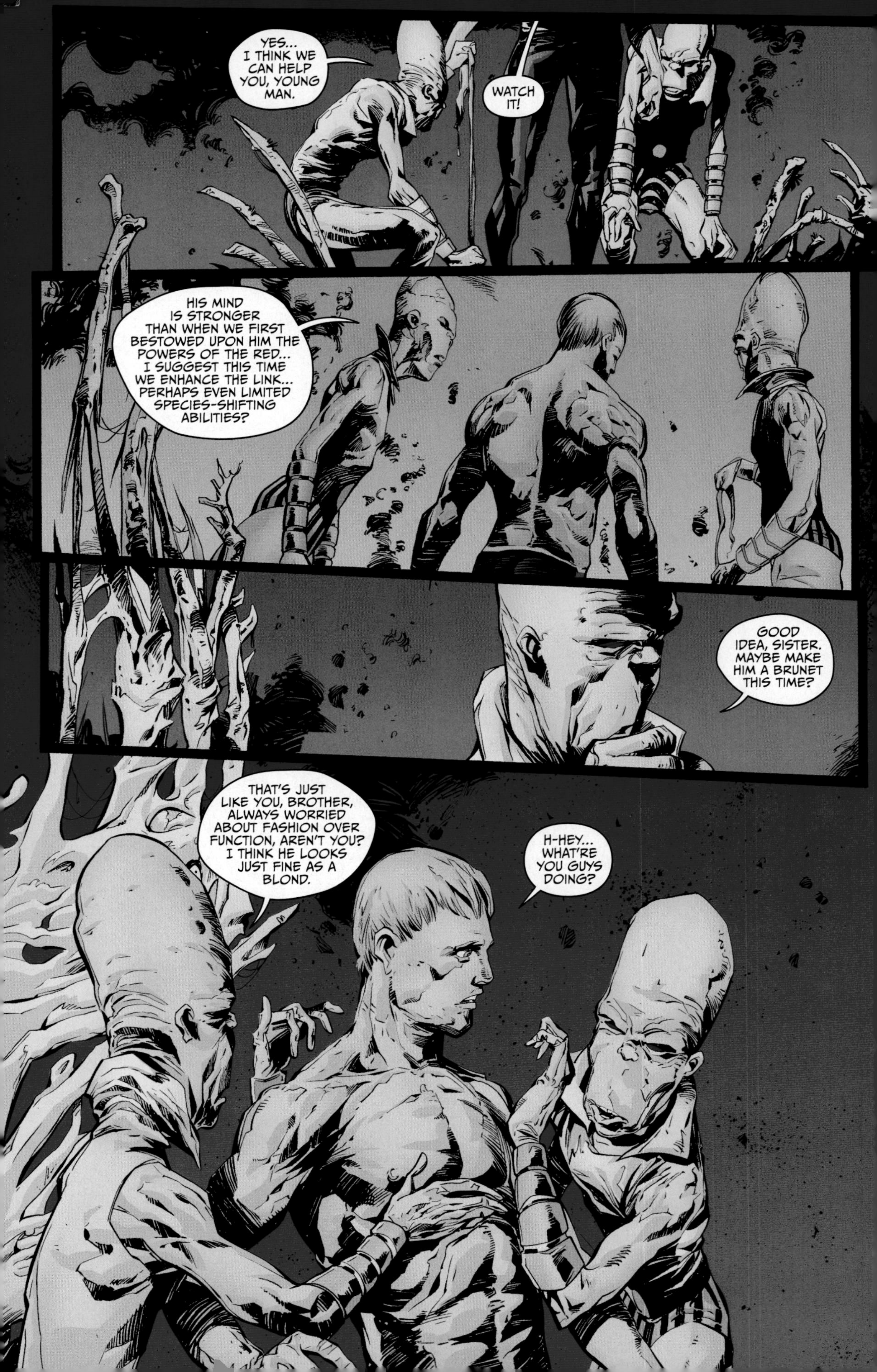
YES... I THINK WE CAN HELP YOU, YOUNG MAN.
WATCH IT!
HIS MIND IS STRONGER THAN WHEN WE FIRST BESTOWED UPON HIM THE POWERS OF THE RED... I SUGGEST THIS TIME WE ENHANCE THE LINK... PERHAPS EVEN LIMITED SPECIES-SHIFTING ABILITIES?
GOOD IDEA, SISTER. MAYBE MAKE HIM A BRUNET THIS TIME?
THAT'S JUST LIKE YOU, BROTHER, ALWAYS WORRIED ABOUT FASHION OVER FUNCTION, AREN'T YOU? I THINK HE LOOKS JUST FINE AS A BLOND.
H-HEY... WHAT'RE YOU GUYS DOING?

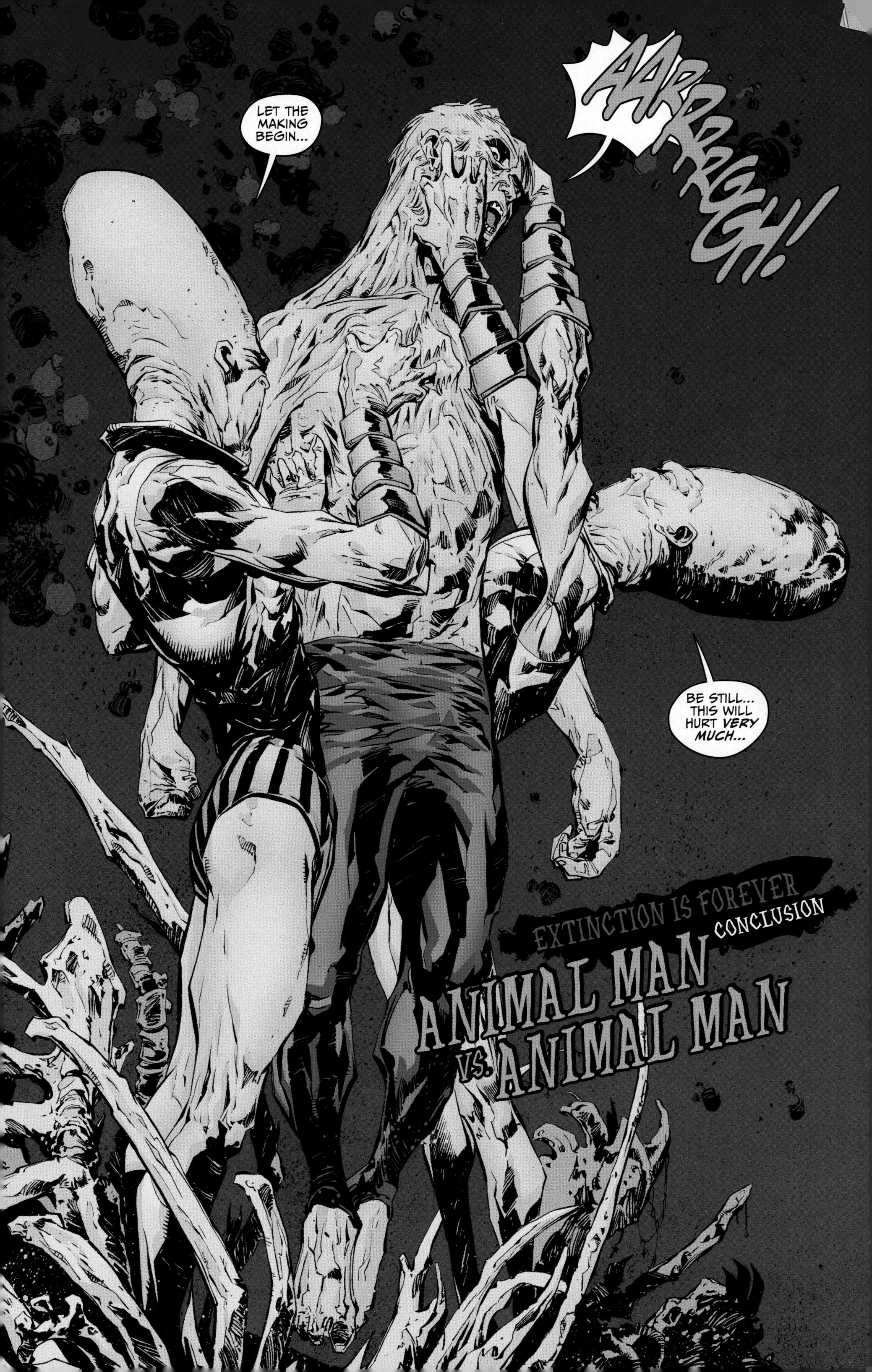
LET THE MAKING BEGIN...
AARRRGH!
BE STILL... THIS WILL HURT VERY MUCH...
EXTINCTION IS FOREVER CONCLUSION
ANIMAL MAN VS. ANIMAL MAN

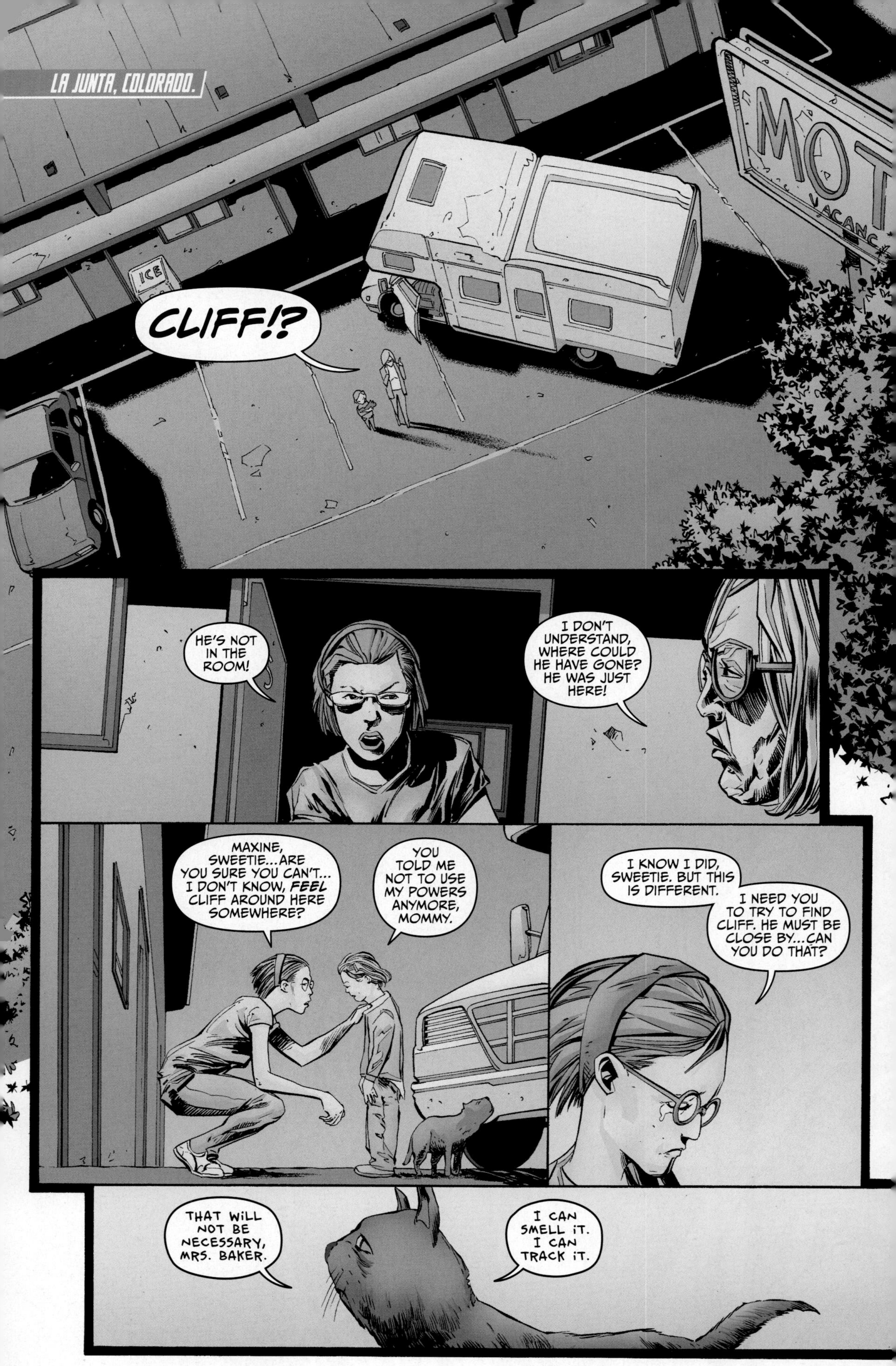
LA JUNTA, COLORADO.
ICE
MOT
VACANC
CLIFF!?
HE'S NOT IN THE ROOM!
I DON'T UNDERSTAND, WHERE COULD HE HAVE GONE? HE WAS JUST HERE!
MAXINE, SWEETIE...ARE YOU SURE YOU CAN'T... I DON'T KNOW, FEEL CLIFF AROUND HERE SOMEWHERE?
YOU TOLD ME NOT TO USE MY POWERS ANYMORE, MOMMY.
I KNOW I DID, SWEETIE. BUT THIS IS DIFFERENT.
I NEED YOU TO TRY TO FIND CLIFF. HE MUST BE CLOSE BY...CAN YOU DO THAT?
THAT WILL NOT BE NECESSARY, MRS. BAKER.
I CAN SMELL IT. I CAN TRACK IT.

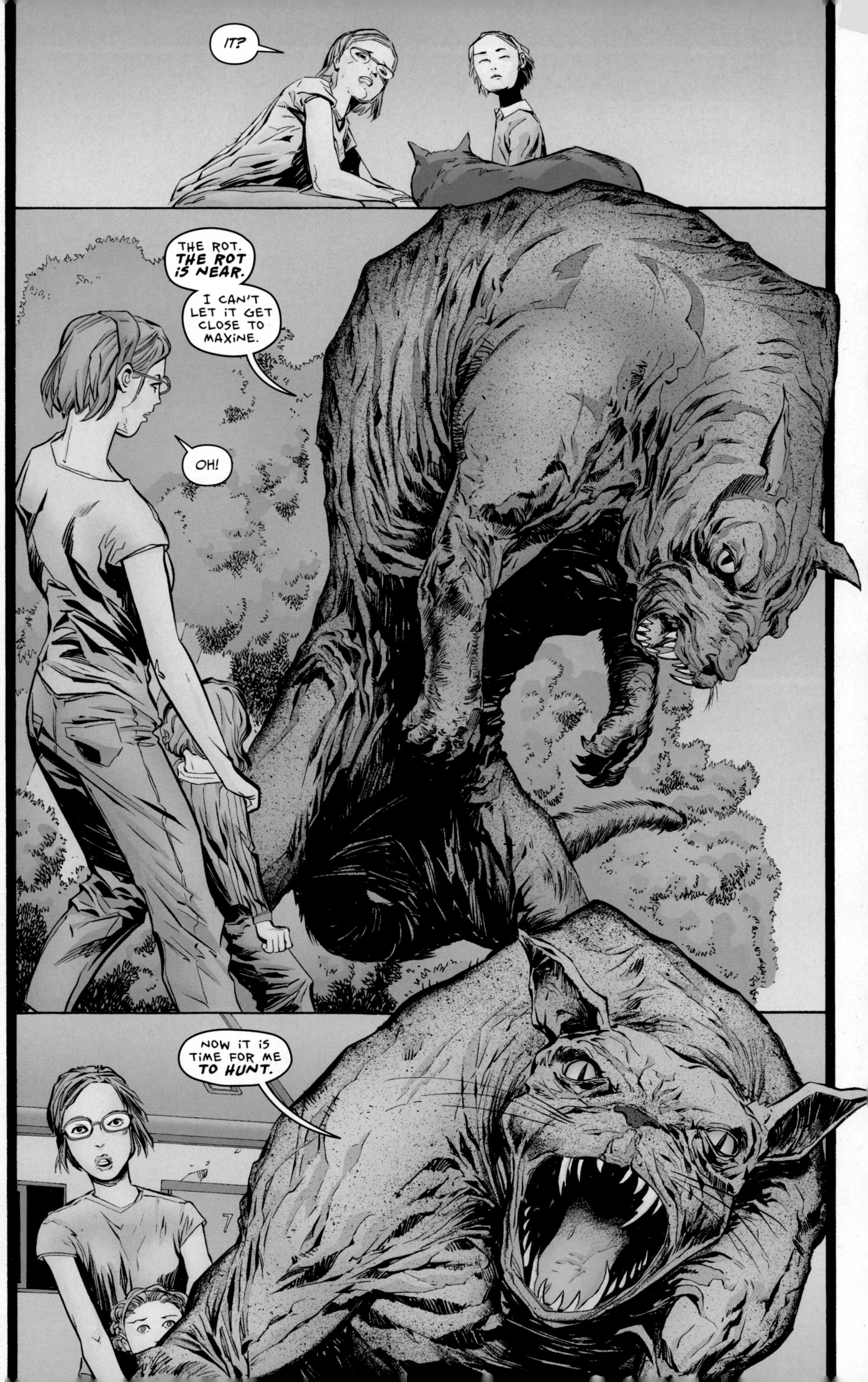
IT?
THE ROT. **THE ROT IS NEAR.**
I CAN'T LET IT GET CLOSE TO MAXINE.
OH!
NOW IT IS TIME FOR ME **TO HUNT.**

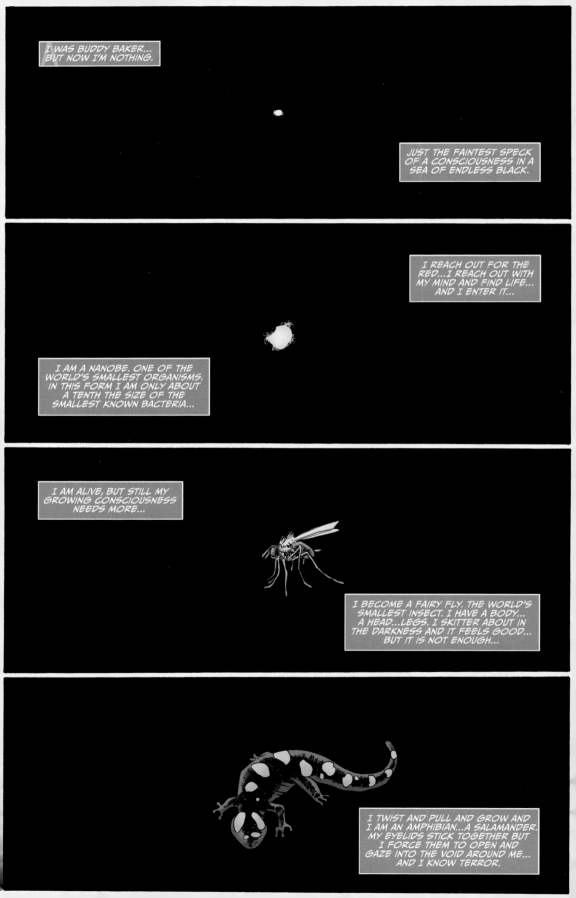

I WAS BUDDY BAKER...
BUT NOW I'M NOTHING.

JUST THE FAINTEST SPECK
OF A CONSCIOUSNESS IN A
SEA OF ENDLESS BLACK.

I REACH OUT FOR THE
RED...I REACH OUT WITH
MY MIND AND FIND LIFE...
AND I ENTER IT...

I AM A NANOBE. ONE OF THE
WORLD'S SMALLEST ORGANISMS.
IN THIS FORM I AM ONLY ABOUT
A TENTH THE SIZE OF THE
SMALLEST KNOWN BACTERIA...

I AM ALIVE, BUT STILL MY
GROWING CONSCIOUSNESS
NEEDS MORE...

I BECOME A FAIRY FLY. THE WORLD'S
SMALLEST INSECT. I HAVE A BODY...
A HEAD...LEGS. I SKITTER ABOUT IN
THE DARKNESS AND IT FEELS GOOD...
BUT IT IS NOT ENOUGH...

I TWIST AND PULL AND GROW AND
I AM AN AMPHIBIAN...A SALAMANDER.
MY EYELIDS STICK TOGETHER BUT
I FORCE THEM TO OPEN AND
GAZE INTO THE VOID AROUND ME...
AND I KNOW TERROR.

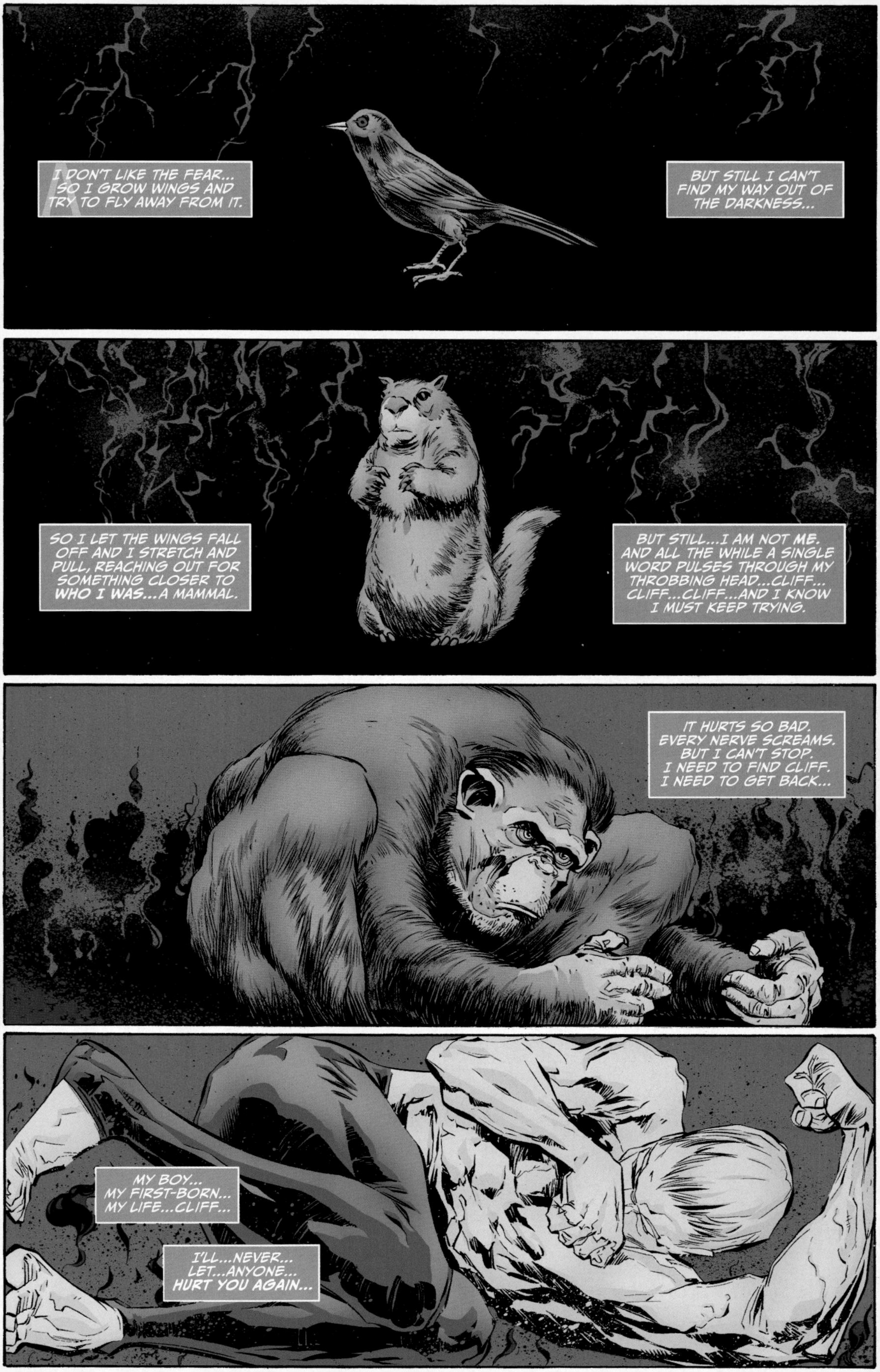
I DON'T LIKE THE FEAR... SO I GROW WINGS AND TRY TO FLY AWAY FROM IT.
BUT STILL I CAN'T FIND MY WAY OUT OF THE DARKNESS...
SO I LET THE WINGS FALL OFF AND I STRETCH AND PULL, REACHING OUT FOR SOMETHING CLOSER TO WHO I WAS...A MAMMAL.
BUT STILL...I AM NOT ME. AND ALL THE WHILE A SINGLE WORD PULSES THROUGH MY THROBBING HEAD...CLIFF... CLIFF...CLIFF...AND I KNOW I MUST KEEP TRYING.
IT HURTS SO BAD. EVERY NERVE SCREAMS. BUT I CAN'T STOP. I NEED TO FIND CLIFF. I NEED TO GET BACK...
MY BOY... MY FIRST-BORN... MY LIFE...CLIFF...
I'LL...NEVER... LET...ANYONE... HURT YOU AGAIN...

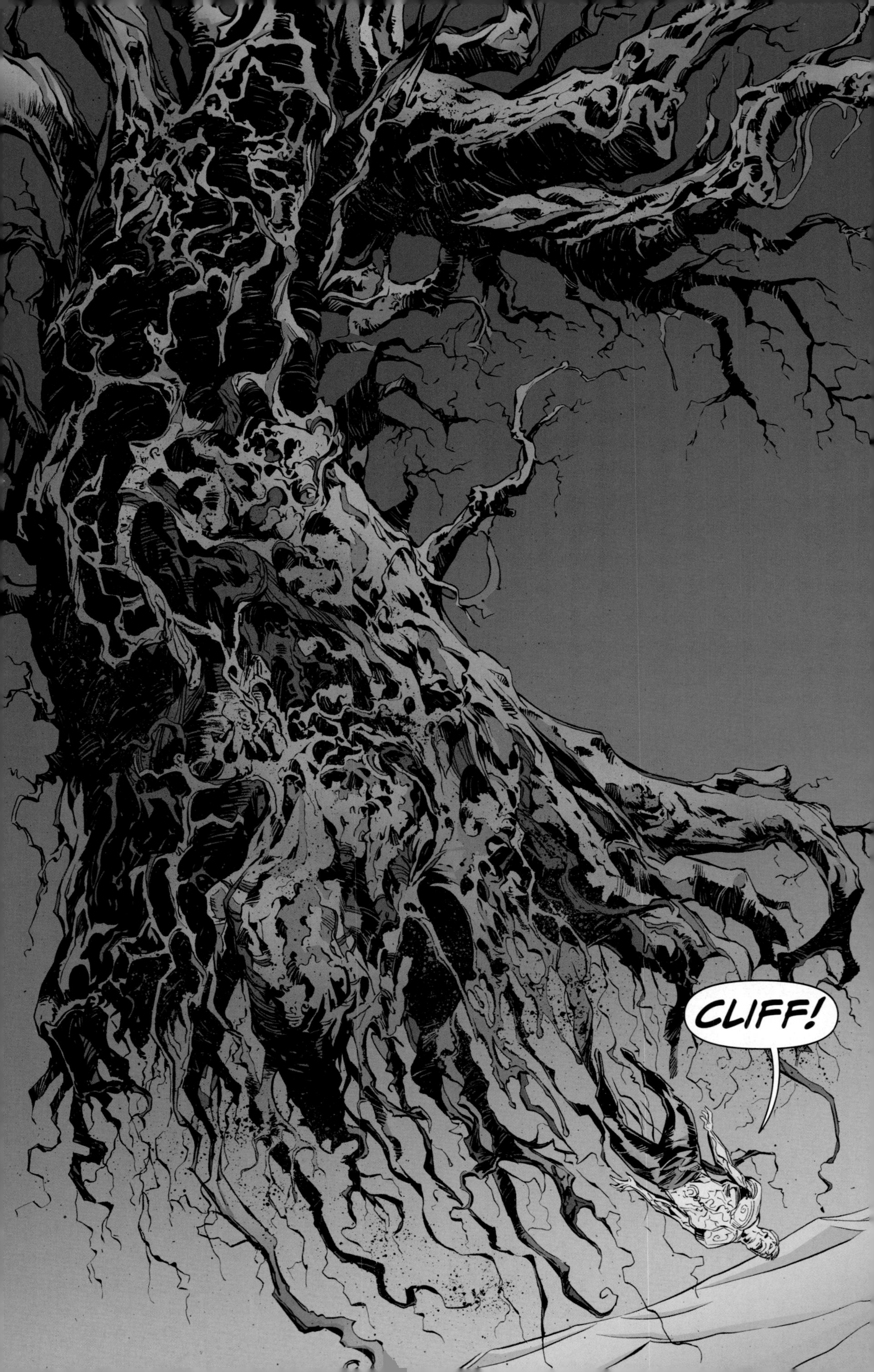
CLIFF!

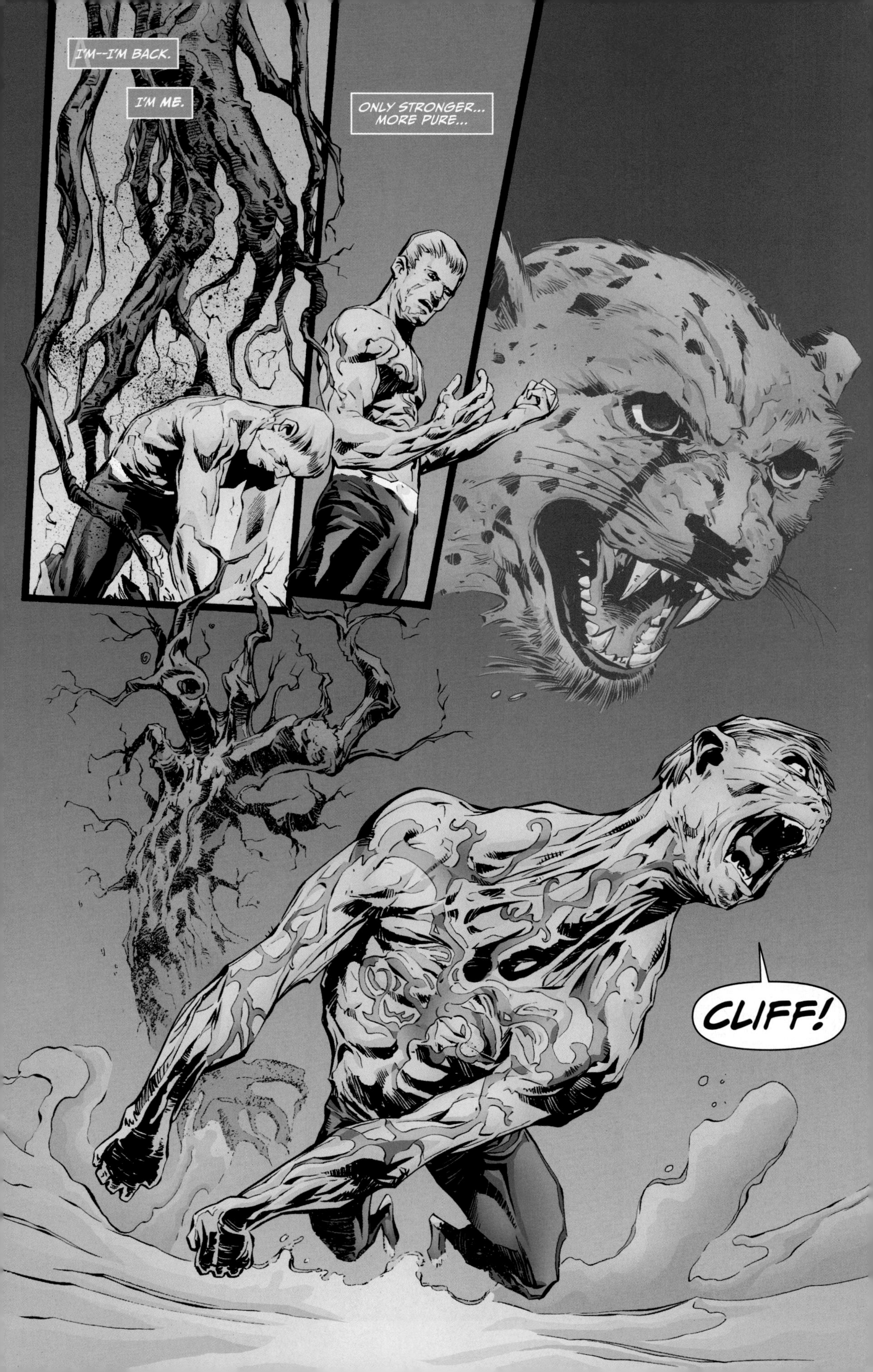
I'M--I'M BACK.
I'M ME.
ONLY STRONGER... MORE PURE...
CLIFF!

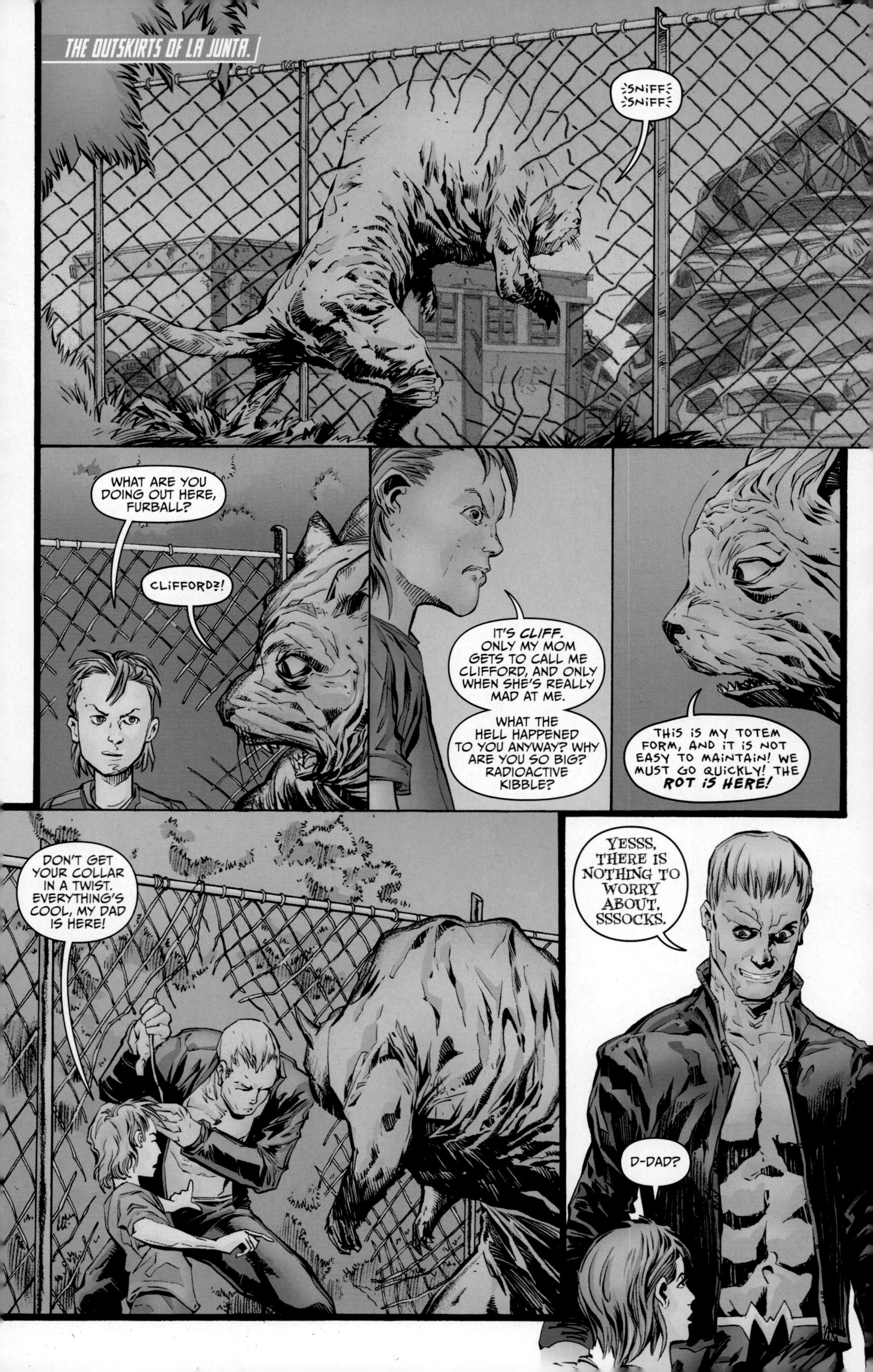
THE OUTSKIRTS OF LA JUNTA.
SNIFF SNIFF
WHAT ARE YOU DOING OUT HERE, FURBALL?
CLIFFORD?!
IT'S CLIFF. ONLY MY MOM GETS TO CALL ME CLIFFORD, AND ONLY WHEN SHE'S REALLY MAD AT ME.
WHAT THE HELL HAPPENED TO YOU ANYWAY? WHY ARE YOU SO BIG? RADIOACTIVE KIBBLE?
THIS IS MY TOTEM FORM, AND IT IS NOT EASY TO MAINTAIN! WE MUST GO QUICKLY! THE ROT IS HERE!
DON'T GET YOUR COLLAR IN A TWIST. EVERYTHING'S COOL, MY DAD IS HERE!
YESSS, THERE IS NOTHING TO WORRY ABOUT, SSSOCKS.
D-DAD?

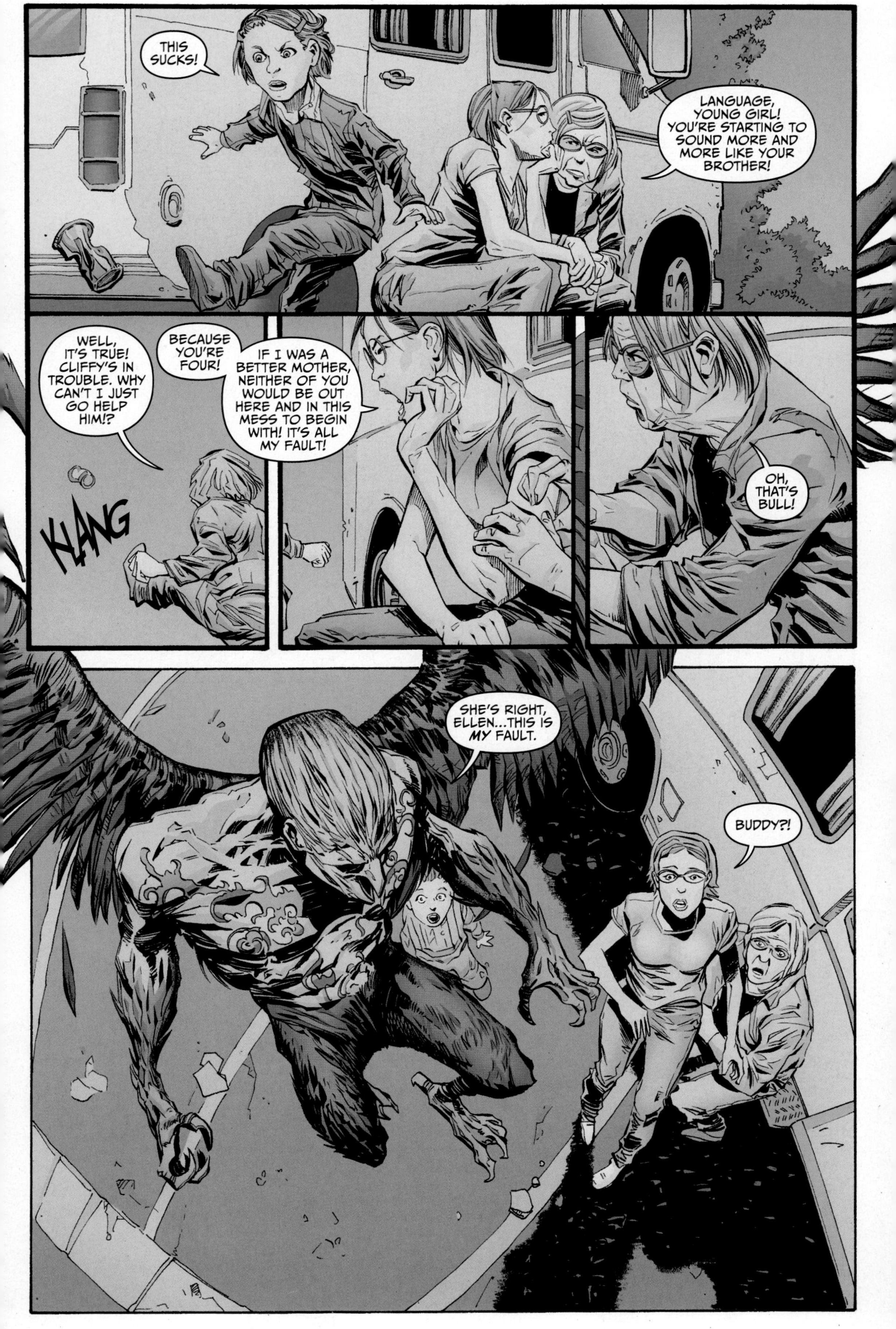
THIS SUCKS!
LANGUAGE, YOUNG GIRL! YOU'RE STARTING TO SOUND MORE AND MORE LIKE YOUR BROTHER!
WELL, IT'S TRUE! CLIFFY'S IN TROUBLE. WHY CAN'T I JUST GO HELP HIM!?
BECAUSE YOU'RE FOUR!
KLANG
IF I WAS A BETTER MOTHER, NEITHER OF YOU WOULD BE OUT HERE AND IN THIS MESS TO BEGIN WITH! IT'S ALL MY FAULT!
OH, THAT'S BULL!
SHE'S RIGHT, ELLEN...THIS IS MY FAULT.
BUDDY?!

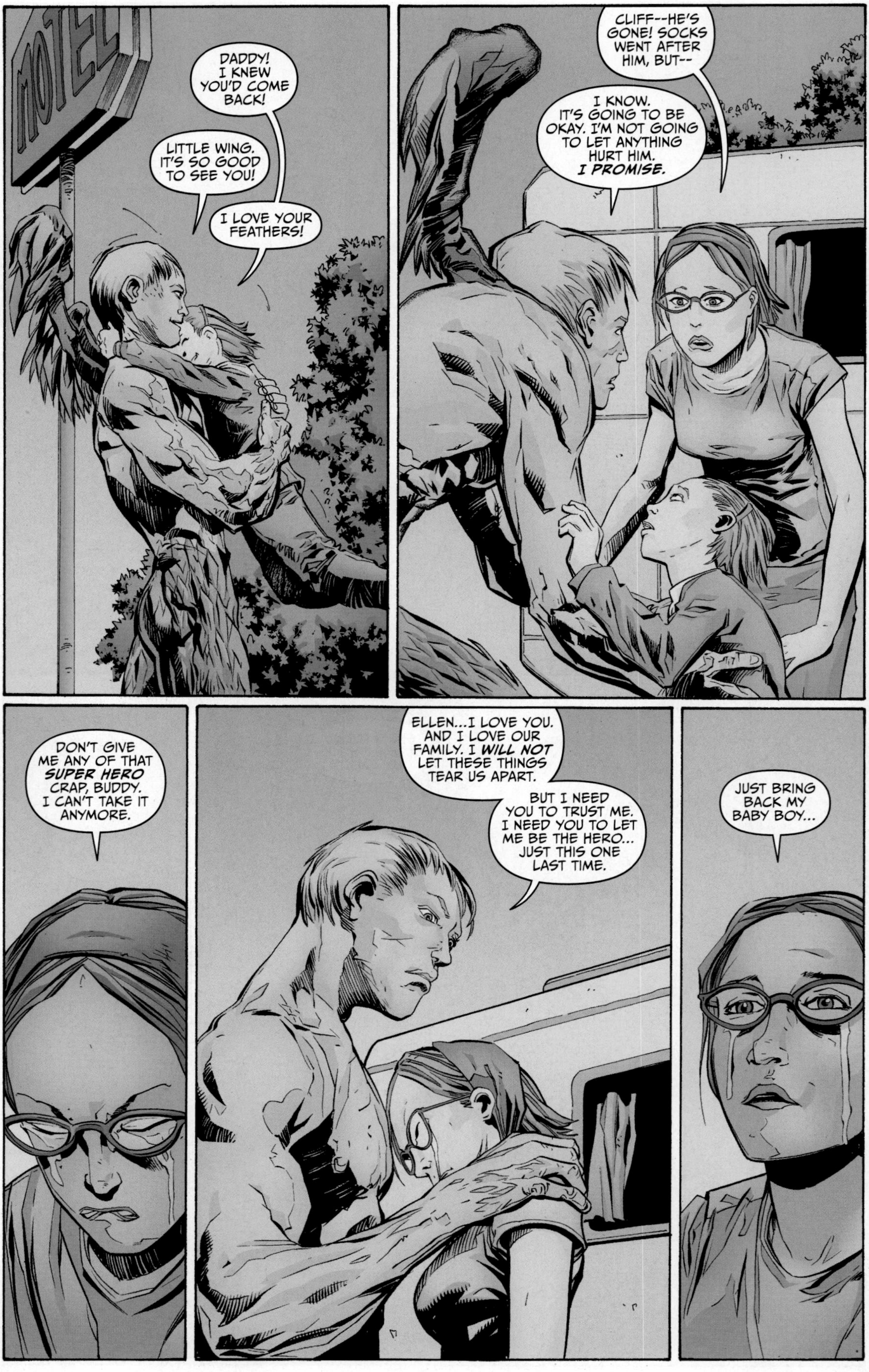
MOTEL
DADDY! I KNEW YOU'D COME BACK!
LITTLE WING. IT'S SO GOOD TO SEE YOU!
I LOVE YOUR FEATHERS!
CLIFF--HE'S GONE! SOCKS WENT AFTER HIM, BUT--
I KNOW. IT'S GOING TO BE OKAY. I'M NOT GOING TO LET ANYTHING HURT HIM. I PROMISE.
DON'T GIVE ME ANY OF THAT SUPER HERO CRAP, BUDDY. I CAN'T TAKE IT ANYMORE.
ELLEN...I LOVE YOU. AND I LOVE OUR FAMILY. I WILL NOT LET THESE THINGS TEAR US APART.
BUT I NEED YOU TO TRUST ME. I NEED YOU TO LET ME BE THE HERO... JUST THIS ONE LAST TIME.
JUST BRING BACK MY BABY BOY...

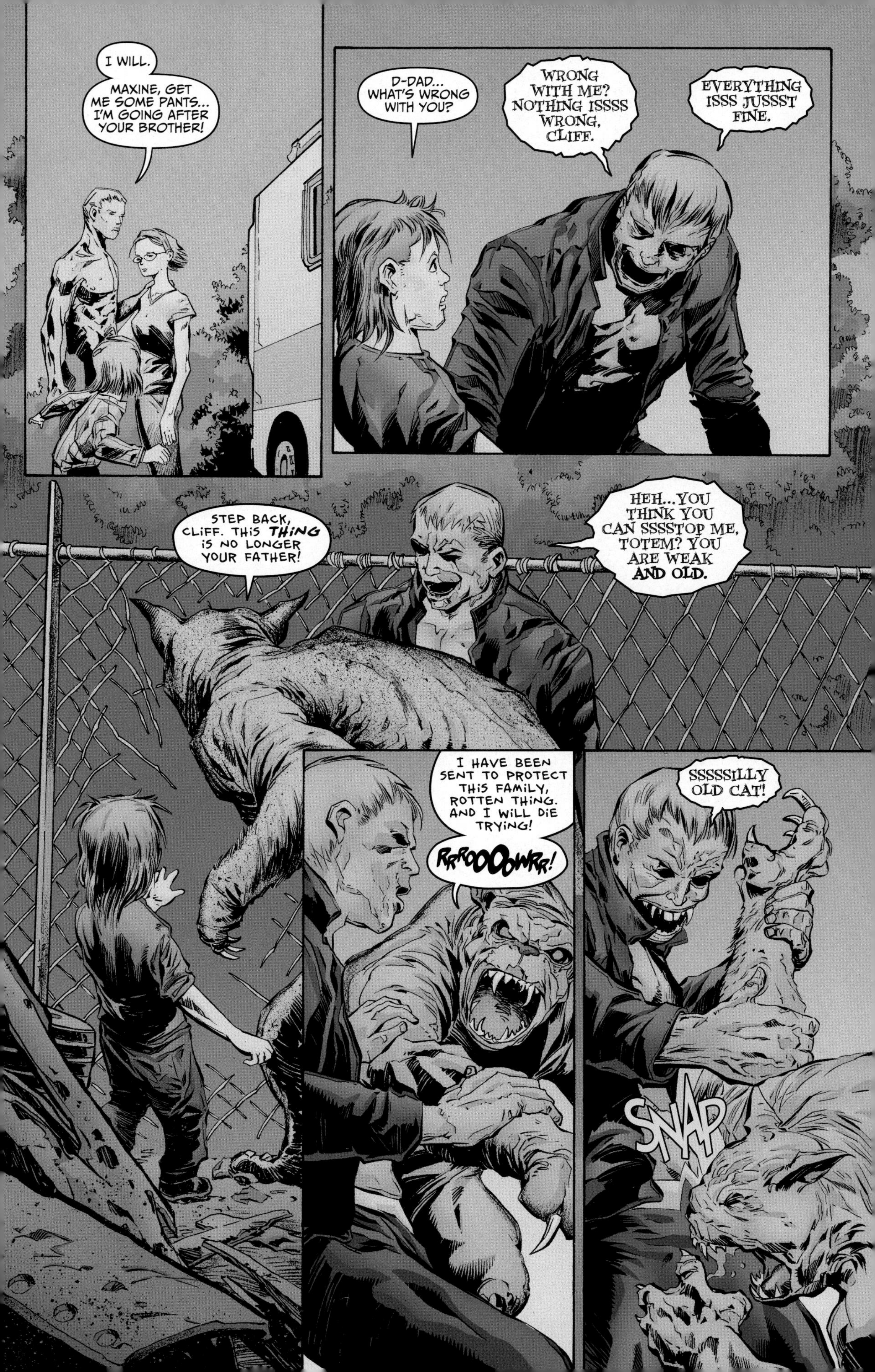
I WILL.
MAXINE, GET ME SOME PANTS... I'M GOING AFTER YOUR BROTHER!
D-DAD... WHAT'S WRONG WITH YOU?
WRONG WITH ME? NOTHING ISSSS WRONG, CLIFF.
EVERYTHING ISSS JUSSST FINE.
STEP BACK, CLIFF. THIS THING IS NO LONGER YOUR FATHER!
HEH...YOU THINK YOU CAN SSSSTOP ME, TOTEM? YOU ARE WEAK AND OLD.
I HAVE BEEN SENT TO PROTECT THIS FAMILY, ROTTEN THING. AND I WILL DIE TRYING!
RRROOOOWRR!
SSSSSILLY OLD CAT!
SNAP

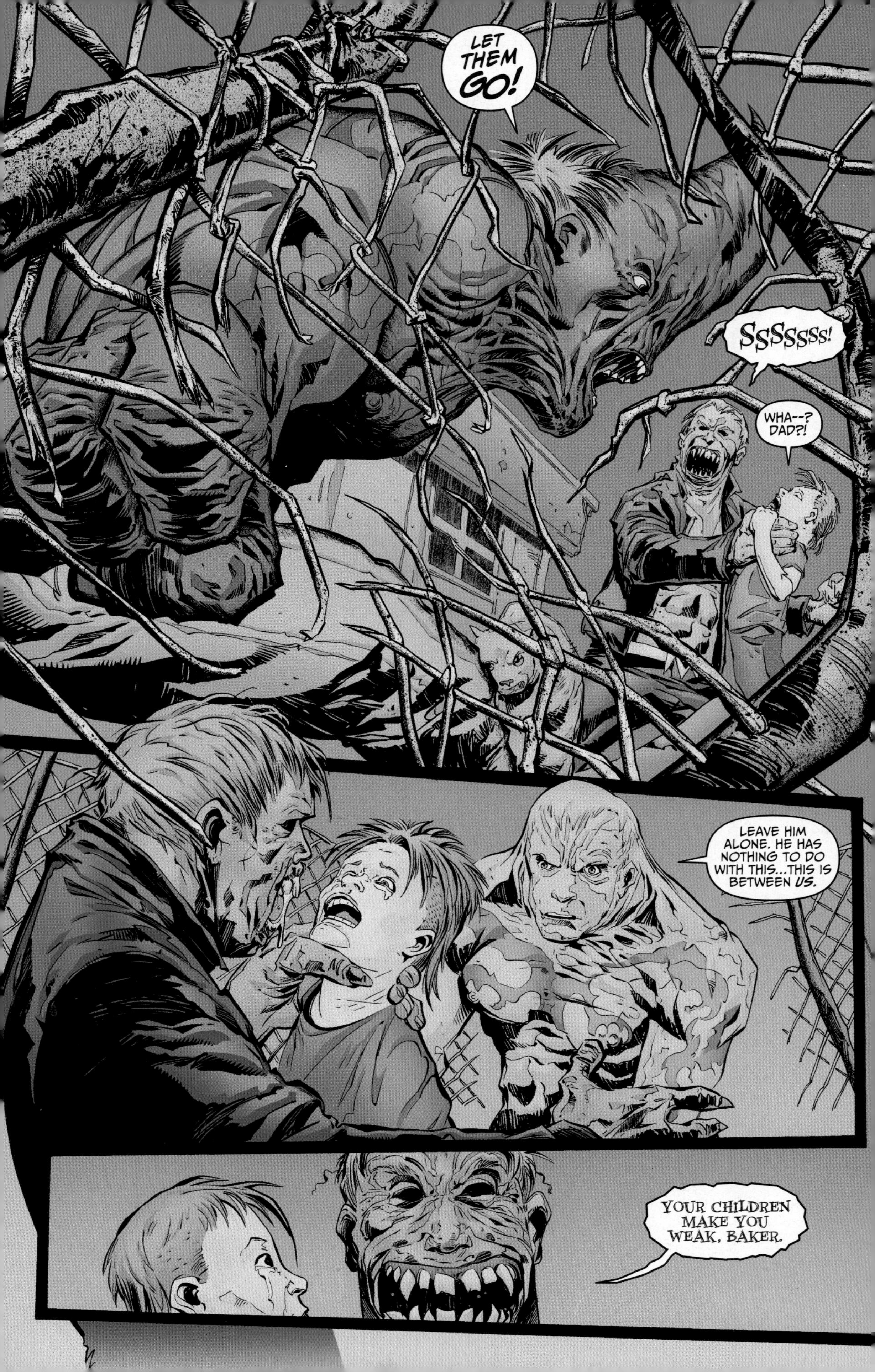
LET THEM GO!
SSSSSSS!
WHA--? DAD?!
LEAVE HIM ALONE. HE HAS NOTHING TO DO WITH THIS...THIS IS BETWEEN US.
YOUR CHILDREN MAKE YOU WEAK, BAKER.

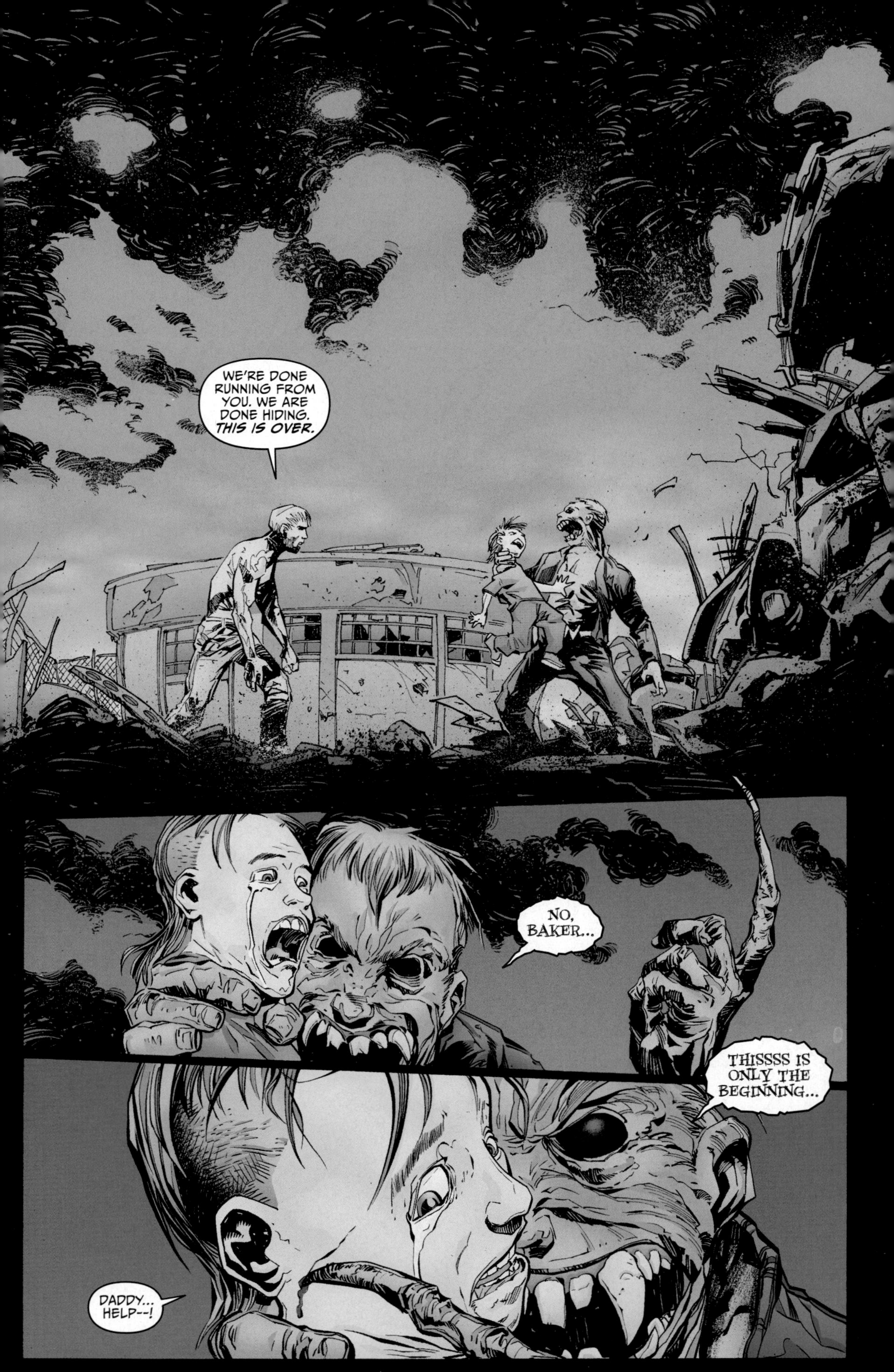
WE'RE DONE RUNNING FROM YOU. WE ARE DONE HIDING. *THIS IS OVER.*
NO, BAKER...
THISSSS IS ONLY THE BEGINNING...
DADDY... HELP--!

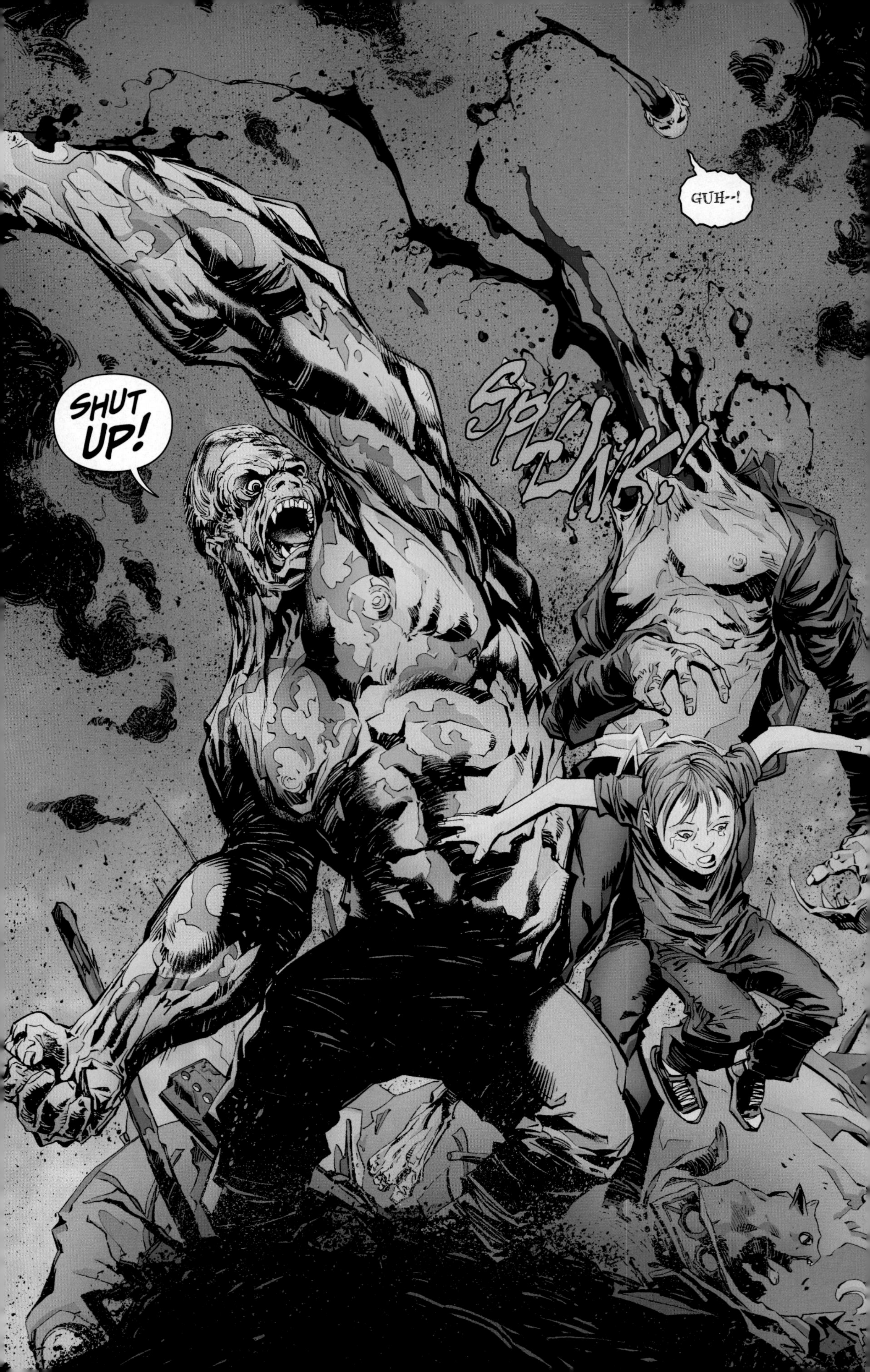
SHUT UP!
SPLUNK!
GUH--!

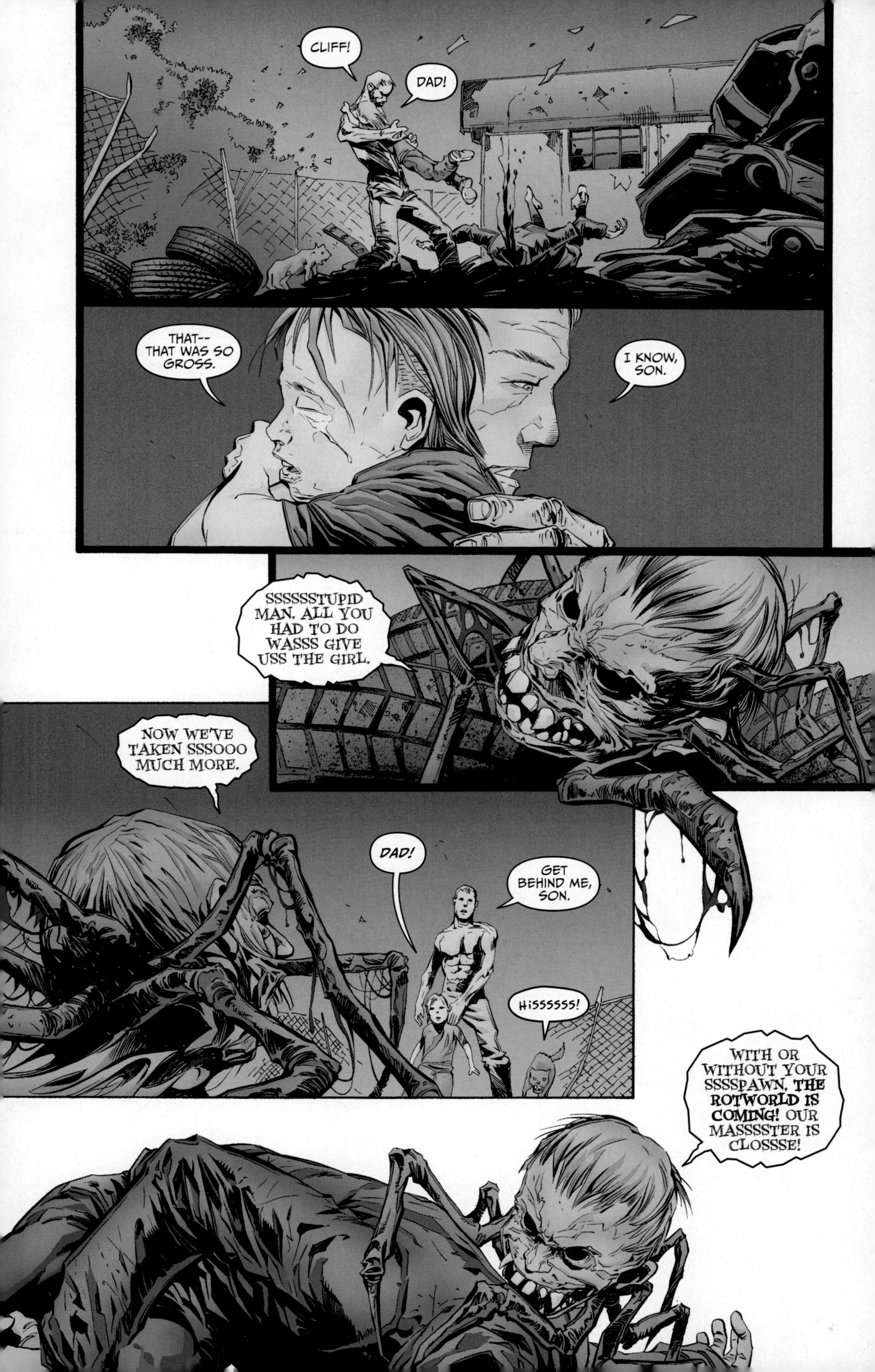
CLIFF!
DAD!
THAT-- THAT WAS SO GROSS.
I KNOW, SON.
SSSSSSTUPID MAN. ALL YOU HAD TO DO WASSS GIVE USS THE GIRL.
NOW WE'VE TAKEN SSSOOO MUCH MORE.
DAD!
GET BEHIND ME, SON.
HISSSSSS!
WITH OR WITHOUT YOUR SSSSPAWN, THE ROTWORLD IS COMING! OUR MASSSSTER IS CLOSSSE!

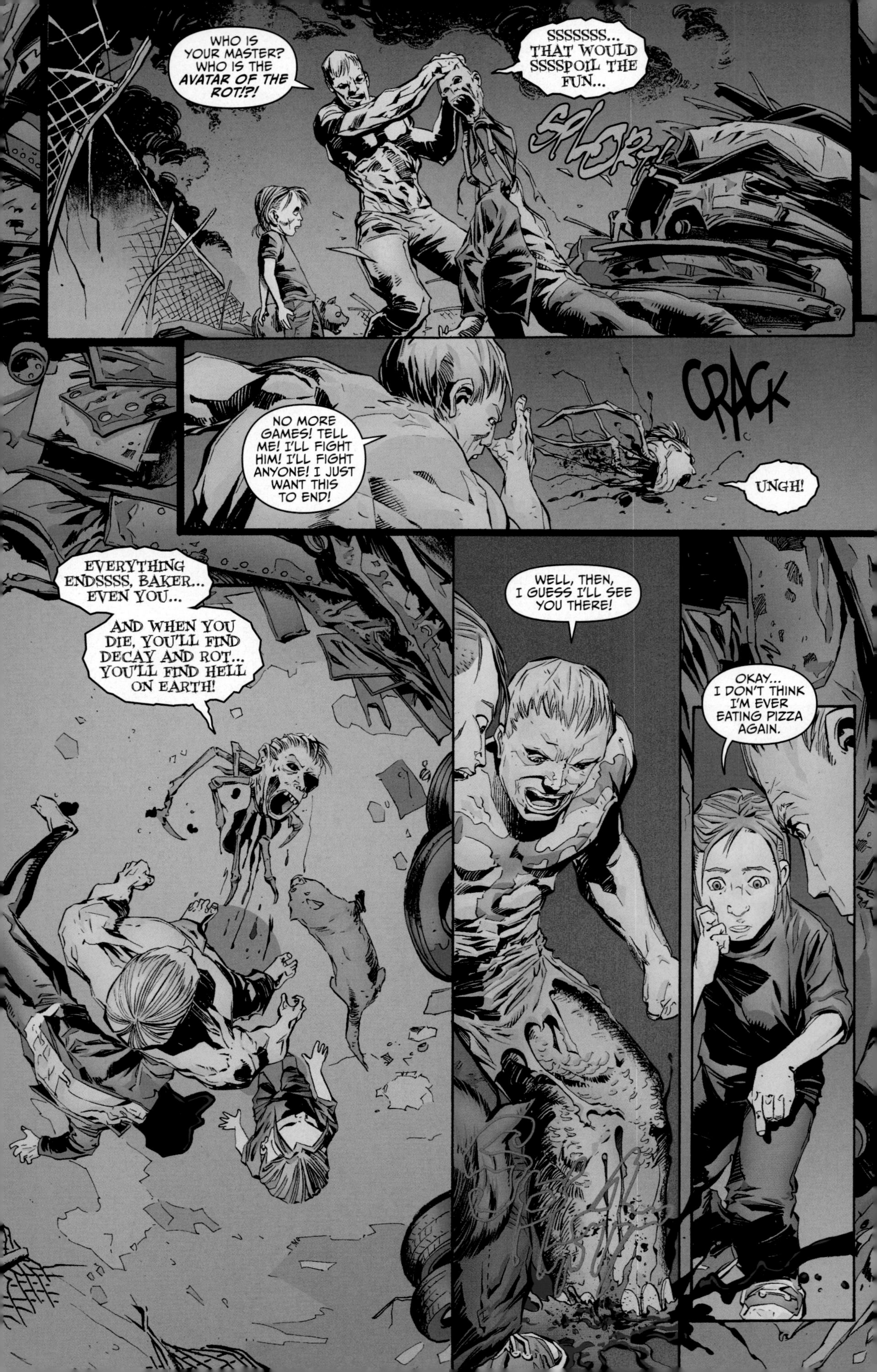
WHO IS YOUR MASTER? WHO IS THE AVATAR OF THE ROT!?!
SSSSSSS... THAT WOULD SSSSPOIL THE FUN...
SPLORCH
CRACK
NO MORE GAMES! TELL ME! I'LL FIGHT HIM! I'LL FIGHT ANYONE! I JUST WANT THIS TO END!
UNGH!
EVERYTHING ENDSSSS, BAKER... EVEN YOU...
AND WHEN YOU DIE, YOU'LL FIND DECAY AND ROT... YOU'LL FIND HELL ON EARTH!
WELL, THEN, I GUESS I'LL SEE YOU THERE!
OKAY... I DON'T THINK I'M EVER EATING PIZZA AGAIN.

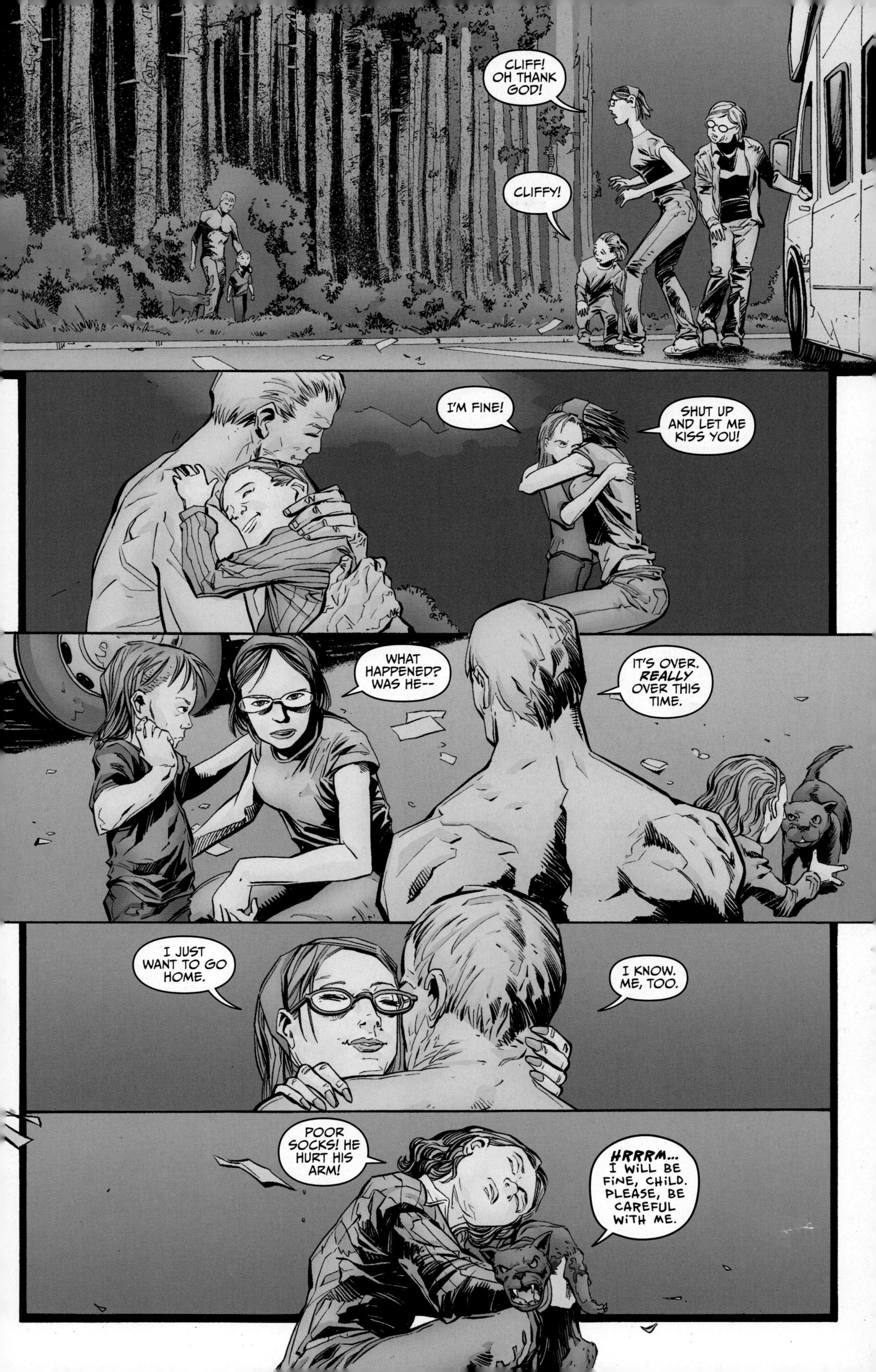
CLIFF! OH THANK GOD!
CLIFFY!
I'M FINE!
SHUT UP AND LET ME KISS YOU!
WHAT HAPPENED? WAS HE--
IT'S OVER. REALLY OVER THIS TIME.
I JUST WANT TO GO HOME.
I KNOW. ME, TOO.
POOR SOCKS! HE HURT HIS ARM!
HRRRM... I WILL BE FINE, CHILD. PLEASE, BE CAREFUL WITH ME.

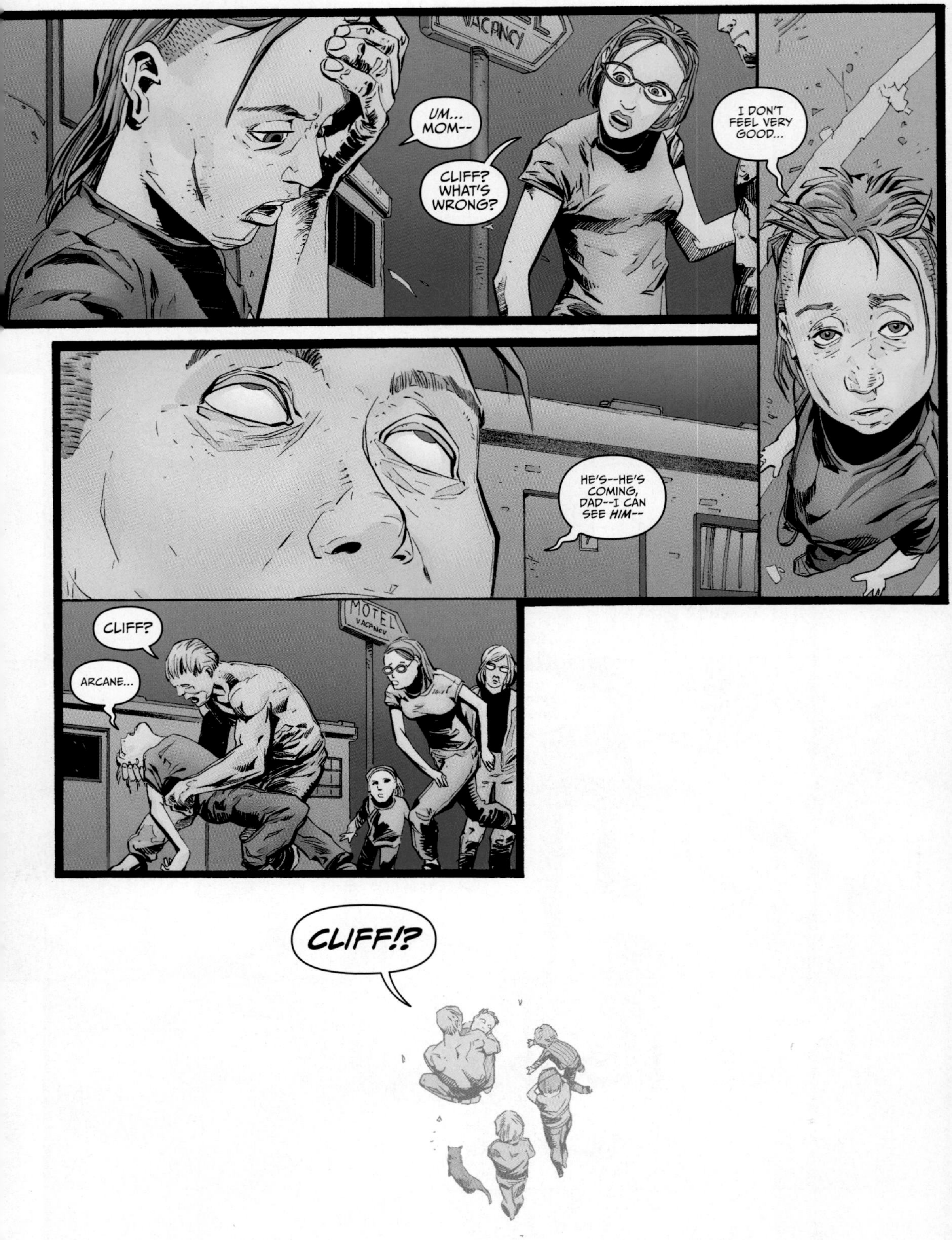

UM... MOM--
CLIFF? WHAT'S WRONG?
I DON'T FEEL VERY GOOD...
HE'S--HE'S COMING, DAD--I CAN SEE *HIM*--
MOTEL
CLIFF?
ARCANE...
CLIFF!?

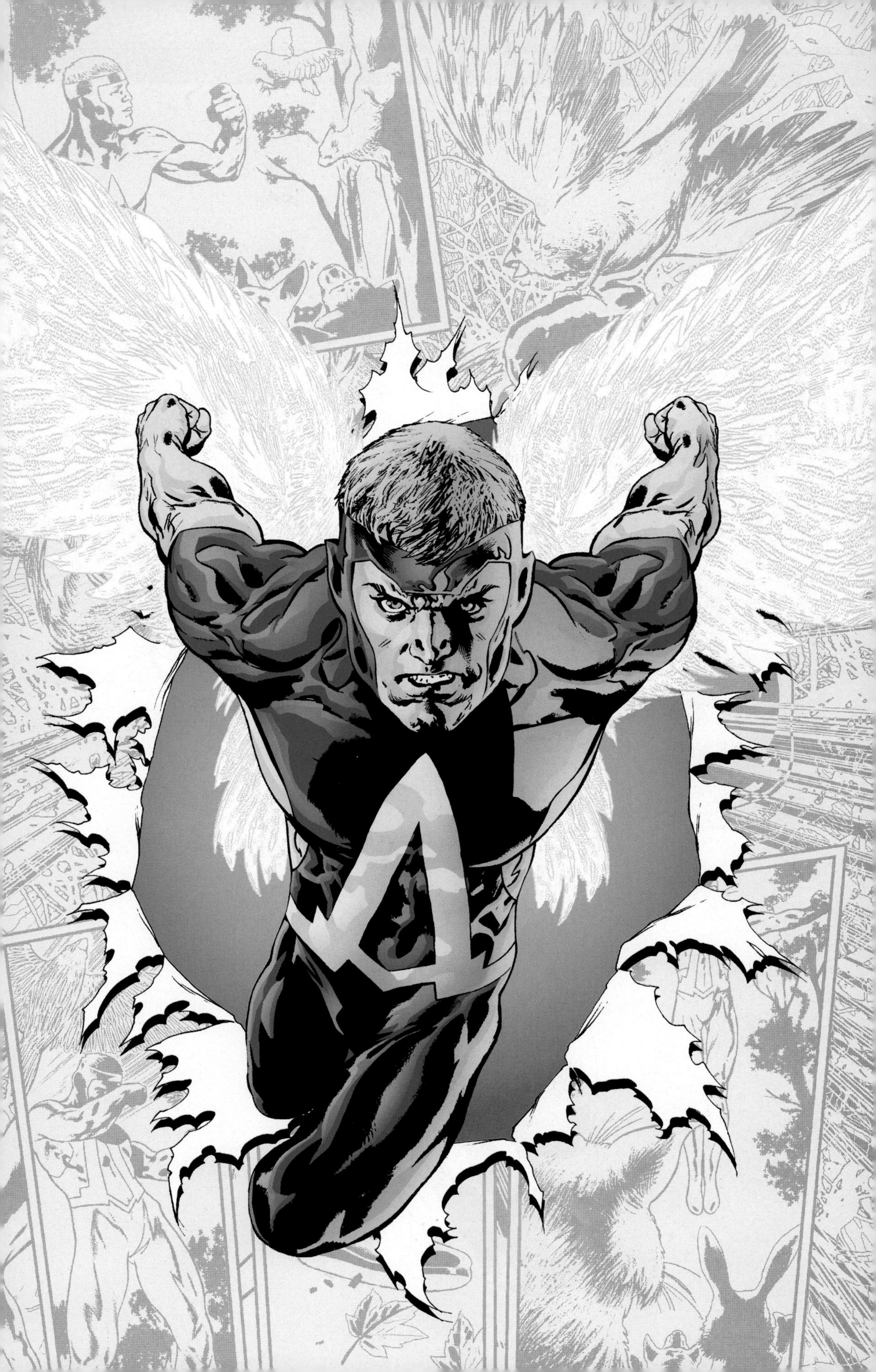

JEFF LEMIRE writer **STEVE PUGH** artist
cover by **STEVE PUGH with LOVERN KINDZIERSKI**

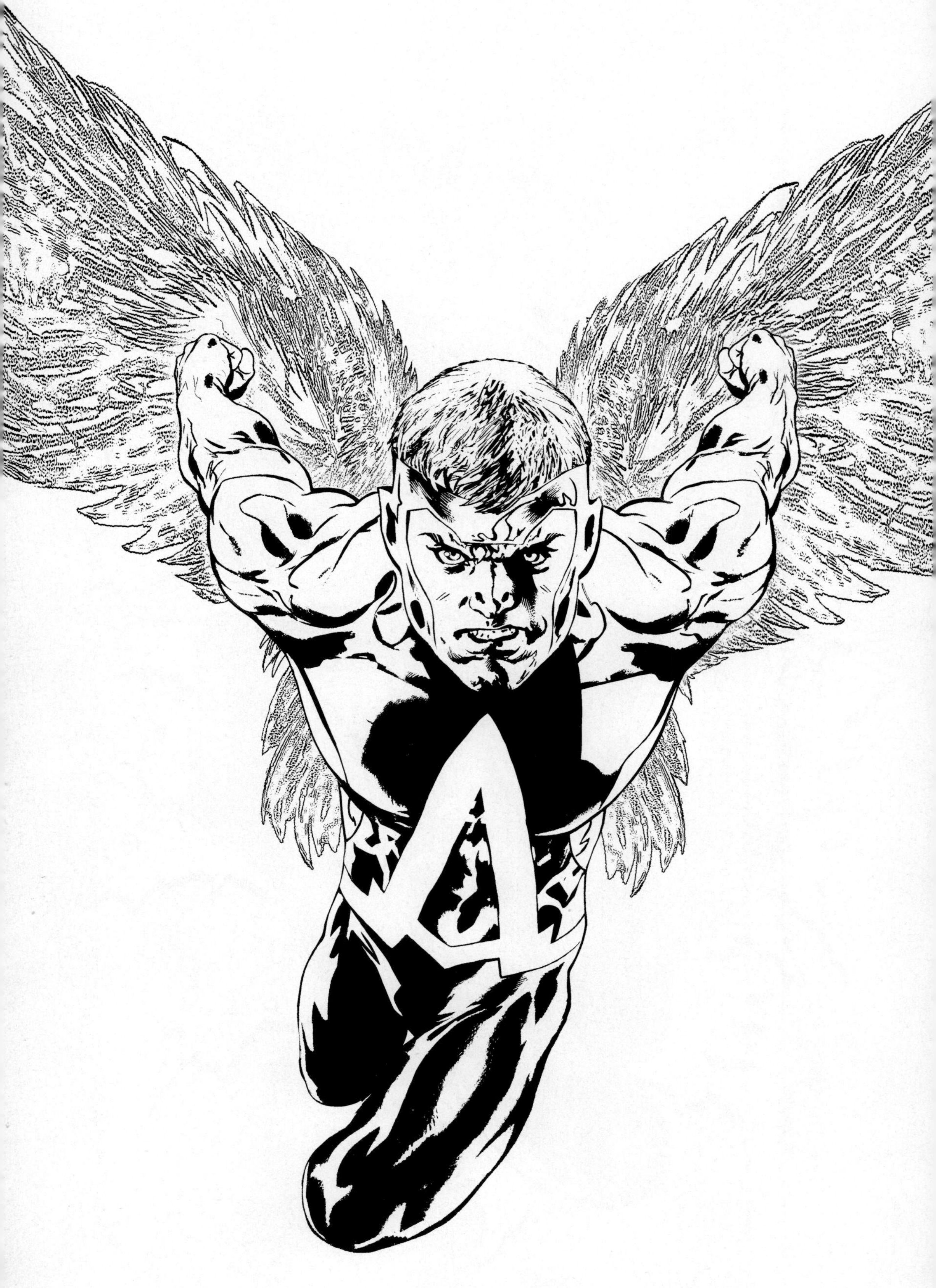

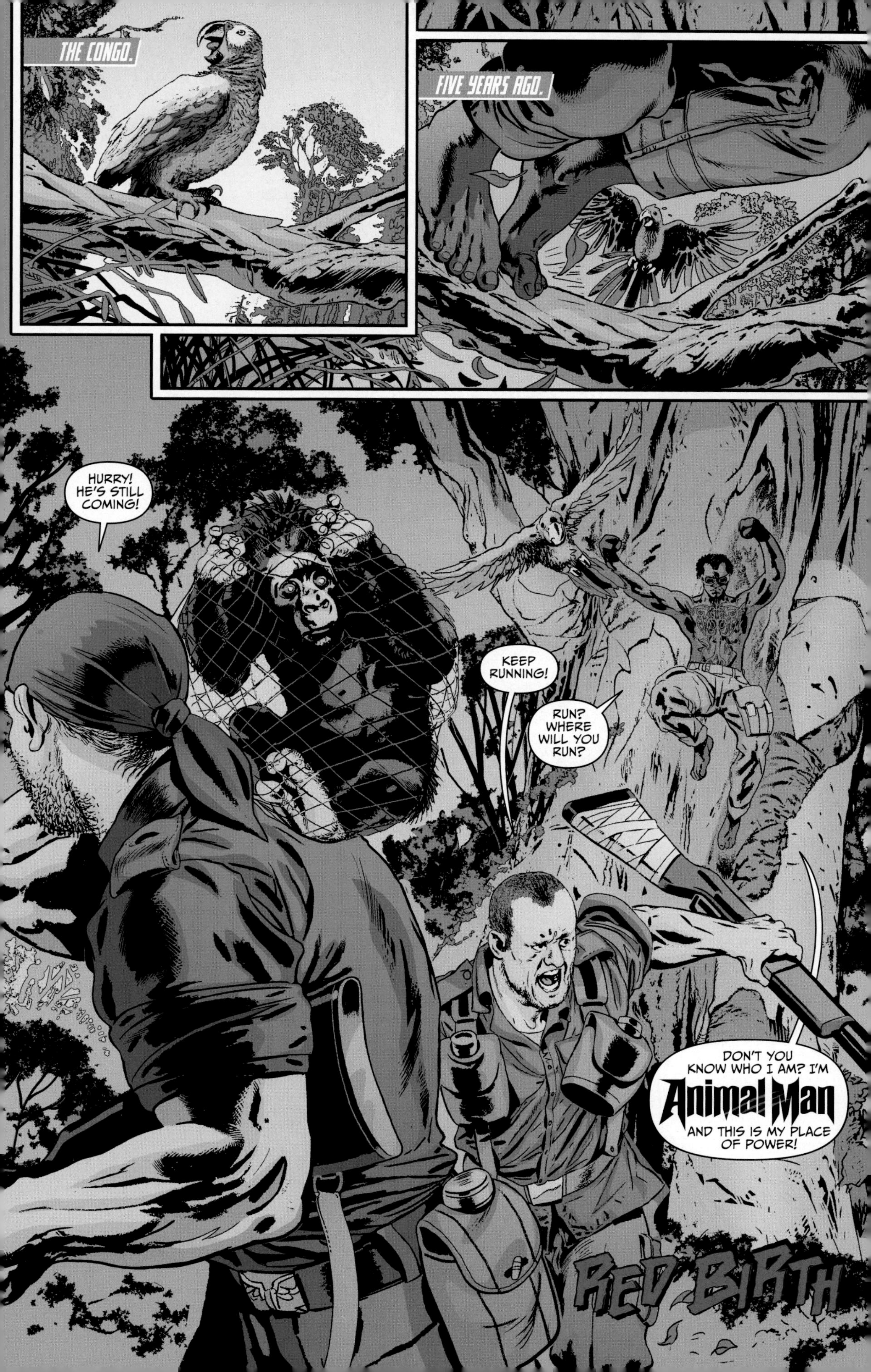
THE CONGO.
FIVE YEARS AGO.
HURRY! HE'S STILL COMING!
KEEP RUNNING!
RUN? WHERE WILL YOU RUN?
DON'T YOU KNOW WHO I AM? I'M Animal Man AND THIS IS MY PLACE OF POWER!
RED BIRTH

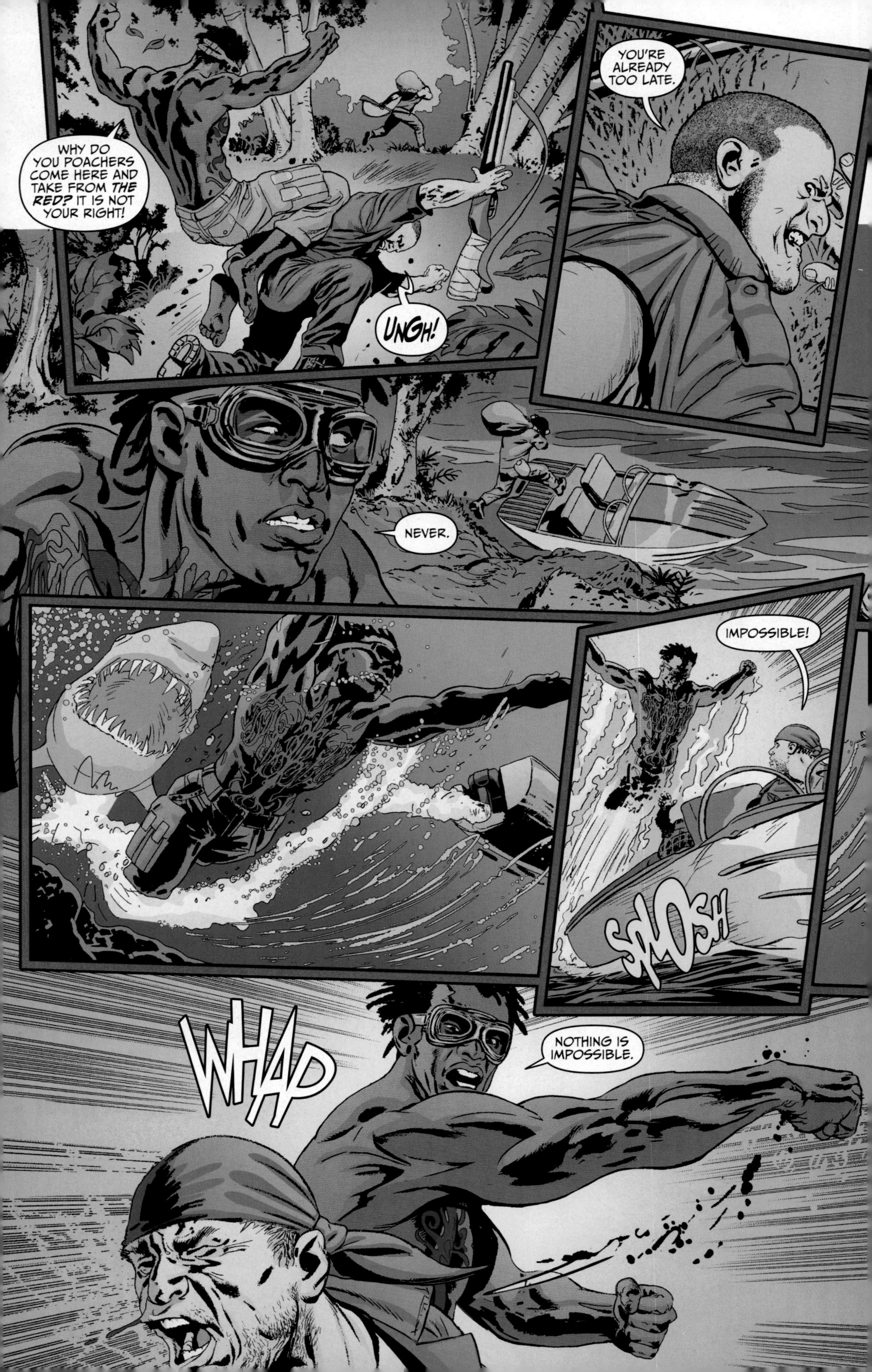
WHY DO YOU POACHERS COME HERE AND TAKE FROM THE RED? IT IS NOT YOUR RIGHT!
UNGH!
YOU'RE ALREADY TOO LATE.
NEVER.
IMPOSSIBLE!
SPLOOSH
WHAP
NOTHING IS IMPOSSIBLE.

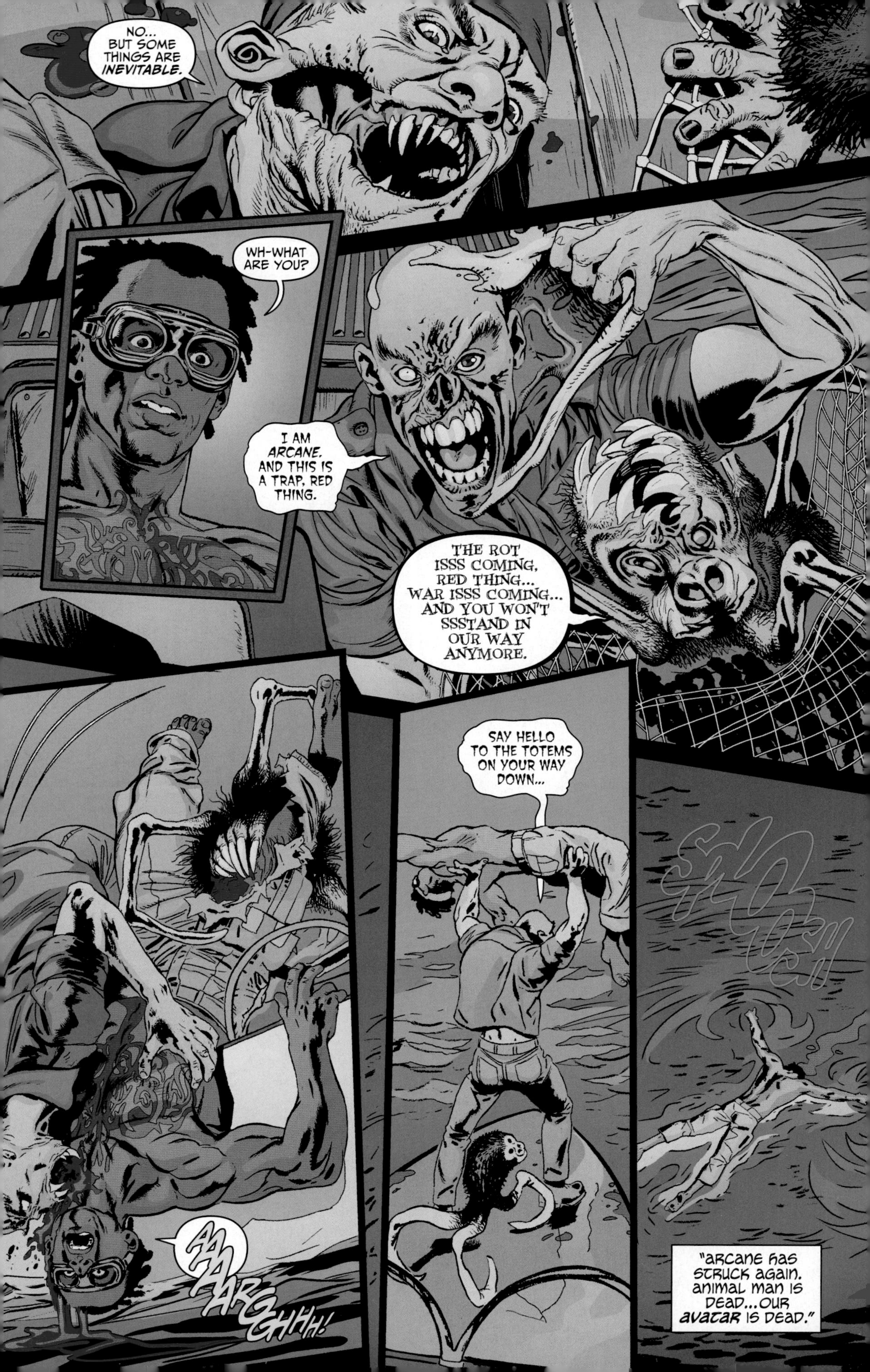
NO... BUT SOME THINGS ARE INEVITABLE.
WH-WHAT ARE YOU?
I AM ARCANE. AND THIS IS A TRAP, RED THING.
THE ROT ISSS COMING, RED THING... WAR ISSS COMING... AND YOU WON'T SSSTAND IN OUR WAY ANYMORE.
AAAARGHHH!
SAY HELLO TO THE TOTEMS ON YOUR WAY DOWN...
"ARCANE HAS STRUCK AGAIN. ANIMAL MAN IS DEAD...OUR AVATAR IS DEAD."

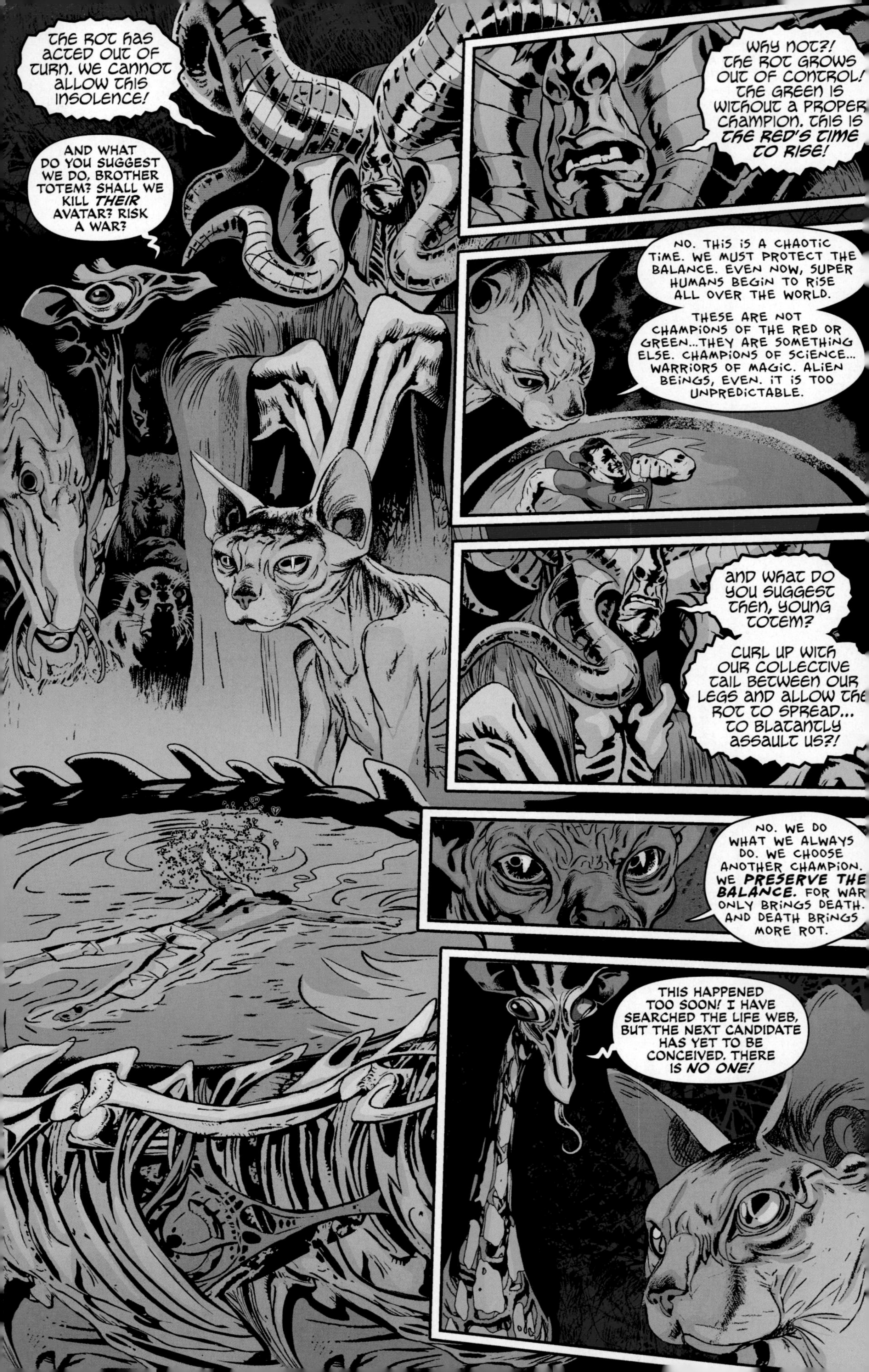
THE ROT HAS ACTED OUT OF TURN. WE CANNOT ALLOW THIS INSOLENCE!
AND WHAT DO YOU SUGGEST WE DO, BROTHER TOTEM? SHALL WE KILL *THEIR* AVATAR? RISK A WAR?
WHY NOT?! THE ROT GROWS OUT OF CONTROL! THE GREEN IS WITHOUT A PROPER CHAMPION. THIS IS *THE RED'S TIME TO RISE!*
NO. THIS IS A CHAOTIC TIME. WE MUST PROTECT THE BALANCE. EVEN NOW, SUPER HUMANS BEGIN TO RISE ALL OVER THE WORLD.
THESE ARE NOT CHAMPIONS OF THE RED OR GREEN...THEY ARE SOMETHING ELSE. CHAMPIONS OF SCIENCE... WARRIORS OF MAGIC. ALIEN BEINGS, EVEN. IT IS TOO UNPREDICTABLE.
AND WHAT DO YOU SUGGEST THEN, YOUNG TOTEM?
CURL UP WITH OUR COLLECTIVE TAIL BETWEEN OUR LEGS AND ALLOW THE ROT TO SPREAD... TO BLATANTLY ASSAULT US?!
NO. WE DO WHAT WE ALWAYS DO. WE CHOOSE ANOTHER CHAMPION. WE **PRESERVE THE BALANCE.** FOR WAR ONLY BRINGS DEATH. AND DEATH BRINGS MORE ROT.
THIS HAPPENED TOO SOON! I HAVE SEARCHED THE LIFE WEB, BUT THE NEXT CANDIDATE HAS YET TO BE CONCEIVED. THERE IS *NO ONE!*

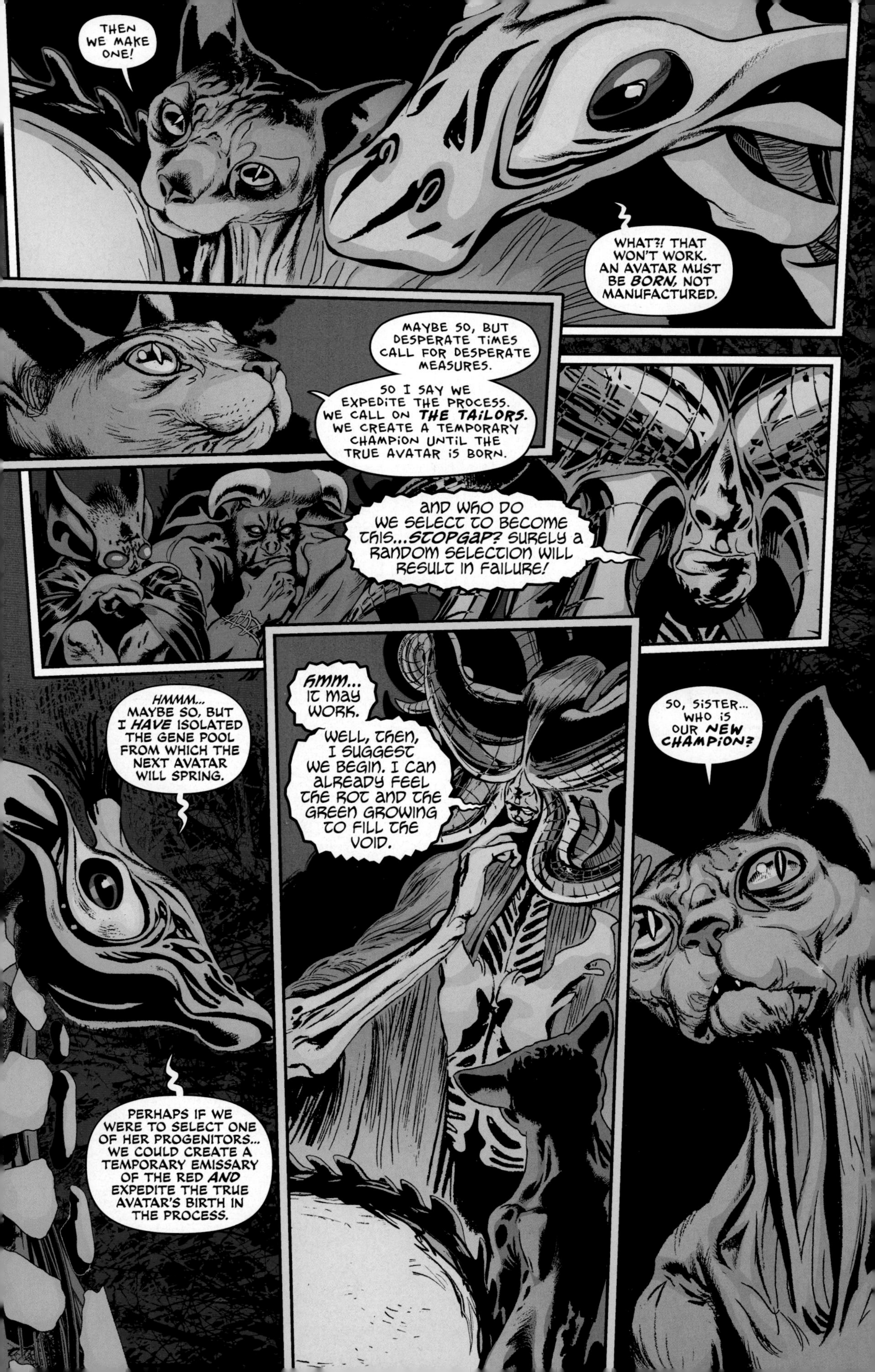
THEN WE MAKE ONE!
WHAT?! THAT WON'T WORK. AN AVATAR MUST BE *BORN,* NOT MANUFACTURED.
MAYBE SO, BUT DESPERATE TIMES CALL FOR DESPERATE MEASURES.
SO I SAY WE EXPEDITE THE PROCESS. WE CALL ON *THE TAILORS.* WE CREATE A TEMPORARY CHAMPION UNTIL THE TRUE AVATAR IS BORN.
AND WHO DO WE SELECT TO BECOME THIS...*STOPGAP?* SURELY A RANDOM SELECTION WILL RESULT IN FAILURE!
HMMM... MAYBE SO, BUT I *HAVE* ISOLATED THE GENE POOL FROM WHICH THE NEXT AVATAR WILL SPRING.
PERHAPS IF WE WERE TO SELECT ONE OF HER PROGENITORS... WE COULD CREATE A TEMPORARY EMISSARY OF THE RED *AND* EXPEDITE THE TRUE AVATAR'S BIRTH IN THE PROCESS.
HMM... IT MAY WORK.
WELL, THEN, I SUGGEST WE BEGIN. I CAN ALREADY FEEL THE ROT AND THE GREEN GROWING TO FILL THE VOID.
SO, SISTER... WHO IS OUR *NEW CHAMPION?*

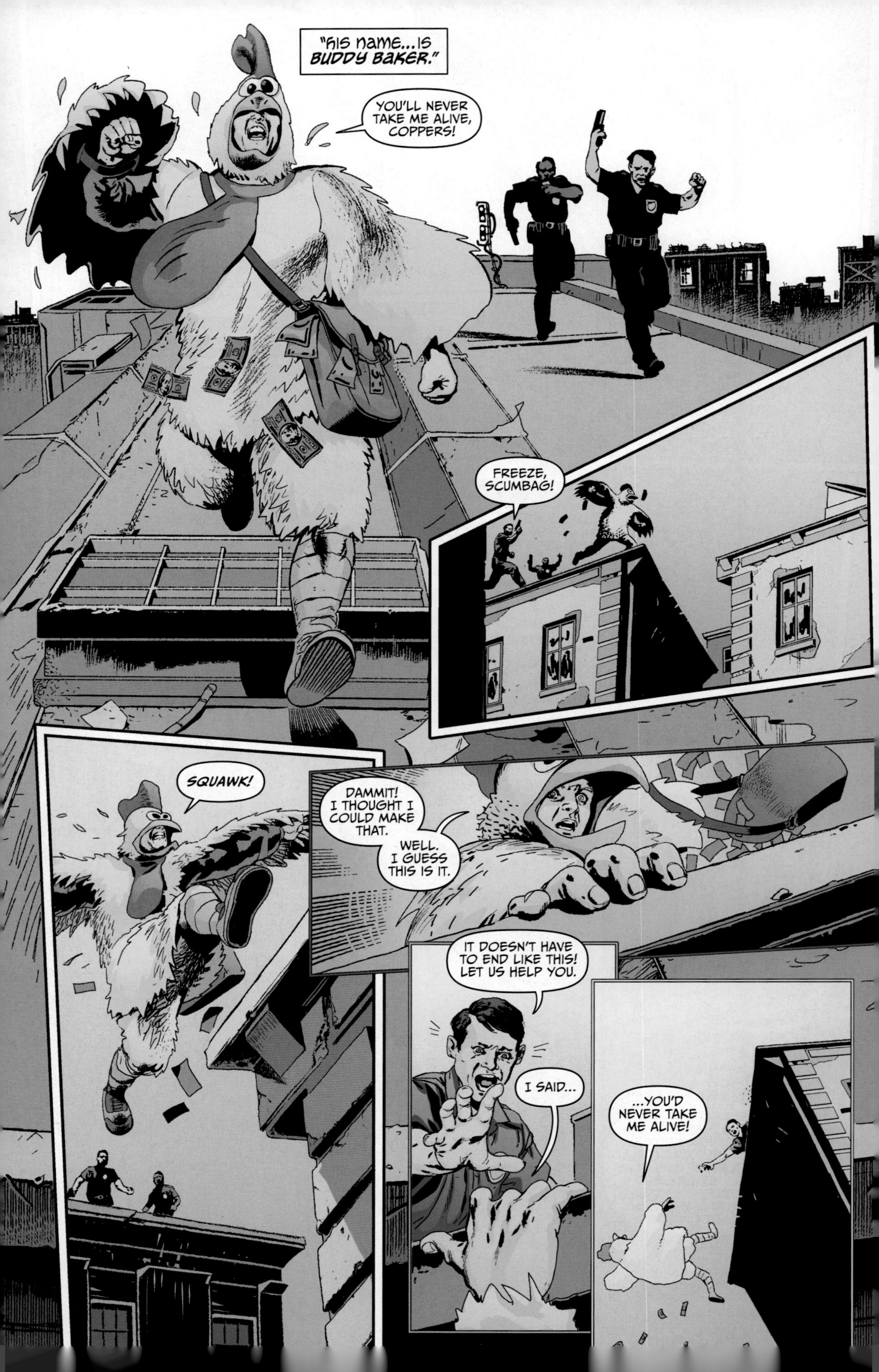
"His name...is BUDDY BAKER."
YOU'LL NEVER TAKE ME ALIVE, COPPERS!
FREEZE, SCUMBAG!
SQUAWK!
DAMMIT! I THOUGHT I COULD MAKE THAT.
WELL. I GUESS THIS IS IT.
IT DOESN'T HAVE TO END LIKE THIS! LET US HELP YOU.
I SAID...
...YOU'D NEVER TAKE ME ALIVE!

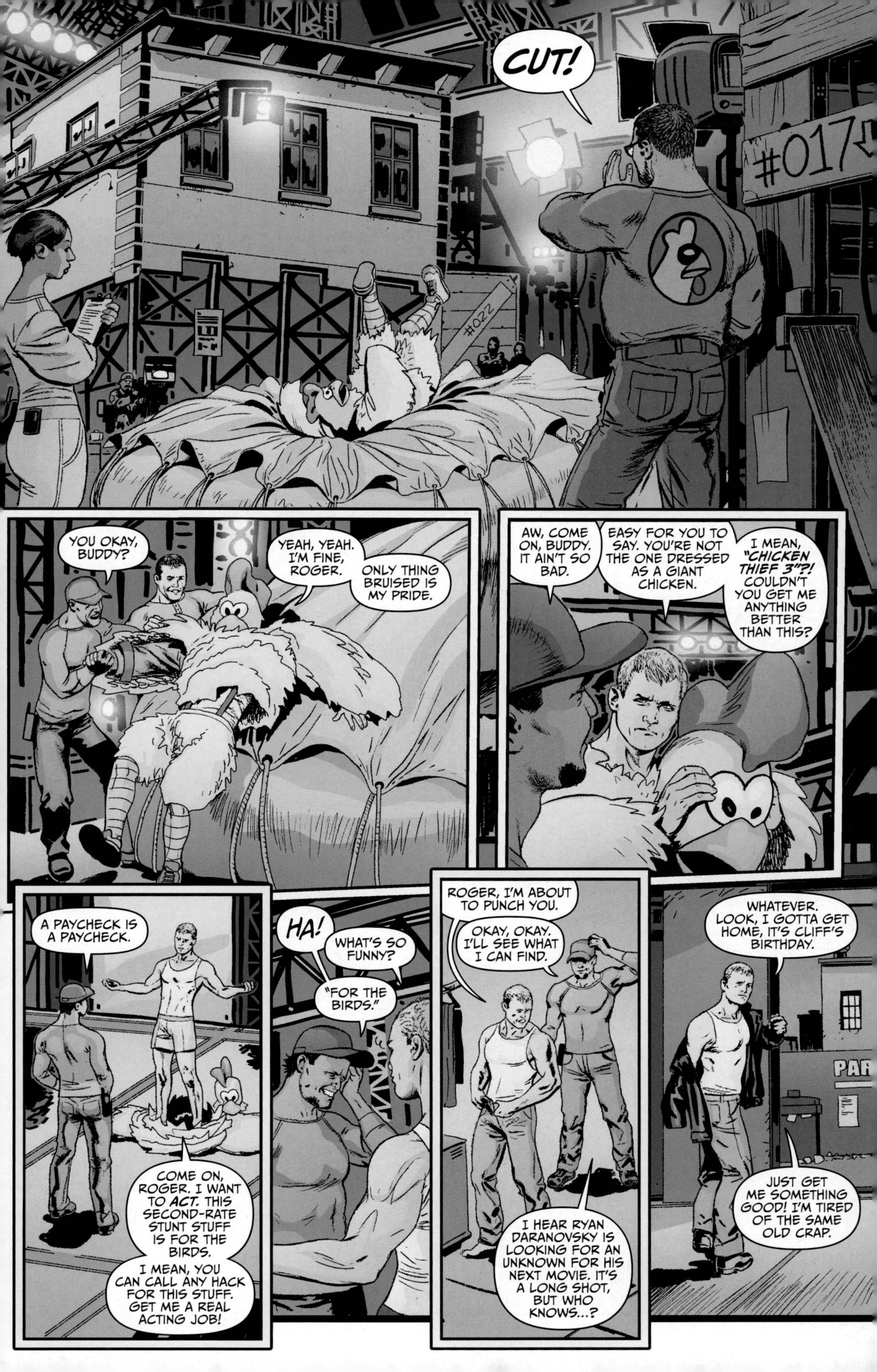
CUT!
#017
#022
YOU OKAY, BUDDY?
YEAH, YEAH. I'M FINE, ROGER.
ONLY THING BRUISED IS MY PRIDE.
AW, COME ON, BUDDY. IT AIN'T SO BAD.
EASY FOR YOU TO SAY. YOU'RE NOT THE ONE DRESSED AS A GIANT CHICKEN.
I MEAN, "CHICKEN THIEF 3"?! COULDN'T YOU GET ME ANYTHING BETTER THAN THIS?
A PAYCHECK IS A PAYCHECK.
COME ON, ROGER. I WANT TO ACT. THIS SECOND-RATE STUNT STUFF IS FOR THE BIRDS.
I MEAN, YOU CAN CALL ANY HACK FOR THIS STUFF. GET ME A REAL ACTING JOB!
HA!
WHAT'S SO FUNNY?
"FOR THE BIRDS."
ROGER, I'M ABOUT TO PUNCH YOU.
OKAY, OKAY. I'LL SEE WHAT I CAN FIND.
I HEAR RYAN DARANOVSKY IS LOOKING FOR AN UNKNOWN FOR HIS NEXT MOVIE. IT'S A LONG SHOT, BUT WHO KNOWS...?
WHATEVER. LOOK, I GOTTA GET HOME, IT'S CLIFF'S BIRTHDAY.
JUST GET ME SOMETHING GOOD! I'M TIRED OF THE SAME OLD CRAP.

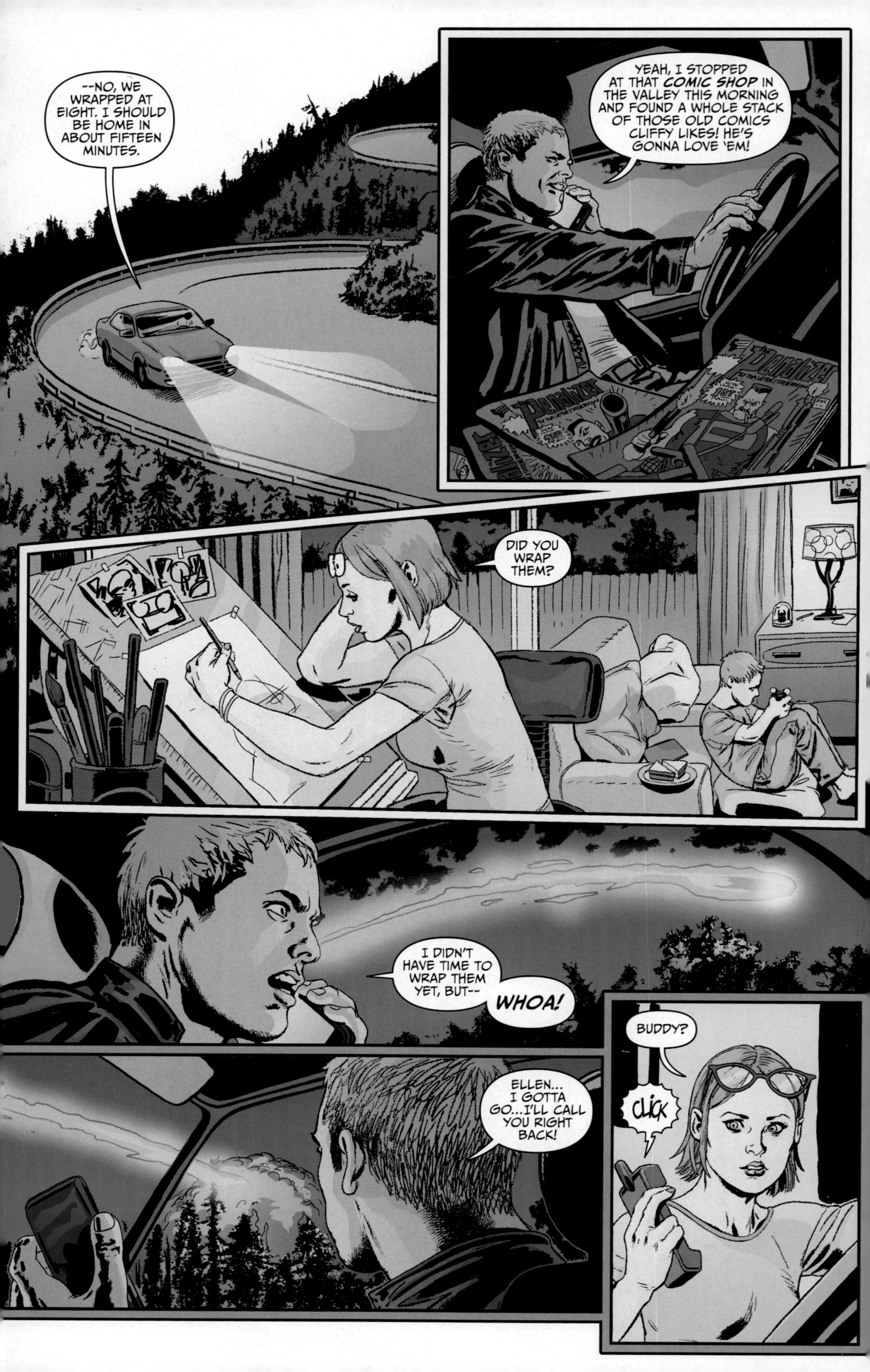
--NO, WE WRAPPED AT EIGHT. I SHOULD BE HOME IN ABOUT FIFTEEN MINUTES.
YEAH, I STOPPED AT THAT COMIC SHOP IN THE VALLEY THIS MORNING AND FOUND A WHOLE STACK OF THOSE OLD COMICS CLIFFY LIKES! HE'S GONNA LOVE 'EM!
DID YOU WRAP THEM?
I DIDN'T HAVE TIME TO WRAP THEM YET, BUT--
WHOA!
BUDDY?
ELLEN... I GOTTA GO...I'LL CALL YOU RIGHT BACK!
CLICK

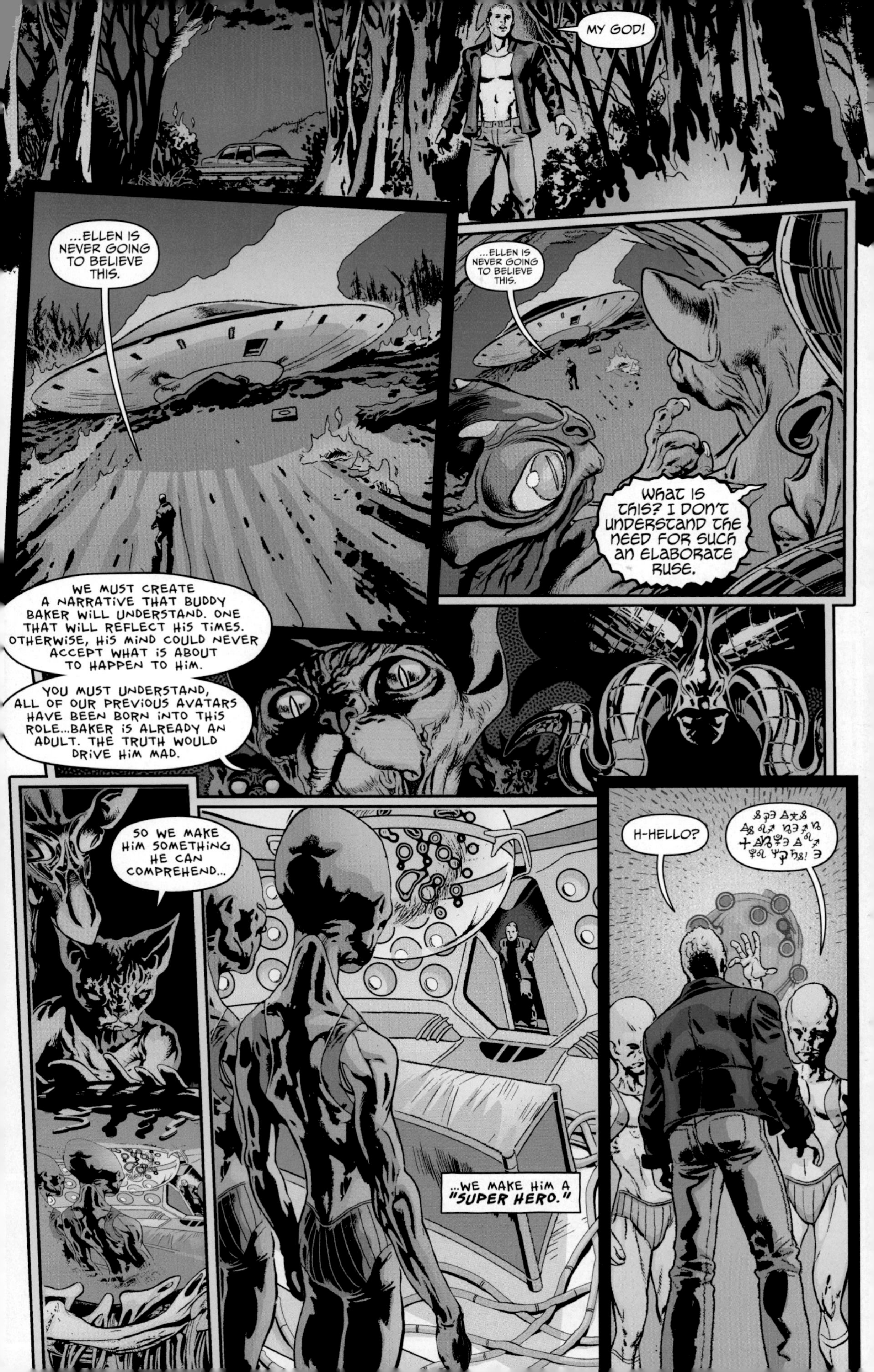

MY GOD!
...ELLEN IS NEVER GOING TO BELIEVE THIS.
...ELLEN IS NEVER GOING TO BELIEVE THIS.
WHAT IS THIS? I DON'T UNDERSTAND THE NEED FOR SUCH AN ELABORATE RUSE.
WE MUST CREATE A NARRATIVE THAT BUDDY BAKER WILL UNDERSTAND. ONE THAT WILL REFLECT HIS TIMES. OTHERWISE, HIS MIND COULD NEVER ACCEPT WHAT IS ABOUT TO HAPPEN TO HIM.
YOU MUST UNDERSTAND, ALL OF OUR PREVIOUS AVATARS HAVE BEEN BORN INTO THIS ROLE...BAKER IS ALREADY AN ADULT. THE TRUTH WOULD DRIVE HIM MAD.
SO WE MAKE HIM SOMETHING HE CAN COMPREHEND...
...WE MAKE HIM A "SUPER HERO."
H-HELLO?

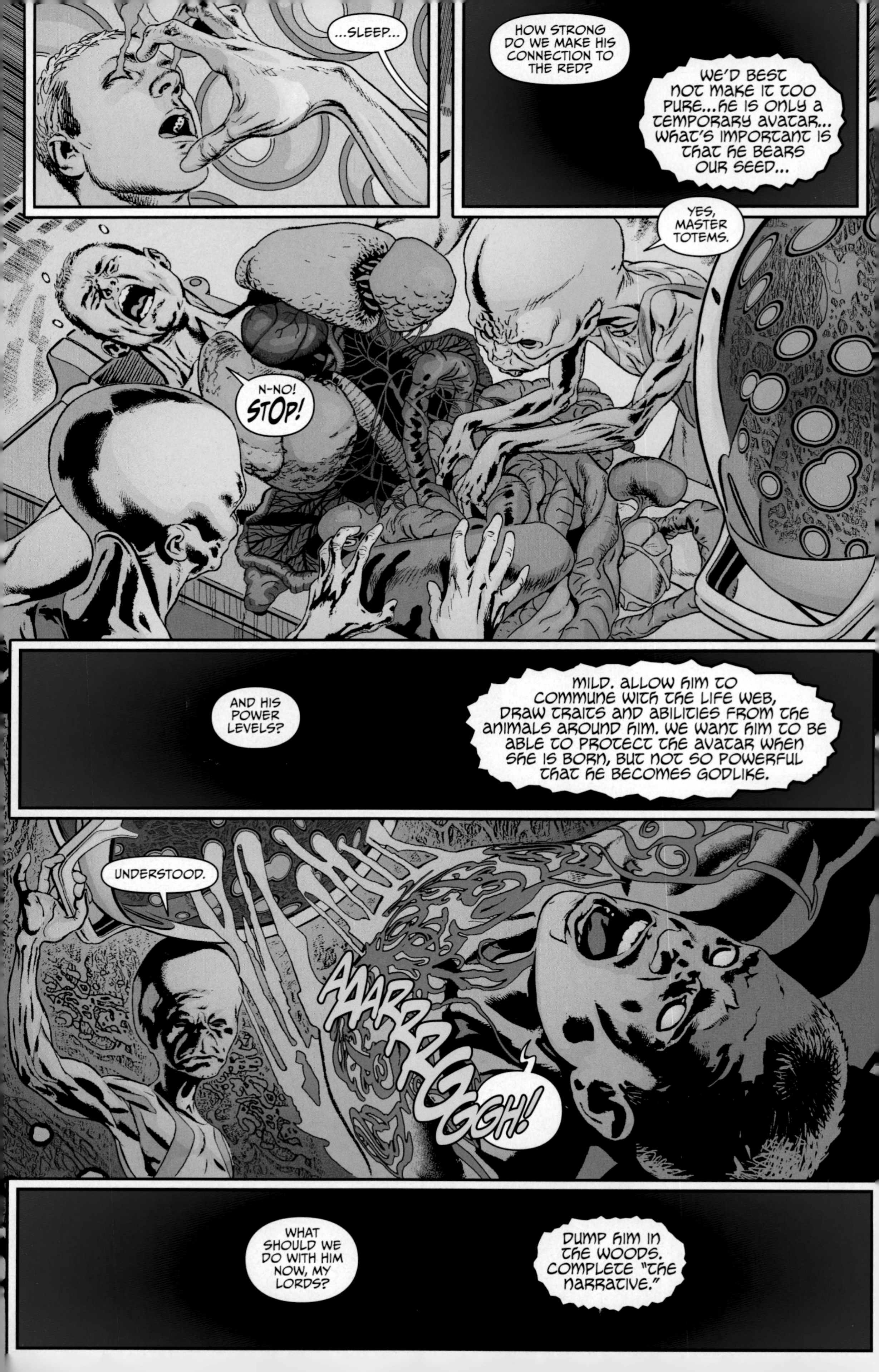
...SLEEP...
HOW STRONG DO WE MAKE HIS CONNECTION TO THE RED?
WE'D BEST NOT MAKE IT TOO PURE...HE IS ONLY A TEMPORARY AVATAR... WHAT'S IMPORTANT IS THAT HE BEARS OUR SEED...
YES, MASTER TOTEMS.
N-NO! STOP!
AND HIS POWER LEVELS?
MILD. ALLOW HIM TO COMMUNE WITH THE LIFE WEB, DRAW TRAITS AND ABILITIES FROM THE ANIMALS AROUND HIM. WE WANT HIM TO BE ABLE TO PROTECT THE AVATAR WHEN SHE IS BORN, BUT NOT SO POWERFUL THAT HE BECOMES GODLIKE.
UNDERSTOOD.
AAARRRGGGH!
WHAT SHOULD WE DO WITH HIM NOW, MY LORDS?
DUMP HIM IN THE WOODS. COMPLETE "THE NARRATIVE."

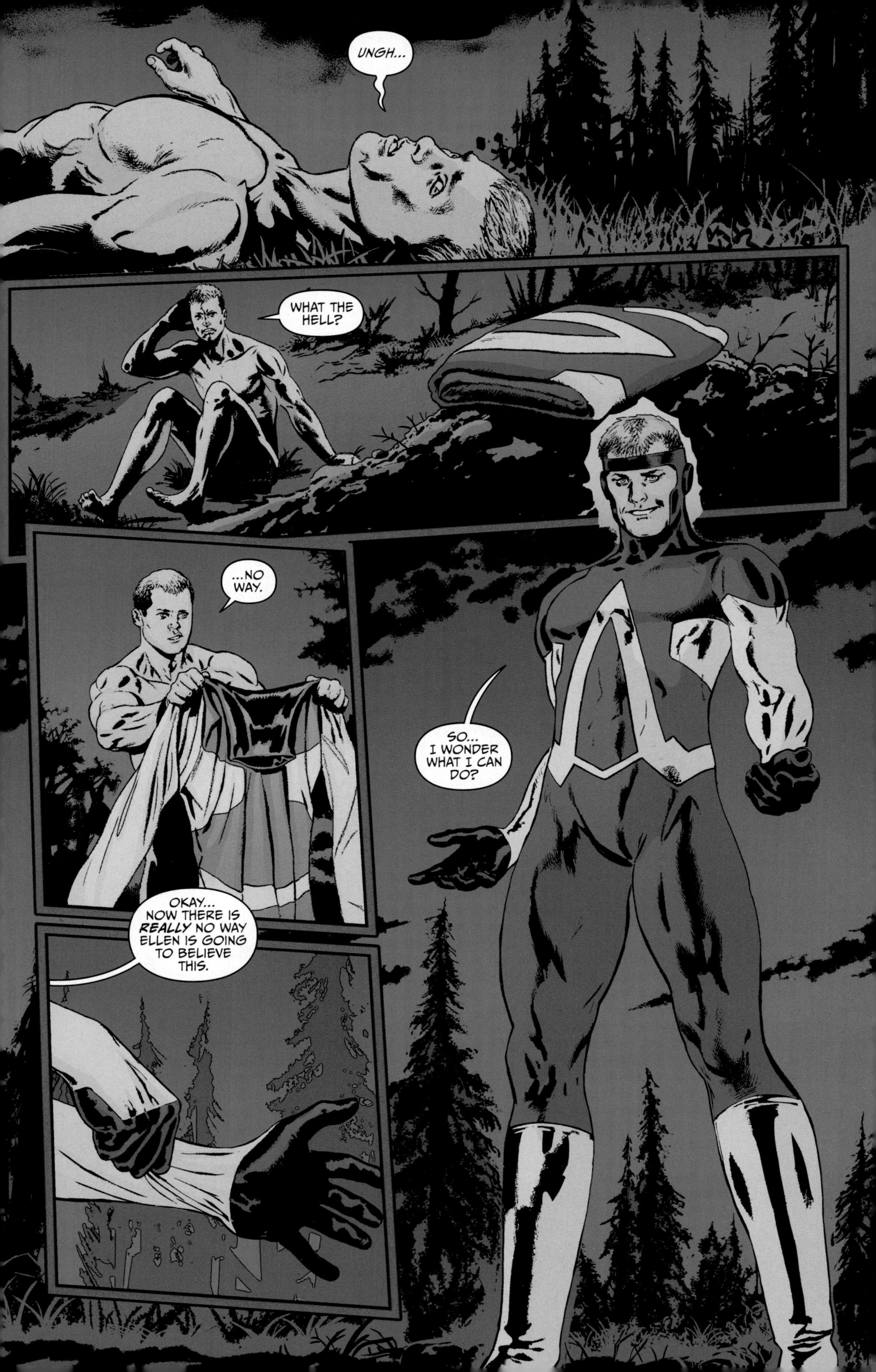
UNGH...
WHAT THE HELL?
...NO WAY.
SO... I WONDER WHAT I CAN DO?
OKAY... NOW THERE IS REALLY NO WAY ELLEN IS GOING TO BELIEVE THIS.

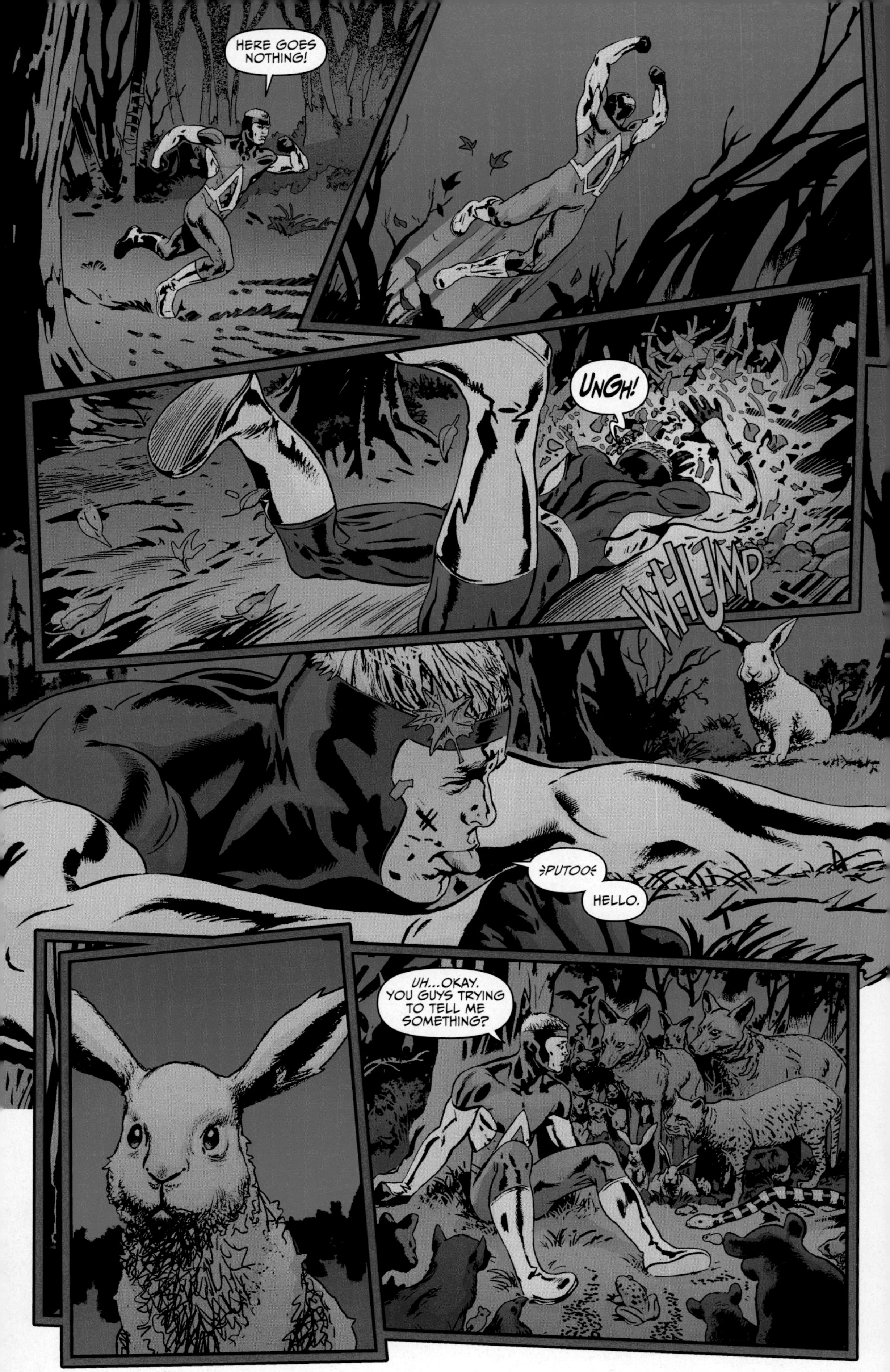
HERE GOES NOTHING!
UNGH!
WHUMP
PUTOO
HELLO.
UH...OKAY. YOU GUYS TRYING TO TELL ME SOMETHING?

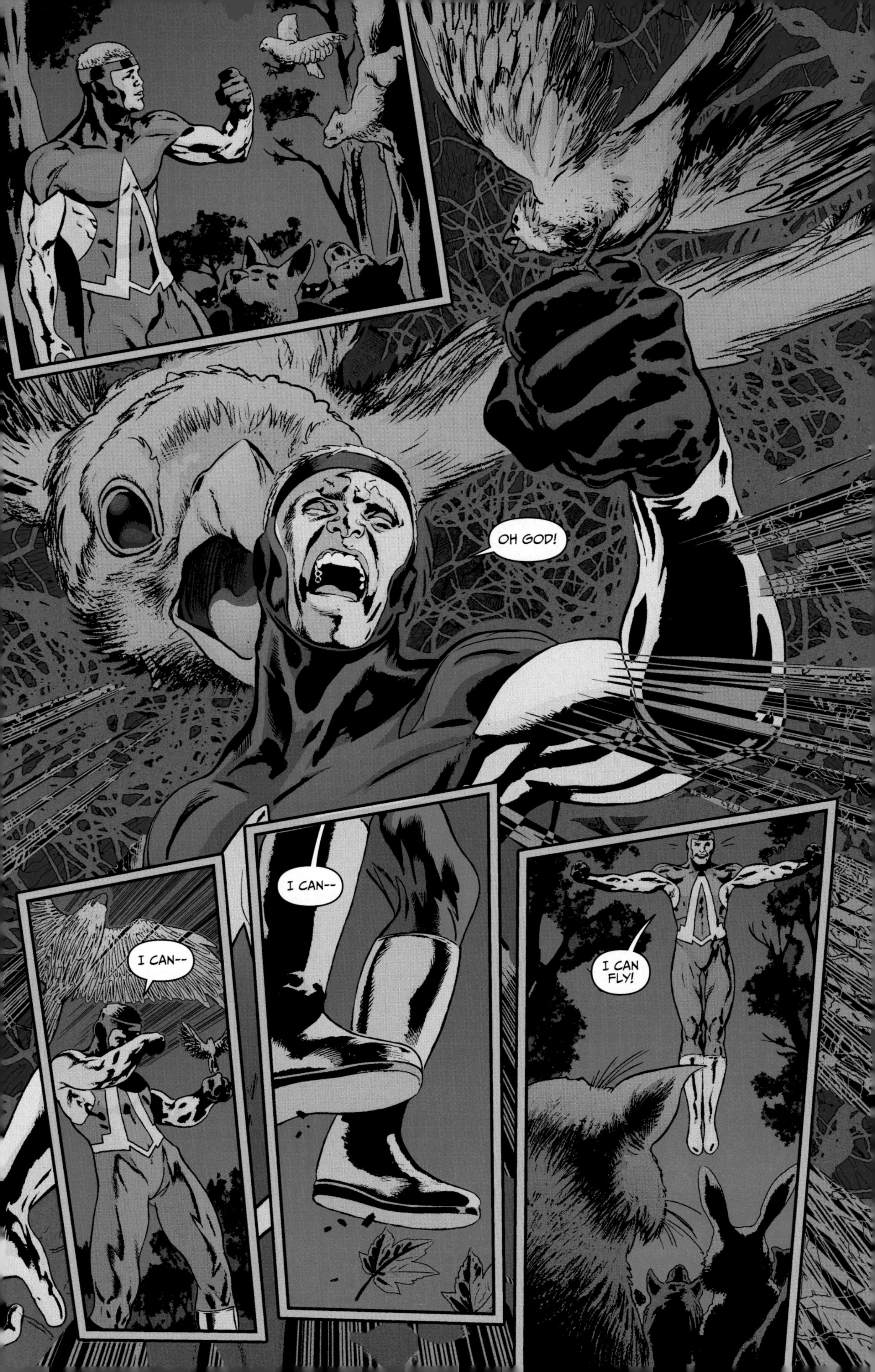
OH GOD!
I CAN--
I CAN--
I CAN FLY!

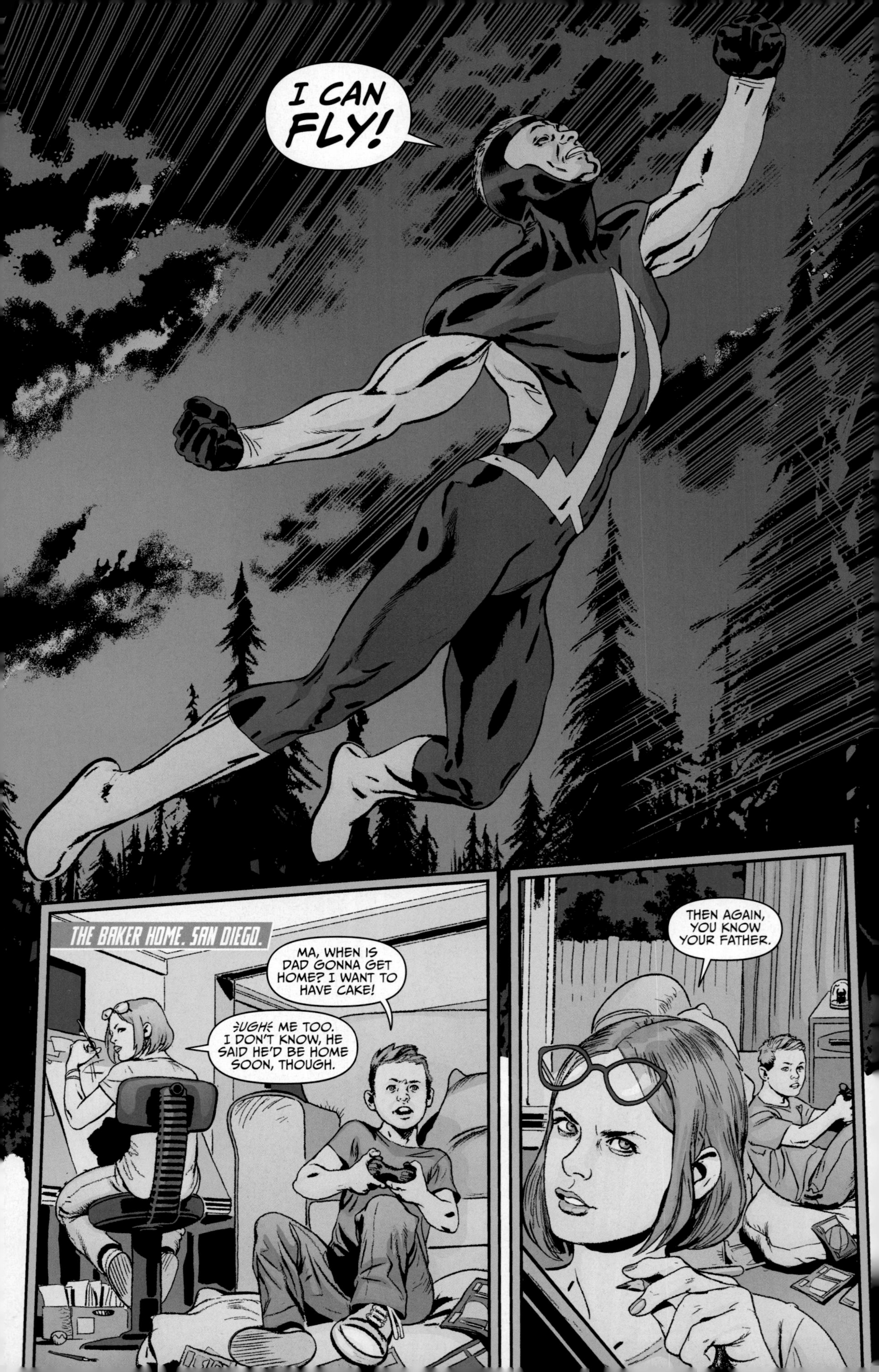
I CAN FLY!
THE BAKER HOME. SAN DIEGO.
MA, WHEN IS DAD GONNA GET HOME? I WANT TO HAVE CAKE!
UGH ME TOO. I DON'T KNOW, HE SAID HE'D BE HOME SOON, THOUGH.
THEN AGAIN, YOU KNOW YOUR FATHER.

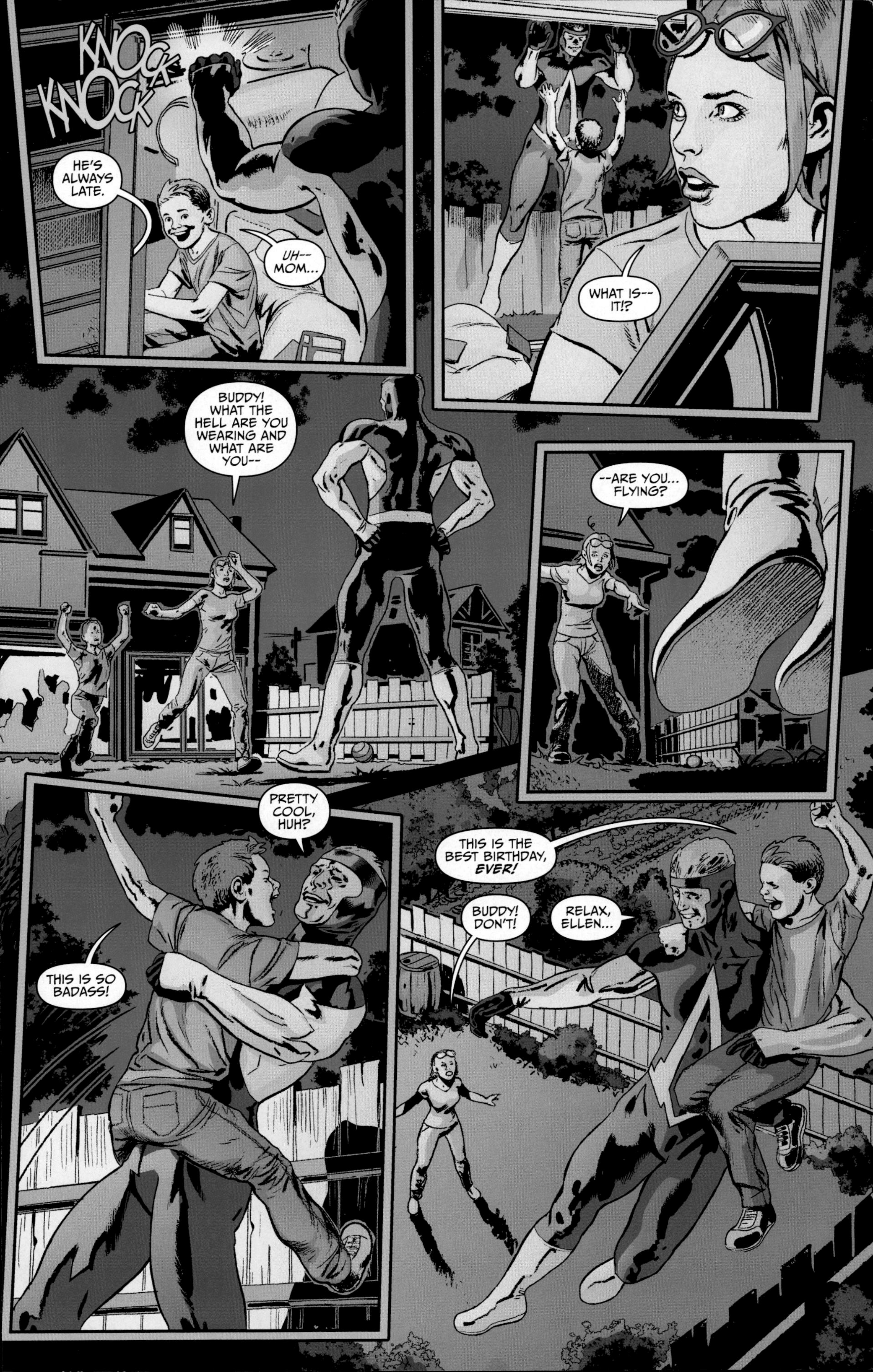
KNOCK KNOCK
HE'S ALWAYS LATE.
UH-- MOM...
WHAT IS-- IT!?
BUDDY! WHAT THE HELL ARE YOU WEARING AND WHAT ARE YOU--
--ARE YOU... FLYING?
PRETTY COOL, HUH?
THIS IS SO BADASS!
THIS IS THE BEST BIRTHDAY, *EVER!*
BUDDY! DON'T!
RELAX, ELLEN...

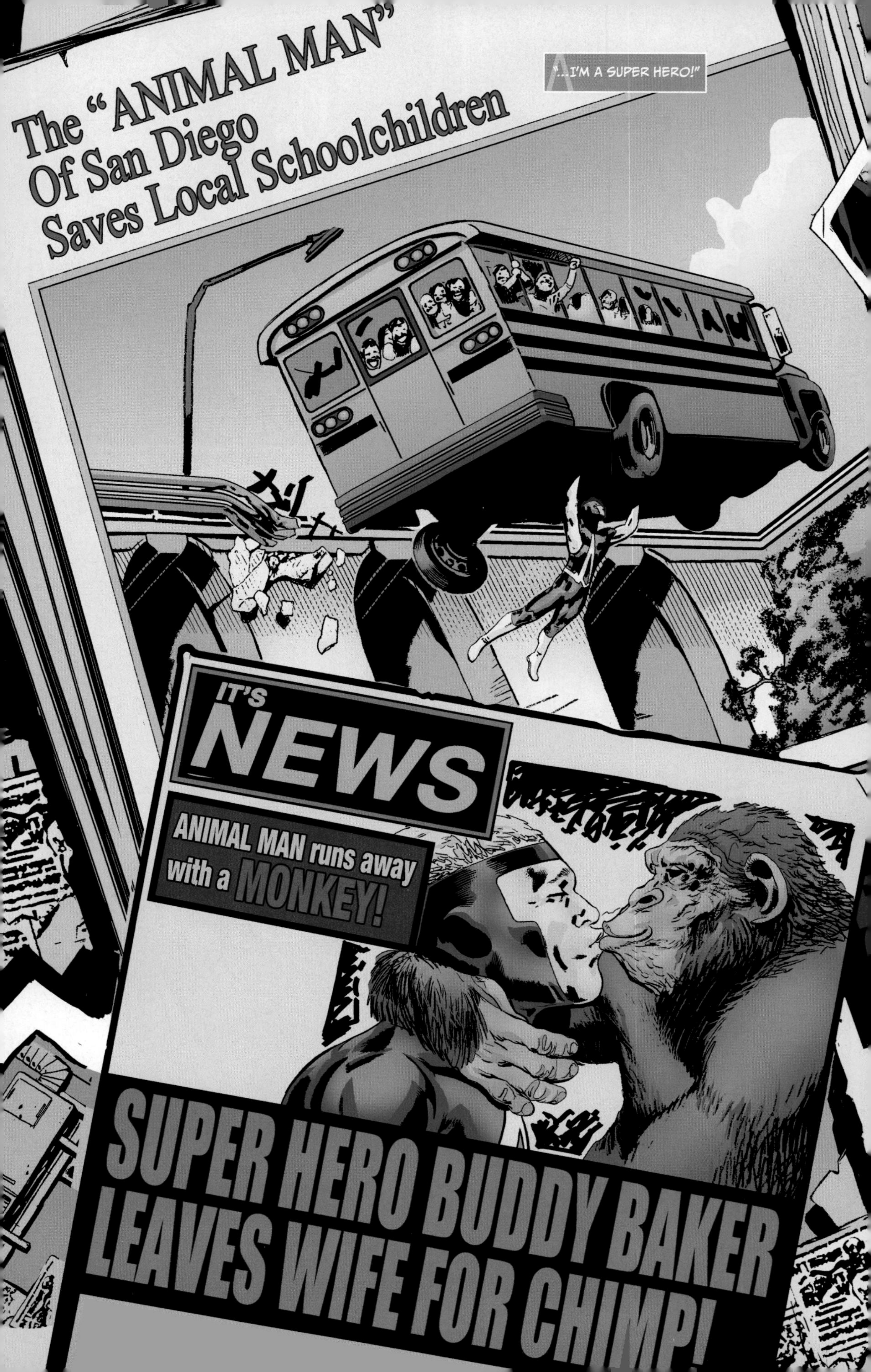
"...I'M A SUPER HERO!"
The "ANIMAL MAN" Of San Diego Saves Local Schoolchildren
IT'S NEWS
ANIMAL MAN runs away with a MONKEY!
SUPER HERO BUDDY BAKER LEAVES WIFE FOR CHIMP!

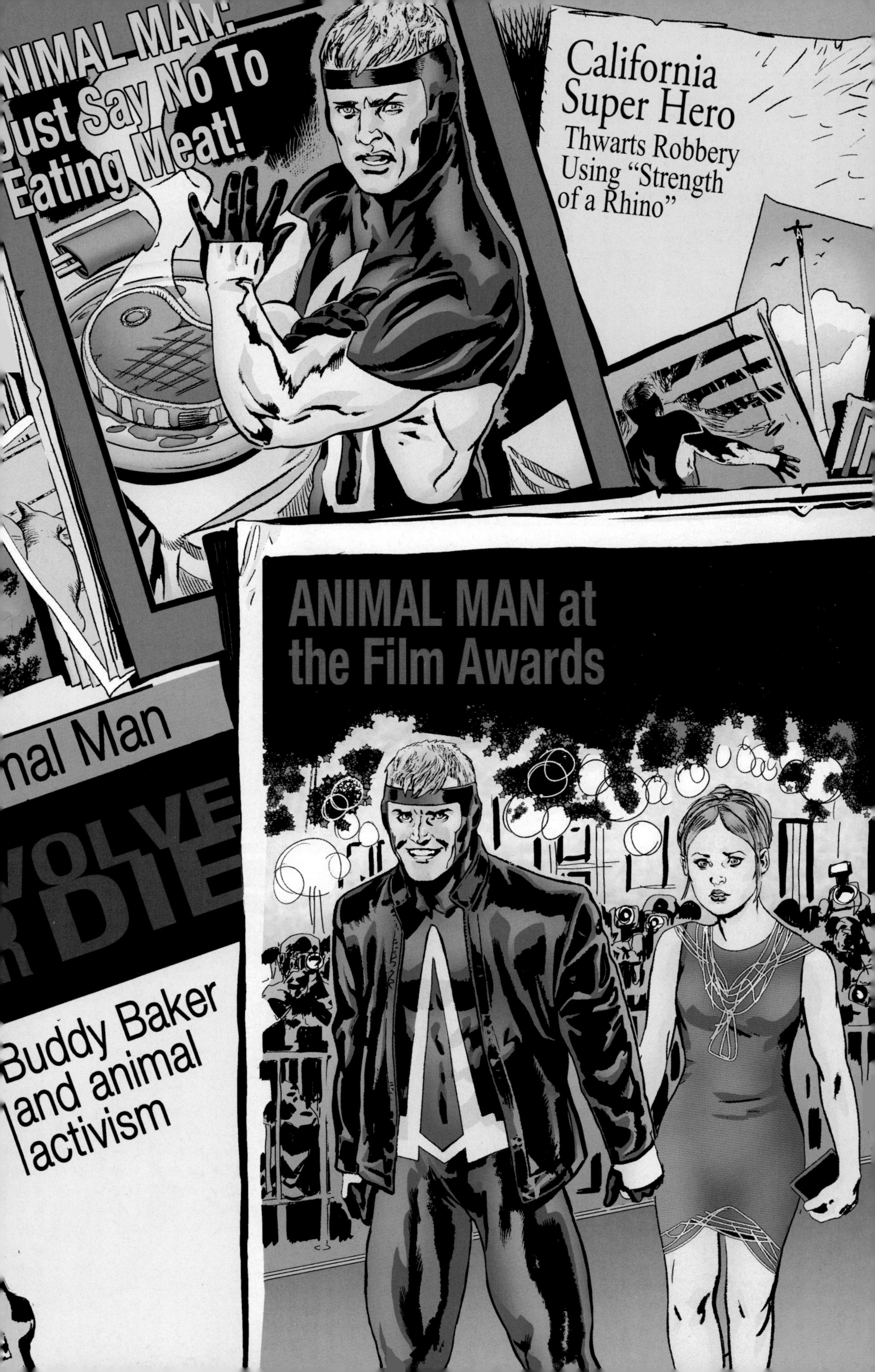
NIMAL MAN:
Just Say No To
Eating Meat!
California
Super Hero
Thwarts Robbery
Using "Strength
of a Rhino"
nal Man
VOLVE
R DIE
Buddy Baker
and animal
activism
ANIMAL MAN at
the Film Awards

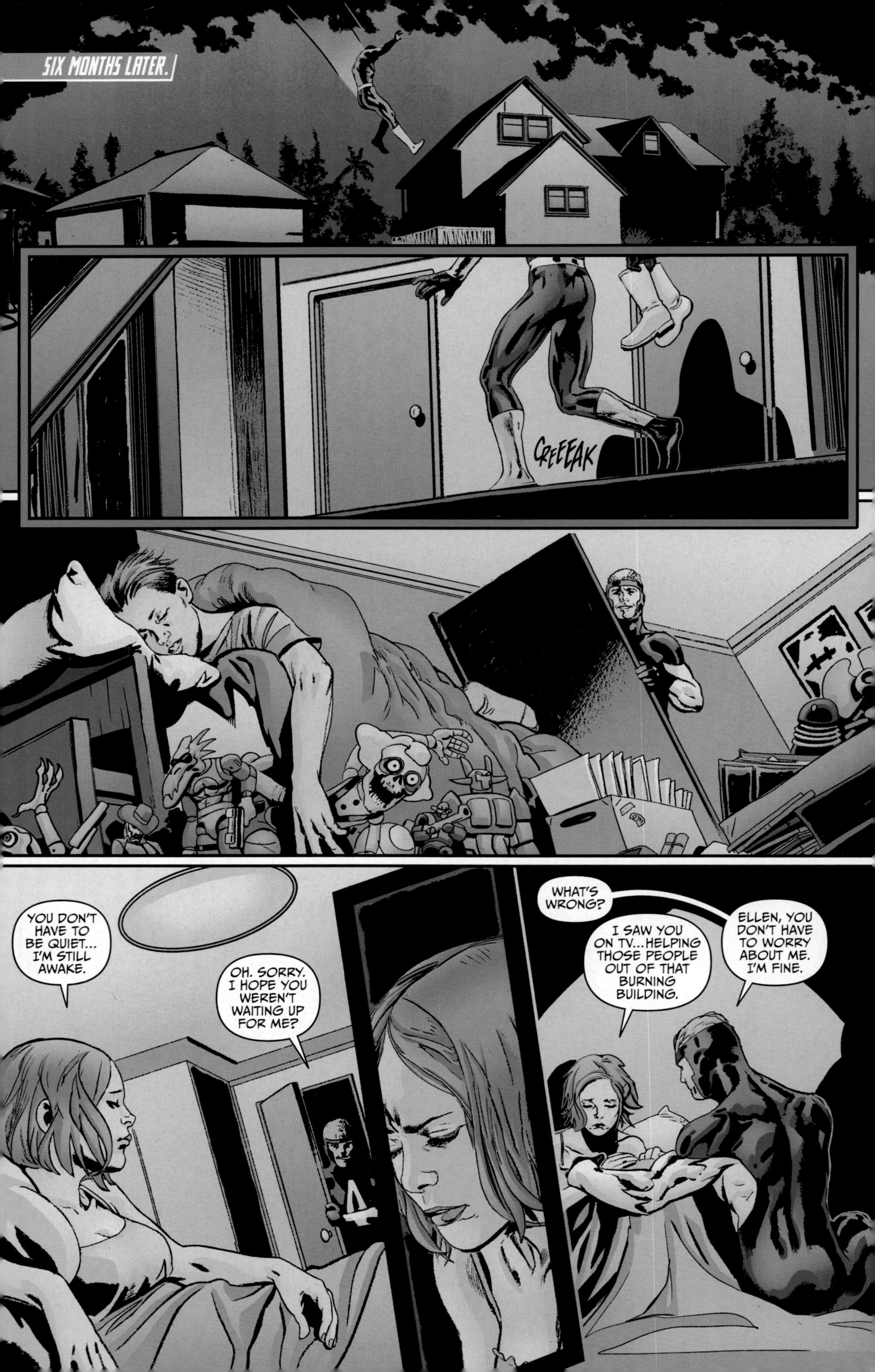
SIX MONTHS LATER.
CREEEAK
YOU DON'T HAVE TO BE QUIET... I'M STILL AWAKE.
OH. SORRY. I HOPE YOU WEREN'T WAITING UP FOR ME?
WHAT'S WRONG?
I SAW YOU ON TV...HELPING THOSE PEOPLE OUT OF THAT BURNING BUILDING.
ELLEN, YOU DON'T HAVE TO WORRY ABOUT ME. I'M FINE.

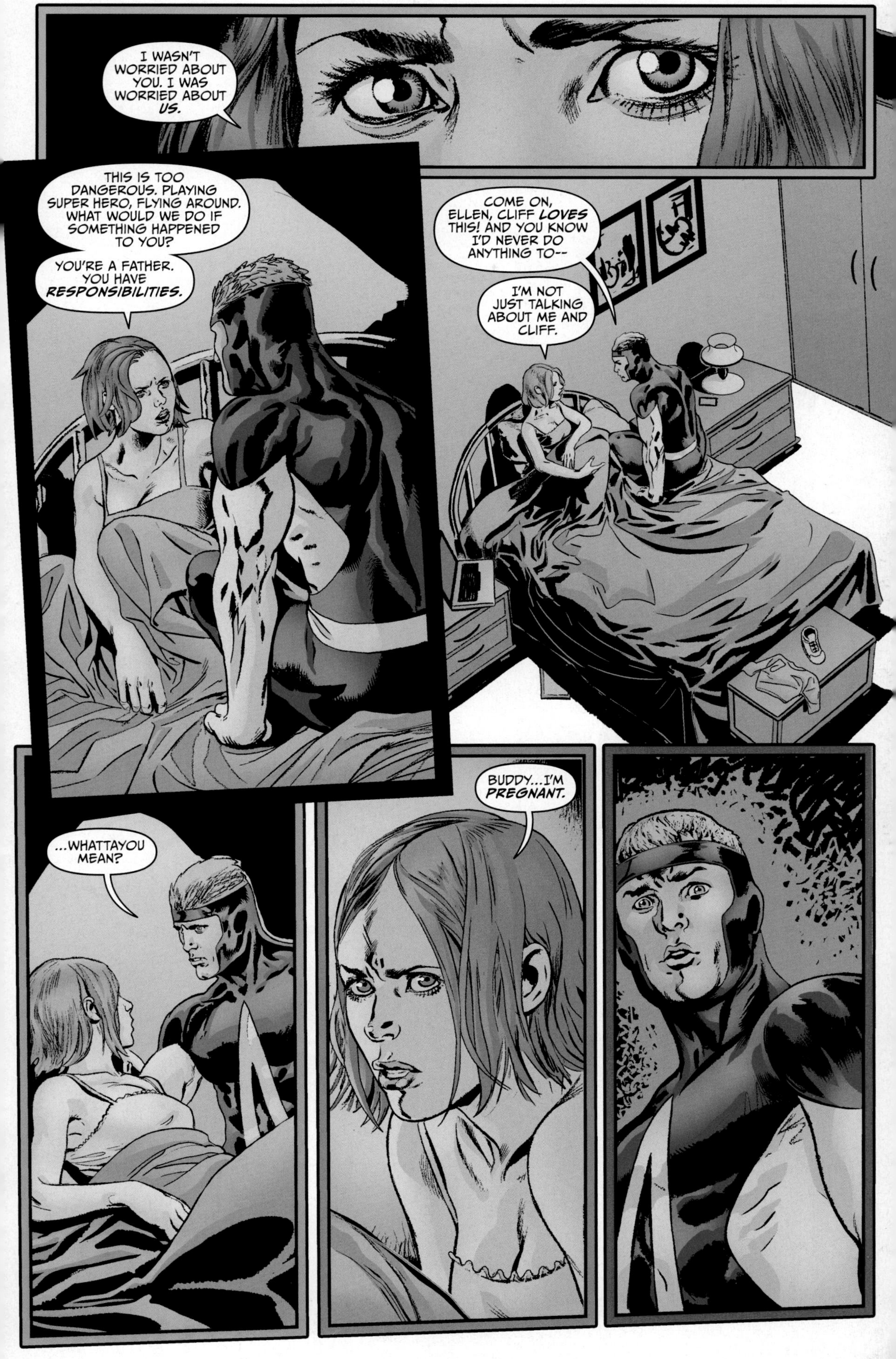

I WASN'T WORRIED ABOUT YOU. I WAS WORRIED ABOUT *US.*
THIS IS TOO DANGEROUS. PLAYING SUPER HERO, FLYING AROUND. WHAT WOULD WE DO IF SOMETHING HAPPENED TO YOU?
YOU'RE A FATHER. YOU HAVE ***RESPONSIBILITIES.***
COME ON, ELLEN, CLIFF ***LOVES*** THIS! AND YOU KNOW I'D NEVER DO ANYTHING TO--
I'M NOT JUST TALKING ABOUT ME AND CLIFF.
...WHATTAYOU MEAN?
BUDDY...I'M ***PREGNANT.***

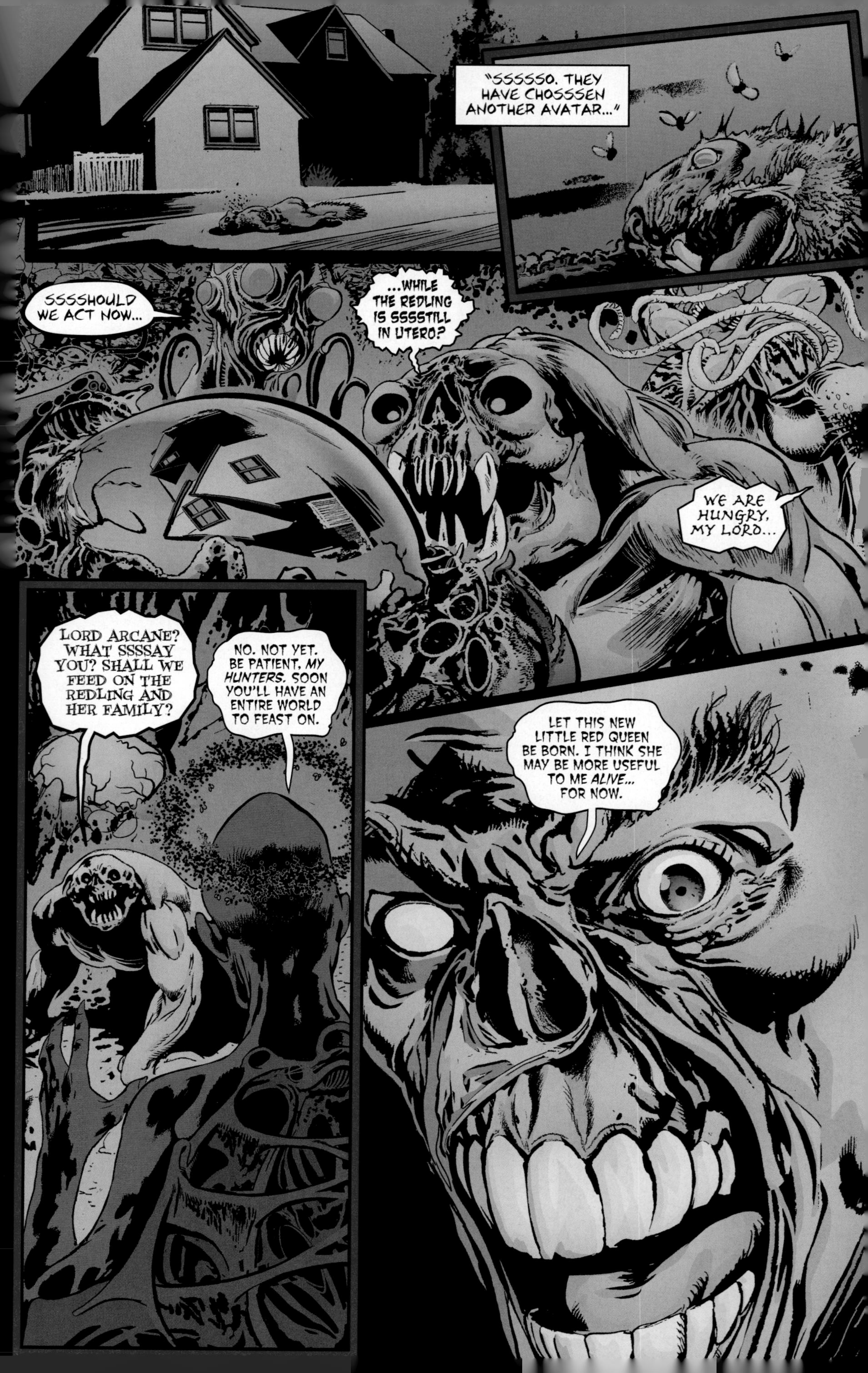
"SSSSSO. THEY HAVE CHOSSSEN ANOTHER AVATAR..."
SSSSHOULD WE ACT NOW...
...WHILE THE REDLING IS SSSSTILL IN UTERO?
WE ARE HUNGRY, MY LORD...
LORD ARCANE? WHAT SSSSAY YOU? SHALL WE FEED ON THE REDLING AND HER FAMILY?
NO. NOT YET. BE PATIENT, MY HUNTERS. SOON YOU'LL HAVE AN ENTIRE WORLD TO FEAST ON.
LET THIS NEW LITTLE RED QUEEN BE BORN. I THINK SHE MAY BE MORE USEFUL TO ME ALIVE... FOR NOW.

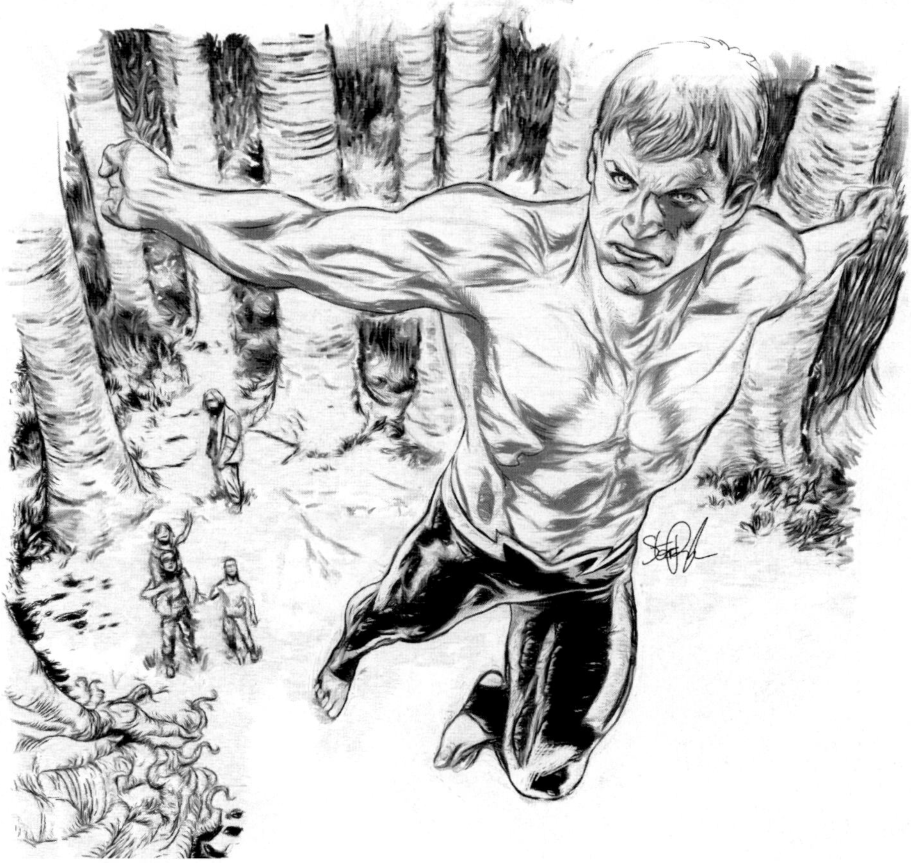

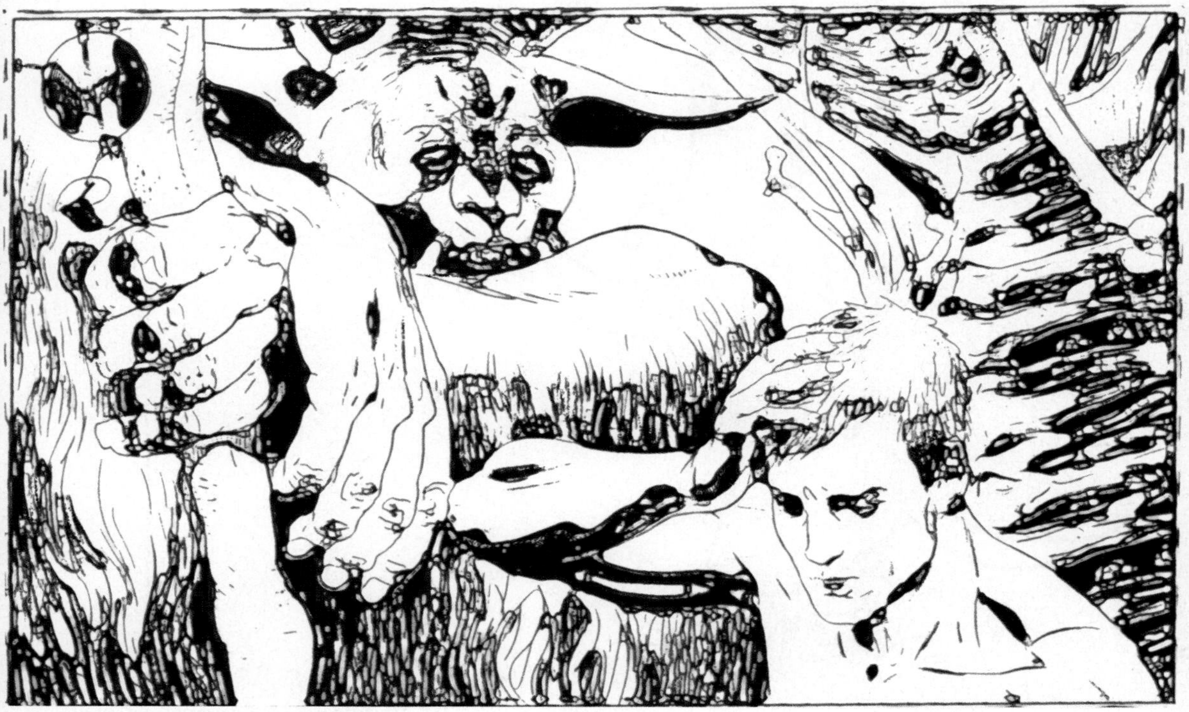

Animal Man sketches by Steve Pugh

Sketches by Steve Pugh

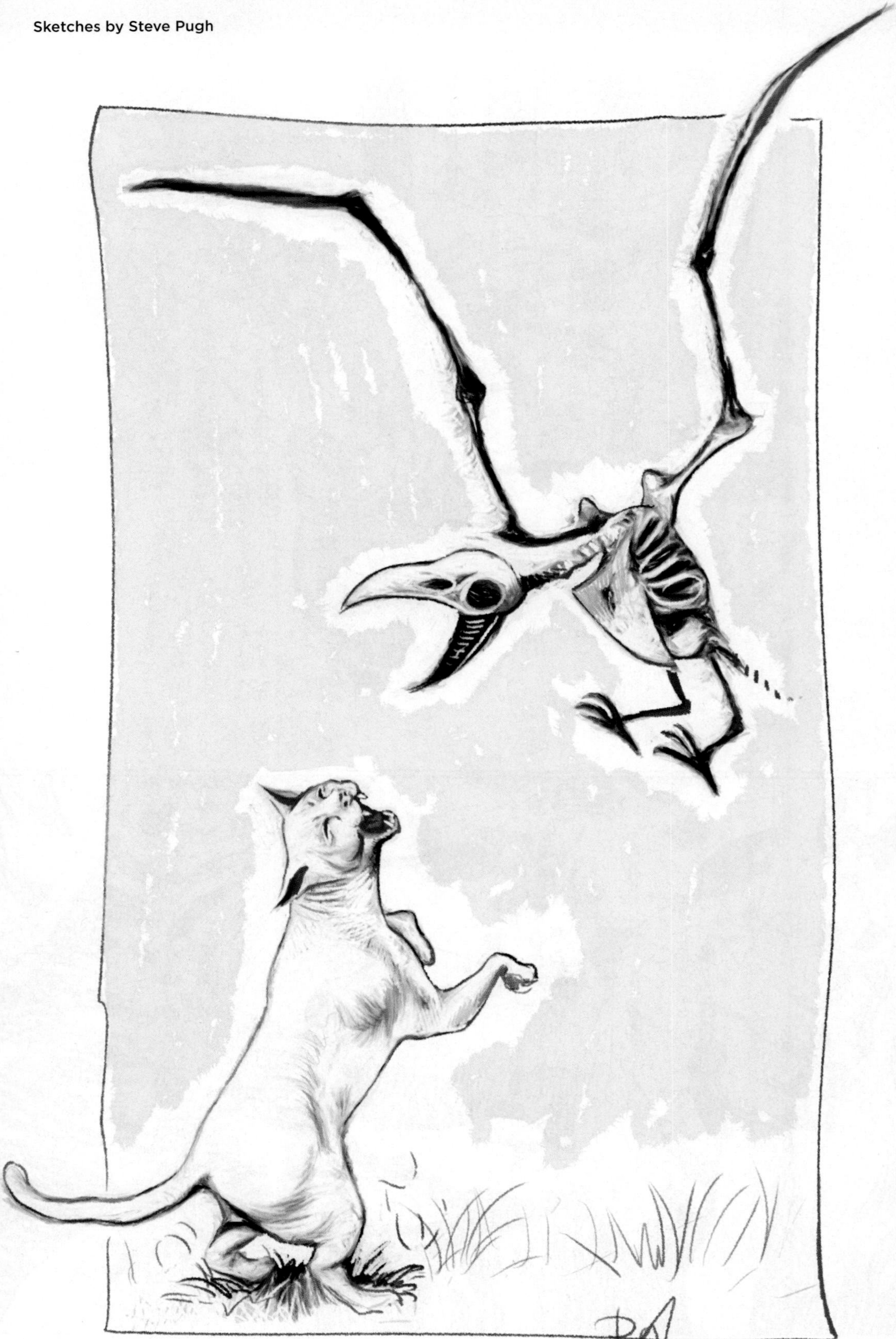

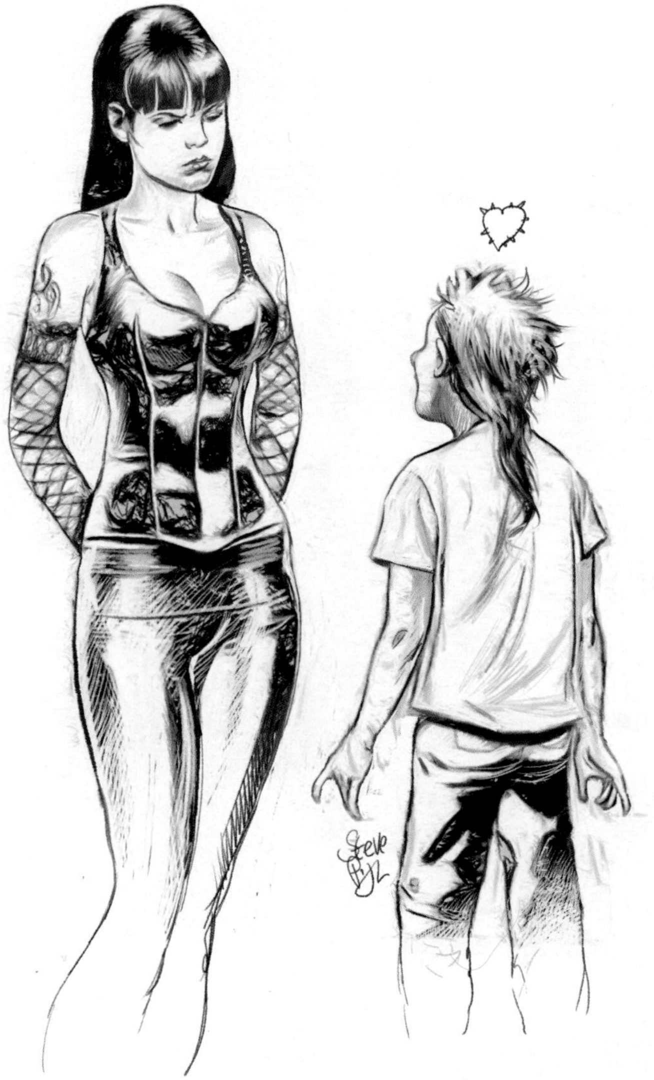

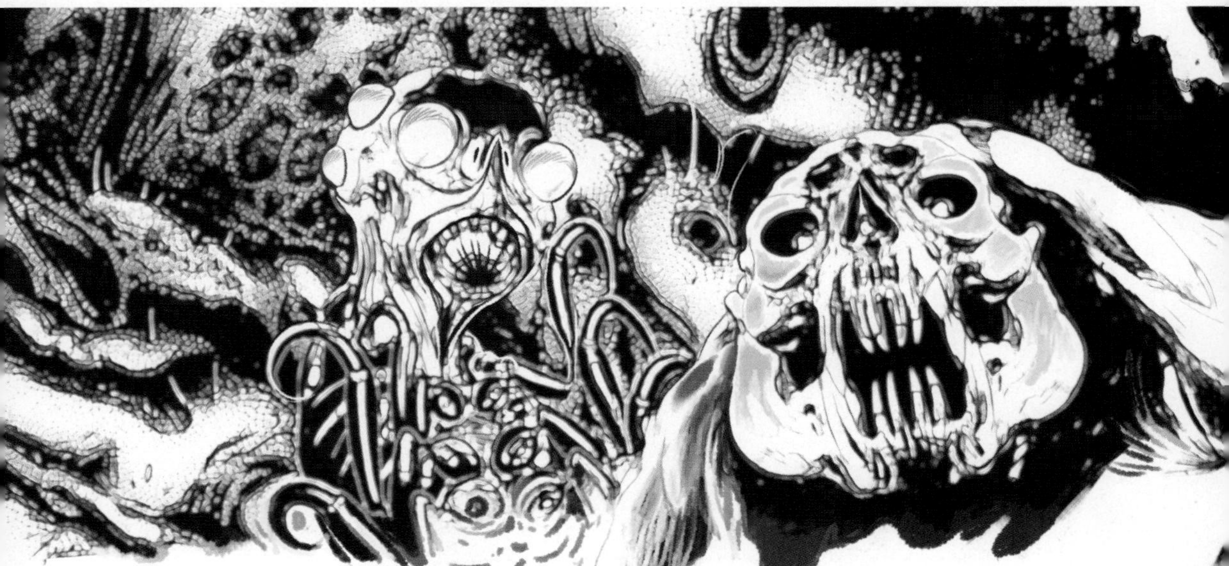

Sketches by Timothy Green II

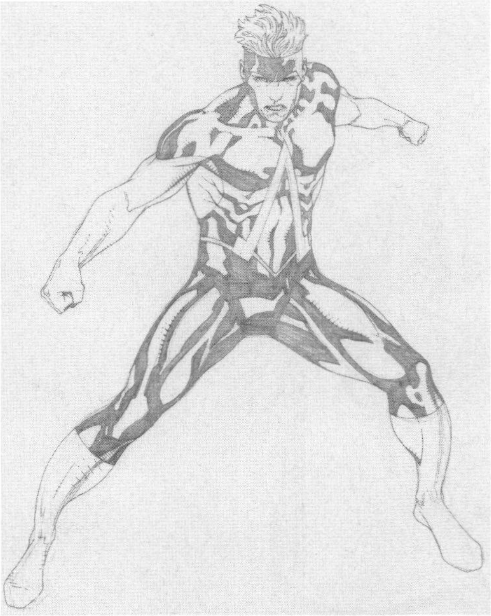

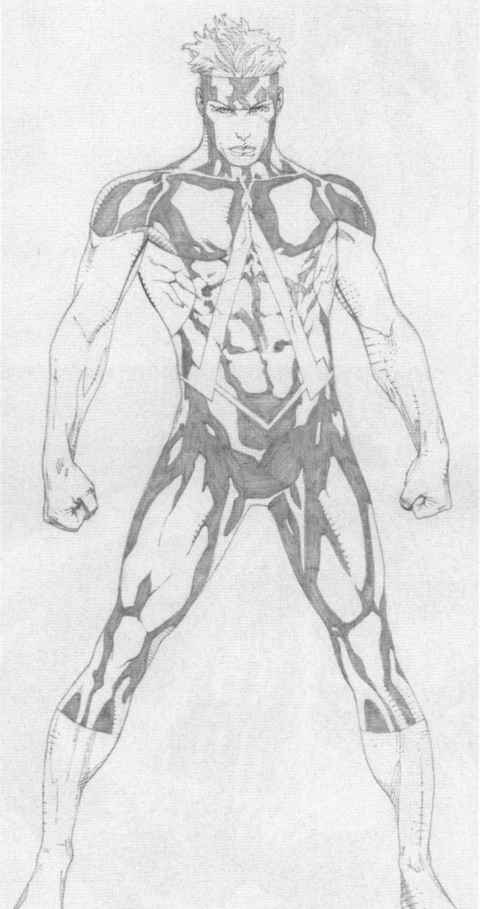

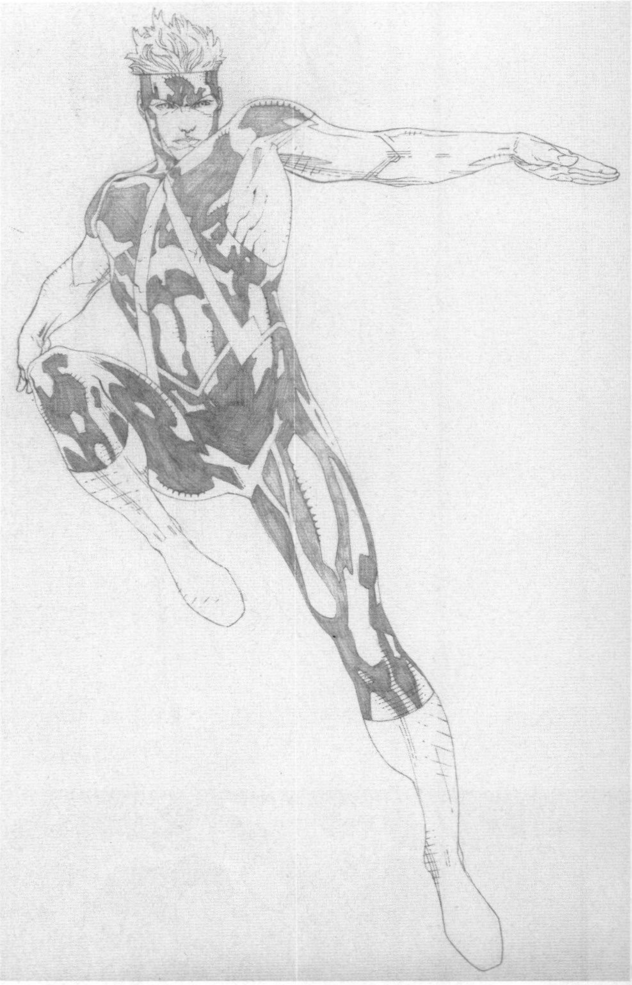

Sketches by Alberto Ponticelli

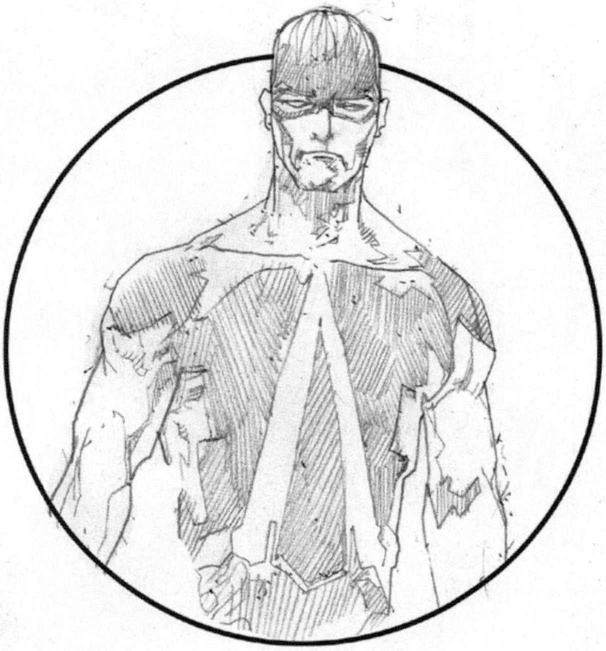

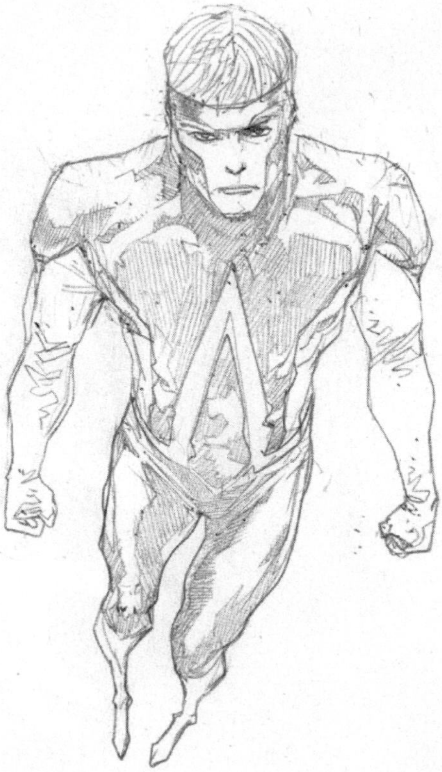

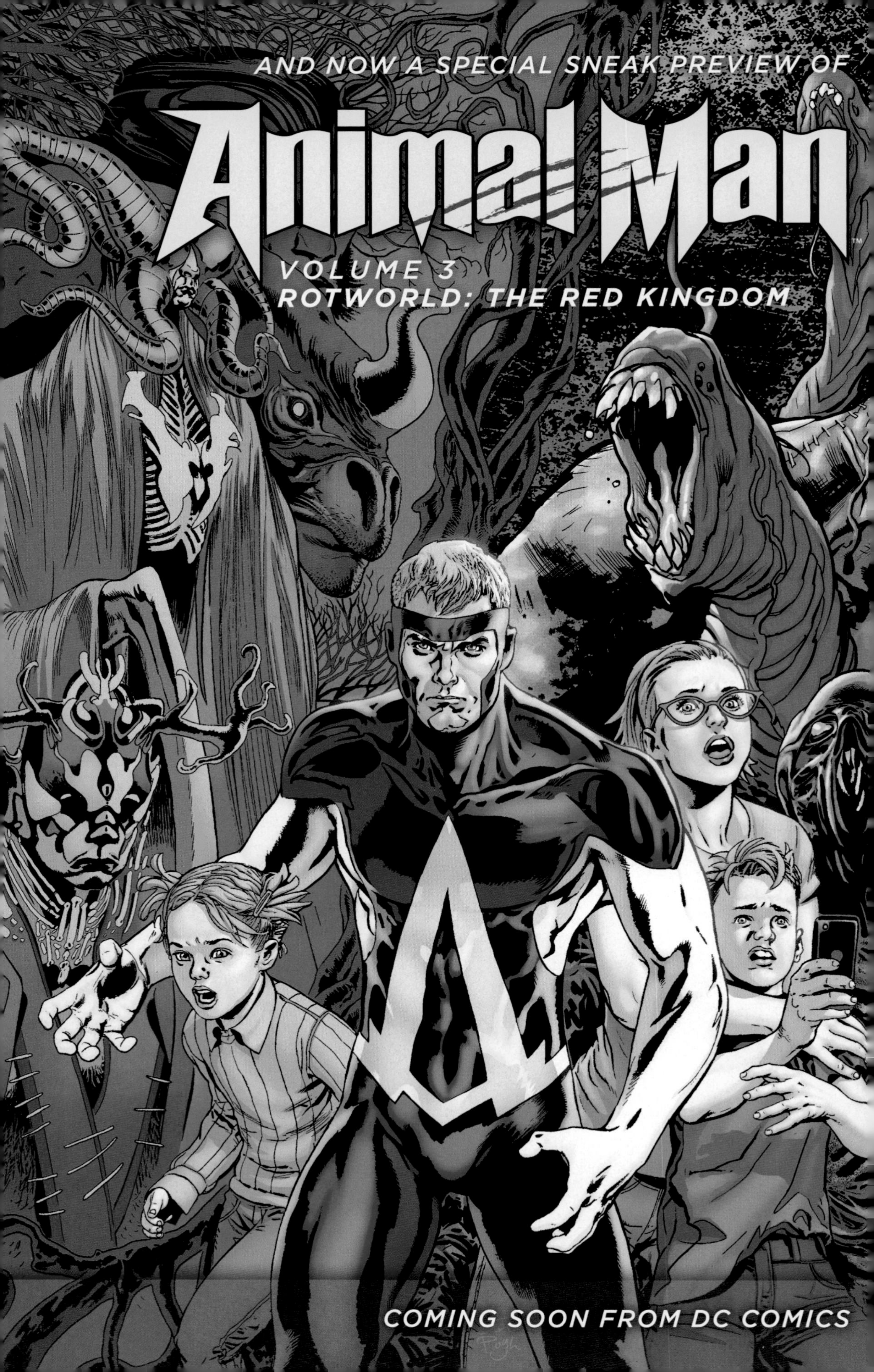
AND NOW A SPECIAL SNEAK PREVIEW OF
Animal Man™
VOLUME 3
ROTWORLD: THE RED KINGDOM
COMING SOON FROM DC COMICS

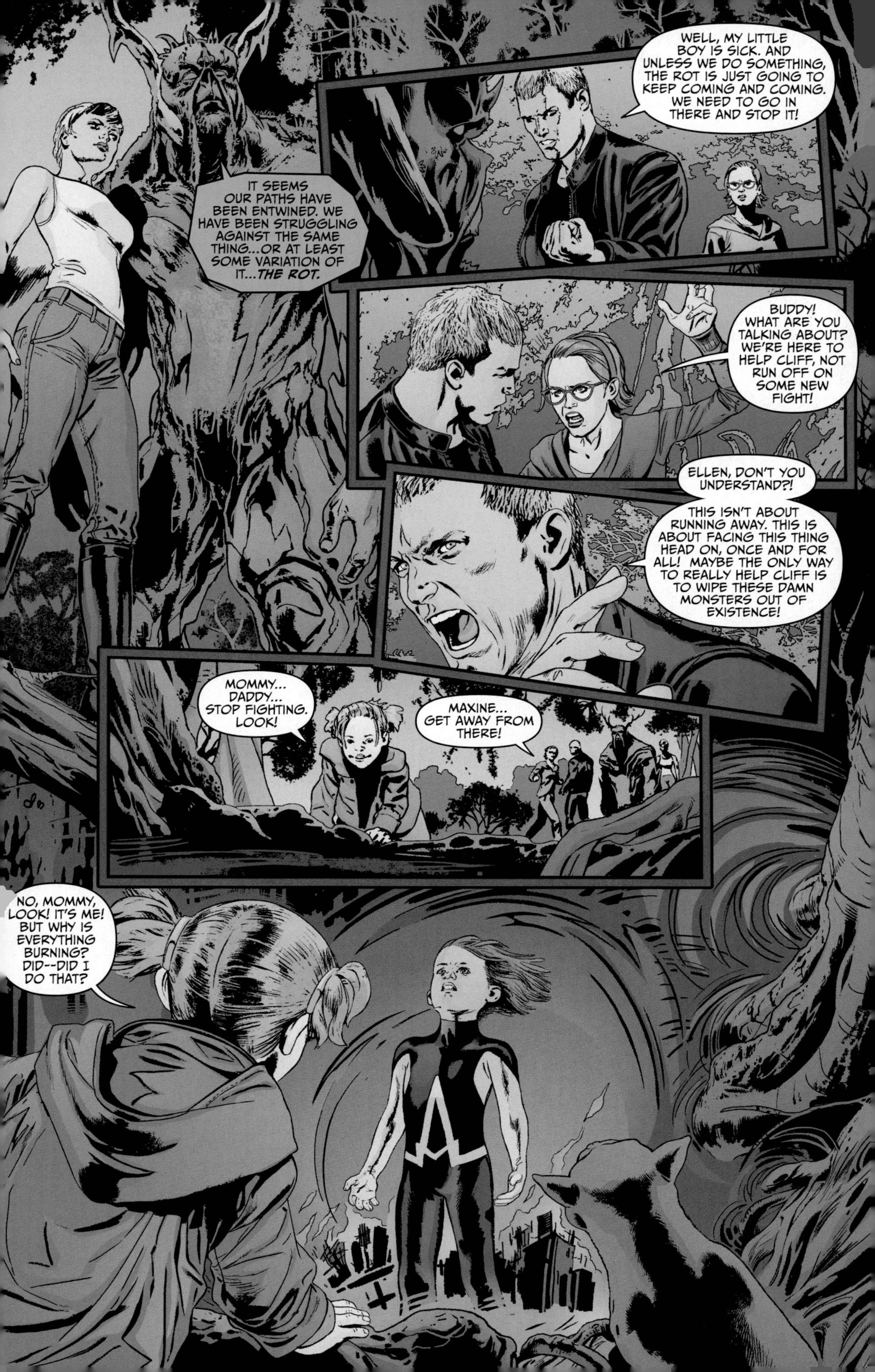
IT SEEMS OUR PATHS HAVE BEEN ENTWINED. WE HAVE BEEN STRUGGLING AGAINST THE SAME THING...OR AT LEAST SOME VARIATION OF IT...*THE ROT*.
WELL, MY LITTLE BOY IS SICK. AND UNLESS WE DO SOMETHING, THE ROT IS JUST GOING TO KEEP COMING AND COMING. WE NEED TO GO IN THERE AND STOP IT!
BUDDY! WHAT ARE YOU TALKING ABOUT? WE'RE HERE TO HELP CLIFF, NOT RUN OFF ON SOME NEW FIGHT!
ELLEN, DON'T YOU UNDERSTAND?!
THIS ISN'T ABOUT RUNNING AWAY. THIS IS ABOUT FACING THIS THING HEAD ON, ONCE AND FOR ALL! MAYBE THE ONLY WAY TO REALLY HELP CLIFF IS TO WIPE THESE DAMN MONSTERS OUT OF EXISTENCE!
MOMMY... DADDY... STOP FIGHTING. LOOK!
MAXINE... GET AWAY FROM THERE!
NO, MOMMY, LOOK! IT'S ME! BUT WHY IS EVERYTHING BURNING? DID--DID I DO THAT?

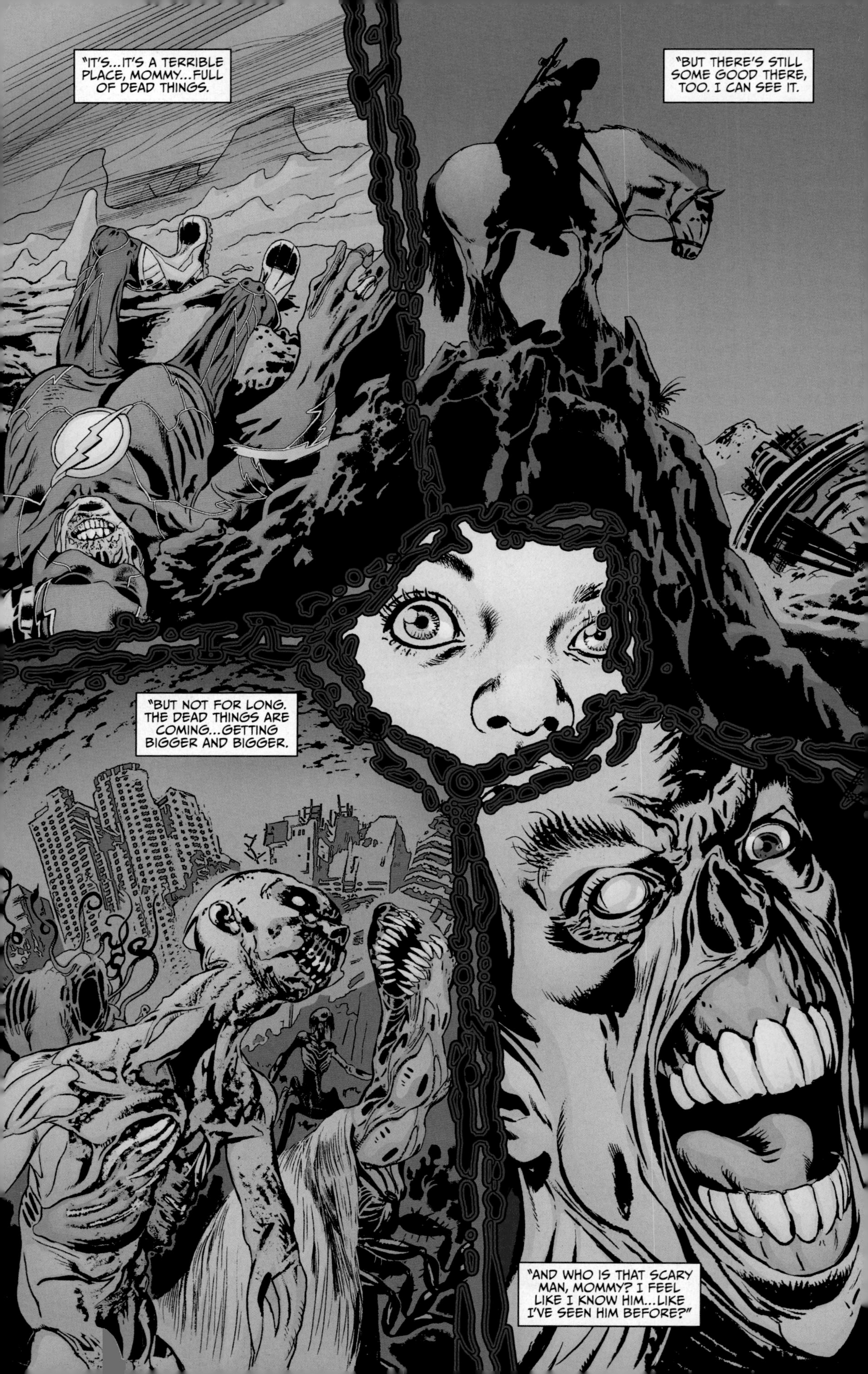
"IT'S...IT'S A TERRIBLE PLACE, MOMMY...FULL OF DEAD THINGS.
"BUT THERE'S STILL SOME GOOD THERE, TOO. I CAN SEE IT.
"BUT NOT FOR LONG. THE DEAD THINGS ARE COMING...GETTING BIGGER AND BIGGER.
"AND WHO IS THAT SCARY MAN, MOMMY? I FEEL LIKE I KNOW HIM...LIKE I'VE SEEN HIM BEFORE?"

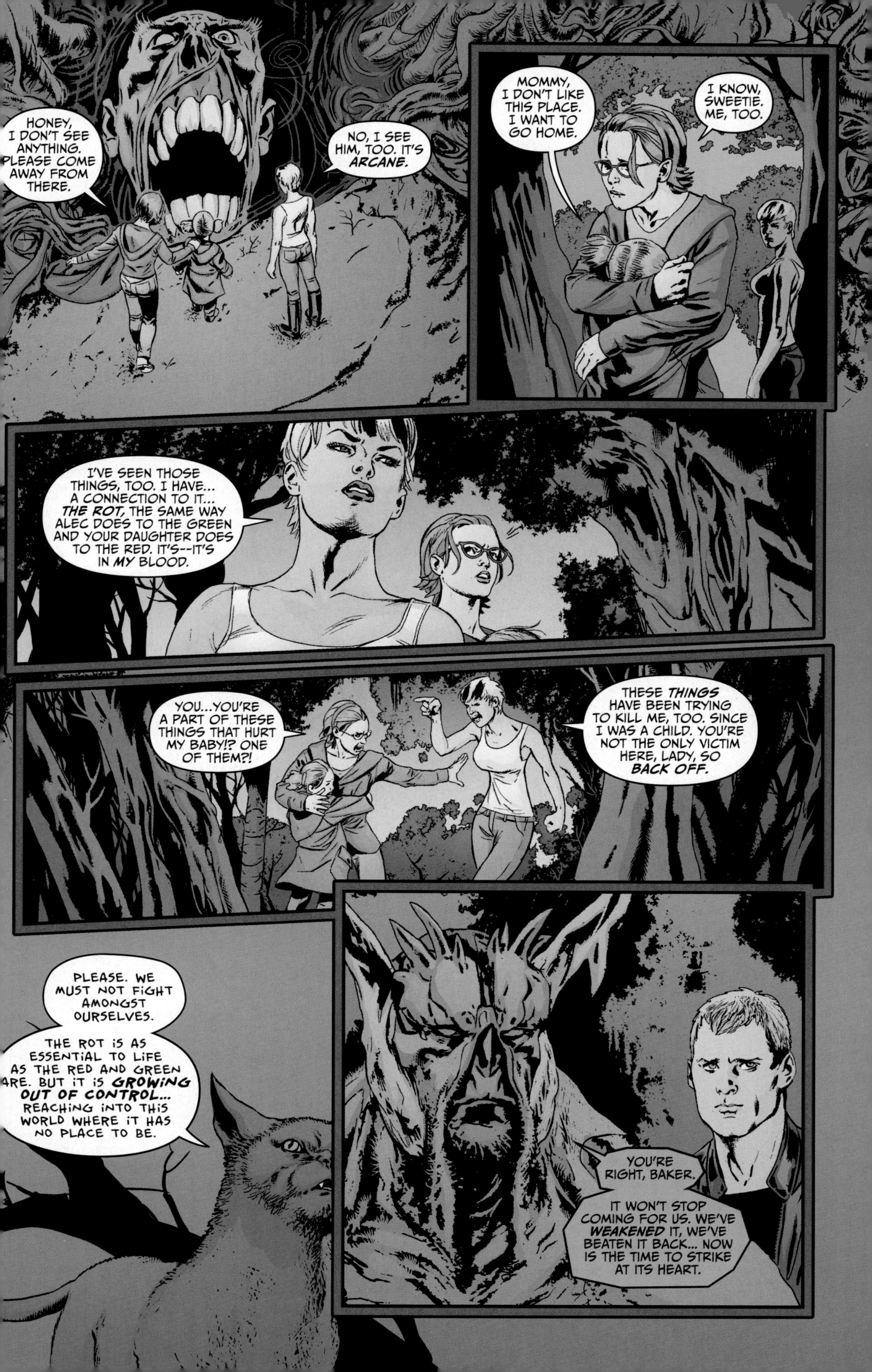

HONEY, I DON'T SEE ANYTHING. PLEASE COME AWAY FROM THERE.
NO, I SEE HIM, TOO. IT'S ARCANE.
MOMMY, I DON'T LIKE THIS PLACE. I WANT TO GO HOME.
I KNOW, SWEETIE. ME, TOO.
I'VE SEEN THOSE THINGS, TOO. I HAVE... A CONNECTION TO IT... THE ROT, THE SAME WAY ALEC DOES TO THE GREEN AND YOUR DAUGHTER DOES TO THE RED. IT'S--IT'S IN MY BLOOD.
YOU...YOU'RE A PART OF THESE THINGS THAT HURT MY BABY!? ONE OF THEM?!
THESE THINGS HAVE BEEN TRYING TO KILL ME, TOO. SINCE I WAS A CHILD. YOU'RE NOT THE ONLY VICTIM HERE, LADY, SO BACK OFF.
PLEASE. WE MUST NOT FIGHT AMONGST OURSELVES.
THE ROT IS AS ESSENTIAL TO LIFE AS THE RED AND GREEN ARE. BUT IT IS GROWING OUT OF CONTROL... REACHING INTO THIS WORLD WHERE IT HAS NO PLACE TO BE.
YOU'RE RIGHT, BAKER.
IT WON'T STOP COMING FOR US. WE'VE WEAKENED IT, WE'VE BEATEN IT BACK... NOW IS THE TIME TO STRIKE AT ITS HEART.

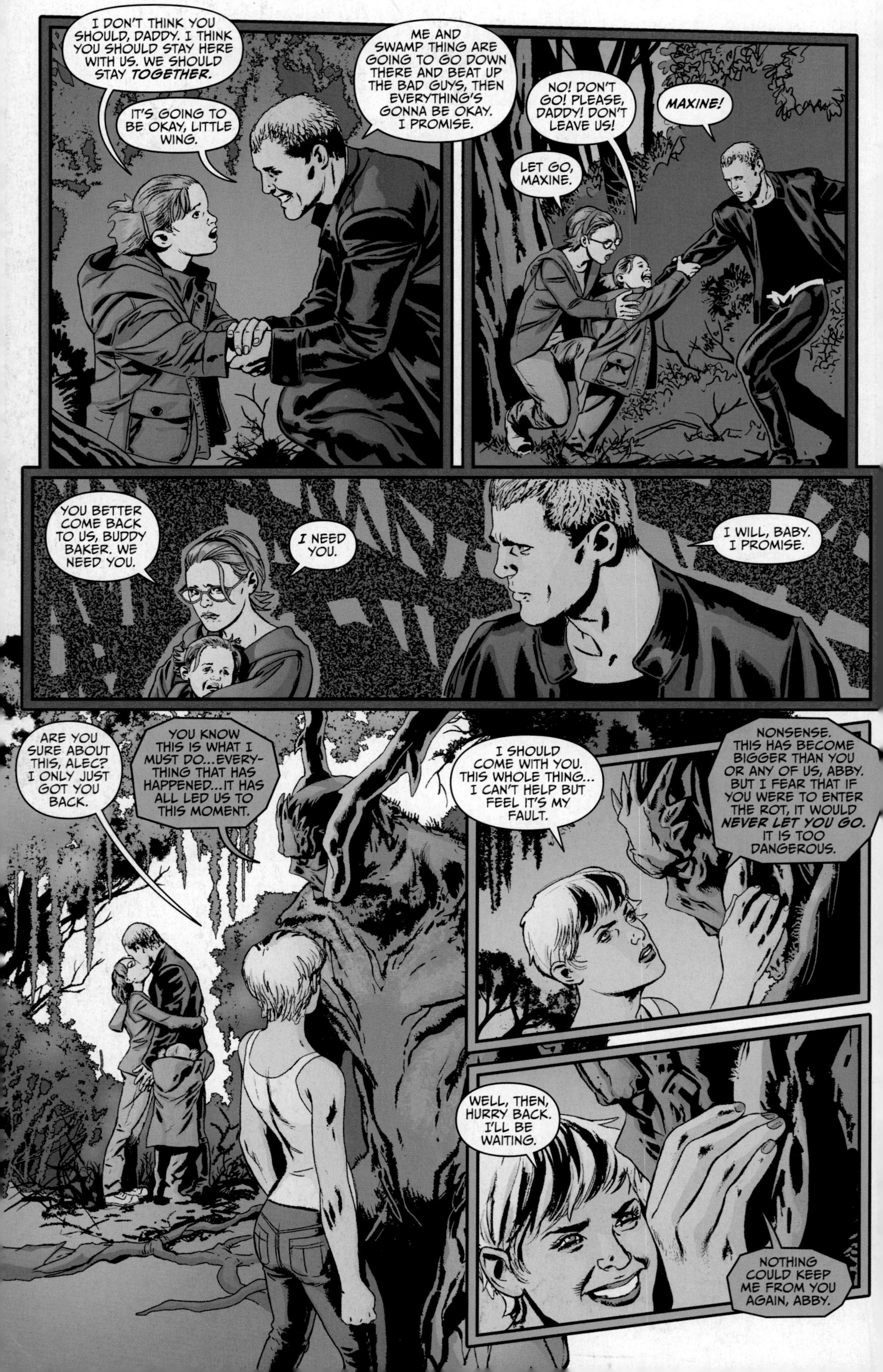
I DON'T THINK YOU SHOULD, DADDY. I THINK YOU SHOULD STAY HERE WITH US. WE SHOULD STAY *TOGETHER.*
IT'S GOING TO BE OKAY, LITTLE WING.
ME AND SWAMP THING ARE GOING TO GO DOWN THERE AND BEAT UP THE BAD GUYS, THEN EVERYTHING'S GONNA BE OKAY. I PROMISE.
NO! DON'T GO! PLEASE, DADDY! DON'T LEAVE US!
MAXINE!
LET GO, MAXINE.
YOU BETTER COME BACK TO US, BUDDY BAKER. WE NEED YOU.
I NEED YOU.
I WILL, BABY. I PROMISE.
ARE YOU SURE ABOUT THIS, ALEC? I ONLY JUST GOT YOU BACK.
YOU KNOW THIS IS WHAT I MUST DO...EVERYTHING THAT HAS HAPPENED...IT HAS ALL LED US TO THIS MOMENT.
I SHOULD COME WITH YOU. THIS WHOLE THING... I CAN'T HELP BUT FEEL IT'S MY FAULT.
NONSENSE. THIS HAS BECOME BIGGER THAN YOU OR ANY OF US, ABBY. BUT I FEAR THAT IF YOU WERE TO ENTER THE ROT, IT WOULD ***NEVER LET YOU GO.*** IT IS TOO DANGEROUS.
WELL, THEN, HURRY BACK. I'LL BE WAITING.
NOTHING COULD KEEP ME FROM YOU AGAIN, ABBY.

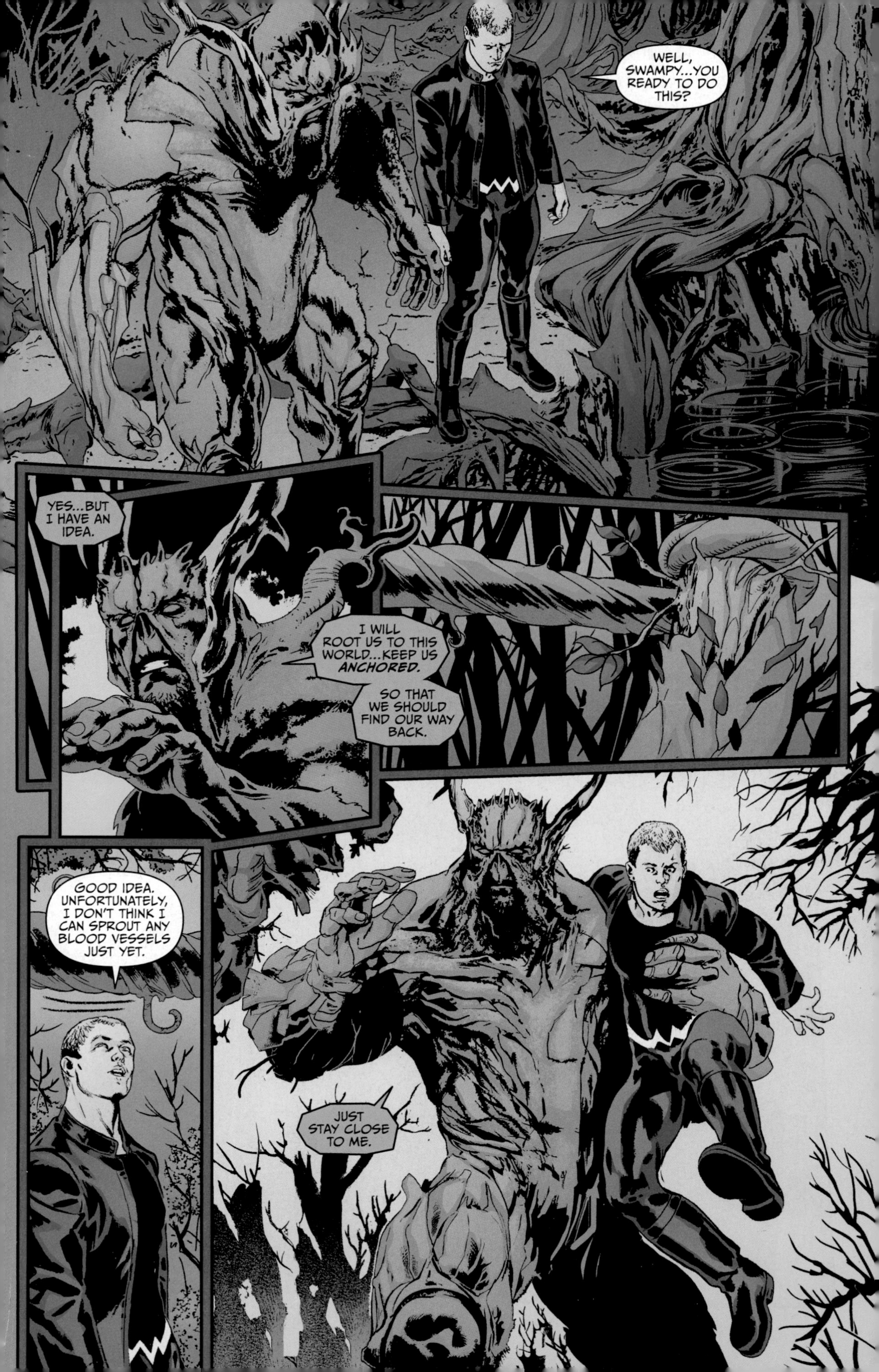
WELL, SWAMPY...YOU READY TO DO THIS?
YES...BUT I HAVE AN IDEA.
I WILL ROOT US TO THIS WORLD...KEEP US ANCHORED.
SO THAT WE SHOULD FIND OUR WAY BACK.
GOOD IDEA. UNFORTUNATELY, I DON'T THINK I CAN SPROUT ANY BLOOD VESSELS JUST YET.
JUST STAY CLOSE TO ME.

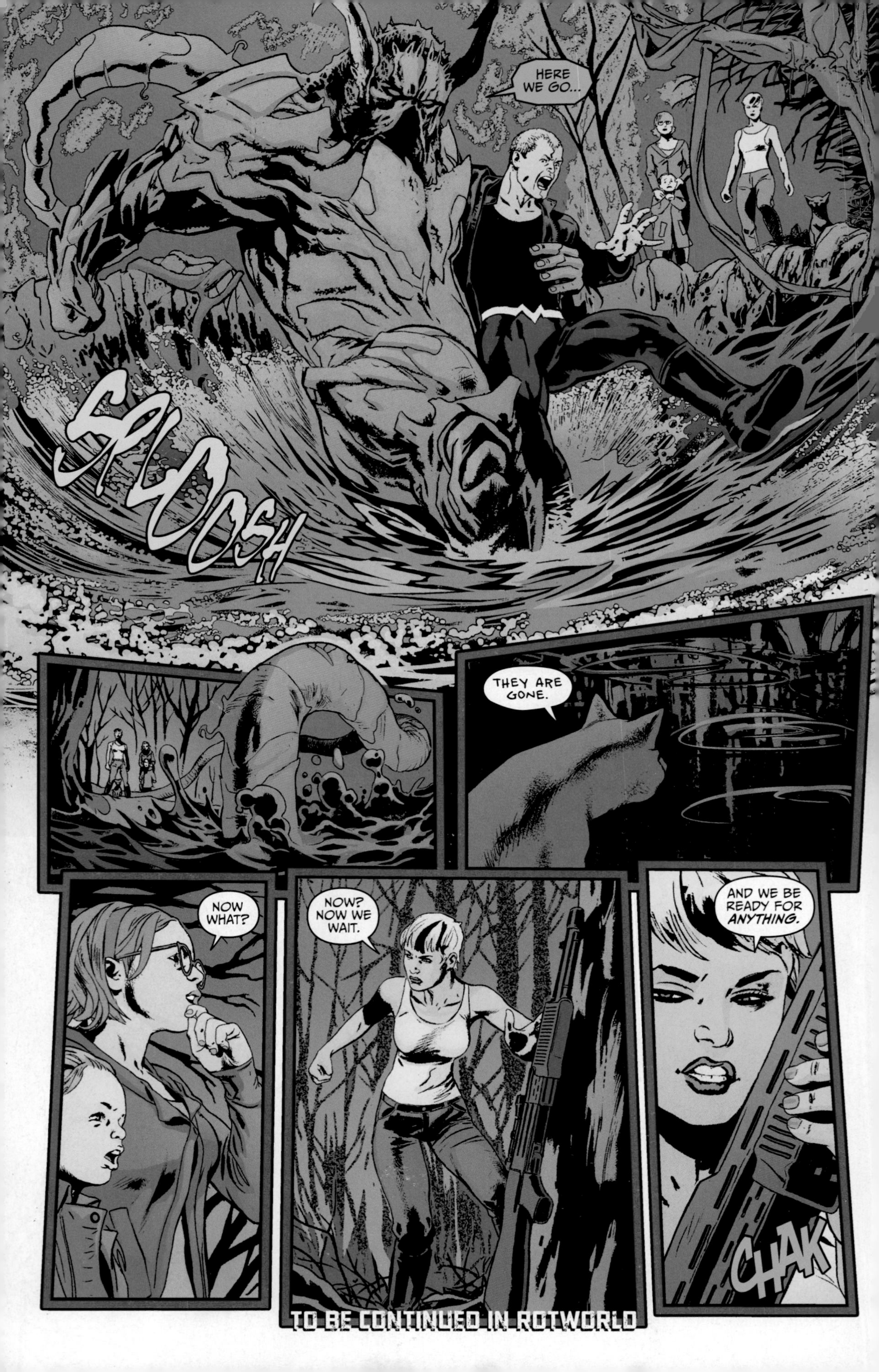
HERE WE GO...
SPLOOSH
THEY ARE GONE.
NOW WHAT?
NOW? NOW WE WAIT.
AND WE BE READY FOR *ANYTHING.*
CHAK
TO BE CONTINUED IN ROTWORLD